JEWS ON ROUTE TO PALESTINE
1934–1944

 JAGIELLONIAN STUDIES IN HISTORY

Editor in chief
Jan Jacek Bruski

Vol. 1

Artur Patek

# JEWS ON ROUTE TO PALESTINE 1934–1944

Sketches from the History of Aliyah Bet
– Clandestine Jewish Immigration

Jagiellonian University Press

The publication of this volume was financed by the Jagiellonian University in Krakow –
Faculty of History

REVIEWER
Prof. Tomasz Gąsowski

SERIES COVER LAYOUT
Jan Jacek Bruski

COVER DESIGN
Agnieszka Winciorek

Cover photography: Departure of Jews from Warsaw to Palestine, Railway Station, Warsaw 1937
[Courtesy of National Digital Archives (Narodowe Archiwum Cyfrowe) in Warsaw]

This volume is an English version of a book originally published in Polish by the Avalon, publishing
house in Krakow (*Żydzi w drodze do Palestyny 1934–1944. Szkice z dziejów alji bet, nielegalnej
imigracji żydowskiej*, Krakow 2009)

Translated from the Polish by Guy Russel Torr and Timothy Williams

ISBN 978-83-233-3390-6
ISSN 2299-758X

www.wuj.pl

Jagiellonian University Press
Editorial Offices: Michałowskiego St. 9/2, 31-126 Krakow
Phone: +48 12 631 18 81, +48 12 631 18 82, Fax: +48 12 631 18 83
Distribution: Phone: +48 12 631 01 97, Fax: +48 12 631 01 98
Cell Phone: + 48 506 006 674, e-mail: sprzedaz@wuj.pl
Bank: PEKAO SA, IBAN PL80 1240 4722 1111 0000 4856 3325

# Contents

# The most important abbreviations and acronyms

AAN – Archiwum Akt Nowych, Central Archives of Modern Records in Warsaw
ADM – Admiralty
CINM – Clandestine Immigration and Naval Museum in Haifa
CO – Colonial Office
col. – column
CZA – Central Zionist Archives in Jerusalem
DDSG – *Deutsche Donau Schiffahrtgesellschaft*, German Association of Danube Navigation
DGFP – *Documents on German Foreign Policy 1918–1945*
FO – Foreign Office
FRUS – *Foreign Relations of the United States. Diplomatic Papers*
HMG – His Majesty's Government
JOINT – American Jewish Joint Distribution Committee
KGPP – Komenda Główna Policji Państwowej, Polish Central Police Command
Mapai – *Mifleget Poalei Eretz Israel*, Party of the Workers of the Land of Israel
Mapam – *Mifleget ha'Poalim ha'Meuhedet*, United Workers Party
M.P. – Member of Parliament
MSW – Ministerstwo Spraw Wewnętrznych, Polish Ministry of Internal Affairs
MSZ – Ministerstwo Spraw Zagranicznych, Polish Ministry of Foreign Affairs
NKVD – *Narodnyy Komissariat Vnutrennikh Del*, Peoples' Commissariat for Internal Affairs
NLI – The National Library of Israel in Jerusalem
NZO – New Zionist Organization
PISM – The Polish Institute and General Sikorski Museum in London
RHL – Rhodes House Library in Oxford
TNA – The National Archives in London
USSR – Union of Soviet Socialist Republics
YVA – Yad Vashem Archives in Jerusalem
ZAM – The Zionist Association in Mauritius

# Introduction

Illegal Jewish immigration to Palestine during the British Mandate was one of the most spectacular enterprises organized by the Jews in the first half of the 20<sup>th</sup> century before the creation of the state of Israel. The Jews called such immigration 'Type B' (*Aliyah Bet*), to differentiate it from the official type (*aliyah*) allowed for by British authorities. *Aliyah Bet* was an indication of the diaspora's longing to return to the Promised Land, and simultaneously a way of fighting the restrictive policy of Great Britain which limited Jewish immigration to Palestine. It was also a form of aid to Jewish refugees from Europe and salvation for Jews menaced by Nazism. In due time *Aliyah Bet* became a national myth, part of the Jews' collective consciousness.

This book deals with *Aliyah Bet* activity in the years 1934–1944. It opens with the organization of the first sea transport of illegal immigrants to set sail for Palestine (the ship *Velos*, in July 1934). That date is considered the symbolic beginning of *Aliyah Bet*, though the phenomenon was known to exist from much earlier. The closing bookend of the book's chronology is December 1944 and the last wartime sea transport (the ship *Taurus*). Thus two entirely different chapters in the history of *Aliyah Bet* form the subject of my analysis: the period when the movement was forming and becoming organized, and the war years – a time of great challenges and even greater difficulties. The book does not address the postwar period (1945–1948), a subject to which a decidedly varied literature has already been devoted;[1] this decision was dictated by the need to focus on issues which had received relatively little attention in previous research.

The work is structured both chronologically and thematically. The introductory chapter attempts to explain the complicated realities of the Middle East, with partic-

---

[1] See for example: Y. Bauer, *Flight and Rescue: Brichah*, New York 1970; M.S. Greenfield, J.M. Hochstein, *The Jews' Secret Fleet. The Untold Story of North American Volunteers Who Smashed the British Blockade*, Jerusalem 1987 (rev. ed. Jerusalem–New York 1999); Z.V. Hadari, *Second Exodus. The Full Story of Jewish Illegal Immigration to Palestine, 1945–1948*, London 1991; Z.V. Hadari, Z. Tsahor, *Voyage to Freedom. An Episode in the Illegal Immigration to Palestine*, London 1985; A. Halamish, *The Exodus Affair. Holocaust Survivors and the Struggle for Palestine*, London 1998; F. Liebreich, *Britain's Naval and Political Reaction to the Illegal Immigration of Jews to Palestine, 1945–1948*, London 2005; N. Stewart, *The Royal Navy and the Palestine Patrol*, London–Portland, Or 2002; G. Thomas, *Operation Exodus. The Perilous Journey from the Nazi Camps to the Promised Land... and Back*, London 2010; I. Zertal, *From Catastrophe to Power. Holocaust Survivors and the Emergence of Israel*, Berkeley–Los Angeles–London 1998.

ular consideration devoted to the factors which determined the Palestinian problem in the Mandate era. Illegal immigration was an integral part of the then-existing order, and the many circumstances which shaped it originated in the preceding years. In the second chapter I present the genesis of *Aliyah Bet*, including the particulars of the organization of the first refugee sea transport in 1934. I consider the reasons why Zionists-Revisionists were initially extremely active in this area and show the dilemmas faced by Yishuv leaders concerning this form of Jewish immigration. My work deals separately with the *Aliyah Bet* of Jews from Poland. Immigrants coming from the Republic of Poland constituted a substantive percentage of illegal immigrants in general, and Polish authorities unofficially supported this so-called "tourist emigration." I endeavor to answer the question as to what motives lay behind these authorities' actions. In the third chapter I discuss the reasons for the intensification of *Aliyah Bet* in the last months before the outbreak of the Second World War. In this context I present Mossad le'Aliyah Bet ("the naval department of Hagana"), the secret organization responsible for illegal Jewish immigration to Palestine in its entirety. I also write about other circles and individuals who, acting independently, allied themselves with *Aliyah Bet* and consider their motives for doing so. Great Britain's position on the inflow of Jewish refugees to Palestine is discussed, as well as Arab reactions. In addition, I approach the question of immigration from the Third Reich, in which context I mention the Zentralstelle für jüdische Auswanderung based in Vienna.

Subsequent chapters address the period of the Second World War. I begin with an attempt to answer the question of how the realities of the time influenced the nature and aims of *Aliyah Bet*, the position of the Yishuv leaders, and the policy of Great Britain. As is known, Palestine and the Middle East played a very important role in London's strategy. I devote a separate section to topics less commonly associated with *Aliyah Bet* in the popular mind, although they were part of it. I have in mind here the secret forms of Jewish influx via the "green border" (mainly from Syria and Lebanon) and what was called *Aliyah Vav*, i.e., willful or legal desertion from the ranks of the Władysław Anders' Polish army (whose troops were stationed for a time in Palestine) by soldiers of Jewish origin who had decided to remain in Eretz Israel. The fifth chapter depicts the circumstances surrounding the deportation of 1580 Jewish refugees to Mauritius by Mandate authorities in December 1940, and describes their five-year exile on this distant island in the Indian Ocean. In the following chapter, I examine the dramatic divisions in *Aliyah Bet*: the tragic fate of Jewish refugees from the "Kladovo" group and the sinking of the *Salvador* (in the Sea of Marmara in December 1940) and the *Struma* (in the Black Sea in February 1942). I reflect on whether these tragedies could have been avoided, and where the responsibility (moral and other) for the deaths of hundreds of unfortunate refugees lay. In the seventh and last chapter, I write about the relaxation of British immigration policy which occurred in 1942 and 1943. I reveal how in changing conditions Mossad le'Aliyah Bet renewed its efforts to organize further transports (by ship) of Jewish refugees. In the Appendix the reader will find a list of the sea transports organized by *Aliyah Bet* in the years 1934–1944.

In my work, I strive to answer the question, what was illegal Jewish immigration? What were the external and internal factors which determined its course, which acted for and against it? What set its tone? What motives drove its organizers and participants? Were these motives consistent over time, or did they change from one period to another? How did *Aliyah Bet* influence Great Britain's Palestinian policy and its relationship with Yishuv before and during the war?

Although various topics concerning illegal Jewish immigration to Palestine have interested scholars, writers and artists before, such interest has largely been focused on particular episodes rich in human drama, such as the tragedy of the *Struma* mentioned earlier or, in the postwar period, that of the *Exodus 1947*.

The first attempts to comprehensively synthesize the history of *Aliyah Bet* appeared relatively early. They were written by the brothers Jon and David Kimche (*The Secret Roads. The "Illegal" Migration of a People, 1938–1948*, London 1954), Bracha Habas (*Portzei ha-shearim. Sipur korotehah shel Aliyah Bet*, Tel Aviv 1957; English edition: *The Gate Breakers*, New York–London 1963) and Chaim Lazar-Litai (*Af-ʿal-pi. Sefer Aliyah Bet*, Tel Aviv 1957). Those books, however, were not scholarly works (they were closer to journalism), and when reading them it is not difficult to establish where the authors' sympathies lie. This can be observed in the selection of arguments, the placement of emphasis, etc. The Kimche brothers and Habas approach the problem from the perspective of the Zionist left, while Lazar-Litai presents the views of the Revisionist movement.

Of scholarly monographs, Dalia Ofer's book *Escaping the Holocaust. Illegal Immigration to the Land of Israel, 1939–1944* (New York 1990), first published in Hebrew in Jerusalem in 1988, is of fundamental importance. This thorough study, based on wide preliminary source research, devotes much attention to the tactics of the Zionist movement. Aryeh L. Avneri's *Mi – „Velos" ʿad „Taurus." Asor rishon le-haʿapalah be-darkhe ha-yam, 1934–1944* (Tel Aviv 1985) [*From "Velos" to "Taurus." The First Decade of Jewish Illegal Immigration 1934–1944*] must also be cited. The work has so far only appeared in Hebrew, which by nature limits its potential readership.

Among other works, Mordechai Naor's popular outline *Aliyah 2, 1934–1948: mekorot, sikumim, parashiyot nivharot vehomer ʿezer/ha – ʿorekh* (Yerushalayim 1988) bears mention. It has also appeared in a shortened English version (*Haapala. Clandestine Immigration 1931–1948*, Tel Aviv 1987; no footnotes or bibliography). *Sefinot be-terem shahar. Sipuran shel sefinot ha-maʿapilim mi "Vilus" ad "Kerav Emek Ayalon." Leksikon ha-haʿapalah, 1934–1948* (Hefa 2004) [*Dawning Ships. The Story of the Clandestine Immigration Ships From "Vilus" to "Ayalon Valley Battle." Dictionary of the Clandestine 1934–1948*] by Shai Horev is a popular, encyclopedic history, with many illustrations and separate entries for each *Aliyah Bet* sea transport. A collection of studies on the subject edited by Anita Shapira, *Haʿapalah: measef letoladot ha-hazalah, ha-berihah, ha-ha'apalah usheerit ha-peleitah* (Tel Aviv 1990), has also only appeared in Hebrew.[2] These works deal only in part with the period surveyed in the present work and, due to their popular nature, may serve only as an introduction to the subject.

Works concentrating on particular sub-divisions within *Aliyah Bet* comprise a separate group. They include studies of illegal immigrants deported to Mauritius (by Ronald Friedmann, Geneviève Pitot and Aaron Zwergbaum, among others),[3] as well as monographs on selected *Aliyah Bet* sea transports. The tragic destinies of the *Struma* and *Mefkura* in particular, ships which sank in the Black Sea in somewhat mysterious circumstances during the war, have attracted historiographers' attention. Israeli, American, German, Rumanian, and Turkish authors have written about these issues, including Douglas Frantz and Catherine Collins, Serban Gheorghiu, Efraim Ofir, Jürgen Rohwer, Shimon Rubinstein, Mihai Stoian, and Çetin Yetkin.[4] Erich Gershon Steiner has written a fictional novel about the disaster on the *Patria* in November 1940.[5]

The basic source materials which I used for this book were from the National Archives in London and the Central Zionist Archives in Jerusalem. The British archives house rich collections of both original documents produced by high-ranking officers in the Foreign Office, Colonial Office and War Office, and translations and transcriptions of materials created by *Aliyah Bet* organizers, Jewish operatives in Palestine, Great Britain and the United States, and immigrants themselves (reports, interrogation transcripts). Reports of the British intelligence services, MI5, must also be mentioned here. I have tried to compare and contrast the information in documents of British provenance with that in Jewish documents from Palestine and the diaspora.

The Central Zionist Archives contain groups of documents created by the Office of the Jewish Agency and its immigration department in London and New York. In the archive I found pre-war British reports revealing Great Britain's attitude to-

---

[2] "Studies in the History of Illegal Immigration into Palestine 1934–1948." See: Zeev Tzahor's review in *Studies in Contemporary Jewry*. Vol. IX: "Modern Jews and Their Musical Agendas." Ed. E. Mendelsohn, New York 1993, pp. 362–364.

[3] R. Friedmann, *Exil auf Mauritius 1940 bis 1945. Report einer "demokratischen" Deportation jüdischer Flüchtlinge*, Berlin 1998; G. Pitot, *The Mauritian Shekel. The Story of the Jewish Detainees in Mauritius, 1940–1945*, Port Louis 1998; A. Zwergbaum, "Exile in Mauritius," *Yad Vashem Studies* (Jerusalem). Vol. IV: 1960, pp. 191–257.

[4] D. Frantz, C. Collins, *Death on the Black Sea. The Untold Story of the "Struma" and World War II's Holocaust at Sea*, New York 2003; S. Gheorghiu, *Tragedia navelor "Struma" şi "Mefkure,"* Constanţa 1998; E. Ofir, *With No Way Out. The Story of the Struma. Documents and Testimonies*, Cluj-Napoca 2003; J. Rohwer, *Die Versenkung der jüdischen Flüchtlingstransporter Struma und Mefkure im Schwarzen Meer (February 1942, August 1944)*, Frankfurt/Main 1965; S. Rubinstein, *Personal Tragedies as a Reflection to a Great Tragedy Called Struma*, Jerusalem 2003; M. Stoian, *Ultima cursă de la Struma la Mefküre*, Bucureşti 1995; Ç. Yetkin, *Struma. Bir dramın içyüzü*, Istanbul 2008.

[5] E.G. Steiner, *The Story of the Patria*, New York 1982.

ward *Aliyah Bet* and materials concerning Jewish refugees deported to Mauritius or interned in the camp at Atlit, as well as a list of several hundred names of *Aliyah Bet* partners or associates for the year 1939. My work was made much easier by the opportunity to use the complete archive of annual bound volumes of *The Palestine Post*, the main English-language Yishuv publication.[6]

I also used materials from other institutions. From the Yad Vashem Archives in Jerusalem I made use of documents concerning the tragic fates of the sea transports *Struma* and *Mefkura* (including a report on the causes of the *Mefkura*'s capsize written by Chaim Barlas, Shaul Avigur and Reuben Resnik). They constitute part of a larger collection documenting the situation of Rumanian Jews at the time of the Holocaust. That institution also keeps interesting materials on immigrants deported to Mauritius, among them refugees' stories, proclamations, petitions, and collections of press clippings. The originals of these documents are the property of The Wiener Library in London and are located there, while Yad Vashem has authorized copies.

At the National Library of Israel in Jerusalem I was able to gain access to several unpublished studies of the *Struma* and *Mefkura* tragedies (works by Tuvia Carmely, Albert Finkelstein, and Shimon Rubinstein).

I studied the Polish chapter of *Aliyah Bet* by means of materials at the Central Archives of Modern Records in Warsaw. This theme is presented mainly in documents from the Ministry of Foreign Affairs and Polish Police Headquarters. A broader context is provided by analyses and reports from Polish consular posts in Palestine, and from the complexes of the Polish Embassy in London and the diplomatic mission in Bern. As Western scholars have given them attention only sporadically, they merit further examination.

One of the most important source publications is *The Holocaust and Illegal Immigration, 1939–1947* (ed. M.J. Cohen, New York–London 1987), from the monumental 39–volume series *The Rise of Israel*, containing facsimiles of over 1,900 documents: from the formation of the Zionist movement to the creation of the state of Israel. In it I found materials from the British, Israeli, and American archives: several dozen concerning various matters relating to *Aliyah Bet*. I also benefited from a collection of accounts, reports, and other documentary materials published in Spanish in Jerusalem under the auspices of the Zionist Organization in 1953, entitled *La Haapala. Compilación de notas y documentos de la Inmigrácion "Ilegal" a Eretz Israel 1933–1948*.

Mention must also be made of the selection of British documents from the collection of the National Archives in London: *Select British Documents on the Illegal Immigration to Palestine (1939–1940)*. The collection, which comprises 11 documents, appeared in the pages of the *Yad Vashem Studies on the European Jewish Catastrophe and Resistance* (Vol. X: 1974. Ed. Leni Yahil) published in Jerusalem.

---

[6]   The daily, under the changed title of *The Jerusalem Post* (since 1950), is published to this day.

Published memoirs and eyewitness accounts constitute a separate category, first and foremost those of organizers of and participants in illegal immigration. I was helped by, among others, the memoirs of Shaul Avigur (head of Mossad le'Aliyah Bet); his associates Ruth Aliav-Klüger, Ehud Avriel, and Munya Mardor; activists and sympathizers of the Revisionist movement: Ludmila Epstein and Wilhelm Perl, et al.[7] All of the above publications are valuable as first-hand testimony, but their plausibility is sometimes less than complete, if only because of the time elapsed between the events narrated and the narration, and consequent coloration of the narrators' perspective by later experiences and political views.

Scholars who are limited to using European languages may find some consolation in the fact that many Israeli monographs and source materials from the relevant period have been published in or translated into English. It should also be remembered that *Aliyah Bet* was of primary interest to Great Britain, which explains the abundance and variety of archival materials produced or available in English. Some were translated from Hebrew or Yiddish to meet the needs of the Mandate authorities and thus kept in British collections.

Through inquiries at archives and libraries I gained access to many materials rarely or never cited by previous scholars. In this context I attempted to fill out the existing bibliography for this subject. In the bibliography I also took into account a selection of about 60 contemporaneous press articles on the events described (e.g. *The Palestine Post*, *The New York Times*, et al.). They in fact contain a great deal of valuable factual information, and have hitherto somehow escaped the historians' attention. Where relevance justified it, I also made use of material recorded on film (in documentary films) or posted on the Internet.

Here I must address the question of what contribution this work brings to research on *Aliyah Bet*. The literature on the subject cited above may give the impression that the topic has to a large degree already been thoroughly covered. Nothing could be further from the truth. I have often been confronted with factual contradictions and insufficient documentation in the existing studies. At times, the same events are perceived in completely divergent ways. Some of the studies (such as the syntheses of the Kimche brothers, Habas or the English version of Mordechai Naor's book), though undoubtedly important and necessary, lack essential footnotes, which makes verifying the information difficult. The present work is therefore not only an attempt to grasp *Aliyah Bet* in its early years, before it became a major political power, in one volume, but also an attempt to gather and set in order the facts and source material. As mentioned above, there is no scholarly monograph which

---

[7]   S. Avigur, *S pokoleniyem khagany*, Tel Awiw 1976 (Hebrew edition: *Im dor ha-Haganah*, Tel Aviv 1962); R. Aliav, P. Mann, *The Last Escape. The Launching of the Largest Secret Rescue Movement of All Time*, London 1974; E. Avriel, *Open the Gates! A Personal Story of "Illegal" Immigration to Israel*. Preface by G. Meir, New York 1975; M.M. Mardor, *Strictly Illegal*. Foreword by D. Ben-Gurion, London 1964; L. Epstein, *Before the Curtain Fell*, Tel-Aviv 1990; W.R. Perl, *Operation Action. Rescue from the Holocaust*. Revised and enlarged edition, New York 1983.

deals comprehensively with pre-war illegal Jewish immigration to Palestine in the English-language literature on the subject. Dalia Ofer's excellent work *Escaping the Holocaust* concentrates on *aliyah* from Europe during the Second World War and for understandable reasons touches only briefly on *aliyah* activity outside of Europe.

In collating information from various sources I had to repeatedly verify facts repeated by other authors, e.g., dates, numbers for *Aliyah Bet* sea transports, and numbers of illegal immigrants among victims. In my extensive footnotes I collated the existing data, divergent in these figures. I made a similar synthesis when making the list of *Aliyah Bet* transports for 1934–1944 located in the Appendices. In contrast to the tables in other works, my list is accompanied by substantial commentary (in the footnotes), drawing attention to the disputes in the literature on the subject.

By its nature, illegal Jewish immigration, a secret undertaking, did not allow for archiving of related documents. The historian is compensated for this lack by the fact that *Aliyah Bet* remained a subject of interest for many countries, thanks to which we have access to source material of diverse provenance.

This study is a shortened version of a book originally published in Polish by the Avalon publishing house in Krakow.[8] The English-language edition omits the Appendix with documents from the British, Israeli and Polish archives. Most of those documents were included in English in the original and there was no need to publish them again here. Illustrations were also omitted. Some sub-chapters were re-edited or condensed. Some fragments of this book appeared first in Israel, on the pages of the Polish-language Tel Aviv weekly *Nowiny Kurier*.

I need to thank all those who in the course of this work's preparation have been kind and helpful to me. I offer heartfelt thanks to the reviewer Prof. Tomasz Gąsowski of the Institute of History at Jagiellonian University in Krakow, as well as to the reviewers of the Polish edition, Prof. Michał Pułaski of the Institute of History at Jagiellonian University and Prof. Janusz Józef Węc of the Institute of Political Science and International Relations at the same university. I wish to thank the Lanckoroński Foundation for the stipend which allowed me to travel to Great Britain twice to conduct research, and Prof. Stanisław Sroka, Director of the Institute of History at Jagiellonian University, for his benevolent financial support which enabled me to travel to Israel and have the work translated into English. And, last but not least, it is my pleasant duty to sincerely thank the translators, Guy Russell Torr and Timothy Williams, who completed the latter task with great care.

---

[8] A. Patek, *Żydzi w drodze do Palestyny 1934–1944. Szkice z dziejów aliji bet, nielegalnej imigracji żydowskiej*, Kraków 2009, pp. 454. The book's publication was noted in, among other: *Nowiny Kurier* (Tel Aviv), 21 V 2009, p. 12; *Midrasz* (Warsaw), No. 2: 2010, pp. 56–57; *Slovanský přehled* (Praha), Nos. 3–4: 2010, pp. 419–421; *Studia Judaica* (Kraków), Nos. 1–2: 2009, p. 368.

# Chapter I: "The old new country"

## 1. Context

When, at the end of the nineteenth century, Palestine started to focus the attention of international politics it had been a component of Ottoman Turkey for almost four hundred years. Jerusalem enjoyed the status of one of the holy cities of Islam, yet the country itself, economically backward and uncivilised, played a marginal role. Not even a separate province, it was considered a part of Syria. When it became clear that Turkey was tottering towards collapse, a series of claimants started to vie for its inheritance.

Of particular interest was the Middle East inhabited by Arabs. Its strategic value had for centuries drawn the attention of various powers. The region's worth lay in its geopolitical positioning between Africa, Asia and Europe, at the crossroads of important communication routes and offering at the time the shortest route from Europe to India. The key junction, the Suez Canal, lay within its environs. In the inter-war years another important factor was to enter into the equation – the huge oil reserves that had been discovered in Iraq and the Arabian Peninsula. The significance of this rudimentary energy resource ("liquid gold") was to rapidly increase.[1] Yet the Middle East is not only geopolitics, this is the region that saw the birth of the three great monotheistic religions and consequently became their spiritual centre. Here are places holy to Jews, Christians and Muslims. This fact has historically determined the fate of this land. While at the same time arousing oppositions that have been the source of the serious tension which has expanded beyond the borders of this part of the world.

The most important link for the region has been Palestine. Not only has it been the bulwark for the Suez Canal but has constituted a natural bridge between it and the Persian Gulf, making it an ideal powerbase for anyone harbouring the idea of control over the Middle East. Rivalry for spheres of influence here has involved Great Britain, France, Russia and Germany, with their endeavours made easier by the weakening of the Ottoman Empire. The furthest advanced in its penetration

---

[1]  For more, see, for example: G. Lenczowski, *The Middle East in World Affairs*, New York 1952; H.L. Hoskins, *The Middle East. Problem Area in World Politics*, New York 1954; B. Schwadran, *The Middle East Oil and the Great Powers*, 3rd ed., New York 1974; E.W. Anderson, *The Middle East. Geography & Geopolitics*, London 2000.

was Great Britain, which had already in the 19th century managed to take effective control over Egypt and the Suez Canal, as well as Cyprus, Aden and the sheikdoms of eastern Arabia. The subjugation of Turkey's Arab provinces of Palestine and Iraq would, it was hoped, allow the British to link up their possessions in this region and safeguard the shortest route to India, "the pearl in the British Crown."

The factor which speeded up the course of events surrounding Palestine was the Zionism that had developed towards the end of the nineteenth century as a nationalist and political movement. Its stimulus had been the conviction that the Jewish problem was a national question and not a social or religious one, and that its solution lay only in the creation by Jews of their own state, preferably in the historic lands of Israel (Eretz Israel). The very name for the movement suggested this, as it referred to the symbolical Biblical designation for Jerusalem and the whole of Palestine, while at the same time expressing the desire of the Chosen Nation for a return to the Promised Land;[2] for "a return," as the Jews here present from the times of the Old Testament had, following the taking of Jerusalem by the Romans in AD 70 and the suppressing of the revolt of Shimeon Bar-Kochba (132–135), mostly been deported and subsequently lived in the Diaspora. Nevertheless the memory and tradition derived from this distant past had been preserved, constituting an important element of Judaism.

Reference was made to these very traditions in projects of varied detail and conceptualisation for the renewed settlement of Jews in their former homeland. This was the effect of political revival amongst Jewish people. This national awakening was, on the one hand, a reaction against the discriminatory anti-Jewish policy of Tsarist Russia and the recurring pogroms (more than 100 occurred in 1881–1882 alone ), and on the other a response to the wave of anti-Semitism in many countries of western Europe (the Dreyfus affair in France). There was a growing conviction that as Jews had failed to obtain full civil rights in the states they lived in, then they should found their own.

This state of affairs was most vividly formulated by the Viennese journalist Theodor Herzl, born in Budapest, in his 1896 book *Der Judenstaat (The Jewish State)*,[3] although he himself – out of diplomatic caution – referred to "national focus" or "national unit," choosing not to specify its content. Herzl, the chief political ideologist of Zionism, saw his theses adopted a year later by the 1st Zionist Congress at its meeting in Basle in Switzerland; during the course of this congress the Zionist Organization was called into being (later the World Zionist Organization) as the ideological and organizational centre of the new movement.

---

[2]  See, for example: L. Stein, *Zionism*, London 1932; W. Laqueur, *A History of Zionism*, London 1972; S. Avineri, *The Making of Modern Zionism. Intellectual Origins of the Jewish State*, New York 1981 (also published in Russian, Jerusalem 2004); H. Edelheit, A.J. Edelheit, *History of Zionism. A Handbook and Dictionary*, Boulder, Col.–Oxford 2000.

[3]  English translation see e.g. T. Herzl, *The Jewish State*, New York–London 1988.

The various projects considered for an alternative Zion (Cyprus, Uganda and even distant Argentina) had no chance of success for they were unable to touch the emotions of the Jewish masses and consequently all such proposals were rejected by the 7th Zionist Congress (1905), which declared that a Jewish national home could come about only in Eretz Israel. A special foundation, Keren Kayemet le'Israel (Jewish National Fund, 1901), was set up which was to assemble funds for the purchase of land in Palestine. Although Zionism did not arouse in Jews general acceptance (some rejected it for ideological reasons, for others it merely constituted Utopianism), it was to gradually gain adherents and draw the attention of the great powers, becoming a factor that had to be taken into political considerations and calculations.

The new movement intensified the inflow of Jewish immigrants to the Holy Land, although it did not initiate the process. The settlement had earlier been supported by idealists such as Sir Moses Montefiore (1784–1885), a Jewish financier from London, or the French millionaire Edmond de Rothschild (1845–1934).[4] Following the pogroms in Russia there began the first wave of immigration (i.e. the first *aliyah*, 1882–1903). This was then joined by flows of refugees from Central and Eastern Europe, as well as from Arab countries. It is worth remembering that the most highly desired destination for this emigration was not Palestine (to date only a mere 3% of all emigrants had headed there) but the United States. For the majority, what counted was leaving, escaping from poverty and anti-Semitism, rather than the destination.

Table 1. Intercontinental migration of Jews 1881–1948

| Destination country | 1881–1914 | | 1915–May 1948 | |
|---|---|---|---|---|
| | 1000s | % | 1000s | % |
| USA | 2,040 | 85.0 | 650 | 41.0 |
| Canada | 105 | 4.0 | 60 | 4.0 |
| South America | 127 | 5.5 | 255 | 16.0 |
| South Africa | 43 | 2.0 | 25 | 1.0 |
| Palestine | 70 | 3.0 | 485 | 30.0 |
| Other countries | 15 | 0.5 | 125 | 8.0 |

The table created from data reported in: S. Della Pergola, *Migrations* [in:] *Encyclopaedia Judaica*, 2nd ed. Vol. 14, Detroit 2007, pp. 208, 210.

---

[4]  J. Kamm, *The Story of Sir Moses Montefiore*, London 1960; R. Aharonson, *Rothschild and Early Jewish Colonization in Palestine*, Lanham 2000. Ibid. further bibliography.

By 1914 at least 70,000 Jews had settled in Eretz Israel. Given the scale of the country as a whole this community (referred to by the Hebrew term *Yishuv*) constituted a tiny minority, although in certain regions like for instance Jerusalem it was to gain a demographic advantage over the Arab population.[5] The enthusiasm and hope was manifested by the names of the new settlements– Rishon le-Zion (First in Zion), Petah Tikva (The Gate of Hope) or Rosh Pina (The Cornerstone).[6]

The popular Zionist slogan of "a country without a nation for a nation without a country" appealed to the imagination.[7] The problem, however, was that this country was not unpopulated. Its inhabitants, the Palestinian Arabs, may not have had a developed sense of separate identity but for many of them Palestine was perceived as their homeland. This gave rise to the danger of clashes in the near future between these two dynamic national movements – Zionism and nascent Arab nationalism. Clashes were unavoidable for the aspirations of both forms of nationalism would turn out to be difficult to reconcile.

One of the few who was to realize the true nature of the problem was Ahad ha-Am (actually Asher Hirsch Ginsberg, 1856–1927), the spokesman of so-called spiritual Zionism. *The Arabs* – he was to write already in 1891 – *at present do not perceive any threat to themselves or their future whatsoever in what we are doing and therefore attempt to profit for themselves from these new arrivals. Yet when the day comes when the life of our people in Eretz Israel has developed to such a degree that to a greater or lesser extent the indigenous population is pushed to the margins then they will be less willing to give up their position so easily.*[8]

An undervaluation of the Arab question was an expression of the mentality and ignorance of the Europeans of the time, convinced of the "civilising mission" of the Old Continent. The fact that Arabs belonged to a completely different culture

---

[5]    In 1880 Jerusalem's population was around 31,000 inhabitants (including 17,000 Jews), while in 1922 – 62,100 (including 34,000 Jews). A.L. Avneri, *The Claim of Dispossession. Jewish Land-Settlement and the Arabs 1878–1948*, New Brunswick–London 1984, p. 255. Cf. M. Gilbert, *The Routledge Historical Atlas of Jerusalem*, 4th ed., London–New York 2008, pp. 33, 39, 49, 53, 67 (data for the years 1845, 1868, 1889, 1905, 1922, 1931, 1944).

[6]    H.M. Sachar, *A History of Israel. From the Rise of Zionism to Our Time*, New York 1988, pp. 26–30, 71–73; Ch. Gvati, *A Hundred Years of Settlement. The Story of Jewish Settlement in the Land of Israel*, Jerusalem 1985, pp. 3–4, 8–26, 32–38. For the distribution of Jewish settlements in Palestine in 1914 see: M. Gilbert, *The Routledge Atlas of the Arab-Israeli Conflict*, 9th ed., London–New York 2008, map 3 ("Jewish Settlement in Palestine 1880–1914").

[7]    Attributed to the writer, resident in London, Israel Zangwill (1864–1926), the son of Jewish immigrants from Russia. A.R. Taylor, *Prelude to Israel. An Analysis of Zionist Diplomacy 1897–1947*, Beirut 1970 (rev. edit.), pp. 31–32; J.H. Udelson, *Dreamer of the Ghetto. The Life and Works of Israel Zangwill*, Tuscaloosa–London 1990, pp. 184–186.

[8]    Quoted after: A. Chojnowski, J. Tomaszewski, *Izrael (Historia Państw Świata w XX wieku)*, Warszawa 2001, p. 20 (translation from the work by S. Avineri, op.cit., p. 123). For more see: G. Antonius, *The Arab Awakening. The Story of the Arab National Movement*, London 1945; N.J. Mandel, *The Arabs and Zionism before World War I*, Berkeley, Cal. 1976; G. Shafir, *Land, Labor and the Origins of the Israeli-Palestinian Conflict 1882–1914*, Cambridge 1989.

and that certain concepts, whose meaning appears obvious to a man of the West (e.g. democracy, nation, society), would be perceived differently here, was lost on them. And the West and Islam were not always able (or willing) to understand the values of the other, interpreting its manifestation on the basis of its own criteria, which resulted in a strengthening of stereotypes and a deepening of conflicts.

# 2. Towards "Pax Britannica"

A series of incidents accelerated the outbreak of the First World War. When Turkey decided to stand on the side of Germany and Austro-Hungary, the prospects for a new division of the Middle East opened up to the fighting powers. The main contracting party was Great Britain, which decisively abandoned the policy of defending the integrity of the Ottoman Empire as its own form of protection against German and Russian expansionism. The British decided to use the growth in independence aspirations amongst the Arabs and to direct them against the Ottoman Empire. They intended through this to obtain two goals: on the one hand, to minimise the consequences of a potential all-Muslim "holy war" to be proclaimed by the Ottoman sultan (who as caliph was the spiritual leader of the Islamic world); on the other hand, to obtain an ally in the fight against Turkey. The choice fell on Sherif Hussein ibn Ali, king of the Hedjaz, who as a descendant of Mohammed and guardian of the Islamic holy places at Mecca and Medina appeared to have a special predisposition for the role of leader of the Arabs. As the price for taking up arms against the Sublime Porte, Great Britain gave him all possible promises concerning the creation of a united Arab kingdom covering Syria, Iraq and the Arabian Peninsula.[9] The problem lay in the fact that these promises had not been specified. Controversy was stirred by, among other things, the question of Palestine's future.

From the point of view of London this was a short-term political solution, although Hussein did crucially incite an anti-Turkish revolt which contributed to British military successes in the Middle East. He did not know that at the same time secret trilateral British-Russian-French negotiations on the division of spheres of influence within the area of the disintegrating Ottoman Empire were taking place. The Arabian part of Turkey was divided by Great Britain and France between themselves, the latter receiving Syria and the Lebanon (the so-called Sykes-Picot Agree-

---

[9]  These promises are to be found in the so-called McMahon-Hussein correspondence (July 1915–March 1916). Henry McMahon was the British High Commissioner in Egypt. For text see: British White Paper. Cmd. 5957 of 1939: *Correspondence between Sir Henry McMahon, His Majesty's High Commissioner at Cairo, and the Sherif Hussein of Mecca, July 1915–March 1916*, London 1939; J.C. Hurewitz, *Diplomacy in the Near and Middle East. A Documentary Record: 1914–1956*. Vol. II, Princeton 1956, pp. 13–17. For more see: E. Kedourie, *In the Anglo-Arab Labyrinth. The McMahon – Husayn Correspondence and Its Interpretations, 1914–1939*, Cambridge–New York 1976; E. Tauber, *The Arab Movements in World War* I, London 1993.

ment of 1916). This agreement constituted a fairly breakneck attempt on the part of London to reconcile its own interests with those of its European allies as well as with the promises made to the Arabs. Little actually remained of these promises, for the future Arab state (or confederation of states) was to be limited chiefly to the inland desert regions, which would anyway be "spheres of influence" for London and Paris. As far as matters concerned Palestine the final "dotting of the i's" was not to take place; instead, what was proposed was its undefined internationalisation.[10]

At the same time the British conducted discussions with the Zionists and at the beginning of November 1917, in secret from the Arabs and the French, supported the Zionist movement's aspirations. This support, which has gone down in history as the Balfour Declaration, took the form of a letter which the head of British diplomacy, Arthur James Balfour, submitted to the hand of the informal leader of the Jewish Diaspora in Great Britain, Lord Walter Rothschild. It stated, among other things, that: *His Majesty's Government view with favour the establishment in Palestine of a national home for the Jewish people, and will use their best endeavours to facilitate the achievement of this object, it being clearly understood that nothing shall be done which may prejudice the civil and religious rights of existing non-Jewish communities in Palestine, or the rights and political status enjoyed by Jews in any other country.*[11]

The writer Arthur Koestler (1905–1983) in commenting on Balfour's declaration has claimed that: *In this document one nation solemnly promised to a second nation the country of a third.*[12] Leaving aside to what degree he was correct, it is difficult not to ask the question as to upon what basis Great Britain considered itself empowered to take such action? Looking from the perspective of Europe it is easy to overlook the fact that the British Empire was not at this time merely a European power, but first and foremost a world one. London's authority stretched over a quarter of all the world's lands, and its interests and commitments were global in nature. From the

---

[10] For more see: E. Kedourie, *England and the Middle East. The Destruction of the Ottoman Empire 1914–1921*, London 1956; J. Nevakivi, *Britain, France and the Arab Middle East 1914–1920*, London 1969; H.M. Sachar, *The Emergence of the Middle East 1914–1924*, London 1970, pp. 152–186; E. Monroe, *Britain's Moment in the Middle East 1914–1971*, 2nd ed., Baltimore, Mar. 1981, pp. 23–49. Text of the agreement: J.C. Hurewitz, *Diplomacy in the Near and Middle East*, pp. 18–22; W. Laqueur, B. Rubin (eds.), *The Israel-Arab Reader. A Documentary History of the Middle East Conflict*, 4th ed., New York–Oxford 1985, pp. 12–15. Borders project: J. Bagot Glubb, *Britain and the Arabs. A Study of Fifty Years 1908 to 1958*, London 1959, p. 69; M. Gilbert, *Atlas historii Żydów*, Kryspinów 1998, map 87 (translation from English: *The Routledge Atlas of Jewish History*, 5th ed., London 1993).

[11] For text see: J.C. Hurewitz, *Diplomacy in the Near and Middle East*, p. 26. For more see: L. Stein, *The Balfour Declaration*, New York 1961; J. Kimche, *The Unromantics. The Great Powers and the Balfour Declaration*, London 1968; R. Sanders, *The High Walls of Jerusalem. A History of the Balfour Declaration and the Birth of the British Mandate for Palestine*, New York 1984. Also the collection of documents *The Rise of Israel. A Documentary Record from the Nineteenth Century to 1948. A Facsimile Series Reproducing Over 1,900 Documents in 39 Volumes*. Vol. 7 and 8: *Britain Enters into a Compact with Zionism 1917*. Ed. I. Friedman, New York–London 1987.

[12] A. Koestler, *Promise and Fulfilment. Palestine 1917–1949*, London 1983, p. 4 (the first edition of this book appeared in 1949). Cf. also: R. Balke, *Izrael*, Warszawa 2005, p. 45.

perspective of this strategy there was no more important question than the Middle East for Britain during the years of the Great War.

The adroit argumentation of the leaders of the Zionist movement, with Chaim Weizmann at the head, continued in this line. Perceiving a chance, in Britain's plans for dismembering Turkey, for the internationalisation of the problem of creating a Jewish state, they started to underline the potential benefits for Britain's interests in the Middle East of a Jewish Palestine.[13]

The Balfour Declaration has left much room for various interpretations. Consciously devoid of precision (how is one suppose to understand the term "national home"?) as well as its legal standing (given that it was addressed to a private individual...), it constituted on the one hand the embodiment of Zionist circles' aspirations, while on the other the seeds of the future Palestinian conflict.

The declaration met with a favourable response in the world of politics for it matched the American president's, Woodrow Wilson's, programme (Fourteen Points) while simultaneously arousing in many states the hope that they would be able to solve their own problems through directing Jewish emigration to Palestine. It equally constituted an important trump in London's efforts to obtain international recognition for its rule over Palestine. In July 1922 the League of Nations formally confirmed the country's mandate to Great Britain. The British then became legally obligated to implement the announcements contained in the Balfour Declaration. The League's decision in point of fact only legalised an already existing state of affairs, for Great Britain had already been ruling Palestine since December 1917 and the actual division of mandates had been made at the conference in San Remo in April of 1920.[14]

# 3. The Gordian knot

The mandate system, created on the basis of Article 22 of the Pact of the League of Nations, sanctioned under the guise of international law the guardianship policy of the victorious powers over former German colonies and the Arab possessions of Turkey. Originally it was to serve in preparing the peoples of these countries for independence while the Mandate formally exerted authority under the control and in the name of the League of Nations. The post-Turkish lands were divided amongst themselves by the British (Palestine and oil-rich Iraq) and the French (Syria

---

[13] See also: Ch. Weizmann, *Trial and Error. The Autobiography of Chaim Weizmann*, London 1950, pp. 223–233; A.R. Taylor, op.cit., pp. 10–26; I. Friedman, *The Question of Palestine. British-Jewish-Arab Relations, 1914–1918*, 2nd ed., New Brunswick 1992; H. Edelheit, A. Edelheit, op.cit., pp. 74–79.

[14] R. Butler and J.P.T. Bury (eds.), *Documents on British Foreign Policy 1919–1939*. Series I. Vol. VIII: *1920*, London 1958, Chapter I: "Proceedings of the Conference of San Remo, April 18–26, 1920." Doc. 15: "British Secretary's Notes of a Meeting of the Supreme Council, held at the Villa Devachan, San Remo, on Saturday, April 24, 1920, at 4 pm," pp. 159–171.

and the Lebanon). The Palestine Mandate initially stretched over both sides of the River Jordan and covered the present-day territories of Israel, Jordan and the Palestinian Autonomy. It was a mandate category A, similarly to Iraq and Syria-Lebanon. This status was allocated to the most developed territories, for which there was envisaged a greater amount of self-government.

The League of Nations' resolution was the first international act in history to recognize Jewish rights to Palestine. The mandate sanctioned the influx of Jews as well as their right to the purchase of land and announced the calling into being of an advisory organ (in 1929 this was to be the Jewish Agency for Palestine), which was to cooperate with the British administration in the building of the future national home.[15]

The reconciling of the interests of the two societies, the Jews and Arabs, turned out to be immensely difficult. For Great Britain undertook obligations of a dual character, and ones to some degree contradictory. On the one hand in relation to all Jews,[16] while on the other in relation to the local Arab population – which resulted from the nature of the Mandate system. And this specificity of the Palestine Mandate in connection with its strategic significance for Great Britain meant that in comparison with other entities of this type it enjoyed a reduced degree of autonomy.

The Balfour Declaration, besides the envisaged short-term benefits, was to bring the British significantly more important problems. Great Britain became a joint participant in the Arab-Jewish conflict, which it itself had, to a certain degree, brought about. The Jews perceived the British obligations as a legal title to Palestine and the creation there of their own state. The Arabs, despite the earlier promises of London, felt cheated and the disappointing experienced was to make the movement more dynamic. As a result, the British found themselves trapped in a tight spot – between the nationalist aspirations of the Jews and the anti-Zionism of the Arabs. In such a situation the Mandate started to manoeuvre between the conflicting arguments of both societies, one time supporting the Jews and another the Arabs. In practice that meant that they had to give up on long-term policy in favour of short-term solutions, a problem which was to characterize London's policies in Palestine.[17]

---

[15] Text of the Palestine Mandate see: *Palestine Mandate*, Cmd. 1785, London 1922 [The Jewish Agency for Palestine], *Book of Documents submitted to the General Assembly of the United Nations relating to the Establishment of the National Home for the Jewish People*, New York 1947, pp. 39–49; M. Wight, *British Colonial Constitutions 1947*, Oxford 1952, pp. 99–106; J.C. Hurewitz, *Diplomacy in the Near and Middle East*, vol. II, pp. 106–111; W. Laqueur, B. Rubin (eds.), op.cit., pp. 34–42.

[16] In as far as talk was of "rebuilding" the Jewish national home, perforce it must have related to the entire Jewish nation. This is admitted to by, among others, prime minister James Ramsay MacDonald in a letter to Chaim Weizmann of the 13 II 1931 (*the undertaking in the Mandate is an undertaking to the Jewish people and not only to the Jewish people of Palestine*), and also the future head of government Winston Churchill. [The Jewish Agency for Palestine], *The Jewish Case before the Anglo-American Committee of Inquiry on Palestine as presented by the Jewish Agency for Palestine. Statements and Memoranda*, Jerusalem 1947, pp. 284–285.

[17] There is an immense array of books on the history of the Palestine Mandate. For example: A. Baumkoller, *Le mandat sur la Palestine*, Paris 1931; N. Bethell, *The Palestine Triangle. The Struggle be-*

Initially Great Britain supported the idea of a "Jewish National Home," for it provided a chance for the social and economic activation of Palestine, strategically important but economically backward. The new arrivals with their capital provided just such a chance. A gesture towards the Jews was, among other things, the recognition of Hebrew – next to English and Arabic – as one of the three official languages, employment in the Mandate administration of people of Jewish origin, the creation of local Jewish self-government, education and many other forms of social-cultural and political life. It is worth adding that also the first High Commissioner, Lord Herbert Louis Samuel (it was said of him that he was *the first Jew to govern the Holy Land since the Romans two thousand years earlier*) did not conceal his Zionist views.[18]

At the same time concessions were being made towards the Arabs. This involved suppressing the dissatisfaction of the Palestinian Arabs, which had been voiced in the spring of 1920. During the disturbances that had occurred at the time, the legendary joint organizer of the Jewish Legion within the framework of the British army, Josef Trumpeldor, had died. In Churchill's so-called White Paper announced in the June of 1922 (Sir Winston Churchill was at the time minister for the colonies) His Majesty's Government had admittedly confirmed its promise of a "national home for the Jews" in Palestine, yet opposed its transformation as a whole into such a home, while it made the levels of Jewish immigration dependent on the "economic capacity of the country;"[19] something that was not discussed in more detail. As viv-

tween the British, the Jews, and the Arabs, 1935–1948, London 1979; N. and H. Bentwich, *Mandate Memories 1918–1948*, New York 1965; M. Buchwajc, *Mandat Ligi Narodów nad Palestyną*, Kraków 1939; R. El-Eini, *Mandated Landscape. British Imperial Rule in Palestine, 1929–1948*, London 2006; T.R. Feiwel, *L'Anglais, le Juif et l'Arabe en Palestine*, Paris 1939; P.L. Hanna, *British Policy in Palestine*, Washington 1942; D. Horowitz, M. Lissak, *Origins of the Israeli Polity. Palestine under the Mandate*, Chicago 1978; A.M. Hyamson, *Palestine under the Mandate, 1920–1948*, London 1950; B. Joseph, *British Rule in Palestine*, Washington 1948; A. Koestler, *Promise and Fulfilment. Palestine 1917–1949*, 2nd ed, London 1983; J. Marlowe, *The Seat of Pilate. An Account of the Palestine Mandate*, London 1959; H. Mejcher (Hg.), *Die Palästina Frage 1917–1948. Historische Ursprünge und internationale Dimensionen eines Nationenkonflikts*. 2. Auflage, Poderborn–München–Wien–Zurich 1993; Y.N. Miller, *Government and Society in Rural Palestine, 1920–1948*, Austin 1985; [Esco Foundation for Palestine], *Palestine: A Study of Jewish, Arab, and British Policies*. Vol. I–II, New Haven 1947; T. Segev, *One Palestine, Complete: Jews and Arabs under the British Mandate*, London 2000; N. Shepherd, *Ploughing Sand. British Rule in Palestine 1917–1948*, London 1999; B. Wasserstein, *The British in Palestine. The Mandatory Government and the Arab-Jewish Conflict 1917–1929*, London 1978. It follows to separately mention the guide to archive collections: P. Jones (ed.), *Britain and Palestine, 1914–1948. Archival Sources for the History of the British Mandate*, Oxford–London 1979.

[18]  Samuel served 1920–1925. See: B. Wasserstein, *Herbert Samuel. A Political Life*, Oxford 1992; S. Huneidi, *A Broken Trust. Herbert Samuel, Zionism and the Palestinians 1920–1925*, London 2001. Quoted after: J. Comay, *Who's Who in Jewish History after the Period of the Old Testament*, 3rd ed. revised by L. Cohn-Sherbok, London–New York 2002, p. 322.

[19]  For the text see: J.C. Hurewitz, *The Middle East and North Africa in World Politics. A Documentary Record*. Vol. II: *British-French Supremacy 1914–1945*, 2nd ed., New Haven–London 1979, pp. 301–305; British White Paper, Cmd. 1700 of 1922: *Palestine. Correspondence with the Palestine Arab Delegation and the Zionist Organization*, London 1922, pp. 17–21; *Great Britain and Palestine 1915–*

idly as this was expressed, London's intention was not for Palestine to become *as Jewish as England is English*, which was a clear allusion to the known statement by Chaim Weizmann made during the time of the Paris Peace Conference.[20]

Not long afterwards a subsequent step was taken: the removal, with the agreement of the League of Nations, of a significant part of the Mandate from the resolutions of the Balfour Declaration. This referred to the land situated to the east of the River Jordan, referred to as Transjordan, representing a reduction in the area available for Jewish settlement. Transjordan, located on the crossroads of the routes linking the Arab countries in Asia and Africa as well as on the route between the Suez Canal and the Persian Gulf, constituted an important link in the British defense system in this region of the world. Nominal power was entrusted to the son of Hussein ibn Ali (the leader of the Hedjaz), Abdullah, desiring to reward the Hashemite family for the help afforded Britain during the war with Turkey. The younger brother of Abdullah, Feisal (who in the summer of 1920 had had to escape from the French in Syria) was given the throne of Iraq. In this way the British partially kept the promises they had made in the McMahon-Hussein correspondence, in obtaining Hashemite's support for their sphere of influence in the Middle East.[21]

Churchill's White Paper, with all the concessions made in favour of the Arabs, in no way changed the fundamental content of the Mandate, which is why it was rejected by them. The discontent of the Arab population was aroused by the successive increase in Jewish immigration as well as the increase in their possessions in Palestine, as this brought with itself an inevitable change in the distribution of forces. In the course of the first ten years more than one hundred thousand Jews arrived, admittedly less than the Zionists had hoped for but enough to influence the population proportions in the Mandate. Of a greater magnitude was to be the immigration of the subsequent decade, and in particular the years 1933–1939. At this time the borders of Palestine were crossed by around 215,000 Jews. In 1934 and 1935 alone more Jews settled here (104,200) than in the whole of the previous decade. As a result, the Jewish population of the mandate grew more than five times, from 83,800 in 1922 to 445,500 in 1939, while its percentage share in the population as a whole

---

*1945*. Ed. by The Royal Institute of International Affairs. Information Papers No. 20, London–New York 1946, pp. 155–158 (appendix III). It is worth looking at M.J. Cohen, *Churchill and the Balfour Declaration: The Interpretation, 1920–1922* [in:] U. Dann (ed.), *The Great Powers in the Middle East 1919–1939*, New York–London 1988, pp. 91–108.

[20] Weizmann expressed then that the term "Jewish National Home" he understands as: *to make Palestine as Jewish as England is English or America American*. Quoted after: G. Kirk, *A Short History of the Middle East. From the Rise of Islam to Modern Times*, 7th ed., London 1964, p. 152.

[21] The assignment of thrones was decided at the conference in Cairo in 1921. A.S. Klieman, *Foundation of British Policy in the Arab World: The Cairo Conference of 1921*, Baltimore 1970. On the beginnings of Transjordan see: M.C. Wilson, *King Abdullah, Britain and the Making of Jordan*, Cambridge 1987, pp. 39–59.

**Table 2. Population of Palestine in the Mandate period**

| Year | In total | Muslims | Jews | Christians | Others |
|------|----------|---------|------|------------|--------|
| 1922 | 752,048 | 589,177 | 83,790 | 71,464 | 7,617 |
| 1927 | 917,315 | 680,725 | 149,789 | 77,880 | 8,921 |
| 1932 | 1,052,872 | 771,174 | 180,793 | 90,624 | 10,281 |
| 1937 | 1,401,794 | 883,446 | 395,836 | 110,869 | 11,643 |
| 1942 | 1,620,005 | 995,292 | 484,408 | 127,184 | 13,121 |
| 1947 | 1,933,673 | 1,157,423 | 614,239 | 146,162 | 15,849 |

The table created from data reported in: *Great Britain and Palestine 1915–1945*, p. 61; R. Bachi, *The Population of Israel*, Jerusalem 1974, p. 399.

**Table 3. Jewish immigration to Palestine for the years 1881–1948 (in 1000s)**

| Years | Number of immigrants |
|-------|----------------------|
| 1881–1914 | around 70 |
| 1919–1923 | 35.1 |
| 1924–1932 | 88.4 |
| 1933–1939 | 215.2 |
| 1940–1945 | 54.1 |
| 1946–15 V 1948 | 56.5 |
| In total for the years 1919–1948 | 449.3 |

The table formulated on the basis of works cited above (table 2) and in footnote 22. The dates given in the table corresponds with the subsequent so called *aliyas*. One may also find different data.

grew from 11% to over 29%. If it had not been for the limitations placed by the British administration the number of new immigrants would have been even greater.[22]

The immigrants came chiefly from the countries of Central and Eastern Europe, where the difficult economic situation and the overcrowding of small towns with a large proportion of Jews, as well as anti-Semitic feeling, had created an atmosphere

---

[22] M. Wischnitzer, *To Dwell in Safety. The Story of Jewish Migration Since 1800*, Philadelphia 1948, pp. 141–223; *The Political History of Palestine under British Administration (Memorandum by His Britannic Majesty's Government presented in July, 1947, to the United Nations Special Committee on Palestine)*, Jerusalem 1947, pp. 6–9, 14–17; H.M. Sachar, *A History of Israel*, pp. 144–154.

conducive to emigration. Others were pushed to emigrate by ideological considerations. Over a half of European immigrants came from Poland.[23]

Before the First World War the stream of emigrants had been largely directed across the ocean, but in the 1920s emigration to the USA became severely curtailed. The world economic crash of 1929 and the bankrupting of many Jewish merchants and craftsmen in the countries of the Diaspora, as well as the subsequent coming to power of Adolf Hitler and the beginnings of discrimination against Jews in Germany meant that a willingness to emigrate to the more peaceful Palestine was expressed by individuals who were often noticeably removed in their thinking from the principles of the Zionist movement. Palestine appeared, in the figurative and literal sense, as the desired "promised land." This lost paradise was an important determinant in Jewish identity.

These desires also had a strong religious aspect. God-fearing Jews would face in the direction of Jerusalem when at prayer, asking the All Mighty for a return of the exiles to Zion, and at the end of the annual service to mark the feast day of Pesah (Passover) they sought solace in the words: *Next year in Jerusalem*. This longing for the Promised Land was the main binding factor that linked Jews from various parts of the world, even if they were externally dissimilar and spoke different languages.

Immigration occurred on the basis of certificates which the British Mandate distributed to the Zionist Organization (and later the Jewish Agency). Preference was given to materially independent individuals, with professional qualifications, and representatives of freelance professions.[24] The scale of immigration (in terms of the number of certificates issued), although it was to have been conditioned by the "economic capacity of the country," did in actual fact change as a result of the political situation in Palestine and neighbouring Arab countries.

Jewish land holdings became highly concentrated. In the course of twenty years it increased twofold and in 1940 – according to various estimates – the Yishuv already had at its disposal from 1/10th to 1/6th of efficiently used agricultural land, chiefly in the fertile coastal strip and Galilee.[25] The majority of the land was obtained from

[23] Arrivals from Poland for the years 1923–1937 constituted 41.2% of all the Jewish immigrants to Palestine. J. Tomaszewski (ed.), *Najnowsze dzieje Żydów w Polsce w zarysie (do 1950 roku)*, Warszawa 1993, p. 165. For the years 1919–1937: 42% (*Great Britain and Palestine*, p. 66).

[24] *Foreign Relations of the United States* (subsequently FRUS). *Diplomatic Papers 1937*. Vol. II, Washington 1954, pp. 918–920 (*The Consul General at Jerusalem (Wadsworth) to the Secretary of State. Jerusalem, 17 XI 1937*); W. Szczepański, *Palestyna po wojnie światowej. Światła i cienie*, Kraków 1923, pp. 294–296. For more on the shaping of the Mandate's immigration policy and its circumstances see: M. Mossek, *Palestine Immigration Policy under Sir Herbert Samuel. British, Zionist and Arab Attitudes*, London 1978.

[25] M. Aumann, *Land Ownership in Palestine 1880–1948*, 3rd rev. ed., Jerusalem 1976; K. Stein, *The Land Question in Palestine 1917–1939*, Chapel Hill 1984; H. Edelheit, A. Edelheit, op.cit., pp. 351–354. See maps: "Żydowska własność ziemska w Palestynie 1942" [in:] M. Gilbert, *Atlas historii Żydów*, map 106 as well as "Jewish-owned Land in Palestine by 1942" [in:] W. Laqueur, *A History of Zionism*, p. 569.

Table 4. Jewish immigration according to the main countries of origin (in 1000s)*

| Country | 1919–1923 | 1924–1931 | 1932–1938 | 1939–1945 | 1946–1948 | 1919–1948 |
|---|---|---|---|---|---|---|
| Poland | 9.2 | 38.6 | 89.3 | 15.9 | 17.1 | 170.1 |
| Romania | 1.4 | 4.1 | 10.5 | 8.9 | 16.2 | 41.1 |
| Germany | 0.5 | 1.0 | 35.9 | 14.2 | 1.4 | 53.0 |
| USSR | 13.4 | 14.9 | 5.5 | 0.8 | 0.3 | 34.8 |
| Czechoslo-vakia | 0.1 | 0.4 | 3.9 | 8.3 | 4.1 | 16.8 |
| Hungary | 0.3 | 0.3 | 1.3 | 3.7 | 4.7 | 10.3 |
| Turkey | 0.5 | 1.3 | 2.2 | 4.2 | 0.1 | 8.3 |
| Bulgaria | 0.3 | 1.2 | 1.1 | 3.2 | 11.2 | 17.1 |
| Yemen | 0.2 | 2.5 | 7.0 | 4.7 | 0.1 | 14.6 |

* As a result of rounding up the data to one place after the decimal point, the value shown in the final column could minimally differ from the arithmetical sum of the values in the preceding columns.

The table created from data reported in: C. Goldscheider, *Israel's Changing Society. Population, Ethnicity and Development*, Boulder, Col. 1996, p. 47; *Encyclopedia of Zionism and Israel*, vol. 1, p. 538. Cf. also V. Meniker, *Osnovnye pokazateli ekonomicheskogo i sotsialnogo razvitiya Izrailya 1948–1991. Statisticheskiy obzor*, Yerusalim 1992, pp. 29–32.

Arab owners, feudal lords often living permanently outside of the Mandate itself. From their point of view it was more beneficial for the short term to have a concrete and sizeable block of capital (for the price of land grew quickly) than money from rent. But the sale of plots to Jews meant the displacement of the local Arab lessees.

The fundamental problem turned out to be the qualitative difference between the two groups of people, which were divided by a recognisable gulf in so called perceived levels of civilization. On a relatively small patch of land, a society developed in a European style of life encountered a local society, semi-feudal in character, with a strong clan structure. The Arabs yielded to the Jews with their education and professional skills. In addition there were differences in mentality, social position and religious discrepancies. The result of the influx of immigrants and their capital, as well as the practical application of the technological achievements of the West, increased this distance all the more. In such a situation the discrepancy in standards of living between the local Arab population and the Jewish settlers, which for some gave rise to pride in their achievements and for others to frustration and envy, deepened.

# 4. Yishuv

The Jewish population, as opposed to the Palestinian Arabs, became relatively quickly well organized and an efficiently functioning unit of marked autonomy ready to build state structures. Yishuv had at its disposal its own economy and structures of socio-cultural and political life, independent from the Arab part.[26] It had its own secular and religious self government (the National Council, *Vaad Leumi*, selected by the elective Assembly of Representatives, *Asefat ha'Nivharim*), a trade union movement (The General Federation of Jewish Workers in the Land of Israel, Histadrut), a system of education and science (including the Hebrew University in Jerusalem) as well as paramilitary forces in the form of the conspiratorial Hagana founded in 1920, which effectively defended Jewish settlements and later became the germ of the Israeli armed forces.[27] Self sufficiency in agriculture was ensured by the efficient kibbutz system (agricultural communities) and moshavas (social cooperatives). Agricultural settlement was an important part of Zionist ideology and the Israeli ethos. Jews in the Diaspora were generally associated with trade and Zionism wanted to change this image. The future settlers – pioneers (Hebrew 'halutzim') were prepared, while still in the Diaspora, within the framework of the so-called *hakhshara* (Hebrew 'training,' 'preparation'), organizing vocational courses, the learning of Hebrew etc.[28]

Equally important in the process of creating the Yishuv identity was the effective revival of Hebrew (*Ivrit*), which for almost two thousand years had been considered as a dead language. In the popularisation of the "old-new language" there was perceived a chance for a harmonious integration of Jewish immigrants – the religious and the secular – from Europe and other parts of the world. This aim was also to be served by making the first names and surnames of those newly arrived Hebrew in form.

The Jewish political landscape was highly developed. The majority of parties had come into being during the Diaspora or continued to draw on traditions originating therein. A key role was played by the Zionist movement, internally diverse and encompassing a series of currents, secular and religious, from the Marxist left to the radical right. The anti-Zionist position was held by, among others, the religious ultra

---

[26] See for more e.g. M. Burstein, *Self-government of the Jews in Palestine since 1900*, Tel Aviv 1934 (reprint: Westport, Conn 1976); B. Halpern, J. Reinharz, *Zionism and the Creation of a New Society*, New York–Oxford 1988; H.M. Sachar, *A History of Israel* (Chapter 7: "Building the Jewish National Home"); J.C. Hurewitz, *The Struggle for Palestine*, New York 1976 (Chapter 3: "The Political Structure of the Yishuv"); also the selection of documents: *The Rise of Israel*. Vol. 16: *The Jewish Yishuv's Development in the Interwar Period*. Ed. by A.S. Klieman, New York–London 1987.

[27] Cf. Y. Slutsky, *Khagana – Evreyskaya boevaya organizatsiya v Eretz-Israel'*, Tel-Aviv 1978; E. Golomb, *The History of Jewish Self-defense in Palestine (1878–1921)*, Tel Aviv [1947?] (the author, from Wołkowysk near Białystok, was a co-founder and leader of Hagana for many years).

[28] For more see: A. Paetz, K. Weiss (Hg.), *"Hachschara." Die Vorbereitung junger Juden auf die Auswanderung nach Palästina*, Potsdam 1999.

Orthodox (for according to them the revival of Israel could not be the work of human hands) as well as the Communists. The most important force of the Yishuv period was the social-democratic Party of the Workers of the Land of Israel, formed in 1930 within the framework of the consolidation of the Zionist workers' movement, (Mifleget Poalei Eretz Israel, abbreviated as Mapai). Mapai controlled Histadrut, Hagana and the majority of the Jewish institutions in Palestine. The radical right comprised the so-called Revisionists, advocates of the Judaicization of the whole of Palestine. Having criticised the Zionist Organization's long-term policy of compromise in relation to the Mandate, they broke with it in 1935 and created the separate New Zionist Organization. The "military arm" of the Revisionists, the National Military Organization (Irgun Zvai Leumi, abbreviated as Etzel) rejected what they saw as the low-key methods of Hagana activities, and accepted political terror. The members of both of these currents, Socialists and Revisionists, in truly hating each other, left behind a psychological chasm that turned out to be difficult to bridge.[29]

The position of Yishuv and the programme of the Zionist movement was strengthened by the formation of the Jewish Agency as the legally recognised representative of Palestinian Jews in relation to the Mandate authorities, the League of Nations and the international community. From 1929 onwards its composition included the representatives of other political directions than just Zionist, from both Palestine and the Diaspora. The Agency was responsible for the practical matters of realising the idea of a "Jewish National Home" through which it was to become the unofficial government of Yishuv, with its own diplomatic service and numerous departments. The British hoped that through the help of this body they would be able to solve the increasingly complex internal problems of Palestine.[30] Two schools of political thought clashed within the Agency and Yishuv, the mouthpieces of which were Chaim Weizmann (head of the Zionist Organization) and David Ben-Gurion (the executive chairman of the Jewish Agency, the leader of Mapai and Histadrut). The first was an idealist placing hope in close cooperation with Great Britain. The second, a pragmatist and tactician, one who equally did not say "no" to the British but who selected his political instruments in relation to changing conditions. Both are considered by Israeli historiography as the "founding fathers" of Jewish statehood.[31]

---

[29] Y. Shapiro, *The Formative Years of the Israeli Labour Party. The Organization of Power, 1919–1939*, London 1976; P.Y. Medding, *Mapai in Israel. Political Organization and Government in a New Society*, Cambridge 1972; Y. Shavit, *Jabotinsky and the Revisionist Movement 1925–1948*, London 1988; L. Brenner, *The Iron Wall. Zionist Revisionism from Jabotinsky to Shamir*, London 1984.

[30] *Palestine. A Study of Jewish, Arab, and British Policies*, pp. 422–427 (the part: "Formation of the enlarged Jewish Agency"); A.R. Taylor, op.cit., pp. 45–48; Ch. Weizmann, op.cit., pp. 376–389.

[31] After the founding of Israel, Weizmann became its first president (till 1952), and Ben-Gurion prime minister (for the years 1948–1954, 1955–1963). Amongst the biographical works it is worth mentioning: J. Carmichael, M.W. Weisgal (eds.), *Chaim Weizmann. A Biography by Several Hands*, London 1962; N. Rose, *Chaim Weizmann. A Biography*, London 1987; J. Reinharz, *Chaim Weizmann. The Making of a Zionist Leader*, New York–Oxford 1985 as well as R. St. John, *Ben-Gurion. A Bi-*

# 5. Polarization

Palestinian Arabs were not served by the internal antagonisms and rivalry for leadership between two influential clans, the Husseini who were adherents of radical methods, and the Nashashibi who had a more conciliatory approach with regard to the Mandate. The Arabs rejected the possibility of undertaking formalized political cooperation with Great Britain (including the rejection of the creation of an Arab Agency). It was understood in the short term as a mark of protest against the Jewish presence in Palestine.[32] This was to come back to haunt them later, for the local Arabs unlike the Jews had not created the substructure of their state. Admittedly the Arab inhabitants of Palestine also took advantage of the economic development of the Mandate (which had been brought about by Jewish colonisation) but the balance of profits lay on the side of the Yishuv. The conflict developed from the economic into the political.

One man who played a major hand in creating the psychological chasm between the Palestinians and Yishuv was Haj Amin al-Husseini, the Grand Mufti, as anti-British (although it was on London's recommendation that he became the religious leader of the Palestinian Muslims in 1921) as he was a pathological anti-Semite.[33] Playing the nationalist note and fighting against conciliatory circles and advocates of compromise with the Jews (e.g. the Nashashibi clan) he succeeded in radicalising the Palestinian movement, which he desired to subordinate to Husseini and incorporate into pan-Islamic circles. It is difficult not to resist the reflection that had the decisive voice belonged to the conciliatory ruler of Transjordan, there might have been more peace in the country...

A prognostication of trouble was the Arab riots that occurred in 1929, the worst in years. The direct cause was the increasingly religious clash between the Jews and Muslims against the background of access to the Wailing Wall,[34] but these disturbances were to quickly spill over into the entire mandate, resulting in over 200 fa-

---

*ography*, Garden City, NJ 1971; M. Bar-Zohar, *Ben-Gurion*, London 1978; S. Teveth, *Ben-Gurion. The Burning Ground, 1886–1948*, Boston 1987.

[32] The Arabs, in rejecting the offer to create an Arab Agency explained that *they had never recognised the status of the Jewish Agency and had no desire for the establishment of an Arab Agency on the same basis.* Quoted after: *Palestine. Termination of the Mandate 15th May, 1948. Statement prepared for public information by the Colonial Office and Foreign Office*, London 1948, p. 6.

[33] It is said that in his hatred for Jews he surpassed even Hitler. During the war he established cooperation with countries of the Axis Powers. Cf. the biographies: J.B. Schechtman, *The Mufti and the Führer. The Rise and Fall of Haj Amin el-Husseini*, New York 1965; K. Gensicke, *Der Mufti von Jerusalem. Amin el-Husseini und die Nationalsozialisten*, Frankfurt am Main 1988; Z. Elpeleg, *The Grand Mufti. Haj Amin al-Hussaini, founder of the Palestinian National Movement*, London 1993.

[34] Cf. *The Wailing Wall Controversy and the Course of the Disturbances* [in:] *Palestine. A Study of Jewish, Arab, and British Policies.* Vol. 2, pp. 597–614; *Report of the Commission on the Palestine Disturbances of August 1929 presented by the Secretary of State for the Colonies to Parliament by command of His Majesty*, London 1930.

talities. The actual socio-economic basis for the clashes is not in doubt, something confirmed by the special government commission called into being by London. The British, in following its recommendations, undertook an attempt to modify their policy towards Palestine and in 1930 published a subsequent "White Paper."[35] This suggested a limitation to Jewish immigration and land acquisition, which aroused protests in Jewish circles and in effect forced James Ramsay MacDonald's government to withdraw from the plan. This was an important signal for the Arab side not to trust the British. The Jews also started to treat the mandate authorities with increasing suspicion.[36]

The situation spiralled out of control in 1936 when violent Arab riots directed equally at Jewish settlers and the mandate administrators took place. The insurrection which started in the April 1936 with a general strike, was to last, in various forms (manifestations, sabotage, the boycott of government institutions, political terror, attacks on Jewish settlements, etc.), for almost three years. The short-term success of the Arabs was determined by their consolidation and the creation of the Arab Higher Committee, a coalition of several groupings with the Grand Mufti at the head.[37] The lasting result of these events was the deepening isolation of both parts of the country (Jewish and Arab), as a consequence of which each led a separate existence. The British found themselves in a situation with no way out. On the one hand they understood why the Jews wanted to emigrate from Europe, on the other they saw what violent resistance the immigration was arousing from the Arabs.

A special Royal Commission was sent to the Mandate to look into a solution to the Palestinian puzzle, headed by the experienced diplomat William Robert Wellesley, Lord Peel, a former minister for India. The extensive four-hundred page report published in 1937 announced that it was impossible to reconcile the aspirations of both communities, and suggested as a remedy the division of the mandate territory into two states, Jewish and Arab, with the latter planned to be joined to Transjordan.[38] The division was intended to be conducted on the basis of the existing state

---

[35] From the surname its signatory, the Secretary of State for the Colonies, Sidney Webb, Lord Passfield (1859–1947), it was called the "Passfield White Paper." For the text see: British White Paper. Cmd. 3692 of 1930: *Palestine: Statement of Policy by His Majesty's Government in the United Kingdom*, London 1930; *Book of Documents*, pp. 64–85.

[36] Ch. Weizmann, op.cit., p. 335; B. Joseph, op.cit., pp. 135–136; R. Ovendale, *The Origins of the Arab-Israeli Wars*, 3rd ed., London–New York 1994, pp. 71–76; H. Edelheit, A. Edelheit, op.cit., pp. 144–149.

[37] For more detail see: T. Bowden, "Arab Rebellion in Palestine 1936–1939," *Middle Eastern Studies* (London). Vol. 11: 1975. No. 2, pp. 147–174; N. Bethell, op.cit., pp. 39–61; J.C. Hurewitz, *The Struggle for Palestine*, pp. 67–72, 81–85; B. Morris, *The Road to Jerusalem. Glubb Pasha, Palestine, and the Jews*, London 2003, pp. 33–55 (Chapter "The Arab Revolt 1936–1939"). The course of the conflict is illustrated in maps in: M. Gilbert, *The Routledge Atlas of the Arab-Israeli Conflict*, maps 18–21, 24, 25.

[38] Full text: *Palestine Royal Commission. Report. Presented by the Secretary of State for the Colonies to Parliament by Command of His Majesty. July, 1937*. Cmd. 5479, London 1937; reprint edition: *The Rise of Israel*. Vol. 24: *The Royal Commission Report, 1937*. Ed. by A.S. Klieman, pp. 9–424. For more detail see: M.J. Cohen, *Palestine: Retreat from the Mandate. The Making of British Policy,*

of affairs. The Jews were to receive Galilee which was to a significant degree already inhabited by them as well as the larger part of the coastal strip from the border with Lebanon to Tel Aviv, and further south in the direction of Gaza. The Arabs were awarded almost three quarters of the Mandate – including the Negev, Samaria, and Judea, a part of the coast in the region of Gaza as well as access to the port of Jaffa. London reserved for itself, in the form of a mandate, an enclave covering the central part of the country with Jerusalem and Bethlehem as well as a corridor linking it with the Mediterranean in the area of Jaffa. In addition, the British maintained control over, among other things, the port of Haifa. This allowed them to exert influence on the future of both states, and considering the actual subordination of Transjordan, the newly dealt cards in essence did not noticeably change Great Britain's position in this area.[39]

Nevertheless, neither the Palestinian Arabs nor the Jews were prepared for the proposed compromise. The former, concentrated around the Grand Mufti, rejected it decisively, opting for sovereignty in the whole of Palestine.[40] The report also did not gain the full support of the Jewish side as it went against their statehood aspirations. This was why the Jews postulated further negotiations and demanded, among other things, sovereign rights in Jerusalem as well as the attachment of the northern Negev, a potential economic hinterland and a place for future immigrants, to their territory.[41]

Due to the lack of compromise, the impasse in Palestine deepened. Chaos within the country intensified. The British responded by declaring a state of emergency and brought in additional military units. The Palestinian conflict had started to expand beyond the framework of a local conflict and become internationalized, affecting the mood within the entire Middle East. Hitler's Germany and Mussolini's Italy attempted to harness Arab dissatisfaction, as London's growing problems in this strategic region were to their advantage, and the political emancipation of the Islamic world could turn out to be an effective counterbalance to British influences. Both states undertook a cautious offensive in the Middle East, something borne out by, among other things, German attempts to provide help, in the form of armaments, to the Palestinian insurgents. A part of the Arab elites contemplated forging cooperation with the Axis countries as a means of pressurising Great Britain. The Grand

---

[39] 1936–1945, London 1978, pp. 10–65; M. Pułaski, "Próba podziału Palestyny w roku 1937 a problem emigracji Żydów" [in:] A. Pankowicz (ed.), Wojna i polityka. Studia nad historią XX wieku, Kraków 1994, pp. 109–119; Palestine. A Study of Jewish, Arab, and British Policies, pp. 799–875; Ch. Sykes, Cross Roads to Israel. Palestine from Balfour to Bevin, 2nd ed., London 1967, pp. 164–189.

[39] See maps: J. Bagot Glubb, op.cit., p. 152; A. Shlaim, The Iron Wall. Israel and the Arab World, London 2001, p. 20; Encyclopaedia Judaica, 4th ed., Jerusalem 1978, Vol. 13, col. 36; M. Gilbert, The Routledge Atlas of the Arab-Israeli Conflict, map 22.

[40] Only the Emir of Transjordan was inclined to accept the plan of division, which one cannot be surprised at given that it envisaged the incorporation into his country of the greater part of Palestine. J. Nevo, King Abdallah and Palestine. A Territorial Ambition, Oxford 1996, pp. 34–35.

[41] S.L. Hattis, The Bi-National Idea in Palestine During Mandatory Times, Haifa 1970, pp. 168–187; D. Ben-Gurion, The Peel Report and the Jewish State, London 1938.

Mufti of Jerusalem, al-Husseini, took advantage of the opportunity to forge contacts with the Nazis.[42]

At the same time, growing tension in Europe (the Anschluss of Austria, the Munich crisis), and the threat of the Reich's gaining Arab support, induced the British to verify their Palestinian policy. Thus, already before the end of 1938, Great Britain had withdrawn from its plan of dividing Palestine. This was the result of a subsequent commission, the Partition Commission, which sought to delineate the borders between the Arab and Jewish part. Despite the presentation of three variations on the division, the conclusion was that the Peel Commission Partition Plan could not be implemented as none of the solutions guaranteed national uniformity or economic self-sufficiency for the proposed states.[43] An attempt at a compromise was the conference called in London in February 1939 with the participation of the representatives of the Palestinian Arabs and Jews, and five Arab countries: Egypt, Iraq, Saudi Arabia, Transjordan and Yemen (the English indirectly recognised the Palestinian issue as a general Arab one). The conference was peculiar, for the Arab delegates did not agree to sit at the same table with the Jews, and so the Mandate had to conduct separate negotiations with each group The failure of negotiations, given the fundamental difference in positions, surprised no one.[44]

London decided on a political manoeuvre. Given the threat of an outbreak of war in Europe, this involved ensuring at least the neutrality of the strategically important Arab world.

This manoeuvre was announced in the White Paper of the 17th of May 1939, which in effect withdrew Great Britain from the Balfour Declaration.[45] Under the pretence of compromise it constituted a classic product of political conditions. Contrary to the Peel Commission report, into whose preparation until recently so much effort had been put, it envisaged the creation within the course of a decade of a bi-national Palestinian State with a constant and clear Arab majority. The Jewish community was to constitute no more than one third of its population. Significant restrictions on the acquisition of land by Jews and on Jewish immigration were pro-

---

[42] See, among others, Ł. Hirszowicz, *III Rzesza i arabski Wschód*, Warszawa 1963 (English language version: *The Third Reich and the Arab East*, London 1966); F.R. Nicosia, *The Third Reich and the Palestine Question*, New Brunswick 2000; A. Hillgruber, *The Third Reich and the Near and Middle East, 1933–1939* [in:] U. Dann (ed.), op.cit., pp. 274–282.

[43] For the text see: J. Woodhead, "The Report of the Palestine Partition Commission," *International Affairs* (Oxford), No. 2: 1939, pp. 171–193. Cf. also P.L. Hanna, op.cit., pp. 131–140; H. Mejcher (Hg.), op.cit., pp. 272–274.

[44] Y. Bauer, *From Diplomacy to Resistance. A History of Jewish Palestine 1939–1945*, New York 1973, pp. 16–51; FRUS 1939. Vol. IV, pp. 720–722: *The Ambassador in the United Kingdom (Kennedy) to the Secretary of State. London, 1 III 1939*; S.L. Hattis, op.cit., pp. 201–206; *The Political History of Palestine under British Administration*, pp. 26–27; N. Bethell, op.cit., pp. 61–65.

[45] This document is known equally as the MacDonald White Paper after the signatory of the document, the British Colonial Secretary Malcolm MacDonald (1901–1981, the son of the first Labour Prime Minister of Great Britain, James Ramsay MacDonald).

posed. Only seventy-five thousand Jews were to settle in the Mandate within the course of the next five years, with any further influx to be dependent on the agreement of the Palestinian Arabs. The guarantees already made of protection for the Yishuv interests were to be merely formal in nature for if the British plan were to succeed, the Arabs would control the future state.[46]

It would be difficult not to note that Great Britain's policy underwent an interesting evolution: from support of the idea of a "Jewish National Home" (Balfour's declaration, the Palestine Mandate), through the concept of its moderation (Passfield's "White Paper") to the actual withdrawal from further steps in this direction.[47]

The resolutions of the "White Paper" were rejected by both sides of the conflict, including the decisive majority of Arabs, although they did so partly for tactical reasons. The Jews understood it as a breaking of promises made, while the expression of their opposition was a broadening of the civil disobedience movement against the mandate administration.[48] If previously it had been the Arabs who had revolted against British governments, now the matter of MacDonald's "White Paper" had reversed the roles, with the Mandate finding a new political opponent. The legal validity of the "White Paper" was not recognised by the Permanent Mandates Commission of the League of Nations,[49] and was also opposed by the labour opposition and future Prime Minister Winston Churchill.[50] Yet this course of action was to remain in force right up until the end of the British presence in Palestine, i.e., until 1948.

---

[46]  For the text see: British White Paper. Cmd. 6019 of 1939: *Palestine: Statement of Policy*, London 1939; *The Rise of Israel*. Vol. 27: *The Darkest Year 1939*, doc. 25: *The 1939 White Paper, May 1939*, pp. 302–313; "Palestine Statement of Policy by H.M.G. Official Communiqué No. 2/39," *The Palestine Post*, 18 V 1939, pp. 3 onwards; *Great Britain and Palestine*, pp. 167–174; J.C. Hurewitz, *Diplomacy in the Near and Middle East*. Vol. II, pp. 219–226; W. Laqueur, B. Rubin (eds.), op.cit., pp. 64–75.

[47]  G. Sheffer, *Principles of Pragmatism. A Revaluation of British Policies toward Palestine in the 1930s* [in:] U. Dann (ed.), op.cit., pp. 109–127.

[48]  "Memorandum on behalf of the Jewish Agency for Palestine by Chaim Weizmann to High Commissioner for Palestine Harold MacMichael, 31 May 1939, to be forwarded as evidence to the Palestine Mandate Commission protesting the policy in the White Paper" [in:] *The Rise of Israel*. Vol. 28: *Implementing the White Paper*, doc. 4, pp. 10–26; "World Jewry's Response" [in:] *The Rise of Israel*. Vol. 27, doc. 31–38, pp. 350–545; Ch. Weizmann, op.cit., pp. 493–507. Cf. also the Central Archives of Modern Records in Warsaw [Archiwum Akt Nowych, subsequently AAN]. Poselstwo RP w Bernie 153 (The Polish Republic's diplomatic mission in Bern), pp. 12–16. Report of the consul of the Polish Republic in Tel Aviv to Department P.III of the Ministry of Foreign Affairs in Warsaw *on the matter of the Jewish reaction to the 'White Paper'* (1 VI 1939).

[49]  "Report by the Permanent Mandates Commission on the policy of the 1939 White Paper made at the thirty-sixth session of the commission, 1939" [in:] *The Rise of Israel*. Vol. 27, doc. 29, pp. 338–342; "Letter from Chaim Weizmann to Dr. Nahum Goldmann, 30 May 1939, on debates in the House of Commons and in the League of Nations' Permanent Mandates Commission on White Paper" [in:] *The Rise of Israel*. Vol. 28, doc. 3, pp. 7–9; "White Paper not in Accordance with League's View of Mandate," *The Palestine Post*, 25 VIII 1939, pp. 9–12.

[50]  "Speech by Winston Churchill in the House of Commons, 23 May 1939, and comments by other members of Parliament" [in:] *The Rise of Israel*, Vol. 27, doc. 28, pp. 331–337; *Parliamentary Debates (Hansard). House of Commons. Official Report. 5th Series*. Vol. 347, London 1939 [further: *Parliamentary Debates (Commons)*], 22 and 23 V 1939, coll. 1937–2190.

# Chapter II: Illegal or independent immigration?

## 1. The dispute over terminology

When the British had become convinced that further access to oil could not be reconciled with further Jewish immigration they placed their sympathies on the side of the Arabs (there were after all tens of millions of them in the Middle East) and started to gradually withdraw from the promises made to Jews in the Balfour Declaration. In practice this meant limiting Jewish immigration to Palestine. The Jews understood London's policy as a breaking of the promises made to them and they started to organize immigration by means other than those legally available. They defined it – as opposed to the *aliyah* allowed by the Mandate authorities – as "type B immigration," that is, *Aliyah Bet*.

*Aliyah Bet* is a term derived from Hebrew. *Aliyah*, the word for the influx of Jews to Palestine (then, beginning in 1948, to Israel), also means "growth, increase, augmentation," e.g. an increase in temperature, the raising or rising of something, promotion at work, etc. Many religious Jews believed that the process of leaving the Diaspora constituted a mystical means of bringing oneself closer to perfection. "Bet" is the second letter of the Hebrew alphabet and in combination with the word "aliyah" connotes something secret and illegal.

The immigrants who took this route were called *ma'apilim*, from the Hebrew *ha'apala* – doggedly raising themselves upwards, ascending through effort or the overcoming of difficulties. Within the context of Jewish immigration *ha'apala* is a term used specifically for the illegal forms of immigration that occurred during the period of the British mandate, and evokes the related strenuous effort and difficulties. The concepts of *Aliyah Bet* and *ha'apala* are used interchangeably and both lie within the framework of the wider concept of *aliyah*, i.e. immigration to Eretz Israel.[1]

---

[1] M. Syrkin, *Blessed is the Match. The Story of Jewish Resistance*, Philadelphia 1947, p. 310; *New Encyclopedia of Zionism and Israel*. Vol. 1. Ed. G. Wigoder, London–Toronto 1994, p. 48 (entry: *Aliyah*); *Encyclopaedia Judaica*, 4th ed., Jerusalem 1978. Vol. 8, col. 1248 (entry: *Illegal Immigration*). The term *ha'apala* is used today, among other things, in the context of climbing to the top of something or reaching the final stage in a tournament.

In a similar way, through the utilization of subsequent letters of the Hebrew alphabet, there arose such terms as *Aliyah Gimmel* ("type C immigration," illegal, with the use of force) and *Aliyah Dalet* ("type D immigration," on the basis of false documents or the multiple use of the self same documents by new people every time).[2]

The British consistently perceived this form of immigration as "illegal immigration" or "illicit," as it was contrary to the procedures determined by them. This matter was viewed differently from the Jewish side. *What was termed illegal immigration* – wrote one of the *Aliyah Bet* activists – *became the proven way of rescuing Jews and of overcoming the barriers set up by the infamous White Paper. Those barriers were intended to prevent our settling [...] in our homeland.*[3] Which is why Jews referred to *ha'apala* as "unauthorised," "clandestine" immigration, and its organizers as "the gate breakers,"[4] reserving the term 'illegal' rather for McDonald's "White Paper" (1939).[5] This matter of terminology only appears on the surface to be secondary. In point of fact it proves that the same issues appeared differently from British and Jewish perspectives. Insofar as the British took their mandate to Palestine from international law, i.e., from manmade sources, the Jews in turn claimed that their mandate was derived from the Bible, in other words from God's law. These differences in position were to impose themselves on the course of developments in Palestine, and consequently on attitudes along the London–Yishuv line.

## 2. Without formalised frameworks

The phenomenon of illegal immigration had been known since the days when Palestine was part of Turkey. Amongst the participants in subsequent *aliyah*, beginning in 1882–1903, there had been many who, thanks to various dodges and pretexts (bribes, pilgrimages to sacred places etc.), had managed to settle in Eretz without the permission of the Turkish authorities. Obtaining such permission would after all have been difficult, considering the tense relations between Russia and Turkey, and it was from Russia that the overwhelming bulk of immigrants derived. Many would-be immigrants were stopped at the border and had to go back. Others attempted to reach Palestine by sea, in small boats and under cover of night. Many succeeded. Those who were less fortunate and were apprehended by the Turks, if they did not

[2]  A. Halamish, *The Exodus Affair. Holocaust Survivors and the Struggle for Palestine*, London 1998, p. 293; I. Zertal, *From Catastrophe to Power. Holocaust Survivors and the Emergence of Israel*, Berkeley–Los Angeles–London 1998, pp. 139, 333.
[3]  Quoted after: M.M. Mardor, *Strictly Illegal*. Foreword by David Ben-Gurion, London 1964, p. 53.
[4]  Cf. the telling title of Bracha Habas' book, *The Gate Breakers*, New York–London 1963.
[5]  *Of course we rejected the White Paper unanimously. We declared it illegal*, wrote the subsequent first president of Israel. Quoted after: Ch. Weizmann, *Trial and Error. The Autobiography of Chaim Weizmann*, New York 1949, p. 413.

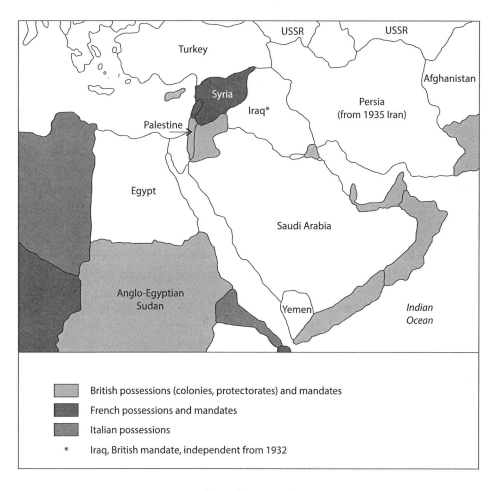

**Map 1.** The Midlle East in the 1930s

Author's study

have an argument at their disposal in the form of cash, consequently had to face deportation.[6]

Not all of those sent back gave up. Sometimes instead of returning to their own countries they travelled to Beirut, where they tried once again, this time by land, to enter Palestine. The trade in passports mushroomed. Documents which certified that the holder came from Bulgaria, Tunisia or another country recognising the authority of the Sultan were much sought-after.

The situation was to change after the First World War when Palestine fell to Great Britain as a mandate of the League of Nations and the British made checking documents for a condition of Jewish settlement. As long as the influx of immigrants was not mass in nature (in the 1920s there settled here around 100,000 Jews), the British saw no cause for worry. But the situation was to change in the following decade. The growth in immigration brought with it a change in the power structure in Palestine and in effect polarized relations within the Mandate. Mass *aliyah* was opposed by both the British (for they feared it would weaken their position in the region) and the Palestinian Arabs (for the idea of Eretz Israel collided with their own political aspirations). For this reason, when it became clear that not all potential immigrants would be able to settle in the Mandate, illegal Jewish immigration started to develop.

Initially this did not involve formalised frameworks. Some came as tourists and remained in the country.[7] Others arrived to study and simply did not leave. Some decided on fictitious "paper" marriages with citizens of the Mandate or those in possession of an immigration visa. In accordance with the Palestine Citizenship Act of 1925, the spouse of a person holding Palestinian citizenship automatically acquired such citizenship and could not be deported. Such formal marriages occurred both in Palestine and beyond its borders. There were also cases of candidates for immigrant status receiving – in the form of a temporary deposit – the sum of money required for applying for a certificate.[8] There were noted cases of forged entry documents as well as multiple use of the same documents by new people every time. Small groups would force their way through the "green border" to Palestine from Lebanon and Syria. To the countries of the Levant came immigrants with French visas, including those from Romania and Poland. They were helped to cross the border by local

---

[6] Ş. Batmaz, "Illegal Jewish – Immigration Policy in Palestine (Periods of 1st and 2nd Constitutional Monarchy)," *Turkish Studies* (Ilford). Vol. 3/1: Winter 2008, pp. 219–229. Cf. also: R. Sanders, *Shores of Refuge. A Hundred Years of Jewish Emigration*, New York 1989, pp. 121–122; H.M. Sachar, *A History of Israel. From the Rise of Zionism to Our Time*, New York 1988, pp. 29, 34–35.

[7] Those settled in this way were termed by the Jewish Agency as "irregular" immigrants, explaining that they had crossed the border of the Mandate in a manner in accordance with the law. [The Jewish Agency for Palestine], *Memorandum submitted to the Palestine Royal Commission on behalf of the Jewish Agency for Palestine*, London 1936, p. 109.

[8] The National Archives, London (subsequently TNA). CO 733/454/2 (pp. 26–28). *Memorandum on (A) Jewish Illegal Immigration into and (B) Jewish Emigration from Palestine by the Commissioner for Migration and Statistics* (October 1945?). Central Zionist Archives, Jerusalem (subsequently CZA). S 25/22701. *Note of illegal immigration* (September 1938?).

Jewish settlers in Upper Galilee. Others were helped, for an appropriate fee, by Arab fishermen and guides from Jaffa and Haifa.[9] The specifics of Palestinian conditions meant that it was not easy for the Mandate to be informed of the actual scale of this phenomenon.

A sizeable group among the illegal immigrants were participants in the Maccabiah tournament, i.e. Jewish sporting competitions known as the Jewish Olympics. In 1932 about 25,000 Jews came from abroad to the Maccabiah, sportsmen and tourists. The majority of them remained in Palestine. The story was to repeat itself, though not on the same scale, four years later in 1936.[10]

According to the report of Lord Peel's Royal Commission, for the period 1932–1933, around 22,400 Jews settled illegally in the Mandate. The majority (17,900) were "travellers" who had stayed in the country without permission.[11] The largest group of so-called illegal tourists were from Poland. In the autumn of 1933 it was estimated that there may even have been ten thousand of them in Palestine.[12] "Palestinian tourism" was not a coordinated phenomenon. It was organized, usually under the facade of "trips," not only by travel agencies but sporadically and for financial profit by various Jewish organizations from the Diaspora not having anything in common with tourism as such whatsoever. Amongst these were political parties, newspaper editorial boards, youth organizations and private individuals.[13] As long as the size of this immigration was small, the British tolerated it. They reacted when the numbers of immigrants started to significantly increase.

In order to limit the size of "tourist immigration," in November 1933 the mandate authorities introduced a deposit of £60 taken from each person applying for a tourist visa to Palestine. In the case of an extended unlawful stay in the Mandate the sum would be appropriated. A return ticket also had to be shown. At the same time the border guard was strengthened on the side of the Syrian Transjordanian border.[14]

---

[9] *A Survey of Palestine. Prepared in December 1945 and January 1946 for the information of the Anglo-American Committee of Inquiry*. Vol. I, Jerusalem 1946, pp. 209–210, 216; TNA. CO 733/255/11 (p. 117). *Report by the Deputy Commissioner of Migration and Statistics. Government of Palestine, following a tour in September 1934. Edwin Samuel, London 19 X 1934*.

[10] Ibidem; M. Gilbert, *Israel. A History*, London 1999, p. 79.

[11] *Palestine Royal Commission. Report. Presented by the Secretary of State for the Colonies to Parliament by Command of His Majesty. July, 1937*. Cmd. 5479, London 1937, p. 290; [Esco Foundation for Palestine], *Palestine. A Study of Jewish, Arab, and British Policies*. Vol. 2, New Haven 1947, p. 682.

[12] AAN. Ambasada RP w Londynie 902 (The Embassy of the Polish Republic in London) (p. 60). Report of Dr Bernard Hausner, the Consul General of the Polish Republic in Tel Aviv, to the Consular Department of the Polish Ministry of Foreign Affairs in Warsaw, 28 X 1933.

[13] Ibidem, p. 64, Report of Dr. Bernard Hausner "on the matter of tourism to Palestine" to the Consular Department of the Polish Ministry of Foreign Affairs in Warsaw, 21 IX 1932.

[14] TNA. T 161/1107. S. 3854/1, *From FO to the Secretary to the Treasury, 25 XI 1933*.

# 3. The position of the leaders of Yishuv

It is peculiar that *Aliyah Bet* did not immediately gain the support of the leaders of the Jewish Agency. It was feared that these activities could not only harm the relative improvement in relations with the British so far achieved, but also influence the immigration quotas which, for the years 1933–1936, were among the highest since the creation of the Mandate.[15] Not without significance is the fact that the British authorities, motivated by humanitarian considerations, had initially legalised the stay in Palestine of those who had arrived or stayed unlawfully, ignoring the relevant procedures.[16] They could use the existing immigration quotas.[17] After all the number of such people grew with each year. If in 1930 the stay of 695 had been legalised, and then a year later the number was already 939, while in 1934 it had risen to 4,114 illegal Jewish immigrants.[18]

Support for *Aliyah Bet* on the part of the Yishuv leadership was not conducive to the tactical cooperation of the mandate authorities with Hagana after the outbreak in 1936 of the Arab uprising. The British agreed at the time to create a Jewish police force, and later, auxiliary intervention units, the so-called Special Night Squads. They were to serve in the defense of strategic objects like the oil pipeline from Kirkuk (Iraq) to Haifa. The commander of this unit, Captain Orde Charles Wingate, a Christian Zionist and mystic called "Lawrence of Judea," created from it a crack commando style formation, while the experience gained by Jewish youth later turned out to be highly valuable.[19]

---

[15] For the years 1933–1936 the British issued in total 164,300 certificates, i.e. over 30,000 more than for the whole period 1919–1932. FRUS 1939. Vol. IV, p. 772: *Memorandum by Mr. J. Rives Childs of the Division of Near Eastern Affairs. Washington, 3 VI 1939*; *Great Britain and Palestine 1915–1945*. Ed. by The Royal Institute of International Affairs. Information Papers No. 20, London–New York 1946, p. 63; *The Political History of Palestine under British Administration (Memorandum by His Britannic Majesty's Government presented in July, 1947, to the United Nations Special Committee on Palestine)*, Jerusalem 1947, pp. 8, 15.

[16] CZA. S 25/22701. *Control and legalization of illegal immigrants* (19 XI 1937).

[17] See also: FRUS 1939. Vol. IV, p. 745: *The Consul General at Jerusalem (Wadsworth) to the Secretary of State. Jerusalem, 3 V 1939*; A. Tartakower, K.R. Grossmann, *The Jewish Refugee*, New York 1944, p. 71.

[18] AAN. Ambasada RP w Londynie 271 (The Embassy of the Polish Republic in London) (pp. 81–84). A letter of Zdzisław Kurnikowski, the Consul General of the Polish Republic in Jerusalem, to the Consular Department of the Polish Ministry of Foreign Affairs, Department E II in Warsaw of 1 II 1935.

[19] J. Slutsky, *Khagana – Evreyskaya boevaya organizatsiya v Eretz-Israel'*. Kn. 1, Tel-Awiw 1978, pp. 294–303; E.N. Luttwak, D. Horowitz, *The Israeli Army 1948–1973*, Cambridge, Mass. 1983, pp. 14–16. For more detail see: Ch. Sykes, *Orde Wingate*, London 1959.

**Table 5. Persons who remained in Palestine without permission and subsequently legalised their stay, 1933–1935**

| Year | Month | In total* | Jews |
|---|---|---|---|
| 1933 | January–March | 1,580 | 1,390 |
| | April–June | 550 | 457 |
| | July–September | 614 | 536 |
| | October–December | 132 | 82 |
| 1934 | January–March | 595 | 490 |
| | April–June | 1,234 | 1,051 |
| | July–September | 1,650 | 1,447 |
| | October–December | 1,389 | 1,127 |
| 1935 | January–March | 1,029 | 897 |
| | April–June | 1,188 | 1,061 |
| | July–September | 1,290 | 1,127 |
| | October–December | 921 | 719 |
| | In total | 12,172 | 10,384 |

* For the period January 1933–December 1934 there were among them 239 Muslims and 920 Christians.

The table created from data reported in: AAN. Ambasada RP w Londynie 271 (The Embassy of the Polish Republic in London) (pp. 16–107): *Reports of the Consul General of the Polish Republic in Jerusalem for the years 1932–1935.*

Even though matters of immigration were of central importance to Zionist interests, the Yishuv leadership of the time was dominated by the view that for the moment it was difficult to talk about mass settlement of Jews from the Diaspora. It was claimed that the country first needed to be prepared, and those who could help in the development of Palestine brought in, while the scale of immigration should be correlated with Yishuv's economic potential. Priority was given to young people, with vocational qualifications. Here a role could have been played by the experience of economic collapse in Palestine that had occurred in the second half of the 1920s (following the fourth *aliyah*). Immigration then fell significantly, while re-emigration rose (in 1927 around 2,700 Jews settled in Palestine while 5,100 left the country).[20]

---

[20] *Great Britain and Palestine*, p. 63; *The Political History of Palestine*, p. 8. Emigration from Yishuv was defined with the term *yerida* (from the Hebrew for *descent*) and was considered a reproachful act.

Not all Zionist activists shared this point of view. Amongst those advocating the mass influx of settlers were Berl Katznelson (a co-founder of Histadrut and an ideologist of Mapai) and Yitzhak Tabenkin, one of the leaders of Ha'Kibbutz Ha'Meuhad (United Kibbutz, a federation of kibbutzim connected with the Zionist left).[21] Both underlined the fact that British immigration regulations affected first and foremost Jews from central and Eastern Europe, where their situation was constantly deteriorating. Katznelson, who in 1933 had visited Jewish communities in Europe, argued that the time had come for Yishuv to start being an advocate in Jewish matters and give practical help to Jews from the Diaspora in fulfilling their desire to settle in Palestine.[22]

# 4. The first transport

The initiative was taken by Zionist youth activist groups from Poland, Hehalutz and Betar. They acted independently of each other, in the way that both groups had acted independently in mutual rivalry. The members of Hehalutz recognised the hegemony of the world Zionist Organization and the Jewish Agency. Betar (an acronym from Brit Trumpeldor – the Trumpeldor Alliance) was a youth annex of Zionists-Revisionists. These young people, regardless of their political affiliations, represented in their position on immigration a far more radical stance than their fathers.

The hopes that the members of Hehalutz had placed on an increase in immigration quotas at the beginning of the 1930s gave way to disillusionment. For it turned out that the number of certificates that they had been allotted within the framework of the general pool not only was below that required but gradually reduced their participation in *aliyah*. Partial responsibility for this state of affairs lay with the Jewish Agency, which in the hope of winning over the religious party Mizrachi, had, in 1933, agreed to a change in the distribution of certificates, reducing by 50% of the pool the allocation previously reserved for Hehalutz.[23] At the same time the number of potential immigrants had risen – thousands of Hehalutz members underwent many months of training in various occupations (particularly agriculture) which was designed to prepare them for their departure for Palestine. In the 1930s, in Poland alone, there were several dozen Hehalutz camps where young people acquired a trade, became acquainted with Hebrew and also underwent a course of

---

[21]  A. Patek, *Emigracja typu B (alija bet) do Palestyny przed II wojną światową* [in:] K. Pilarczyk (ed.), *Żydzi i judaizm we współczesnych badaniach polskich*. Vol. IV, Kraków 2008, p. 296.

[22]  D. Ofer, *Escaping the Holocaust. Illegal Immigration to the Land of Israel, 1939–1944*, New York 1990, pp. 7–8. Cf. B. Katznelson, *Sobre la costa* and I. Tabenkin, *Hemos sido crueles* [in:] *La Haapala. Compilación de notas y documentos de la Inmigrácion "Ilegal" a Eretz Israel 1933–1948*. La Selección del material y su traducción fueron realizadas por Moshé Kitrón, Jerusalem 1953, pp. 11–12 and 29–30.

[23]  D. Ofer, *Escaping the Holocaust*, p. 9.

military training.[24] In this situation it was decided not to count on the Jewish Agency but to start organizing illegal immigration, though it was not labeled as such, on the premise that a Jew in Palestine *is no stranger, no intruder, no immigrant. He is at home.*[25] The undertaking started to take on real forms when it gained the support of the leader of Hagana, Eliyahu Golomb, and help was promised by emissaries from Palestine. The immigrants were to reach their goal by sea. With time this form of *aliyah* was to turn out to be the most effective.

However, the transport was not able to sail out of Poland. The journey would have lasted too long, it would have been necessary to sail around a large piece of Europe and this would surely have made it impossible to keep the whole endeavour secret. A possible option was to sail from a Mediterranean port. Initially Italy was considered, finally, however, Greece was chosen for its more favourable geographical location.[26] A small ship, *Velos*, was bought and preparatory work undertaken. The soul of the undertaking were two Yishuv emissaries, Yosef Barpal and Yehuda Braginski. They knew the local reality well. They had been born in Russia and spent their childhood and youth there, and in the 1920s they had jointly organized the Hehalutz movement – Barpal in Romania, Braginski in Poland. They also had experience in the illegal transportation of Jews (from post-revolutionary Russia).[27]

Meanwhile in Poland recruitment of future immigrants was underway. The group was organized by Braginski and Ze'ev Shind, a subsequent emissary from Palestine. And for him the reality around him was far from alien as he was working in a country he knew from childhood. 350 Hehalutz members were mobilised. After their transfer to Athens by train in the July of 1934, *Velos* set course for Palestine. Officially this was to be a holiday trip. After several days, the ship arrived at its destination, in the environs of Tel Aviv, where it was awaited by a Hagana group, who helped the arrivals ashore. The first organized *Aliyah Bet* transport was a success.[28]

The success of the mission led to its continuation. Yet the Jewish Agency's approach to these plans was one of caution and only a few of the Zionist leaders, like

[24] AAN. MSZ 9935 (pp. 17–18). *Protokół z konferencji odbytej w M.S.Z. w dniu 5 lipca b.r.* [1939] *w sprawie obozów chalucowych i emigracji turystycznej żydów (Minutes of the conference of the 5th of July [1939] on the question of Hehalutz camps and the tourist emigration of Jews).*

[25] Quoted after: D. Ben-Gurion, *Rebirth and Destiny of Israel.* Edited and translated from the Hebrew under the supervision of M. Nurock, New York 1954, p. 122.

[26] Like in 1934 Edwin Samuel of the Palestine department of migration reported to the Colonial Office, Greece was at that time the main point for dropping illegal Jewish immigrants to Palestine. TNA. CO 733/255/11 (p. 115). *Report by the Deputy Commissioner of Migration and Statistics, Government of Palestine, following a tour in September 1934. Edwin Samuel, London 19 X 1934.*

[27] Braginski is the author of the remembrance book *Am hoter el hof*, Tel Aviv 1965 (in Hebrew).

[28] Cf. Jananiá, *El episodio „Velos"* and M. Zeevi, *Días en el „Velos"* in the collection of documents *La Haapala. Compilación de notas y documentos,* pp. 12–20. Incorrect date for the trip (1933) in: D. Ben-Gurion, *Israel. A Personal History,* London 1972, p. 52. Cf. also the concise note in Shai Horev's lexicon, *Sefinot be-terem shahar. Sipuran shel sefinot ha-ma'apilim mi "Vilus" ad "Kerav Emek Ayalon." Leksikon ha-ha'apalah, 1934–1948 (Dawning Ships. The Story of the Clandestine Immigration Ships From "Vilus" to "Ayalon Valley Battle"),* Hefa 2004, pp. 31–32 (headword: "Vilus").

Eliyahu Golomb and Berl Katznelson, supported these intentions. *Velos* next trip was in September 1934. Once again there were 350 persons on board, mainly Jews from Poland. For reasons of safety the departure point was moved to Varna in Bulgaria. At the Dardanelles, however, the transport was tracked down by the British, who made it clear that they would not allow the ship to reach Palestine. It was necessary to interrupt the journey and dock at one of the Greek ports, where they intended to wait for a more opportune moment. But a subsequent attempt to reach Palestine failed, although the immigrants (in November) did manage to sail close to the Mandate. The *Velos,* turned back by the British border guards, sailed aimlessly for ten weeks, unsuccessfully trying to dock at one of the Mediterranean ports. Greece refused to receive the failed immigrants' "phantom ship," as the vessel over time began to be called.[29] *Not a single rich and so-called democratic state, claiming humanism and Christian love, wanted to accept this tragic transportation.*[30] Finally they found themselves back in Poland. For a time they spent their days at temporary camps in south-east Poland, from where, thanks to the help of the Jewish Agency, they managed to legally emigrate to Palestine within the framework of immigrant quotas. The failure of the undertaking stopped the *Aliyah Bet* activities of Hehalutz for several years.

# 5. Revisionist *Ha'apala*

In the very same year of 1934 the first marine transportation of illegal immigrants was also organized by Betar.[31] The Revisionists felt themselves discriminated against by the Jewish Agency in the distribution of immigration certificates. It was claimed that the Mapai Zionists dominant in the Agency limited the number of these documents for their ideological opponents in order to gain hegemony in Jewish society in Palestine. The situation deteriorated following the official split in 1935 and the creation of the New Zionist Organization. Henceforth, Betar was passed

[29] Cf. B. Habas, op.cit., p. 13; J. and D. Kimche, *The Secrets Roads. The "Illegal" Migration of a People 1938–1948*, London 1954, p. 21 (the name of the ship as "Vellos," similarly in M. Naor, *Haapala. Clandestine Immigration 1931–1948*, Tel Aviv 1987, pp. 4–5); *Walka o prawo powrotu do Ojczyzny (maapilim)*. Ed. by Ichud Hanoar Hacijoni-Akiba, Łódź 1948, p. 8.

[30] Quoted after: W.T. Drymmer, "Zagadnienie żydowskie w Polsce 1935–1939," *Zeszyty Historyczne* (Paris), No. 13: 1968, p. 60.

[31] According to Ludmila Epstein, connected with the Zionist-Revisionist movement, the Revisionists organized the first *Aliyah Bet* sea transport eleven years earlier in 1923. The boat was called *Nili* and set sail from Marseilles with 23 Jewish pioneers on board. The next with 250 Betar members was to sail from Danzig (via Marseilles and Alexandria). It was not possible to confirm this information in other sources. Otherwise the author (a relative of the movement's leader Vladimir Jabotinsky, who was her uncle) is not consistent for twice when writing about *Nordia* she gives a different date (on p. 73 we have the year 1928, while on p. 13 the year 1934). L. Epstein, *Before the Curtain Fell*, Tel-Aviv 1990, pp. 11–13, 72–73.

over in the official distribution of these certificates.[32] A solution appeared to be a Revisionist *ha'apala*.

The question of *aliyah* occupied an important place in the Revisionist programme. Their leader, a former journalist of one of the Odessa newspapers and a joint organizer of the Jewish Legion that had fought within the British army against the Turks, Vladimir Jabotinsky supported the mass emigration of Jews to Palestine and considered that Great Britain should be fought if it restricted *aliyah* and supported the Arabs. He treated the hostile attitudes of Palestinian Arabs towards Zionism as the natural course of things, although he foresaw the coexistence of Jews and Arabs in Eretz Israel, which was to cover the lands on both sides of the Jordan (i.e. including Transjordan). He was an advocate of a policy of "active defense," including retaliation, and proclaimed the need for speedy organization of Jewish armed forces, something essential for the creation of a state. Irgun, whose creation he brought about, adopted an even more radical position. Jabotinsky, at the end of the 1930s, concentrated his attention on the idea of "an evacuation" of the maximum number of Jews from Eastern Europe to Palestine (and tried to persuade the governments of Poland and Romania accordingly).[33]

Foreseeing the Hitlerian tempest, he argued that the only solution to the Jewish problem in Europe was immigration to Eretz Israel. *Free immigration* – he claimed – *is helping to win a country for a homeless rabble and to make the rabble a nation.*[34]

Hence various forms of illegal influx were supported. So it was, for example, during the Jewish Olympics. Several thousand immigrants managed to travel via a land route through Lebanon and Syria.[35] In the struggle across the "green border" from the side of Upper Galilee they were helped by among others, armed groups of Betar from Rosh Pina (a settlement to the north of Lake Tiberias). The main smuggling point was in the region of Mishmar Ha'Yarden, close to the Golan Heights.[36] 30–40 people were smuggled in at a time, making use of, among others, the local Circassians with their expert knowledge of the terrain. Some immigrants found shelter in one of the Circassian villages in Upper Galilee.[37] A large percentage of those who

---

[32] Y. Lapidot, *The Irgun's Role in Illegal Immigration*, p. 1 [in:] Jewish Virtual Library (http://www.jewishvirtuallibrary.org/jsource).

[33] We shall add that Jabotinsky (1880–1940) combined the features of a politician and an intellectual. He wrote novels, poems (chiefly in Russian), translated Dante into Hebrew. See: J.B. Schechtman, *The Life and Times of Vladimir Jabotinsky*. Vol. 1–2, Silver Spring, Mar. 1986; J. Nedava, *Vladimir Jabotinsky. The Man and his Struggles*, Tel Aviv 1986; S. Katz, *Lone Wolf. A Biography of Vladimir (Ze'ev) Jabotinsky*, New York 1996. In Polish cf. the pamphlet: I. Bernstein, *Włodzimierz Żabotyński jako pisarz i myśliciel. Studjum psychologiczno-literackie*, Warszawa 1935.

[34] Quoted after: L. Epstein, op.cit., p. 8; Y. Lapidot, op.cit., p. 2.

[35] CZA. S 25/22701. *Note of illegal immigration* [September 1938 ?].

[36] Y. Lapidot, op.cit.; H. Lazar, *The Revisionist Immigration* [in:] M. Naor, *Haapala*, pp. 9–11.

[37] Palestinian Circassians came from the Caucasus region, from where they emigrated in the second half of the 19th century, after the collapse of the anti-Russian Shamil rebellion. As Muslims they found shelter in the Ottoman Empire. A part of them were settled by Sultan Abdülhamid II in two

arrived were Betar supporters. With time the British strengthened the defense of the Mandate's northern border. A greater number of patrols as well as cunning ambushes gradually paralysed this means of immigrant smuggling. The solution remained the sea.

The fate of the first sea transport of Zionists-Revisionists is a ready made film script. These immigrants, on the whole Betar members from Poland, were to reach Palestine on board the Greek ship *Cappollo*, capable of transporting at most 100 people. The embarking took place during the summer of 1934 on one of the islands in the Aegean. The undertaking was supported by the movement's leadership from Warsaw and Danzig. After several days the greedy captain announced to the passengers that they were starting to run out of coal, water and food. He hoped that in this way he would force the passengers to pay more. The ration of food was reduced. The immigrants started to become agitated. Meanwhile in Tel Aviv preparations were underway to receive the transport. The plan had been for a boat to sail out to the passengers and to set them ashore at a certain distance from the coast. Rough waves and darkness however thwarted these designs. The captain took the approaching boat to be a British patrol and decided to elude it. For four subsequent nights the *Cappollo* unsuccessfully approached the shore and every time the frightened crew demanded a withdrawal. In the end the captain gave up and the ship returned to Greece. The unsuccessful immigrants, hungry and exhausted, had to step ashore on one of the Greek islands where they were arrested by the local police and taken to the nearest port, from whence, with the help of the Greek branch of the Revisionists, they sailed to Athens.[38]

Meanwhile the search was on for another ship. The choice fell on the *Union*, the vessel used to transport cement to Palestine. The ship set off in August 1934 with 117 Jewish passengers along with the crew. The journey passed without incident. For reasons of safety the passengers were to transfer to smaller boats as they approached the coast. A hundred immigrants made it ashore without any problems. Under cover of night they made it to nearby Tel Aviv and there dispersed. While the last 17 were being transported the boat started to leak. This prolonged the operation and allowed the British to arrest the group. The captain along with the crew was also detained. After a time they were all deported to Greece.[39] This failure, along with the increasing number of unsuccessful attempts to smuggle people overland, discouraged the Revisionists from organizing this type of undertaking for several years.

---

villages in Galilee – Kfar Kama and Rihaniya, where live to this day about 3000 of their descendants. D. Wasserstein, *The Druzes and Circassians of Israel*, London 1976 (pamphlet published by the Anglo-Israel Association).

[38]  H. Lazar, op.cit., pp. 12–13.

[39]  Ibidem, p. 14. Dalia Ofer maintains that the "Union" mission was a total success (op.cit., p. 11). According to Lenni Brenner (*Zionism in the Age of the Dictators*, Westport, Conn. 1983, Chapter "Illegal Immigration") as well as the *New Encyclopedia of Zionism and Israel* (vol. 1, p. 648) the majority of immigrants were apprehended by the British and subsequently interned.

# 6. "For Jews the world divides itself into two places…"

*Aliyah Bet* gradually gained wider support, also from the Yishuv leadership. This occurred for several reasons. After the outbreak of the Palestinian uprising in 1936, Great Britain imposed serious limitations on immigrant influx. The number of certificates fell almost six fold from 61,900 to 10,500 in 1937.[40] Weizmann, in his reaction to this policy, formulated the oft-quoted remark that for Jews the world is divided into places "where they cannot live" and places "where they cannot leave."[41]

Meanwhile the situation of Jews in Europe worsened dramatically. The Nazis introduced formal measures persecuting the Jewish population. Following the Reichstag's passage of the Nuremberg Laws (September 1935), German Jews became second class citizens. Persecution intensified, with its culmination on the 9th of November with the Night of Broken Glass (Kristallnacht), when the Nazis burnt hundreds of synagogues and 91 people were killed. Worry was aroused by the deteriorating economic situation of Jewish communities and the manifestations of anti-Semitism in many countries of Central and Eastern Europe.

A subsequent event was the economic crisis of the 1930s. Admittedly this did not only affect Jews *but in Eastern Europe they were amongst the extremely poor, in occupations especially dependent on the general pace of economic life, and were therefore susceptible to the blow. […] Moreover there was directed against them (through the mechanism of aggression transfer, often intentionally amplified) the tensions generated by the crisis; the normal fate, known from many countries and epochs, of a minority in conditions of crisis. This situation was not helped by the fact that Jews were a 'go-between minority' (trade, services) and it was therefore easy targets for resentment.*[42]

After the annexation of Austria (March 1938) tension rose in Europe. The flow of Jewish refugees from Germany and Austria grew. Before the outbreak of war in September 1939, their number had risen above 329,000.[43] These people went mainly to neighbouring countries though some crossed the ocean to the United States, Canada, Argentina, Brazil, to South Africa. These were joined by Jews looking for opportunities to earn money from the countries of central Europe that had been hit by the economic crisis.

---

[40] *Great Britain and Palestine 1915–1945*, p. 63; *The Political History of Palestine*, pp. 15, 33; M. Wischnitzer, *To Dwell in Safety. The Story of Jewish Migration Since 1800*, Philadelphia 1948, p. 290.

[41] M. Kula, "Porozmawiajmy jeszcze raz, na spokojnie, o syjonizmie," *Dzieje Najnowsze* (Warszawa), No. 2: 1987, p. 111. The wording first appeared in *The Manchester Guardian*, 23 V 1936.

[42] Quoted after: M. Kula, op.cit., p. 109.

[43] Data after: CZA. Z 6/1567. *The problem of German refugees*, p. 3. For more detail see: B. Eckert (Hg.), *Die jüdische Emigration aus Deutschland 1933–1941. Die Geschichte einer Austreibung*, Frankfurt/Main 1985; H.A. Strauss, "Jewish Emigration from Germany. Nazi Policies and Jewish Responses," *Leo Baeck Institute Year Book* (London). Vol. 25: 1980, pp. 313–361, Part II – Vol. 26: 1981, pp. 343–409; N. Bentwich, *The Refugees from Germany, April 1933 to December 1935*, London 1936.

And both the former and the latter were welcomed reluctantly, with attempts to send these illegal arrivals back.[44] On the one hand it is difficult not to understand the policy of states like France and Czechoslovakia, wrestling as they were with their own problems. Their position resulted simply from a desire to defend their own job market from foreign competition, from individuals generally deprived of a livelihood. On the other hand these directives worsened the tragic lot of Jewish refugees.

On the long list of countries interested in solving the refugee problem was also the United States, where the largest and the strongest Diaspora was located. Washington did not want, for various reasons, to take the full responsibility onto itself. In July 1938, therefore at the initiative of the President of the United States, Franklin Delano Roosevelt, an international conference on the problem of Jewish refugees was convened at the French resort of Evian-les-Bains on Lake Geneva. Delegations from 32 countries took part in the conference, from Europe, both Americas, and Australia. Among them delegates represented those countries where Jewish refugees had found temporary shelter as well as those states with extensive and underpopulated areas in which Jews could potentially settle. There were also delegates from Yishuv and the Diaspora, in total representing 21 Jewish organizations.[45]

The Intergovernmental Committee on Political Refugees recently convoked with its secretariat in London, even started negotiations with the German government, fated to end in fiasco.[46] Western European countries made it clear that they had already taken enough political refugees and that they had to protect their labour markets. The delegates from Latin America warned of the recklessness of opening borders to all immigrants and explained that their countries required first and foremost farming settlers and that they were not in a position to absorb such a large number of merchants and petty craftsmen. Others, mindful of relations with Berlin, carefully avoided the most heated polemics addressed at Nazi Germany.

In such a situation there was almost no choice and immigration to Palestine appeared in the eyes of many Jews to be the only solution. Also in the eyes of the anti-Zionists. *I remember an Austrian colleague arriving at the moment of Anschluss* – recalled the historian and diplomat Elie Barnawi – *a Communist whose violent anti-Zionist utterances somewhat irritated me. I asked him: "Given that, why have you come here? Who forced you?" He looked at me and in bewilderment said: "But there simply was nowhere else for me to go."*[47]

---

44  S. Wolf, "Słowa a czyny. Po historycznej debacie w Izbie Gmin," *Nasz Przegląd* (Warszawa), 26 XI 1938 (press cutting in AAN. Ambasada RP w Londynie 966, p. 97).

45  CZA. Z 6/1567. *Evian Conference*, pp. 1–2.

46  For more detail see: T. Sjöberg, *The Powers and the Persecuted. The Refugee Problem and the Intergovernmental Committee on Refugees*, Lund 1991; memorandum of the Jewish Agency: [The Jewish Agency for Palestine], *Memorandum submitted to the Inter-Governmental Conference on Refugees, 6th July, 1938*, London 1939 (reprint in: *The Rise of Israel*. Vol. 19, doc. 31, pp. 430–436).

47  Quoted after: E. Barnawi, "60 lat samotności (the interview was conducted by J. Alia, H. Guirchoun, R. Backmann)," *Forum* (Warszawa). No. 5: 2008, p. 16. Reprint from *Le Nouvel Observateur* (Paris), 29 XI 2007.

Even the USA and Canada, which had traditionally been open to immigrants, were very selective at this time in their immigration policy in relation to Jews, which was not to change even in the light of the obvious persecution being carried out by the Third Reich.[48] Jews, along with refugees of other nations and victims of persecution, did not constitute a desired category of individuals.

What conditioned such a policy by Washington? Anti-Semitism or a fear of the economic consequences of an influx of immigrants and a rise in unemployment? Indifference and pacifism or their own understanding of responsibility to the state? Each of these was to play its part. When in the 1930s immigration law was tightened it was justified in terms of the defense of national security. Initially this referred to a desire not to deepen the economic crisis which had hit America in the years 1929–1933. Later they did not want to endanger Roosevelt's "New Deal." And later still, following the outbreak of war, the idea that relaxing visa regulations could be used not only by Jews but also German spies and agents.[49]

The symbol of this policy was the dramatic history of the more than 930 passengers of the *St. Louis*, refugees from Germany, who in May of 1939 attempted to find safety in Cuba and in the USA. An unsuccessful attempt, even though the majority had guaranteed financial support in the United States on the part of families or friends. The ship had to leave Havana and return to Hamburg.[50]

In these circumstances the existing tactics of the Jewish Agency were of little use. The conviction arose that further cooperation with the Mandate would be pointless, and that the Mandate itself was not credible. For had not Lord Robert Peel's Royal Commission report announced in 1937 a proposed division of Palestine between Arabs and Jews, only for the British to officially withdraw from this plan a year later? It had withdrawn – for it had harboured the hope that given the threat of an outbreak of war in Europe it would be able to ensure, if not favour, then at least neutrality for the strategically important Arab East, where, for some time now, the penetration of the Axis Powers had increased.[51]

[48] Cf. for example R. Breitman, A.M. Kraut, *American Refugee Policy and European Jewry, 1933–1945*, Bloomington 1987.

[49] For more detail see: N.L. Zucker, N. Flink Zucker, *The Guarded Gate. The Reality of American Refugee Policy*, New York 1987; R. Daniels, *Coming to America. A History of Immigration and Ethnicity in American Life*, New York 1990.

[50] Eventually the unfortunate travellers were taken by Great Britain, France, Belgium and Holland. For more detail see: G. Thomas, M. Morgan Witts, *Voyage of the Damned*, New York 1974 (also Polish edition, *Rejs wyklętych*, Zakrzewo 2010); S. Miller, S.A. Ogilvie, *Refuge Denied. The St. Louis Passengers and the Holocaust*, Madison 2006; R. Sanders, *Shores of Refuge*, pp. 459–467 (Chapter 54: "The Course of the St. Louis"). A fictionalised version of events was presented in 1976 in the British film *Voyage of the Damned* directed by Stuart Rosenberg.

[51] For more detail see: Ł. Hirszowicz, *III Rzesza i arabski Wschód*, Warszawa 1963, pp. 39–69, and particularly the selection of documents in the collection: *Documents on German Foreign Policy 1918–1945* [subsequently DGFP]. Series D. Vol. V, London 1953, documents 561–592, pp. 746–814.

# 7. "Af al pi"

The first attempt at a secret drop of illegal immigrants by sea, after an interval of several years, took place in the spring of 1937. The leading light behind the operation was neither a member of Hehalutz nor a Revisionist but the young idealist Moshe Galili (originally Moshe Krivoshein), a sympathizer of the New Zionist Organization.[52] He believed that the perspective of leaving for Eretz Israel would return hope and meaning in life to poverty-stricken refugees from the Third Reich. He had come across the problem of refugees in France, where he had arrived from Italy after studying there in 1936. He tried to interest Zionist activists from France, Belgium, Italy and Greece in his plan, but without success. More luck was to be had in Vienna, where he made contact with the local leaders of the Revisionist movement, Dr Wolfgang von Weisl and Dr Paul Haller. The proposals of this young enthusiast aroused interest. The undertaking, which was given the codename 'Af al pi' (from the Hebrew 'in spite of all'),[53] required, however, a lot of money. This was promised but under the condition that first Galili organized a small transport and if he successfully reached Palestine with it then the operation would be continued. A small, well-equipped Greek two-mast ship, *Kosta*, was purchased. This was to take in total 15 immigrants, members of Betar and other Zionist organizations.[54]

The group set sail from Piraeus in March 1937. On board was also Galili. The journey dragged as the engine broke down easily. To make matters worse a storm broke loose and smashed a mast. Shelter had to be sought. A course for Haifa was charted. Officially *Kosta* was to only sit out the storm here. Anchored by one of the breakwaters, Galili managed to get ashore unnoticed. In Haifa he contacted the local Revisionist cell. A plan for disembarkation was devised. The local power station was to cut the power supply so that under cover of darkness the passengers could be safely brought ashore. The success of the mission constituted the green light for 'Af al pi'. There was, however, one problem. Galili, as an illegal incomer, was unable to leave Palestine easily in order to return to Europe. The problem was resolved in a daring but simple fashion. First he forced his way to Syria via the "green border" so as to return – now legally – over the mandate's border and then to embark to Greece.

Upon arrival in Athens he made contact with the local Diaspora as well as sailing circles, with a view to future transports. The most fruitful of these turned out to be

---

[52] W. von Weisl, *Illegale Transporte* [in:] J. Fraenkel (ed.), *The Jews of Austria. Essays on their Life, History and Destruction*, London 1967, pp. 166–167; W.R Perl, *Operation Action. Rescue from the Holocaust*, New York 1983, pp. 14–17, 24–29; Ch. Lazar-Litai, *Af'-al-pi. Aliyah 2. shel tenu'at Z'abotinsky*. Berit hayale ha-Etsel 1988, p. 16 (here the surname in the form Kriboshein).

[53] This was one of the slogans of the Revisionist movement: *Mass immigration to Palestine despite all the difficulties*. Quoted after: Vladimir Jabotinsky's proclamation, *Na obydwu frontach (mój apel do Narodu Żydowskiego)*, in the collections of AAN. MSZ 9916, pp. 39–41.

[54] Ch. Lazar-Litai, op.cit., p. 128. A somewhat different number of immigrants (16) can be found in the work of W.R. Perl, op.cit., p. 405.

the meeting, now in Vienna, with the head of the Austrian branch of Betar, Mordechai Katz. A strategy of action was decided upon. Galili was to organize the transports, Katz and the Betars the groups of immigrants.[55] The first group, 54 people, set off in August 1937. In 1938 three more went. All reached their goal. According to Dalia Ofer, up until September 1938, Galili was to have dropped a total of 359 Jews in Palestine, mostly Betar members from Poland and Austria. The boarding took place at Mediterranean ports in Greece (Piraeus), Italy (Fiume) and Albania (Durrës).[56]

Internal discrepancies connected with, among other things, finances and the provenance of the immigrants (Galili had initially supposed that they would come from the Third Reich) led to the suspension of the cooperation but not the operation itself, which was to be continued by the Betars and Revisionists.[57] Up until the outbreak of the war in September 1939 they organized (partly with the help of similarly minded people and private organizations) a subsequent dozen or so transports with around 10,000 illegal immigrants, chiefly from Germany and Austria.[58]

With the aim of coordinating action, the Merkaz le'Aliyah (Centre for Aliyah) was created in Paris in January 1939. One of its founders was Eri Jabotinsky, the son of the movement's leader. He worked with, among others, Hillel Kook, Shlomo Yaakobi, Eliyahu Glazer, Josef Katznelson, Abraham Stavsky and Yitzhak Rozin. Jabotinsky (Betar) was responsible for land transports to the port of departure, Rozin (Irgun) for sea transport and the safe unloading in Palestine, while Katznelson took responsibility for the financial side of the undertaking.[59] *Aliyah Bet* operations were usually protected by the paramilitary groupings of Irgun (Irgun Zvai Leumi, The National Military Organization). To deceive the British patrols, transports tried to reach the Palestinian shore under the cover of night. Radio contact was made with the Irgun unit waiting at shore and operational details were agreed upon. If the ship was not able to reach the shore the passengers were transferred at sea to small boats. Subsequently the immigrants were transferred to a safe place (e.g. to

---

[55] For more detail see: H. Rosenkranz, *Verfolgung und Selbstbehauptung. Die Juden in Österreich 1938–1945*, Wien 1978, pp. 108–110; W. von Weisl, op.cit., pp. 166–167; L. Epstein, op.cit., pp. 15–18.

[56] D. Ofer, *Escaping the Holocaust*, pp. 12–13, 323. Other data is given by H. Lazar (6 transports up until June 1938, 641 immigrants – Cf. pp. 18–19) and M. Naor (5 transports up until June 1938, 545 immigrants – Cf. p. 109). Different again may be found in Y. Lapidot, op.cit., p. 2 (6 transports, 545 immigrants).

[57] A picture of the involvement of Revisionists in *Aliyah Bet* is presented in the work of Chaim Lazar-Litai, *Af-'al-pi. Sefer aliyah bet*, Tel Aviv 1959 (in 1988 there appeared a new edition, the already cited work entitled *Af-'al-pi. Aliyah 2. shel tenu'at Z'abotinsky*; also the English edition: *Despite it all*, translated and adapted from the Hebrew by G. Wachsman, New York 1984).

[58] According to D. Ofer (op.cit., p. 14) the Revisionists and private individuals in the period 1938–September 1939 organized a drop of around 12,000 illegal immigrants. Yaacov Shavit (*Jabotinsky and the Revisionist Movement 1925–1948*, London 1988, pp. 218 and 376) increases this number to 15,000. Yehuda Bauer and Nana Sagi ("'Illegal' Immigration" [in:] *New Encyclopedia of Zionism and Israel*, p. 648) estimate the participation of the Revisionists to be 6,000 transported people.

[59] D. Ofer, *Escaping the Holocaust*, p. 71; M. Naor, *Haapala*, p. 20.

nearby kibbutzim) and were then dispersed to the extent that conditions allowed for it. Here of immense help were the grass roots members of Yishuv, inhabitants of towns and farming settlements. In order to outwit the British, the services of informers, corrupt mandate officials, smugglers, prostitutes and wandering Bedouins were employed. This tactic was later also adopted by Hagana.[60]

Merkaz le'Aliyah turned out, however, to be a body that was limited in its effectiveness and which did not play the role expected of it. Up until the outbreak of the war it had prepared only two transports – *Parita* (850 immigrants) and *Naomi Julia* (1130). Preparing such an operation was far from easy. It involved not only the hiring of a ship but equipping it to transport hundreds of people, ensuring supplies of fuel, food and drinking water, organizing safe transportation of the immigrants to the departure point. All of this with utmost discretion. This required a sizeable financial investment. It was also not easy to find a crew, as serving *Aliyah Bet* could result in the confiscation of the boat and a prison term, or, at best, a fine.

*Parita* and *Naomi Julia* were chartered from a Greek ship-owner. The first was moored in Marseilles and the second at Braila in Romania, but the plan was for both vessels to set sail from Romania. Part of the loading of the *Parita*[61] was to take place in France at a safe distance from the port of Marseilles, near the small island of Chateau d'If.[62] The refugees were brought aboard in small boats. They included Jews from France, Belgium and Holland. In Romania they were joined by others from Central Europe. The *Parita* set sail for Palestine in July 1939. After six days, in the region of Cyprus, the passengers were to transfer to smaller fishing boats. The plan, however, failed. The supplies of food and fuel ran out. They were partly replenished on Rhodes. The *Parita's* odyssey lasted 41 days. The immigrants did manage to reach the shore in Tel Aviv (during the night of the 22nd of August 1939) but found British soldiers already waiting for them on the beach.[63] However, after a week of internment the refugees were released and were allowed to stay in the Mandate.[64]

Equal misfortune was to attend the journey of *Naomi Julia*. The ship left the Romanian port of Sulina at the end of August 1939. After three weeks, on the 19th of September, as it approached the coast of Lebanon it was taken by the British. Fearing that they would be turned back to sea, the immigrants took up passive resistance.

---

[60]  TNA. CO 733/429/4 (p. 5). *Statement by an illegal immigrant. VII 1940.*

[61]  The name of this ship is sometimes confused with the *Patria*, sunk by Hagana in the port at Haifa in November 1940. Cf. an incorrect title under the photograph of the *Parita* in D. Ofer, *Escaping the Holocaust*, p. 133.

[62]  See memoires of Ludmila Epstein (op.cit., p. 36).

[63]  TNA. CO 733/395/1. *Particulars of ships and groups of illegal immigrants en route to, or preparing to depart for Palestine*, pp. 163–165; H. Lazar, op.cit., pp. 20–22. Yehuda Lapidot presents a different version. According to him the ship *under cover of darkness, it anchored some fifty meters from shore. Thousands thronged the beach and helped bring the immigrants to shore in small boats.* Y. Lapidot, op.cit., p. 3.

[64]  Cf.: "The S.S. Parita Beached at Tel Aviv on Tuesday," *The Palestine Post*, 24 VIII 1939, p. 2; "Parita Refugees Released," *The Palestine Post*, 1 IX 1939, p. 1.

They destroyed the supplies of drinking water and started to wreck the ship. Some jumped into the water to swim to shore. Finally the refugees were interned. They were freed after a month and allowed to stay in Palestine within the framework of the immigration quotas.[65]

The Revisionist activists in Poland, Austria or Romania involved in *Aliyah Bet* found themselves under the pressure of the moment. The number of refugees from Germany and those wanting to leave Europe was growing. This in turn motivated them to act immediately, sometimes independently, without coordination with the Paris centre.

# 8. The Polish chapter

*Aliyah Bet* also aroused interest on the part of the Polish authorities,[66] who, guided by internal considerations, supported the emigration of the Jewish population (as well as other ethnic minorities and economically underdeveloped groups). The emigration of Jews (who constituted about 10% of the population)[67] was motivated by a desire to solve internal economic and social problems. Jewish emigration from Poland had, however, as Jerzy Tomaszewski writes, one additional aspect, *connected with the growing radicalism of the so-called nationalist camp, which used anti-Semitic demagogy in the fight for influence with the government as well as instigating attacks on Jews. The undertaking of efforts to promote Jewish emigration could therefore have later served the political interests of the governing camp, which attempted to weaken, possibly by gaining the cooperation of some of its factions, the position of the right.*[68] In the second half of the 1930s Polish government policy took a gradual turn to the detriment of Jews, one manifestation of which was the project for "racial cleansing" among employees of state institutions as well as within key areas of Polish

---

[65] FRUS 1939. Vol. IV, Washington 1955, pp. 805, 807: *The Consul at Jerusalem (Steger) to the Secretary of State. Jerusalem, 21 IX 1939*.

[66] Usually these matters are taken up on the margins of broader reflections on Jewish society in Poland. Cf. L. Weinbaum, *A Marriage of Convenience. The New Zionist Organization and the Polish Government 1936–1939*, New York 1993; E. Melzer, *No Way Out. The Politics of Polish Jewry, 1935–1939*, Cincinnati 1997. In Polish: A. Patek, "Nielegalna emigracja żydowska z II Rzeczypospolitej do Palestyny," *Zeszyty Naukowe Uniwersytetu Jagiellońskiego. Prace Historyczne* (Kraków), No. 136: 2009, pp. 114–125.

[67] According to the census of 1931 there lived in Poland 3,113,900 Jews. J. Tomaszewski, *Niepodległa Rzeczpospolita* [in:] *Najnowsze dzieje Żydów w Polsce w zarysie (do 1950 roku)*, Warszawa 1993, p. 157. For more detail see: Sz. Bronsztejn, *Ludność żydowska w Polsce w okresie międzywojennym. Studium statystyczne*, Wrocław 1963.

[68] J. Tomaszewski (ed.), "Ministerstwo Spraw Zagranicznych Rzeczypospolitej Polskiej wobec Żydów, 1938–1939 (dokumenty)," *Polski Przegląd Dyplomatyczny* (Warszawa). Vol. 3: 2003. No. 1 (11), p. 198.

cultural life (various levels of education, the press, film, radio).[69] These plans, luckily, did not reach fruition.

Attitudes toward emigration were very clear amongst the Jews living in Poland. As Laurence Weinbaum has claimed, perhaps every fifth Jewish inhabitant was interested in leaving.[70] They were induced to emigrate by the difficult economic situation in the country, including unemployment as well as the extremely large percentage of people living from trade and crafts, in which Jews were traditionally employed. Even in the more developed western regions of the country the number of trade enterprises exceeded the real needs of the economy. In the 1930s the Jews faced the consequences of the world economic crisis, the threat from the Third Reich, and intensified anti-Jewish propaganda from nationalist groups. The imposing of limitations on Jews such as restrictions in trading on Sundays and the creation of the so-called "bench ghettos" (which forced Jewish students to occupy designated seats in lecture halls) or the introduction of "numerus clausus" whereby the number of Jewish students at Polish institutions of tertiary education was limited, caused concern. A hostile mood against Jews was manifested in, e.g., economic boycotts as well as in acts of open aggression (the pogroms in Przytyk and Mińsk Mazowiecki in 1936, and in Brest on the Bug in 1937 to name three).[71]

There were also ideological motives for emigration – the building of a national home in Palestine. In the period 1921–1937 almost 400,000 Jews left Poland,[72] a third of whom were to settle in the Holy Land. The number of those who wanted to emigrate exceeded realistic possibilities. Following the Wall Street Crash of 1929 the USA and other countries started to protect their labour markets from immigrant workers. In turn the Arab card started to take on increasing importance in the Palestinian policy of Great Britain, which was difficult to reconcile with the massive Jewish influx.

Warsaw became worried about British immigration limitations and tried to persuade the British to relax this policy. The Polish foreign minister, Józef Beck, addressing a closed session of the Council of the League of Nations, spoke of the interest in Palestine as a territory for Jewish colonisation, concluding that the Polish government would strive to obtain for this country the maximum possible absorption capacity. At this time a division of the Mandate into an Arab and Jewish part

[69]  Ibidem, p. 204; AAN. MSZ 10004 (pp. 131–135). A note entitled: "Sprawa żydowska w resorcie MSZ oraz innych urzędach centralnych" (The Jewish question in the Ministry of Foreign Affairs and other central [government] offices), first half of February 1939.

[70]  L. Weinbaum, op.cit., p. 166.

[71]  E. Melzer, op.cit., Chapters 4 and 5 (pp. 53–80); E. Mendelsohn, *Żydzi Europy środkowo-wschodniej w okresie międzywojennym*, Warszawa 1992, pp. 104–120 (translation from English: *The Jews of East Central Europe between the World Wars*, Bloomington 1983).

[72]  J. Tomaszewski, *Niepodległa Rzeczpospolita*, pp. 168–175; R. Żebrowski, *Dzieje Żydów w Polsce 1918–1939. Wybór tekstów źródłowych*, Warszawa 1993, pp. 7–8; K. Bojko, "Emigracja polskich Żydów do Palestyny i Państwa Izrael od końca wieku XIX do czasów współczesnych," *Portolana. Studia Mediterranea* (Kraków). Ed. by D. Quirini-Popławska. Vol. 3: 2007, pp. 393–398.

was being considered, and the Polish government desired to introduce the question of Jewish emigration into these discussions. During his stay in Geneva Beck arranged a meeting with the British foreign minister, Anthony Eden, to whom he explained the reasons for Polish interest in the Palestinian problem. He intentionally focused on the economic motive to avoid any suspicion of anti-Semitism.[73]

Given Great Britain's reluctance to change its position, potential overseas territories were considered for the settlement of Polish Jews. Among those considered was Madagascar, which belonged to France. The absence of alternative directions for emigration and possibilities for their successful realisation amongst Jews inclined the Polish authorities to support the Zionist programme.[74]

The project announced by Vladimir Jabotinsky in 1936 for the evacuation, within the course of ten years, of one and a half million Jews from Eastern Europe to Palestine (including around 700,000 from Poland) met with genuine interest on the part of the Polish government.[75] *Our position is entirely at one with that of the Zionists-Revisionists Jews and organizations akin to them* – wrote Wiktor Tomir Drymmer, the head of the Consular Department at the Ministry of Foreign Affairs, a close colleague of Józef Beck.[76] The secret agreement concluded with the Zionists-Revisionists included a broad range of cooperation.

The Revisionists received, among other things, financial help and military training from the authorities. At Polish military camps in Rembertów, Andrychów, Warsaw, Pińsk and Zofiówka in Volynia (eastern Poland), under the watchful eye of Polish officers, soldiers of Hagana and Irgun Zvai Leumi were also trained. There they became acquainted with the principles of sabotage and conspiracy. Palestinian Jews also took part in the courses. They came to Poland by various routes, some on false passports, others as tourists. For reasons of secrecy the course participants dressed in civilian clothes and were forbidden to appear in public places or to make contact with the local Jewish population even if they had relatives in Poland. The future fighters were provided with weapons which were later smuggled into Palestine.[77]

---

[73] M. Pułaski, "Próba podziału Palestyny w roku 1937 a problem emigracji Żydów" [in:] A. Pankowicz (ed.), *Wojna i polityka. Studia nad historią XX wieku*, Kraków 1994, p. 118; G. Zalewska, "Sprawa emigracji żydowskiej z Polski w drugiej połowie lat trzydziestych w świetle materiałów polskiego MSZ," *Dzieje Najnowsze* (Warszawa). No. 1: 1988, pp. 99–103.

[74] Cf. the memorandum *Czy istnieją możliwości masowej kolonizacji żydowskiej poza Palestyną?* (1938) in the collections of AAN. MSZ 9909, pp. 4–11.

[75] On the project see: W. Żabotyński [V. Jabotinsky], *Państwo Żydowskie*, Warszawa–Kraków–Poznań–Łódź [1937], pp. 131–132, 142–143.

[76] Quoted after: E. Kossoy, "Żydowskie podziemie zbrojne w Palestynie i jego polskie powiązania," *Zeszyty Historyczne* (Paris), No. 157: 2006, p. 66.

[77] L. Weinbaum, op.cit., Chapter 7: "Military Aid" (pp. 123–163); W.T. Drymmer, op.cit., pp. 71–72; Y. Shavit, *Jabotinsky and the Revisionist Movement 1925–1948*, London 1988, p. 38; W. Chmielewski, *Bojownicy Ziemi Świętej. W II RP przygotowywali się do walki o powstanie Izraela*, „Nowiny Kurier" (Tel Aviv), 26 V 2006, pp. 10–11.

As Aleksander Klugman writes, *the transportations were camouflaged as duty-free furniture and household equipment* for Jewish immigrants from Germany.[78]

When, in the second half of the 1930s, the possibilities of legal emigration to Palestine started to be restricted, the significance of *Aliyah Bet* grew. In 1938 only 3357 Jews from Poland settled in the Mandate, nine times fewer than in 1935. This situation did not satisfy either the expectations of the Polish side or the Jewish population.[79] The Revisionists especially counted on cooperation with Polish government circles in the area of *haʿapala*. As has been mentioned, they claimed that they were discriminated against by the Jewish Agency in the distribution of immigration certificates. Help from the Polish side took various forms, for example enabling Jews to leave "in a tourist capacity," and they cooperated with the Jewish side in organizing rail transports of emigrants to the Romanian port of Constanta, where ships waited for them to sail to Palestine.

One such undertaking is recalled by Marek Kahan, an activist from the Polish Revisionists branch. This was a secret transport of a 250 strong group of Jewish young people via Romania in December 1938. The emigrants were helped by the Polish Ministry of Foreign Affairs which supplied them with free passport booklets. *Equipped with passports, the group, using the cheapest possible transport available, arrived in Constanta. There a freight ship to Palestine awaited them, upon which the free passports were collected to be returned to the Polish authorities. What is more [...] the Ministry of Finance had given permission for 40 pounds sterling to be given by the Polish National Bank to each individual at the official exchange rate (of 25 zlotys rather than the market price of 40).*[80]

"Tourist emigration," as it was defined by the Polish authorities, lasted for the whole interwar period, but intensified in the 1930s. According to a report of the Polish Consulate in Tel Aviv, in the autumn of 1933 around 10,000 "illegal tourists" from Poland came to Palestine.[81] They left the country on the basis of legal passports, while entry into the Mandate took place on the basis of a tourist visa. This action was supported by tourist agencies and various Jewish organizations. The most active were the "Turgal" Association attached to the "Hehalutz" youth union, the tourist section of the Zionists-Revisionists youth weekly "Unzer Welt," the tourist section of the "Maccabi" sports association as well as a similar section of the *Hamagshim* journal, gathering Hehalutz organizations of general, radical and re-

---

[78]    Quoted after: A. Klugman, *Izrael ziemia świecka*, Warszawa 2001, p. 235.

[79]    L. Weinbaum, op.cit., p. 174.

[80]    Quoted after: E. Kossoy, op.cit., pp. 70–71. The vessel was called *Delpa* (a different spelling *Dalfa* also occurs, Cf. D. Ofer, *Escaping the Holocaust*, p. 323; P.H. Silverstone, *Aliyah Bet Project* (http://www.paulsilverstone.com/immigration/Primary/Aliyah/shiplist1.php). The transport successfully reached Palestine.

[81]    AAN. Ambasada RP w Londynie 902 (p. 60). Report of Dr. Bernard Hausner, the Consul General of the Polish Republic in Tel Aviv, on the question of illegal tourists, to the Ministry of Foreign Affairs in Warsaw. Consular Department, Tel-Aviv 28 X 1933.

Table 6. "Tourist emigration organizations"

| Name | Turgal | "Unzer Welt" | Poltour | Hamags-zim | Gazeta Gospo-darcza | Orbis | Others |
|---|---|---|---|---|---|---|---|
| Number of people who emigrated 1938–1.03.1939 | 2,902 | 2,156 | 743 | 401 | 273 | 239 | 591 |

The table created from data reported in: AAN. MSZ 9909 (p. 45). Message for the Head of the Emigration Policy Department, Ministry of Foreign Affairs, on the matter of Jewish tourist emigration [May 1939?].

ligious Zionists. "Tourist emigration" was also conducted by the travel agencies Orbis, Poltour as well as the Head office of Jewish Light Industry and Crafts in Poland (Centrala Drobnego Przemysłu i Rzemiosła Żydowskiego w Polsce) and its organ *Gazeta Gospodarcza*.[82]

It is worth noting that this emigration was headed not only towards Palestine but also to countries overseas and to the western part of Europe. The voyages took place officially under the facade of "trips" or "individual tourist visits" and were announced as such in newspapers.[83]

The mechanism of "tourist emigration" is presented (in relation to the activities of the Revisionists) by a report of the Provincial State Police Department in Brest on the Bug.[84] *According to the information obtained for the territory of the entire State, not excluding the town of Pińsk, there is to be conducted illegal emigration of chiefly young people to Palestine through the Zionists-Revisionists organization. Recruitment of candidates for emigration will be organized by N.N. residing in Warsaw. In the area of the town of Pińsk the representative is Lejba Dworkin, a member of the Zionists Revisionists organization at Albrechtowska Street. The aforementioned person is to organize all the formalities connected with the departure, provide instructions etc. Young people wishing to go to Palestine and being unable to do so legally, or who desire to avoid military service, should report to Dworkin Lejba, and the said will deal with the situation accordingly. Each emigrant must pay 750 zlotys towards the cost of the journey, possess proof of Polish citizenship as well as a document issued by the administrative authorities of the 1st resort allowing for travel abroad as a tourist (to*

---

[82]   AAN. KGPP 258 (p. 4). Letter of Wacław Żyborski, director of the Department at the Ministry of Foreign Affairs in Warsaw on the matter of so called tourist emigration to Palestine, Warsaw 15 VI 1939.

[83]   Cf. "Do Palestyny turystyczne przejazdy indywidualne (...)," *5-ta Rano. Pismo codzienne żydowsko--polskie* (Warszawa), 19 XII 1938, p. 2 (press cutting in the collections of AAN. MSW 1069, p. 22).

[84]   AAN. KGPP 258 (p. 11). Report of the Provincial State Police Department in Brest (on the Bug) to Main Command. Department IV. Central Investigation Service in Warsaw. Brest on the Bug, 17 III 1939.

*Romania or another state from where ships depart). Individuals not being members of the Zionists-Revisionist organization will not be sent for fear of disclosing information. Each candidate who obtains the necessary documentation in Pińsk will travel to Warsaw to the designated location from whence, upon having arranged the relevant formalities, he will be sent to that country for which permission has been granted him as a tourist. In the said country a representative will report to him, take care of formalities, issue a passport on another surname and give the name of the vessel on which passage is to take place. On this craft several dozen emigrants from various parts of Poland are gathered allegedly going on a pleasure cruise heading for the port at Tel Aviv. There in the night they will leave the ship and on shore will be waiting for them Jewish young people, resident in Palestine, who will aid them in their further journey.*[85]

Particularly active in the organization of illegal emigration to Palestine were Zionists-Revisionists.[86] The majority of their members and sympathisers departed through the intermediacy of the Tourist Department of the weekly "Unzer Welt." This department was formed in 1938 on the basis of permission granted by the Ministry of the Interior and had the right to arrange trips to the countries of South America, Belgium, France, Sweden, Albania and the Belgium Congo. "Tourists" received departure visas to these countries. Formalities were sorted out at the newspaper's headquarters in Warsaw.[87] Passports *were issued without the need to prove that the applicant was a Polish citizen, which in certain cases made the departure to Palestine possible for citizens of other states.*[88] The members of Betar could count on free passports.[89] Costs were dealt with in advance. Amongst the organizers of the Revisionist *Aliyah Bet* from Poland was a law graduate of Warsaw University, Menachem Begin, a subsequent leader of Irgun and Prime Minister of Israel.[90] *Our nation today is experiencing a historic moment –* he wrote. *Its fate is in the balance. Either it will be able to win its fight for a free homeland in which to start a new life or it will remain in captivity to die.*[91]

The Ministry of the Interior looked kindly on this immigration, instructing provincial administrative departments not to cause any difficulties, and police authori-

---

[85]   Ibidem (full text published in: A. Patek (ed.), "Żydowska 'emigracja turystyczna' z Polski do Palestyny w 1939 roku – dokumenty," *Studia Historyczne* (Kraków), No. 1 (213): 2011, pp. 87–89.

[86]   On the activities of the Hehalutz movement, which organized, among others, the transport on the *Velos* in 1934 see the subchapter "The First Transport."

[87]   AAN. KGPP 258 (p. 7). Report of the Investigation Department of the Provincial State Police Department in Brest on the Bug to Central Command Department IV in Warsaw. Brest on the Bug, 31 III 1939.

[88]   A. Klugman, op.cit., pp. 242, 244; L. Weinbaum, op.cit., pp. 186–187.

[89]   The decision was taken by the Ministry of Internal Affairs 27 XII 1937. AAN. KGPP 258 (p. 7). Report of the Provincial State Police Department in Brest on the Bug, 31 III 1939.

[90]   "Af-al-pi-magbit," *Trybuna Narodowa* (Kraków–Lwów–Warszawa), 9 XII 1938, p. 8. *Trybuna Narodowa* (*The National Tribune*) was a Jewish weekly linked with the Revisionists.

[91]   M. Begin, *Jedyna droga*, Warszawa 1936, pp. 15–16.

ties were instructed to *not frighten anyone from leaving by trifling investigations.*[92] The Finance Ministry agreed to provide foreign currency for those departing in the sum of 400 zlotys a person (the market rate for a dollar was 5.28 zlotys).[93] The possibility of increasing this amount was discussed as well as also an allotment of 100 thousand zlotys to support "tourist emigration."[94]

A conference at the Ministry of Foreign Affairs on the 5th of July 1939 was devoted to the problems of "Palestinian tourism." It was proposed that the trips should be concentrated in the hands of responsible Jewish institutions so as to eliminate suspicious middlemen, who, in a dishonest way, were trying to make money from illegal emigration.[95] When Great Britain restricted immigration to Palestine, every single certificate started to count. In accordance with the rule of supply and demand certificates were subject to abuse. Shady dealers would earn from 5 to 10 pounds on every "tourist," organizing transports without preparation or consultation with Yishuv.[96] Complaints came from those cheated, mostly poor people who had often sold off a large part of their possessions in order to pay for the "excursion."[97]

As documents of the Ministry of the Interior testify, the British mandate authorities deported to Poland a certain number of emigrants on the grounds of "illegally remaining in Palestine."[98] Admittedly, the number of those deported from the Mandate was not large (for example, in 1937 just 157 Jews were deported from the Mandate to various countries, and in 1938 – only 46),[99] yet this fact still caused concern among the Polish authorities. In the summer of 1939 they even considered the possibility of depriving 10,000 "tourists" of their citizenship so as to avoid their return.[100]

---

[92]  Quoted after: AAN. KGPP 258 (p. 5). Letter of W. Żyborski, director of the Department at the Ministry of Internal Affairs to provincial offices. Warsaw 15 VI 1939; also – ibidem (p. 1), Letter of the Head of the Ministry of Internal Affairs Department to the Central State Police Department. Department IV. Warsaw 12 V 1939.

[93]  AAN. MSZ 10004 (pp. 206–207). *Notatka w sprawie aktualnych zagadnień żydowskich.* (*A memo on the matter of current Jewish questions,* May 1939?). Zloty exchange rate after: Cz. Brzoza, *Kraków między wojnami. Kalendarium 28 X 1918–6 IX 1939,* Kraków 1998, p. 391 (data for 4 IV 1939).

[94]  AAN. MSZ 9909 (p. 44). Message for the Head of the Emigration Policy Department...; L. Weinbaum, op.cit., p. 186. Enquiry at the Archiwum Akt Nowych in Warsaw (the Central Archives of Modern Records) did not result in a categorical explanation of the matter. It is not be to excluded that the realisation of these intentions was cut short by the war.

[95]  AAN. MSZ 9935 (p. 19). Minutes from a conference held in the Ministry of Foreign Affairs on 5th July 1939.

[96]  AAN. MSZ 10008 (p. 17). *Sprawozdanie z podróży służbowej do Palestyny, odbytej w czasie 4–18 maja 1939 r.*

[97]  AAN. KGPP 258 (pp. 82–83). A letter of Max Gitman (Tours, France) to the Polish consul in Paris, 1 XII 1937.

[98]  AAN. MSW 1508 (p. 87). Letter of Jan Gajewski, head at the Warsaw Government Section to the Ministry of Internal Affairs on the matter of the deportation of Gordon Hirsz, Warsaw 5 XII 1936. It is worth looking at the whole file for it contains a series of documents on the deportation of Polish citizens from Palestine for the years 1925–1939.

[99]  *Great Britain and Palestine,* p. 64.

[100]  AAN. MSZ 10004 (p. 207). *Notatka w sprawie aktualnych zagadnień żydowskich.* (*A memo on the matter of current Jewish questions,* May 1939?).

**Table 7. Tourist emigration from Poland to Palestine January 1938–February 1939 according to month**

| | January | 247 | July | 335 |
|---|---|---|---|---|
| | February | 356 | August | 622 |
| | March | 285 | September | 51 |
| 1938 | April | 366 | October | 165 |
| | May | 112 | November | 157 |
| | June | 489 | December | 780 |
| | In total: 3,965 | | | |
| | January | 1,969 | Combined for the period January 1938–February 1939: 7,323 | |
| 1939 | February | 1,389 | | |
| | In total: | 3,358 | | |

The table created from data reported in: AAN. MSZ 9909 (p. 45). Message for the Head of the Emigration Policy Department...

**Table 8. Jewish emigration from Poland in 1938**

| | | |
|---|---|---|
| | overseas | 6,232 |
| | Palestine | 3,357 |
| Legal | Europe | 100 |
| | in total | 9,589 |
| | Palestine | 3,965 |
| | non-Palestinian | 850 |
| Illegal | in total | 4,815 |
| | combined | 14,404 |

The table created from data reported in: AAN. MSZ 9909 (p. 48). Message for the Head of the Emigration Policy Department...

The Consular Department of the Ministry of Foreign Affairs estimated that in 1938 around 4,000 "tourist emigrants" left Poland for Palestine, while in the first quarter of 1939, a further six thousand left.[101] If this data is reliable, it appears that

---

[101]   Ibidem, (pp. 206–207); L. Weinbaum, op.cit., p. 198.

from amongst the general *ma'apilim*, arrivals from Poland constituted a very sizeable percentage.

Attention was drawn to the intensification in emigration after December 1938. On the one hand this showed the enhanced cooperation between Polish government circles and the New Zionist Organization; on the other, it resulted from fears of a Polish-German war.

The activities of the Polish side required special care as "tourist emigration" was directed against a state with which Warsaw was involved in a military alliance. The situation was complicated by the tensions in Europe. The threat of armed conflict with Germany loomed, and Poland was counting on the support of Great Britain in the event of hostilities.

It was extremely important for the Polish authorities that the Jewish side exercise the utmost discretion in this cooperation and that it did not publically suggest Polish support for the endeavour. *From the moment when illegal immigration becomes publically propagated in the press and at meetings* – we read in a note from a discussion of Jan Wagner (the under secretary of the Consular Department of the Ministry of Foreign Affairs) with Vladimir Jabotinsky – *the Polish authorities will have to implement restrictions both with regard to internal legislative acts as well as diplomatic intervention on the part of Great Britain.*[102]

The Ministry of the Interior directed an order to subordinate organs for them to exert pressure on the Jewish press so that the actual purpose of the "tourist trips" was not revealed.[103] In accordance with the guidelines of the Consular Department of Emigration Policy of the Ministry of Foreign Affairs of the 27th of August 1939: *a) the participation of official circles should be limited to a minimum – and even in formally explicable matters it follows to avoid openness, b) tourist emigration should be conducted only in small groups, which do not draw attention to themselves, c) the organizers of group excursions should change the transit routes as a result of Great Britain's vigorous efforts in Romania to block tourist emigration to Palestine.*[104]

It seems that Great Britain was not aware of the actual scale of Warsaw – New Zionist Organization cooperation. This is indirectly shown by an official letter of Alec Walter George Randall of the Foreign Office, sent to Clifford Norton, the British consul in Warsaw, on the 28th of July 1939. Randall, in referring to reports from various sources, writes that a significant part of the illegal immigrants are from Poland, and have left the country *probably in organized groups*. He correctly points to the Revisionists as the main motor of *Aliyah Bet* but by proposing access for the Polish side to evidence confirming this activity he appears to exclude the possibility

---

[102]  AAN. MSZ 9918 (p. 124). *Notatka z rozmowy p. Dr. Wagnera z p. Włodzimierzem Żabotyńskim* (*A memo from a conversation of Dr Wagner with Mr. Vladimir Jabotinsky*, Warsaw, 14 VI 1939).

[103]  AAN. MSZ 9935 (pp. 18–19). Minutes from a conference held in the Ministry of Foreign Affairs on 5th July 1939.

[104]  AAN. MSZ 9935 (p. 10). A letter of Jan Wagner, deputy of the Consular Department of Emigration Policy to the Nationality Department of the Ministry of Internal Affairs of the 27 VIII 1939.

of Warsaw's cooperation in this undertaking.[105] The diplomatic representatives of the United Kingdom repeatedly intervened in Warsaw and other capitals of Central Europe (particularly in Bucharest) in order to stop the stream of illegal refugees.[106] *His Majesty's Government sincerely is of the belief that the Polish Government will do everything in its power* – we read in a note of the Foreign Office directed to the Polish ambassador in London, Edward Raczyński – *to cooperate on averting illegal immigration to Palestine insofar as it is organized or has its origins in the territory of Poland.*[107]

The help provided by the pre-war Polish authorities to *Aliyah Bet* could be interpreted as based on a desire "to get rid of the Jews" by means of their emigration to Palestine. Even if the cooperation with the Revisionists was otherwise largely short-term in nature, increasing Jewish emigration as away of weakening the influences of other Jewish groups was indeed Warsaw's strategy. An entwining of circumstances aided the discovery of common ground, although not necessarily dictated by common aims. For it was Zionist circles that proclaimed the slogan of emigration to Palestine. For them, this represented their aspiration to build their own state in the land of Israel.

---

[105] L. Weinbaum, op.cit., pp. 194–195.

[106] FRUS 1939. Vol. IV, pp. 790–791: *The Consul General at Jerusalem (Wadsworth) to the Secretary of State. Jerusalem, 21 VII 1939*; AAN. MSZ 9933 (pp. 61–63). A Foreign Office note to the Polish ambassador in London, Edward Raczyński, 2 VIII 1939.

[107] AAN. MSZ 9933 (p. 68). Translation of the Foreign Office note to Ambassador Raczyński, 2 VIII 1939.

# Chapter III: On the eve of war

## 1. Mossad – "the maritime department of Hagana"

The effectiveness of *Aliyah Bet* was dependent on the organizational efficiency of the movement. Towards the end of 1938, upon the initiative of Hagana and with the blessing of the Jewish Agency, Mossad le'Aliyah Bet (literally the Institute of B Immigration and in English also as the Organization for Illegal Immigration)[1] was created, with its headquarters in Paris. In effect it was an arm of Hagana and was to deal with all matters connected with the illegal transfer of immigrants (such as the purchase of ships and their conversion for the needs of transportation, the hiring of crews, obtainment of finances, the selection and enlisting of immigrants, obtaining travel documents, the safe arrival at destination, etc.).[2] At its head was Shaul Meirov (Avigur), one of the founders of Hagana[3] and a man without whom *Aliyah Bet* would

---

[1] It is worth noting that there is a lack of consistency in the writing of this institution's name. Cf. for example: Mossad Le'Aliyah Beth (Z.V. Hadari, *Second Exodus. The Full Story of Jewish Illegal Immigration to Palestine, 1945–1948*, London 1991), Ha-Mossad le-Aliyah Bet (A. Halamish, *The Exodus Affair. Holocaust Survivors and the Struggle for Palestine*, London 1998, p. 294), Ha'mossad Le'Aliya Bet (I. Zertal, *From Catastrophe to Power. Holocaust Survivors and the Emergence of Israel*, Berkeley–Los Angeles–London 1998, p. 333), Mossad le'Aliyah Bet (F. Liebreich, *Britain's Naval and Political Reaction to the Illegal Immigration of Jews to Palestine, 1945–1948*, London–New York 2005, p. 305), Mossad le-Aliyah Bet (M. Gilbert, *Israel. A History*, London 1999, p. 96), Mossad le-Aliya Bet (Y. Bauer, N. Sagi, "'Illegal' Immigration" [in:] *New Encyclopedia of Zionism and Israel.* Vol. 1. Ed. by G. Wigoder, London–Toronto 1994, p. 648), Mosad le-Aliyah Bet (*Encyclopaedia Judaica*, vol. 8, col. 1249), Mossad L'Aliya Bet (M. Naor, *Atlit. "Illegal immigrant" detention camp. A story of a time and place*, Mikveh Israel 2010, p. 18).

[2] The Institute for Immigration B was formally established in April 1939. Cf. D. Ofer, *Escaping the Holocaust. Illegal Immigration to the Land of Israel, 1939–1944*, New York 1990, p. 43. An incorrect date is given by Yoram Kaniuk, *Commander of the Exodus*, New York 1999, p. 209 (1934), Alan R. Taylor, *Prelude to Israel. An Analysis of Zionist Diplomacy 1897–1947*, Beirut 1970 (rev. edit.), p. 74 (1937) and Eugene J. Cohen, *Rescue. 2500.000 Jews Were Liberated by Mossad From Europe, North Africa and Asia – 1932–1990. 300 Stories and Photographs*, New York 1991, p. 14 (1937).

[3] Shaul Avigur (Meirov, 1899–1978) of Dyneburg in Livonia, settled in Palestine in 1912. From 1922 he was in the Hagana leadership and jointly created its intelligence services. As the head of Mossad le'Aliyah Bet he brought tens of thousands of Jewish refugees from Europe to Palestine. After the creation of Israel he worked closely with the Prime Minister and Minister of Defense David Ben-Gurion. During the war for independence he organized supplies of arms for the Israeli Army from Europe and the USA. In later years he was active in promoting free emigration for Jews from the USSR. The author of the memoires *Im dor ha-Haganah*, Tel Aviv 1962 (Russian translation:

not have been what it was. Politically and personally linked to the leaders of Yishuv (Eliyahu Golomb and Moshe Shertok were his brothers-in-law) he was of a more practical than political disposition and was at his best in secret matters requiring discretion. He had a wide range of experience during his long years of service within the structures of Hagana.

Thanks to him Mossad (from the Hebrew – 'institute'; it not to be confused with the Israeli secret service bearing the same name, which was created in 1951) was later to play a key role in the organization of illegal immigration to Palestine.

Who were Mossad's people? In the main they were recruited from the kibbutz movement Ha'Kibbutz Ha'Meuhad. Among them were members of Histadrut and the Hehalutz movement from Palestine and the Diaspora. They were in their early twenties and thirties. Many of them came from the kibbutzim in Upper Galilee and the Arab part of Palestine. This Arab neighbourhood, and the awareness of an uncertain tomorrow, shaped their character. Amongst Meirov's collaborators were, among others: David Nameri, Ze'ev Shind, Yosef Barpal, Zvi Yehieli, Shmarya Zameret, Yehuda Arazi, Moshe Averbuch, Yehuda Braginski, Pino Ginsburg and Ruth Klueger, the only woman in the leadership of the Institute of B Immigration. Yehuda Arazi ("Alon") would after the war head Mossad's operations in Italy, Averbuch ("Agami") in Romania, and Zameret ("Meyuhas") in France. Barpal ("Kadmon") was to become Avigur's right hand man and Mossad's treasurer, Nameri ("Hofshi") would be responsible for contact with Palmach, while Ze'ev Shind ("Danny") with the Diaspora in the USA. The latter, as an emissary of the Jewish Agency in Istanbul (for the years 1942–1944), was to play an important role in the transport of Balkan Jews via Turkey. Yehieli carried out special missions. A knowledge of several languages (Hebrew, Yiddish, Romanian, German and English) enabled him to travel through the Middle East, Turkey, and Europe. He was to prepare, among other things, a group of Jewish parachutists – volunteers from Palestine, who would at the end of the war, in collaboration with the British, be taken to occupied Europe to carry out acts of sabotage.[4]

Their head was a supporter of Ben-Gurion, while they themselves on the whole were closer to the more radical Tabenkin.[5] The oldest – Meirov, Barpal and Braginski – were born at the end of the nineteenth century, the youngest – Ginsburg and Klueger – in the second decade of the twentieth. Almost all of them, from the elev-

---

*S pokoleniyem khagany*, Tel Aviv 1976). He took the surname Avigur (Hebrew 'Father of Gur') to commemorate the death of his son Gur Meirov, who died aged 17 in July 1948 during the war with a coalition of Arab states. T. Szulc, *The Secret Alliance. The Extraordinary Story of the Rescue of the Jews Since World War II*, New York 1991, pp. 13, 192–193. Cf. biographic entry: E. Hoter, *Avigur (Meirov) Shaul* [in:] *New Encyclopedia of Zionism and Israel*, vol. 1, p. 148; *Encyclopaedia Judaica*, vol. 1, col. 968; J. Comay, *Who's Who in Jewish History after the period of the Old Testament*, 3rd ed. revised by L. Cohn-Sherbok, London 2002, pp. 31–33.

4   After I. Zertal, op.cit., pp. 171–177, 327–332; *The Mossad's People* [in:] *The Darien Dilemma* (http://www.dariendilemma.com/eng/ people/mossad).

5   As Ze'ev Venia Hadari notes: *Avigur was involved in Mapai whilst most of us who worked with him were from the other political stream.* Z.V. Hadari, op.cit., p. 22.

en listed, were born in Europe: in Poland, Russia and Romania. One came from the American Diaspora (Zameret) and one from the German (Ginsburg).

As Idith Zertal writes, the germ of the group (which then formally took on the structure of Mossad) had come into being about a year and a half earlier and was the work of the supporters of Yitzhak Tabenkin, the leader of Ha'Kibbutz Ha'Meuhad (United Kibbutz). *This group was assigned two functions: to undermine the restrictive British quotas on Jewish immigration to Palestine and to force radicalization of the political leadership of the Zionist movement itself, which, according to Tabenkin, was [...] cooperative with the British government.*[6] This referred to relations with the British government. There is an absence of documents confirming the creation of such a group by Ha'Kibbutz Ha'Meuhad. According to Zertal this could have resulted from a set of key decisions taken in confidence, for the group was initially to have a dual profile – it activities were *directed toward the British and also toward the central Zionist leadership.*[7]

Mossad was a conspiratorial cell. It was formed by a group of people who knew each other well and who trusted each other. The agents came from various countries and spoke various languages. It would have been impossible for the operation to succeed in any other way. Candidates for service in Mossad were carefully selected. The best agents for secret operations were individuals with strong personalities and tough characters. Their missions were carried out "undercover," sometimes they pretended to be journalists or students, at other times representatives of Jewish religious organizations.[8]

It is worth noting as an aside that the Palestinian section of Mossad had its headquarters almost right under the noses of the British, in the very centre of Tel Aviv (at Allenby Street), in a building housing the offices of Histadrut. This location, on the surface at odds with conspiratorial principles, turned out to be a wise choice. Though British intelligence was quick to find out about the "maritime department of Hagana" and was able to acquire detailed information about the planned transports of immigrants and the activities of Mossad emissaries in European countries, it was unable to locate the section in its two small rooms and was unable to crack its structures.[9] Nine years later, in July 1947, the British – as one of their confidential reports testifies – knew only that the *Palestine H.Q. of HAGANA's illegal immigration organization is either in TEL AVIV or JERUSALEM.*[10]

---

[6]   I. Zertal, op.cit., pp. 153–154. This work initially appeared in Hebrew entitled *Zehavam shel ha'Yehudim. Ha' Hagirah ha'Yehudit ha'machtartit le'Erets Yisra'el, 1945–1948*, Tel Aviv 1996.

[7]   Ibidem, p. 154.

[8]   TNA. CO 537/2398. *Illegal Immigration Review No. 2. Period 16th June–15th July 1947. Top Secret*, pp. 3–4.

[9]   Z.V. Hadari, op.cit., pp. 20–21; A. Rabinovich, "In the Name of Isaiah and Balfour," *Jerusalem Post*, 22 V 1991, p. 5.

[10]  TNA. CO 537/2398. *Illegal Immigration Review No. 2. Period 16th June–15th July, 1947. Top Secret*, p. 3.

Mossad le'Aliyah Bet was formally independent of the Jewish Agency, for as the legally recognised representative of Yishuv it was unable to support an illegal institution. In practice, however, it exerted influence on it, if only through the fact that its leaders jointly participated in the cyclical meetings during which the organization's policy was decided on. The Agency's authority was recognised by Hagana, Mossad's actual head. This interdependent network meant that the Jewish Agency combined legal and conspiratorial activities. Although Hagana had something in the nature of a maternal relationship to Mossad, while Meirov operated as its leader's right arm, the Institute of B Immigration enjoyed sizeable autonomy, particularly after the war. Meirov obviously consulted with Golomb and Hagana when planning his actions, but he was the genuine head of Mossad.

Besides Avigur, the leadership of the Institute of B Immigration comprised Eliyahu Golomb and Berl Katznelson, both from Mapai. In 1944 its composition was broadened to include representatives of other political parties within the make-up of the Jewish Agency's executive.[11] Formally Mossad's ruling authority was composed of seven members: four from Mapai and one each from Ha'Shomer Ha'Tzair, Ha'Oved Ha'Tziyoni and Ha'Poel Ha'Mizrachi.[12] Mapai's numerical advantage was short-lived as already in the very same year Yehuda Braginski left the party's ranks, connecting himself with the more left-wing and secessionist Achdut Ha'Avoda (new), while a few months later, in May 1945, Golomb died.

After the war Mossad practically monopolised *Aliyah Bet*. From out of the 65 sea transports which took place from 1945–1948 only one (*Ben Hecht*, March 1947) was not organized by Hagana.[13]

*Ha'apala* required a lot of financing, only a very small portion of which came from the prospective immigrants themselves. The Zionist Organization and the Jewish Agency acted as agents in the search for funding. The Agency's budget had a sizeable sum reserved for illegal immigration. For example, in September of 1939 – as we read in Moshe Shertok's report (the head of the Agency's political department,

---

[11]  Z.V. Hadari, op.cit., p. 31.

[12]  Ha'Shomer Ha'Tzair (The Young Guard) – a youth organization of a leftist-Zionist nature, gradually took shape as a political party. In 1948 together with Achdut Ha'Avoda (new) it gave inception to the Marxist Mapam. Ha'Oved Ha'Tziyoni (The Zionist Worker) – a liberal-democratic grouping entered, in 1948, into the makeup of the newly created Progressive Party. Ha'Poel Ha'Mizrachi (Mizrachi Worker) – a religious Zionist party that emerged from the Mizrachi movement (Spiritual Centre) in 1921/1922. It attempted to reconcile socialist ideology with religious principles. In 1956 it joined with Mizrachi, creating the National Religious Party (Mafdal).

[13]  Zionists-Revisionists organized the transport. More see: M.S. Greenfield, J.M. Hochstein, *The Jews' Secret Fleet*. Rev. ed., Jerusalem–New York 1999, Chapter "Ben Hecht (Abril)," pp. 95–101; M. Liebman, *"Ben Hecht" Purser Poses as Refugee, Tells of Life on Cyprus* (TNA. FO 371/61805/E 3533, press cutting); see also: "Abril Refugees Deported," *The Palestine Post*, 10 III 1947; N. Stewart, *The Royal Navy and the Palestine Patrol*, London–Portland, Or 2002, s. 97–98.

later Prime Minister of Israel 1954–1955) – this was £5,000 sterling which constituted more than a quarter of the Jewish Agency's outlay.[14]

Of immense significance was the support given by the American Jewish Joint Distribution Committee (JOINT). This American Jewish aid organization, founded in 1914, accounted for 75% of the costs incurred by Mossad during the course of the Second World War.[15] The Joint had to act very cautiously. Supporting Mossad meant acting against Great Britain, the United States' closest ally. The leaders of the Committee were therefore very careful to ensure that this sphere of activity remained hidden. Ben-Gurion personally appealed to the American Diaspora for help. *We must and can bring in fifty thousand Jews, one thousand a week* – he wrote in May 1939 to Solomon Goldman, president of the Zionist Organization of America. *Implementation of this plan means the failure of the White Paper, an incalculable reinforcement of the Jewish position and decisive preparedness in case of war.*[16]

A sizeable part of the funds went to the purchase or (more often) hiring of ships and their fitting out for the transportation of refugees. These were mostly Greek craft. Later, when the British had intensified their control of Palestinian territorial waters and imposed sanctions for cooperation in running illegal immigrants, the search for new vessels became more problematic as the owner feared confiscation or fines. This significantly increased the price of a contract. The owners and captains would demand exorbitant fees for participating. The majority of the vessels were not fit for passenger transportation. They were used to transport various cargoes such as coal or cement. It was therefore necessary to carry out alterations, to prepare temporary sleeping areas, toilets, a functional kitchen, etc. There were required quantities of food, drinking water and fuel. There had to be at least one doctor on board.

The crews were only partly recruited from among Jews. At this time Yishuv's possibilities were limited in this area, so sailors of various nationalities were employed. Greeks were particularly numerous, while in the case of transports from Romania and Bulgaria citizens of those countries were as well.[17]

---

[14] CZA. Z 4/31107 (p. 7). *Report on the situation in Palestine, October 1939, delivered by Mr. M. Shertok on his arrival in London. 9.10.39* (this same report also in CZA. Z 4/31108). See also: "Jewish Agency and Aid to 'Illegals'," *The Palestine Post*, 2 VIII 1939, p. 1. Moshe Shertok took the name Sharett in Israel.

[15] Y. Bauer, *My Brother's Keeper. A History of the American Jewish Joint Distribution Committee, 1929–1939*, Philadelphia 1974, p. 287. See also: TNA. CO 537/2398. *Illegal Immigration Review No. 2* (16 VI–15 VII 1947), p. 5.

[16] Quoted after: D. Ofer, "Illegal Immigration During the Second World War: Its Suspension and Subsequent Resumption," *Studies in Contemporary Jewry* (New York–Oxford). Ed. by J. Frankel. Vol. VII: 1991 ("Jews and Messianism in the Modern Era: Metaphor and Meaning"), p. 222.

[17] M. Naor, *Haapala. Clandestine Immigration 1931–1948*, [Tel Aviv 1987], pp. 55–57. See also the remembrance book of David Nameri, one of the Mossad's activist: *Sipuro shel Davidka*, Tel Aviv 1974 (in Hebrew).

What motivated them? Most often simply the opportunity to earn money. For some, ideological factors also played a role. It was customary to evacuate the crew shortly before the transport reached the shore in Palestine. These people were transferred to a previously prepared boat, and the helm was taken over by the escort composed of Hagana personnel accompanying the passengers. This was done so that none of the foreign sailors would be arrested by the Mandate, something that would have certainly made it much harder to recruit replacements.

The escort mentioned was an integral part of the whole operation. It was composed of young Jews from Yishuv, Hagana fighters, members of youth movements, kibbutzniks. They underwent special training, during which they were to learn the arcana of service at sea. The courses were organized by Hagana. After the war the burden of exercises was taken on by the soldiers of Palmach (the elite Hagana assault units formed in 1941) as well as its sea section known as Palyam (an acronym of the Hebrew name 'plugot yam,' maritime companies). The escort had three tasks to perform – preparing the vessel for its journey (which meant kitting it out with all the necessary equipment and planning the route), guaranteeing the peace and safety of the immigrants, as well as organizing the drop-off after reaching Palestine, and if necessary defense if it came to the use of force on the part of the Mandate authorities. Every transport had its own commander, and some even a radio operator. The latter was responsible for maintaining radio contact with the Hagana headquarters in Tel Aviv. A part of the operations were designated as the transportation of ordinary cargo. In order not to arouse suspicion the passengers stayed below deck. Landing points were chosen so as to be as far as possible from British military and police posts, though also near Jewish settlements so that help, if needed, could be called on. This included the beaches in the region of Nahariya, Caesarea, Tel Aviv, Netanya or Nitsanim in the south. The immigrant drops were prepared down to the smallest details. A separate group of people was responsible for the transfer of immigrants ashore, another for their immediate transfer to various Jewish settlements. The whole operation was watched over by a Hagana unit.[18]

Certain vessels, in order to avoid confrontation, anchored before Palestinian territorial waters and the passengers were transferred to smaller boats. They thus tried to mislead the British border guards.[19]

---

[18]  Z.V. Hadari, op.cit., pp. 41–42; S. Shapiro, "Smugglers with a cause," *The Jerusalem Post*, 4 IX 1998, p. 22. One of the Mossad activists Yehuda Arazi (real name Tennenbaum, 1907–1959) born in Lodz in Poland, was to conduct his secret activities under the peculiar cryptonym "Tilhaz Tizi Gesheften" (in abbreviation TTG), being a cluster of words from Arabic and Yiddish (in literal translation "kiss our...").

[19]  TNA. FO 371/24094/W 12164 (pp. 79–80). *From Mr Bateman (Alexandria) to the Egyptian Minister for Foreign Affairs*. 8 XII 1939.

Mossad emissaries had operated before the war in several European capitals including Paris, Vienna, Warsaw, Belgrade, Bucharest, Athens, Rome and Istanbul.[20] They had formed a kind of conspiratorial network and kept in close contact with each other, something possible through radio contact. *Ha'apala* constituted in this way an undertaking of an international dimension.

Mossad emissaries were also installed in the countries of the Levant, in Syria (Damascus, Aleppa) and Lebanon (Beirut). The priority was immigration from Europe, but this could also take place via "backdoor routes," through the Middle East. Syria and Lebanon were under French control, which is why it was considered easier to smuggle people through those countries than through the British-controlled side of Egypt and Transjordan. Jews from Arab countries also made use of this route. In the crossing of the borders Arab smugglers were usually employed. For them, this was a lucrative business – they collected sizeable sums as well as sometimes actually robbing their charges.[21]

The centre that was to play a special role (special for a number of reasons) was Vienna. The local Mossad emissary, the Latvian born Hagana officer, Moshe Averbuch (known better under the name Agami), was to turn out to be one of the most important figures in *Aliyah Bet*. He was to carry out missions for Mossad in Austria as well as in Iran, on the Bosphorus and in the Balkans.[22]

In Vienna the young Zionist activist Georg Überall (Ehud Avriel) cooperated with him.[23] Both organized the first Mossad sea transport which successfully reached Palestine. The immigrants were to travel on the proven Greek ship *Atrato*, for which this was to be the fourth sail in the service of *Aliyah Bet* (the first being in November 1938, see Appendices). As before, the intention this time was to sail from

---

[20]   According to reports from British intelligence, in January 1947 there were to have worked for Hagana 102 emissaries from Yishuv in occupied Germany alone, a further 33 in Italy as well as functioning in Romania, Hungary, France, Poland, Czechoslovakia, Greece and other countries. TNA. CO 537/2398. *Illegal Immigration Review. No. 2*, p. 3.

[21]   J. and D. Kimche, *The Secrets Roads. The "Illegal" Migration of a People 1938–1948*, London 1954, pp. 59–60. In the collections of the Central Zionist Archives in Jerusalem is preserved a list of individuals who helped in the illegal smuggling of Jewish refugees to Palestine. Amongst the 500 surnames a significant part are Arab sounding names. CZA. S 25/ 22701. *List of smugglers of illegal immigrants into Palestine* (1939).

[22]   I. Zertal, op.cit., p. 174.

[23]   Ehud Avriel (real name Georg Überall, 1917–1980) – was born in Vienna, an activist in the youth Zionist organization Blau-Weiss (the name from the colours of the Zionist flag), after Anschluss he cooperated with Mossad le'Aliyah Bet. For the period 1943–1944 he was an emissary on behalf of the Jewish Agency in Istanbul and worked to help Jews in occupied Europe. Later, right up until the creation of Israel, he was connected with the organization of illegal immigration to Palestine. He was an agent in the procuring of arms for Hagana and the Israeli Army during the 1948 war. He worked after the creation of Israel in the diplomatic service in, among other places, Czechoslovakia, Hungary, Romania and Italy. From 1968 to 1972 he headed the World Zionist Organization. Author of the memories *Open the Gates! A Personal Story of "Illegal" Immigration to Israel*. Preface by G. Meir, New York 1975.

an Italian port. The Italians did not, however, agree as they feared that in the case of the immigrants being detained by the British they would be forced to take them back. The choice fell therefore on the Yugoslavian port of Sušak (right on the border with Italy). The ship was to transport 400 Jewish refugees in total, mainly from Germany, Austria and Danzig. Before departure it had to undergo a routine inspection in port. *Atrato* was not a passenger vessel and there consequently was a risk that it would not pass as sea worthy. The decision was taken to take evasive measures. The passengers were to sail out on the tourist vessel *Colorado* (also hired from Greeks) and then out at sea transfer to the more substantial *Atrato*. The transport set off in March 1939. What is interesting is that it was sent with the help of a well-connected Nazi official Wolfgang Karthaus as well as members of the ill-renowned Geheime Staatspolizei (Gestapo).[24]

## 2. "The cooperation of enemies for a common cause"

A paradox of history meant that, at the end of the 1930s, official circles within the Third Reich voluntarily declared their support for *Aliyah Bet*, and one of the instigators of this undertaking was Adolf Eichmann, the man who has gone down in history as the architect of the policy of exterminating European Jews. From today's perspective this story takes a fairly curious turn but it follows to remember that Germany was trying to get rid of its Jewish citizens, in effect forcing those who could to emigrate. In as far as the figure for 1933 was 503,000 Jews by May 1939 this number had dropped to only 214,000.[25] The Third Reich saw the emigration of Jews as an effective way, up to a certain point, of "solving the Jewish question" and constructing a state on the basis of racial criteria. At the same time steps were taken to use the Jewish question in short-term political games both within the Reich and on the international stage. Developments in the Middle East were observed with close attention, and problems for the British in Palestine worked to the Germans' advantage. On the one hand, Berlin's policy forced Jews to fight with the immigration limitations imposed by the Mandate, on the other it stirred up anti-British and anti-Jewish feelings in some Arab circles.[26]

---

[24] Y. Bauer, *Jews for Sale? Nazi-Jewish Negotiations, 1933–1945*, New Haven–London 1994, p. 46; E. Avriel, *Open the Gates! A Personal Story of "Illegal" Immigration to Israel*. Preface by G. Meir, New York 1975, p. 48–61 (Chapter "The Adventures of the Attrato"); J. and D. Kimche, op.cit., pp. 33–35 (vessel name as the *Otrato*). On *Aliyah Bet* through Yugoslavia see: M. Shelah, *Ha-kesher ha-Yugoslavi. Yugoslavyah le-Aliyah Beth, 1938–1948 (The Yugoslav Connection, Yugoslavia and the Illegal Jewish Immigration 1938–1948)*, Tel Aviv 1994.

[25] J. Krasuski, *Historia Rzeszy Niemieckiej 1871–1945*, 4th ed., Poznań 1986, p. 378.

[26] For more detail see: Ł. Hirszowicz, *III Rzesza i arabski Wschód*, Warszawa 1963, pp. 47–57; The Polish Institute and General Sikorski Museum in London (subsequently PISM). A. 11.3/Bl.Wsch./3a–h. File no. 4: "Niemcy a Bliski Wschód" ("Germany and the Near East"), analyses of the Polish Gov-

Unexpectedly the Nazis and Zionists perceived a common ground: the former wanted to get rid of the Jews, the latter to take them to Palestine, saving them from persecution. In 1933 the finance ministry of the Reich concluded an agreement with the Jewish Agency (called the Palestinian transfer or *ha'avara*; from the Hebrew for 'transfer'), thanks to which Jews heading for Palestine – and there were for the period 1933–1941 in total around 55,000 of them – could take with them a part of their possessions in the form of goods produced in Germany. Those in possession of immigration certificates had the possibility of transferring the equivalent of tens of thousands of Marks at a favourable rate of exchange. The transfers were realized through an institution called the Trust and Transfer Office Haavara Ltd. with its headquarters in Tel Aviv. The agreement was in force until the 3rd of September 1939 (i.e. until the declaration of war on Germany by Great Britain) and was to significantly influence Jewish immigration to Palestine.[27] On the Jewish side the chief architect of the agreement was the Zionist left (*we have to give a Zionist answer to the catastrophe which faces German Jewry: to transform this disaster into a chance for developing our country*), while the Revisionists violently attacked it.[28]

An outgrowth of Berlin's policy were the activities of the Zentralstelle für jüdische Auswanderung (Central Office for Jewish Emigration) created by Eichmann in August 1938 with its headquarters in Vienna.[29] Eichmann, a high-ranking SS officer, came to Austria a few days after Anschluss, as the representative of the Gestapo on matters of Jewish emigration.[30] Auswärtiges Amt (the German Ministry of Foreign Affairs) in a circular addressed to diplomatic posts abroad pointed out that *the ultimate aim of Germany's Jewish policy is the emigration of all Jews living on German territory*.[31] It lay in the interests of the Reich if emigration was directed outside of Europe. This could mean a green light for the organizers of *Aliyah Bet*.

---

ernment in Exile's Section for Near and Middle East Studies; E. Marcus, "The German Foreign Office and the Palestine Question in the Period 1933–1939," *Yad Vashem Studies* (Jerusalem). Vol. 2: 1958, pp. 179–204.

[27] W. Feilchenfeld, D. Michaelis, L. Pinner, *Haha'avarah – Transfer nach Palästina*, Tübingen 1972; E. Black, *The Transfer Agreement. The Untold Story of the Secret Pact between The Third Reich and Jewish Palestine*, New York 1984; F.R. Nicosia, *The Third Reich and the Palestine Question*, New Brunswick 2000, pp. 29–49. Cf. also DGFP, pp. 772–777, document 575: *The Reich Foreign Exchange Control Office to the Foreign Ministry, Berlin 7 XII 1937*; ibidem, pp. 785–787, document 580: *Memorandum of Referat Deutschland, Berlin 10 III 1938*.

[28] Quoted after: K. Gebert, *Miejsce pod słońcem. Wojny Izraela*, Warszawa 2008, p. 87.

[29] For more detail see: G. Anderl, D. Rupnow, *Die Zentralstelle für jüdische Auswanderung als Beraubungsinstitution*, Wien–München 2004. Eichmann's activity and his role in the Jewish policy of the Third Reich has been analysed on many occasions. For example see: Q. Reynolds, E. Katz, Z. Aldouby, *Minister of Death. The Adolf Eichmann Story*, London 1961; H. Arendt, *Eichmann w Jerozolimie. Rzecz o banalności zła*, Kraków 1987 (English edition: *Eichmann in Jerusalem. A Report on the Banality of Evil*, New York 1964); D. Cesarani, *Eichmann. Jego życie i zbrodnie*, Zakrzewo 2008 (English edition: *Eichmann. His Life and Crimes*, London 2004).

[30] Eichmann initially opposed the organization of illegal transports. Y. Bauer, *Jews for Sale?*, p. 47.

[31] Quoted after: DGFP, p. 927: document 664: *Circular of the Foreign Ministry, Berlin, 25 I 1939*. Cf. Ł. Hirszowicz, op.cit., pp. 52–53.

The representatives of various currents within *ha'apala* made contact with Zentralstelle für jüdische Auswanderung. Considering that a large number of Jews wanted to leave the Reich, the creation of Zentralstelle would, to a certain degree, meet these aspirations halfway.

In the Central Office's hands lay all matters connected with emigration, including those within the framework of *Aliyah Bet*.[32] The price for emigration was the loss of one's possessions and the covering of the entire cost by the Jews themselves. The cost of the trip for the poorest was paid out of the funds of the richest emigrants. The operation took place with the joint participation of the authorised Reichsvertretung der Juden in Deutschland (National Representative Council of Jews in Germany) and also, in the case of illegal immigration, of the emissaries of Mossad as well as members and sympathisers of the New Zionist Organization.

The German authorities had already earlier agreed to create vocational and agricultural training centres, where specialists sent from Yishuv and other Jewish activists prepared young pioneers (priority was to given to those individuals who were most useful to Yishuv) for departure to Palestine. Zentralstelle participated in, among other things, equipping these centres.[33] Sometimes future immigrants were released from concentration camps. The transports on route to Palestine were to travel through the territory of Slovakia occupied by the Third Reich and from there onwards along the Danube to the Black Sea, usually on hired barges and vessels of the Deutsche Donau Schiffahrtgesellschaft (DDSG, German Association of Danube Navigation).[34] The German side acted as an agent in obtaining transit visas and travel documents, often forged, for which the refugees paid dearly. The rail and river transports were escorted by Nazi functionaries.[35] The paradox was that for the Jews

[32] Besides the works already cited it is worth seeing also: G. Anderl, "Die Zentralstelle für jüdische Auswanderung in Wien, 1938–1943," *David – Jüdische Kulturzeitschrift* (Wien). Jg. 5: 1993. H. 16, pp. 12–19; J. Moser, "Die Zentralstelle für jüdische Auswanderung in Wien" [in:] K. Schmid, R. Streibel (Hg.), *Der Pogrom 1938. Judenverfolgung in Österreich und Deutschland. Dokumentation eines Symposiums der Volkshochschule Brigittenau*, Wien 1990, pp. 96–100.

[33] *When the Zionists sought permission to open vocational training camps for future emigrants Eichmann willingly supplied them with housing and equipment.* Quoted after: H.M. Sachar, *A History of Israel. From the Rise of Zionism to Our Time*, New York 1988, p. 197.

[34] For more detail see: K.J. Ball-Kaduri, "Illegale Judenauswanderung aus Deutschland nach Palästina 1939/1940 – Planung, Durchführung und internationale Zusammenhänge," *Jahrbuch des Instituts für deutsche Geschichte* (Tel Aviv). 4. Band: 1975, pp. 387–421; A. Prinz, "The Role of the Gestapo in Obstructing and Promoting Jewish Emigration," *Yad Vashem Studies* (Jerusalem). Vol. 2: 1958, pp. 205–218; F.R. Nicosia, op.cit., pp. 151–162; H. Rosenkranz, *Verfolgung und Selbstbehauptung. Die Juden in Österreich 1938–1945*, Wien 1978, pp. 121–125; B. Habas, *The Gate Breakers*, New York–London 1963, pp. 47–70. Cf. also the monograph DDSG: J. Binder, *Von Wien zum Schwarzen Meer. Eigenverlag der DDSG*, Wien 1972.

[35] Also the British Colonial Office understood the existing state of affairs. Cf. "Minute by Sir John Shuckburgh, 22 June 1939, alleging Nazi sponsorship of Jewish illegal immigration into Palestine" [in:] *The Rise of Israel*. Vol. 30: *The Holocaust and Illegal Immigration*. Edited by M.J. Cohen, New York–London 1987, pp. 1–2.

in league with Zentralstelle, Great Britain with its legacy of democratic traditions appeared at this time to be a greater enemy than the totalitarian Third Reich. Who could, however, predict the ominous future?

The transit route through Slovakia was not merely dictated by geographical considerations with respect to location. An increasing role was being played in Slovakia by overt nationalistic feelings, and already, during the period of autonomy within the framework of Czechoslovakia (October 1938–March 1939), the first signs of overt anti-Jewish feelings had appeared. This had found expression in the formation of a special commission in January 1939 to "solve the Jewish question." The relevant regulations were to appear following the proclamation of the Slovak State, theoretically independent but actually a German protectorate which gradually turned its Jewish inhabitants into second class citizens. The removal of Jews from certain areas of economic life as well as forced emigration were postulated. The "Jewish code" passed in 1941 was to noticeably intensify the existing regulations.[36]

Slovakia was a transitory stage not only for Jews from the Reich and Austria; refugees from the Protectorate of Bohemia and Moravia, and following September 1939, from Poland, came there as well. The fugitives were helped materially by local Jewish communities. Field kitchens were set up to provide meals for those in need. Collections of money were organized. Expenditures were high. Guards and many other officials had to be paid off. The Slovak authorities also counted on financial benefits from agreeing to allow the organization of transports of illegal immigrants who most often departed from the river port in Bratislava. Thus, until the end of 1939, several thousand Jews, citizens of various states, managed to travel on further.[37]

The outbreak of war in September 1939 made it impossible to carry out the planned transportation of 10,000 Jews from the Reich to Palestine on ships of the German Hapag association (Hamburg-American Lines). The immigrants were to have set off from the port at Emden, sail through the North Sea and the Strait of Gibraltar and, when close to Palestinian waters, transfer to smaller craft organized by Mossad.[38] Another project envisaged the arrival of prospective immigrants at Italian ports from whence they would reach the British Mandate by sea. This was, however, not agreed to by the Italians (for the entire duration of the war not a single *Aliyah Bet* ship was to leave Italy).[39]

By February 1939, through the intermediacy of Eichmann and his office, around 100,000 Austrian Jews had emigrated, several thousand of whom were illegal immi-

[36]  For more detail see: I. Kamenec, *Po stopách tragédie*, Bratislava 1991; I. Lipscher, *Die Juden im Slowakischen Staat 1939–1945*, München–Wien 1980 (Slovak edition: *Židia v slovenskom štáte 1939–1945*, Bratislava 1992).

[37]  J. Tomaszewski, "Początki prześladowania Żydów słowackich," *Zeszyty Majdanka* (Lublin). T. 11: 1993, pp. 15–16.

[38]  TNA. FO 371/25239/W 2743 (pp. 231–237). *Use of Hamburg-Amerika line ships to carry illegal immigrants to Palestine. 16 II 1940.*

[39]  F.R. Nicosia, op.cit., p. 161; D. Ofer, *Escaping the Holocaust*, pp. 100–103.

grants. From January 1939 on, the Zentralstelle started its activities in Berlin (here Mossad's emissary was Pino Ginsburg) based on the Viennese model, under the formal leadership of the Gestapo head Heinrich Müller, and following the annexation of the Czech lands also in Prague.[40]

Eichmann wanted to completely control the organization of immigrant groups. He did not trust Mossad and the Revisionists as he had no influence over their leadership. He therefore started to look for someone who could coordinate all matters related to *Aliyah Bet* in his name and who would be subordinate to him. The decision was made to choose Berthold Storfer, a banker and merchant from a Jewish family from Bukovina.[41]

In March 1939, or a little earlier, Eichmann entrusted Storfer with power of attorney with regard to "immigration B," while the following year (already after the outbreak of war) he extended it to cover all matters of Jewish emigration from the Reich. From then on, Mossad and the Revisionists, as well as other institutions and individuals from Germany and Austria connected with *Aliyah Bet,* had to contact Storfer, whose options were considerable. On Eichmann's recommendation he could reject or change the plans proposed by the organizers of *ha'apala*. He had contacts in banking spheres in Greece, Romania, Slovakia, and Hungary. His interests were looked after in Bucharest by his own brother, in Bratislava and Budapest by his brother-in-law. He maintained contacts with Jewish activists in many countries, including in the Balkans. Storfer continued to conduct his activities until October 1941. The hiring of vessels and their conditions up until their departure were also in his hands. He certainly helped many Jews to leave Austria and Germany. In 1940, when a significant part of Europe found itself under German occupation, he was to play a key role in the *Aliyah Bet* maritime transport of around 3,600 refugees (the ships *Milos, Atlantic* and *Pacific*).[42]

Who was Berthold Storfer? Many saw in him a traitor and Gestapo agent. Others claimed that he was chiefly driven by ambition and a desire for profit. Others still

---

[40] DGFP, p. 935, document 665: *The Chief of the Security Police to the Foreign Ministry, Berlin 14 II 1939*; G. Anderl, "Die 'Zentralstellen für jüdische Auswanderung' in Wien, Berlin und Prag – ein Vergleich," *Tel Aviver Jahrbuch für deutsche Geschichte*. 23. Band:1994, pp. 275–299; J. Milotová, "Die Zentralstelle für jüdische Auswanderung in Prag. Genesis und Tätigkeit bis zum Anfang des Jahres 1940" [in:] M. Kárný, M. Kárná, R. Kemper (Hg.), *Theresienstädter Studien und Dokumente 1997*, Prag 1997, pp. 7–30. See also: A. Szyndler, "Leon Schönker i jego plan emigracji Żydów z rejencji katowickiej z końca 1939 roku," *Studia Judaica* (Kraków). Nos. 1–2: 2009, pp. 237–274.

[41] Cf. G. Anderl, "Berthold Storfer: Retter oder Kollaborateur? Skizzen einer umstrittenen Persönlichkeit. Ein Beitrag zur Geschichte der 'sogenannten illegalen Einwanderung' in das britische Mandatsgebiet," *David – Jüdische Kulturzeitschrift* (Wien). Jg. 9: 1997, H. 35, pp. 15–30.

[42] We present this story in more detail in the chapter "Atlantic – Mauritius." Cf. among others: D. Ofer, "The Rescue of European Jewry and Illegal Immigration to Palestine in 1940. Prospects and reality: Berthold Storfer and the Mossad le'Aliyah Bet," *Modern Judaism* (Baltimore), Vol. 4: 1984. No. 2, pp. 159–181.

– including the passengers of the three ships mentioned – believed that this man helped many Jews.

It is difficult to reach an unambiguous conclusion. The truth is that he worked for Eichmann and the Gestapo. But it is also true that in the conditions of the Reich at that time, all Jewish-related issues had to go through them. It is also important to remember that this cooperation took place before "Endlösung" became the directive of SS policy, although on the other hand Berlin's racist and anti-Semitic colours were under no doubts whatsoever. The line between necessary cooperation and collaboration was an extremely thin one. Did Storfer cross over it? His activities subordinated to Nazi directives (which in any case did not save Storfer from death in the Holocaust) took place within specific frameworks. On the one hand were the persecutors (the Nazis), on the opposite the victims (the Jews). The aim of the former (forced emigration) corresponded with the aspirations of the latter (to leave the Reich). This paradoxical situation of cooperation was neatly formulated by Yehuda Bauer as *enemies with a common interest*.[43]

The chance of saving the Jews from Germany and Austria, which had appeared to be opening up, was, however, not to be made use of. It is true that no one could have foreseen the Holocaust. But it is also true that the West minimised the approaching signals of the Jews' tragedy, as the gates to the majority of democratic countries were shut to larger numbers of Jewish refugees. As Ehud Avriel, one of the organizers of *Aliyah Bet* in Austria, bitterly concluded: *Jewish refugees were an especially unwelcome commodity: the Germans wanted to get rid of them at all cost, and the British refused them admission to territory under their control.*[44] It is very difficult to defend the position taken by British policy. It is worth noting, however, that if one compares Britain's position with that of other countries, then the picture is not so black. For the period 1933–1939 Great Britain accepted around 70,000 Jewish refugees from Germany, Austria and occupied Czechoslovakia (with for a further 10,000 it served as a place of transit), more than any other country on Earth – except the USA.[45] We should also add here those who settled in Palestine or British overseas territories including Cyprus, Kenya, Southern Rhodesia, Malaya, in Hong Kong, and British Guiana.[46]

---

[43] Y. Bauer, *Jews for Sale?*, pp. 44–54. Marxist authors have proposed other view points on these matters, in writing about a "conspiracy" and "political union of Zionism and Nazi Germany." Cf.: *the Palestinian Zionists developed intense activities to draw immigrants from Germany and engaged as a consequence in close cooperation with the Nazi regime*. Quoted after: V.V. Bogoslovskiy et al. (ed.), *Syjonizm – teoria i praktyka*, Warszawa 1975, p. 81 (translation of the Moscow edition of 1973).

[44] Quote after: T. Szulc, op.cit., p. 28.

[45] L. London, *Whitehall and the Jews 1933–1948. British immigration policy, Jewish refugees and the Holocaust*, Cambridge 2003, pp. 11–12. Cf. also A.J. Sherman, *Island Refuge. Britain and Refugees from the Third Reich, 1933–1939*, London 1973. By way of comparison for the entire period of 1933–1944 the USA accepted 240,000 Jewish immigrants, Canada 8,000, Argentina 50,000, Brazil 25,000, Portugal 15,000. M. Gilbert, *Atlas historii Żydów*, Kryspinów 1998, pp. 99–100.

[46] According to the official data of the Colonial Office, for the period March–September 1939, 930 Jewish refugees settled in overseas possessions. The most in Cyprus (291), in Kenya (216)

# 3. "Immigration today is a question of life or death"

With the end of 1938 *Aliyah Bet* began increasingly to attract the attention of the Yishuv leadership. At the meeting of the Jewish Agency on the 13th of November 1938 (immediately after the "Night of Broken Glass" ("Kristallnacht") in Germany, when the Nazis organized an anti-Jewish pogrom) David Ben-Gurion subscribed to the idea of mass Jewish immigration to Palestine. *Without mass aliyah Zionism is condemned to failure and we to the loss of this country.*[47]

What role did he envisage for *ha'apala*? At the time he was not an advocate of *Aliyah Bet* for he saw it had – as he claimed – *destroyed planned immigration*. This referred to the fact that the majority of illegal immigrants were caught by the British, who subsequently allowed them to settle in Palestine but within the framework of the quotas for legal immigration already in force, which meant that fewer of those particularly desired from the point of view of the future Jewish State could come. *Now is the time of Hitler* – he cried during a Mapai meeting in April 1939 – *and immigration today is a question of life and death for hundreds and thousands of Jews.*[48] Here he saw a place for, among others, *ha'apala* as one of the instruments of struggle with the Mandate. Behind organizing dozens of transports and at the same time provoking the British to counteract (and possibly engage in conflict with Hagana) was the intention to win the propaganda battle by showing the international community the indifference of Great Britain, which refused to help "Jewish refugees from Nazi Germany." One practical expression of this approach was to be the attempt proposed by Ben-Gurion to use Hagana units to free over 370 passenger refugees of the ship *Colorado*, which the British intended to deport from the Mandate (August 1939). The main Yishuv activists, including among them Golomb, Shertok, Tabenkin and Katznelson, however, opposed this operation for it could have led to confrontation with British forces and resulted in casualties.[49]

Ben-Gurion's position met with reservations from within the Yishuv leadership, as well as Mossad. It was claimed that illegal immigration should rather guarantee a *maximum quantity* [in the sense of Jews saved] *than maximum publicity*.[50] The difference in views was visible during, e.g., the proceedings of the 21st World Zionist Congress in Geneva in August 1939.[51]

---

and Southern Rhodesia (186). M. Gilbert, "British Government Policy towards Jewish Refugees (November 1938–September 1939)," *Yad Vashem Studies* (Jerusalem). Vol. XIII: 1979, p. 165.

[47] CZA. S 100/25 b. *Minutes of the Jewish Agency*, vol. 25, pp. 6290–6295 (13 XI 1938) and 6296–6299 (14 XI 1938), text in Hebrew.

[48] Quoted after: S. Teveth, *Ben-Gurion. The Burning Ground 1886–1948*, Boston 1987, p. 725.

[49] The refugees were finally not deported, they were interned as was the widespread practice. S. Teveth, op.cit., p. 726; *La Haapala. Compilación de notas y documentos de la Inmigrácion "Ilegal" a Eretz Israel 1933–1948*. La Selección del material y su traducción fueron realizadas por Moshé Kitrón, Jerusalem 1953, pp. 72–81.

[50] Quoted after: W. Laqueur, *A History of Zionism*, p. 531.

[51] CZA. Z 4/ 31046. *Memorandum: a Positive Program. Suggestions for Agenda of World Zionist Congress, Geneva, August 1939* (pp. 1–3); AAN. Poselstwo RP w Bernie 153 (pp. 36–38). *Otwarcie*

The supporters of a conciliatory approach in relation to Great Britain included Chaim Weizmann, Moshe Shertok as well as Yosef Sprinzak, one of the leaders of Histadrut. They proposed, in place of conflict, dialogue with the Mandate, the exertion of pressure and the pointing out that London's policy was at odds with its obligations to the League of Nations. Such an approach was dictated by the conviction that Great Britain was the only state in which the Zionist movement could place any hope, for the *fate of the Jews is entirely in the hands of England*.[52] It was feared that illegal immigration would discredit Zionism. It was believed that by resigning from *Aliyah Bet* it would be possible to count on an agreement with the Mandate with regard to an increase in the official immigration quotas.[53]

In the reality of 1939 the validity of this position was increasingly less convincing. The proverbial "dotting of the i's" was the publication by London on the 17th of May 1939 of a "White Paper" which was an attempt to define Great Britain's current policy in relation to Palestine.[54]

It is worth noting, as the Jewish side strongly underlined, that the Mandate did not place such limitations on Arab immigration. Admittedly its scope was not great, but the economic development of Palestine drew an increasing number of Arabs. According to official data for the period from 1921 to 1944, 30,649 non-Jews, the majority of whom were Arabs, legally settled in the Mandate.[55]

Illegal immigrants also came from neighbouring countries: Egypt, Transjordan, Syria and Lebanon (the crossing of the desert borders was not too difficult).[56] The number of these is not precisely known, though according to official British circles "it was significant."[57] This form of immigration was generally connected with money and was to some extent only temporary. It is worth noting that Mandate statistics rather meticulously noted illegal Jewish arrivals while the information on the influx of Arabs is rather imprecise. This is related to the fact that the latter could cross into the Mandate via a division that was merely a "green border" and not the sea. Anthropologically identical to the Palestinian Arabs they blended into

  *XXI Międzynarodowego Kongresu Sjonistycznego – Genewa, 16.08.1939* (*Opening of the 21st International Zionist Congress – Geneva 16.08.1939*).

[52] Quoted after: PISM. A 11.E/87. *Żydzi w Palestynie 1945* (*Jews in Palestine 1945*). Ministerstwo Spraw Wewnętrznych. Sytuacja żydostwa w świetle żydowskich palestyńskich źródeł politycznych. Londyn, 10 II 1945, p. 4 (*The Ministry of Internal Affairs. The situation of Jewry in the light of Jewish Palestinian political sources*).

[53] D. Ofer, *Escaping the Holocaust*, pp. 18–19.

[54] For more detail see: M.J. Cohen, *Palestine to Israel. From Mandate to Independence*, London 1988 (Chapter 6: "Appeasement in the Middle East: The British White Paper on Palestine, May 1939," pp. 101–128); J.C. Hurewitz, *The Struggle for Palestine* (Chapter 7: "The 1939 White Paper," pp. 94–111).

[55] *Great Britain and Palestine 1915–1945*. Ed. by The Royal Institute of International Affairs. Information Papers No. 20, London–New York 1946, p. 63.

[56] FRUS 1939. Vol. IV, pp. 772–773: *Memorandum by Mr. J. Rives Childs of the Division of Near Eastern Affairs. Washington, 3 VI 1939*.

[57] F. Liebreich, op.cit., p. 31.

the local environment without any problems. Let us here add that the permanent residents of Transjordan and the border regions of Lebanon and Syria could cross the border without any immigration formalities whatsoever, a situation designed to serve the economic activation of territories on both sides of the border.[58]

In effect, it helped the uncontrolled influx into the Mandate. According to Tewfik Bey al-Haurani, the governor of Hauran in Syria, in the course of a few months in 1934, around 30–36,000 Arabs crossed from this province to Palestine in this fashion. Other estimates refer to 20,000.[59]

In accepting these figures as accurate and taking into consideration immigrants from other Arab countries, it might appear that for certain periods the number of Arab immigrants exceeded Jewish ones. The seriousness of the problem is borne out by the number of people deported from Palestine on accusations of violating immigration regulations. It turns out that there were more Arabs among them. Out of 11,601 individuals subjected to this procedure for the period 1934–1939, Jews constituted less than 13%. This tendency also continued after the outbreak of the Second World War.[60]

Table 9. Persons deported from Palestine 1934–1939

| Year | Jews | non-Jews |
|---|---|---|
| 1934 | 772 | 1,635 |
| 1935 | 293 | 2,152 |
| 1936 | 152 | 1,887 |
| 1937 | 157 | 2,218 |
| 1938 | 46 | 1,904 |
| 1939 | 36 | 349 |
| In total | 1,456 | 10,145 |

The table created from data reported in: R. Bachi, *The Population of Israel*, Jerusalem 1974, p. 388; *Great Britain and Palestine 1915–1945*, p. 64.

---

[58] TNA. CO 733/331/3 (pp. 43–51). *Arthur Wauchope, High Commissioner for Palestine to W.G.A. Ormsby-Gore, His Majesty's Principal Secretary of State for the Colonies: "Note on illegal Arab immigration into Palestine with particular reference to Hauranis"* (14 I 1937).

[59] J. Peters, *From Time Immemorial. The Origins of the Arab-Jewish Conflict over Palestine*, London 1985, pp. 318–319; F. Liebreich, op.cit., pp. 31–32. This information is confirmed by the anonymous author of the work *Note of illegal immigration* (probably from September 1938) in the CZA. S 25/22701 (file: "Illegal immigration. Various doc. 1936–39").

[60] For the period 1937–1945 14,458 persons were sentenced for illegally being in Palestine. Amongst whom were 11,902 Muslims, 1,371 Jews and 1,141 Christians. R. Bachi, *The Population of Israel*, Jerusalem 1974, p. 388; *Great Britain and Palestine 1915–1945*, p. 64.

After 1936 the number of illegal Arab immigrants decreased in number while in 1938 a growth in temporary emigration of Arabs to neighbouring countries was noted. This state of affairs was influenced by the destabilization in relations in Palestine following the outbreak of the Arab uprising.[61]

# 4. The intensification of *Aliyah Bet*

The Jews understood the "White Paper"– a classic product of a *circumstance highly unfavourable for the interests of one side while being conducive to the interests of the other*[62] – as a breaking of promises. *The Jews will never accept the closing of the gates of Palestine to them nor will they let their National Home be converted into a ghetto* – announced the Jewish Agency.[63] In Yishuv the movement against the Mandate administration intensified. One of its manifestations was *Aliyah Bet*, which was becoming increasingly understood as a weapon in the struggle for a sovereign Israel as well as a mission to help the Jewish refugees of Central Europe. *Ha'apala* underwent an intensification. During the whole of 1938 the number of *ma'apilim* numbered 3,200–3,400, then in the course of two summer months in 1939 (July–August) the number of those who wanted to illegally enter Palestine reached 8 thousand.[64] There was not a week that went by without some *ha'apala* transport or other being organized.

After the Munich crisis and the fall of Czechoslovakia, when the situation in Europe underwent a period of dramatic tension, individuals and independently operating groups joined in the organization of illegal immigration. Some did so for noble reasons, others, lofty ideals aside, were in the game for the additional amount of cash on offer. The majority were members or sympathisers of the Revisionist movement. They included Paul Haller, Hermann Flesch, Eliyahu Glazer (the Betar leader in Czechoslovakia), Jacques Aron as well as one particularly active member, the Viennese lawyer Wilhelm R. Perl. Perl (1906–1998) was born in Prague but as a young man moved to Austria. Here he studied and started his professional practice. Here he also joined Betar. He gained experience during his cooperation in secret operations with Moshe Galili ("Af al pi"). After the Anschluss of Austria he established contact with Zentralstelle für jüdische Auswanderung and took part in organizing Jewish emigrant groups and in preparing 11 *Aliyah Bet* sea transports. They were to

[61]  CZA. S 25/22701. *Note of illegal immigration* [September 1938 ?].

[62]  AAN. Poselstwo RP w Bernie 153 (p. 9). The Consulate of the Polish Republic in Tel Aviv to Department P. III of the Ministry of Foreign Affairs in Warsaw, 20 V 1939.

[63]  "Britain's Blow Will Not Subdue Jews. Statement of the Jewish Agency for Palestine," *The Palestine Post*, 18 V 1939, pp. 1–2.

[64]  M. Naor, *Haapala*, pp. 109–110. Malcolm MacDonald during a debate in the House of Commons on the 4 X 1939 spoke of 4,892 illegal immigrants arriving in the Mandate for the period from 1 VIII to 30 IX 1939. *Parliamentary Debates* (*Commons*), vol. 351, 4 X 1939, col. 351.

**Table 10. Before and after the "White Paper." *Ha'apala* from Europe in 1939**

| Time of transport | Number of transports | Immigrants (in 1000s) |
|---|---|---|
| January | 2 | 1.1 |
| February | 2 | 1.0 |
| March | 7 | 3.3–3.4 |
| April | 4 | 1.5–1.8 |
| May | 8 | 3.1 |
| June | 5 | 2.9–3.1 |
| July | 3 | 1.7 |
| August | 8 | 6.0 |
| September | – | – |
| October | 2 | 1.6 |
| November | – | – |
| December | 2 | 1.2 |

Author's analysis. The table includes also transports which did not reach Palestine. Given the discrepancies that exist in the works on the subject with regard to number of immigrants, the figures are rounded.

transport more than seven thousand refugees. Three vessels were caught, and one sent back, by the British.[65]

Close to the Jewish Agency was Baruch Konfino (Confino, 1891–1982), an idealist, by profession an ophthalmologist, and a Zionist activist in Sofia. The principles that guided him may be formulated thus: 1) the situation of the Jewish population in Central Europe was dramatically deteriorating, the only solution was emigration to Palestine, through Bulgarian ports; 2) the Diaspora in Bulgaria awaited the same fate as the Jews in Germany and (after the outbreak of war) in the countries occupied by them; 3) the necessity of the moment meant that action had to be immediate. It seems that the political aspect (the struggle with the limitations imposed

---

[65]  In 1940 Perl forced his way into the United States, where he enlisted in the US Army. He describes his activity in the book *The Four-Front War. From the Holocaust to the Promised Land*, New York 1979 (2nd edition: *Operation Action. Rescue from the Holocaust*, New York 1983). Archive materials on the life and activities of Perl were given after his death to The George Washington University in Washington, USA, and are to be found in the Special Collections Research Center, The Gelman Library (inventory no. MS 2026). Of especial significance from the point of view of *Aliyah Bet* are the Rescue of European Jews Files (Box 1, Files 12–31). After: *Guide to the William R. Perl Papers, 1925–1998* (http://www.gwu.edu/gelman/spec/ead/ms2026.xml).

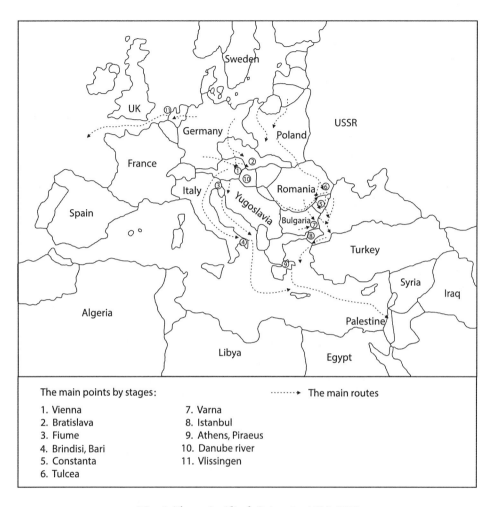

The main points by stages:

1. Vienna
2. Bratislava
3. Fiume
4. Brindisi, Bari
5. Constanta
6. Tulcea
7. Varna
8. Istanbul
9. Athens, Piraeus
10. Danube river
11. Vlissingen

········► The main routes

**Map 2. The main *Aliyah Bet* routes 1934–1939**

Author's study. See also M. Wischnitzer, *To Dwell in Safety. The Story of Jewish Migration Since 1800*, Philadelphia 1948, map on p. 186; M. Gilbert, *Exile and Return. The Emergence of Jewish Statehood*, London 1978, map on p. 224

by the Mandate) did not play a significant role. In any case Konfino, in his book published in 1946 in Bulgaria, does not mention this (although such information appeared in the Israeli edition published 19 years later).[66]

Yet Bulgarian Zionists did not share his fears concerning the future of the Diaspora as the situation in Bulgaria, in comparison with other countries of Central and Eastern Europe, looked relatively favourable. Konfino formed a committee which was to involve itself in illegal *aliyah* to Palestine. It was made up of both left wing Zionists and members of the Revisionist movement. Konfino saw his activities as part of the Zionist *ha'apala;* the development of events, however, meant that he was forced to act independently.[67] Between May and September 1939, Konfino organized (in part jointly with the Revisionists) five transports, which together carried more than 2,000 Jewish refugees. He organized another four after the outbreak of war. Three were captured by the British. The last, *Salvador*, which set off in December 1940, sank during a storm on the Sea of Marmara, taking down with it around 200 people. The largest of the voyages was the *Rudnitchar*. This far from large vessel (a displacement of 269 tons), built in 1872, four times plied its course to Palestine, avoiding detection by British patrols. In total it transported 1638 immigrants.[68] Konfino effectively helped, through his own transports or those organized by other operators, around 4000 Jewish refugees from Germany, Hungary, Bulgaria, Slovakia, Poland and other countries to reach Palestine.[69]

Up until the outbreak of war all the various currents of *Aliyah Bet* (Revisionists, Hehalutz and Mossad as well as private individuals) had prepared over 50 sea transports with around 22,000 immigrants. The majority managed to reach their destination. From the comprehensive list of transports published by the Israeli researcher Dalia Ofer[70] it emerges that 17 amongst them (6,300 immigrants) were sent by Hehalutz and Mossad, while 27 by Revisionists and their sympathisers (12,000

[66]  Cf. B. Konfino, „*Aliyah-Bet.*" *Nielegalna imigraciya. Kratk ocherk za izvshenite nielegalni transporti za Palestina prez 1939/40 god*, Sofiya 1946 (Hebrew edition: *Aliyah Bet me-hofe Bulgaryah*, Yerushalayim–Tel Aviv 1965).

[67]  S. Shealtiel, "The private clandestine immigration operation of Dr. Baruch Confino, 1939–1940," *Shvut. Studies in Russian and East European Jewish History and Culture* (Tel Aviv–Beer Sheva). Vol. 10 (26): 2001, pp. 58–59, 70–71. This article is a fragment of an unpublished PhD thesis defended at Tel Aviv University: *Emigration and Illegal Immigration to Palestine from Bulgaria and via Bulgaria in the years 1939–1945*. Vol. 1–2, Tel Aviv 2001 (the work is in Hebrew, the summary and additional title in English); in the collections of The National Library of Israel in Jerusalem (subsequently NLI, inventory no. S2 = 2003 A 1581).

[68]  TNA. FO 371/24096/W 16279 (p. 92). *Transport of illegal immigrants into Palestine on S.S. „Rudnitchar."* 7 XI 1939; B. Konfino, „*Aliyah-Bet.*" *Nielegalna imigraciya*, pp. 30–33.

[69]  Konfino established this number to be 4,500 („*Aliyah-Bet.*" *Nielegalna imigraciya*, p. 3), according to Shlomo Shealtiel it was 4,000 to 4,500 (*The private clandestine*, p. 120), Dalia Ofer wrote of 3,683 people (*Escaping the Holocaust*, p. 93).

[70]  D. Ofer, *Escaping the Holocaust*, pp. 323–325.

immigrants).[71] The remainder (eight) were organized by others. According to Paul H. Silverstone of the USA, out of the 56 *Aliyah Bet* transports, the Revisionists and their sympathisers prepared 29.[72] In turn Yehuda Bauer and Nana Sagi state that up until the outbreak of war, 41 vessels with 20,500 immigrants on board set out for Palestine, 16 transports each were organized (with around 6,000 refugees) by the Revisionists and Mossad (i.e. Hehalutz and Mossad).[73] If we adopt the estimates of the Mandate authorities that for the period between 1920 and April 1939, 30,000–40,000 illegal immigrants settled in Palestine, it turns out that those who came by sea constituted over half of all *ma'apilim*, and at the end of the 1930s dominated.[74] The greatest numbers came from Central and Eastern Europe – Germany, Poland, Austria, Czechoslovakia, the Free City of Danzig, Romania and Hungary. In 1939 the number of transports from the Third Reich and countries threatened by Germany increased.

The ships usually set sail from the Mediterranean ports of Italy, Greece, Yugoslavia, or from Romania and Bulgaria.[75] Only one voyage set out from Holland. This was the *Dora* with around 480–500 refugees, mainly from Germany. The transport was prepared by Mossad, left Vlissingen in July 1939 and reached Palestine in the middle of August, avoiding interception by the British.[76]

---

[71] The exact same number of transports prepared by activists and sympathisers of the New Zionist Organization is given by the Israeli author Chaim Lazar-Litai. The number of immigrants differs though (13,654). Ch. Lazar-Litai, *Af-'al-pi. Aliyah 2. shel tenu'at Żabotinski*, Berit hayale ha-Etsel 1988, table on p. 128. According to Yaacov Shavit (*Jabotinsky and the Revisionist Movement, 1925–1948*, London 1988, p. 218) the Revisionists were to prepare 25 sea transports with 15,000 illegal immigrants. Kurt Jakob Ball-Kaduri equally subscribes to a similar figure (*Illegale Judenauswanderung*, p. 415; 14,634 to 15,000).

[72] P.H. Silverstone, *Aliyah Bet Project. List 1: 1934–1945* (http://www.paulsilverstone.com/immigration/Primary/Aliyah/shiplist1.php). See also P.H. Silverstone, *Our Only Refuge, Open the Gates! Clandestine Immigration to Palestine, 1938–1948*, New York 1999. This is a 38-page booklet, richly illustrated (35 photographs).

[73] Y. Bauer, N. Sagi, op.cit., p. 648. According to *The Holocaust Encyclopedia* (ed. W. Laqueur, New Haven–London 2001, p. 324) from 1934 to the beginning of the war 18,176 Jews were to have illegally entered Palestine by sea, and according to Mordechai Naor (*Haapala*, p. 104) and the brochure of the *Clandestine Immigration and Naval Museum* (ed. by Clandestine Immigration and Naval Museum in Haifa, without year of issue, subsequently: CINH) – 21,630. We can find a different figure in Shaul Avigur (*S pokoleniyem khagany*, p. 39), yet the figure of 10,000 given by him is clearly an understatement.

[74] TNA. CO 733/454/2 (p. 17). *Cypher Telegram from High Commissioner for Palestine to Secretary of State. No. 140. 7 XI 1945.*

[75] See map "The main Aliyah Bet routes 1934–1939" (p. 83).

[76] TNA. FO 371/24094/W 12123 (pp. 62–65). *Movements of S.S. „Dora" with Jewish refugees on board*; ibidem, W 12183 (pp. 86–88). *Details of S.S. "Dora." From Mr Coverley Price (The Hague) to FO. 19 VIII 1939.* Amongst the passengers were around 120 Polish Jews, who the Third Reich deported in the autumn of 1938 to the region of Zbąszyń, between the line of German and Polish border posts.

Table 11. The largest *Aliyah Bet* sea transports before World War II

| Name of ship | Number of immigrants | Date | Organizer |
|---|---|---|---|
| *Tiger Hill* | 1,417 | VIII–IX 1939 | Mossad |
| *Naomi Julia* | 1,130–1,136 | VIII–IX 1939 | Revisionists |
| *Liesel* | 906–921 | V–VI 1939 | Revisionists |
| *Parita* | 800–850 | VII–VIII 1939 | Revisionists |
| *Aghios Nikolaos* (II) | 795–809 | VIII 1939 | Revisionists (Perl) |
| *Katina* | 773–778 | I–II 1939 | Revisionists (Glazer) |
| *Aghios Nikolaos* | 750 | III 1939 | Revisionists |
| *Geppo* (II) | 750 | II–IV 1939 | Revisionists (Perl) |
| *Geppo* | 734 | XII 1938 | Revisionists (Perl) |
| *Astir* | 699–720 | III–IV 1939 | Revisionists (Haller, Perl) |

Developed on the basis of works cited in footnotes 70, 72 and 73.

As has been already mentioned, a lot of refugees made it to Romania and Bulgaria on smaller vessels by means of the Danube. At that time the river was international in status, which meant that there was no need to apply for transit visas. Others took the rail route to Romania, including, among others, Jews from Poland.

In every case close coordination was essential so as not to draw the attention of British intelligence too early.[77] Occasionally the fugitives would set off in one vessel and after a certain time – already at sea – transfer to another, larger and more seaworthy. Such a "composite" operation had a greater chance of success but it demanded great caution. This was not displayed by the Greek captain of the *Colorado*. In the spring of 1939 the vessel set sail from one of the Yugoslavian ports with several hundred Jews on board, the destination having been given as Mexico. After the transfer of the refugees onto another ship not far off Corfu (i.e. the *Atrato*), the *Colorado* returned to the very same port, after three days and without passengers, which resulted, understandably, in a sensation. As a result the operation had to be suspended.[78]

The potential immigrants were provided with false visas, and the point of destination was often given as a port in South America or even Shanghai. Ships would sail under the flag of Panama, but also Liberia, Brazil and other countries.[79] *Aliyah*

---

[77] FRUS 1939. Vol. IV, p. 773: *The Minister in Rumania (Gunther) to the Secretary of State. Bucharest, 8 VI 1939*; A. Tartakower, K.R. Grossmann, *The Jewish Refugee*, New York 1944, p. 67.

[78] J. and D. Kimche, op.cit., pp. 35–36; E. Avriel, op.cit., p. 54.

[79] TNA. CO 733/394/3 (f. 271). *Palestine: Illegal Immigration. 6 VI 1939.*

*Bet* met with the unofficial support and kindness of many countries. Some saw in the Jewish emigration a solution to internal social and political problems. Others were motivated by humanitarian considerations. Others still anticipated concrete profits (someone had to act as an intermediary in transit, give permission for refugee groups to be organized on their territory, charter ships, turn a blind eye to fake passports and travel documents, etc.). In this way *ha'apala* was helped, directly or indirectly, for ideological or financial reasons, by people of various nationalities.[80]

*Aliyah Bet* operations were not only conditioned by political circumstances but also by lack of sufficient finances. This inevitably affected the character and scope of the operations. It was difficult to buy or charter passenger liners. Old vessels, often built in the 19th century, not adapted to transporting large groups of people and which had difficulties in maintaining sea worthiness and the requirements for journeys at sea,[81] such as river steamers, and even ordinary fishing boats which in no circumstances should take to sea, dominated. Often the passengers had to hide in cramped conditions below deck as the ship was officially transporting cement. The conditions rarely conformed to twentieth century norms. In the holds, where makeshift sleeping areas were organized, it was so stuffy that it was difficult to sleep. Two or three toilets had to suffice for several hundred people. Let us add that amongst the refugees there were many women, children and old people, and it was they who suffered from the conditions the worst. There were cases of seasickness.[82] It was not unknown for a journey to stretch on for many weeks,[83] during which food and water would run out.

Here is how a journey is described by one of the immigrants: *The ship was old and in poor condition; it was dirty, with visible defects. Into this floating tomb there entered 750 people including 250 women and 15 children. In the hold beds were arranged several bunks high. The mattress was a bag filled with straw. We were so crowded together that it was difficult to turn over onto your other side when lying on the mattress. The worst, however, was the air. Sometimes when it rained, all the entrances were closed so the atmosphere was extremely stuffy. On deck two makeshift latrines had been set up.*[84] It is amazing, given such conditions, that people did not lose their heads, that there were not attempts to mutiny, etc.

---

[80]  CZA. S 25/22701. *List of smugglers of illegal immigrants into Palestine* (1939?); E. Ben-Horin, *The Middle East. Crossroads of History*, New York 1943, pp. 175, 178.

[81]  For example, 19th century specifications had, for example: *Struma* (1867), *Rudnitchar* (1872), *Milos* (1878), *Pacific* (1880), *Parita* (1881), *Atlantic* (1885), *Katina* (1892). After P.H. Silverstone, op.cit. (List 1: 1934–1945); idem, *Our Only Refuge*, pp. 35–36.

[82]  "Hundreds of Homeless in Cellars and Ship's Holds," *The Palestine Post*, 14 VI 1939, p. 1.

[83]  For example, the second voyage of the *Velos* lasted over two months (6 IX–13 XI 1934), *Katina* – 4 weeks (18 I–16 II 1939), *Parita* – 41 days (13 VII–23 VIII 1939), *Tiger Hill* – 29 days (3 VIII–1 IX 1939). Cf. footnote 81.

[84]  Quoted after: A. Chojnowski, J. Tomaszewski, *Izrael (Historia Państw Świata w XX wieku)*, Warszawa 2001, p. 22.

It was clear that not all the transports would make it to their goal. Even if they coped with the difficulties of the sea they could be detained by the British Navy. This discomfort was outweighed for most passengers by the hope of returning to Zion. *Everyone, young and old, orthodox and atheists, Russians and Belgians, men and women, all are inspired by one desire, to see the homeland that they have never seen. The nostalgia of their songs that they have sung for two thousand years in their prayers, has seized them and they have set out to reconquer their homeland, as Moses the Master did thousands of years ago.*[85] To various degrees this determination was strengthened by the conviction that a greater risk than a journey by clapped-out tub was staying in Europe where war was drawing near.

Some vessels never made it to their destinations for they fell foul of catastrophe at sea. Such was the fate that befell the steam ship *Geppo* sent by Wilhelm Perl, which sank to the south of Crete (the passengers numbering 750 were luckily saved). In turn the Betar *Rim* was first gutted by fire on the Aegean and then sank to the bottom (3rd of July 1939). The survivors were saved by the Italian ship *Fiume* which took them to Rhodes.[86]

✻✻✻

The role of the organizers of *Aliyah Bet* in saving thousands of European Jews is beyond doubt. With time, after the Second World War, there took root a conviction that *ha'apala* was a part of their, the Zionists and Revisionists', *contribution to the rescue of European Jewry from Hitler.*[87] Without negating the fact that there was no absence of idealists amongst both groups willing to sacrifice themselves for their threatened kin from Central Europe, it still is worth noting that even in 1939 these noble principles were accompanied by immediate considerations related to the applicability of *ma'apilim* in Palestine. The assumption was that they would contribute to building the foundations of Jewish statehood and would strengthen the ranks of Yishuv's military formations. Following the outbreak of the Palestinian uprising this became important. Hence the emphasis placed on young people who prior to arrival in Palestine had undergone specialized instruction (including

---

[85] TNA. WO 275/60. *Translation by 317 Airborne FS Section of a diary, written in French, taken from a passenger on the "President Warfield"* (26 VII 1947), p. 2.

[86] The immigrants finally arrived in Palestine on the 19th of August 1939 on board the *Aghios Nikolaos*. FRUS. Vol. IV, p. 793: *The Consul General at Jerusalem (Wadsworth) to the Secretary of State. Jerusalem, 21 VII 1939*; TNA. ADM 116/4312. *Illegal immigration of Jewish refugees by S.S. "Rim" – flying Panamanian flag. From FO. 23 VI 1939*. Cf. press reports: "400 Refugees Rescued from Blazing Vessel off Rhodes," *The Palestine Post*, 6 VII 1939, p. 1; "840 Refugees from Rhodes Land Here. Rim Disaster Victims and Others in 3 Small Boats," *The Palestine Post*, 20 VIII 1939, p. 1.

[87] L. Brenner, *Zionism in the Age of the Dictators* (the text of the monograph is also available on the Internet at – http://www.vho.org/aaargh/engl/zad/zad.html).

military training). *A correctly thought through, planned emigration should place its main attention on those aged 23 to 37* – wrote Jabotinsky, admittedly with a view to *aliyah* as an entirety.[88]


# 5. Great Britain's position and the Arab voice

The British authorities undertook countermeasures against *Aliyah Bet*. *If we were to countenance the reception of one shipload of illegal immigrants into Palestine* – urged Malcolm MacDonald, Secretary of State for the Colonies, in the House of Commons – *we should at once find that we were faced with a problem with which we could not possibly cope*.[89] In April 1939 the existing regulations in this matter were tightened up. As the existing system of patrolling the coast by the Royal Navy had turned out to be insufficiently effective, a separate police unit was organized and trained to apprehend transports with illegal immigrants; this was to patrol the Palestinian coast both on land and at sea. In case immigrants did not adhere to orders and the vessels were not detained, the use of force was envisaged including the use of live bullets.[90]

The British intercepted and detained some of the transports, turning several back. This was the fate that befell *Sandu*, *Assimi* and *Astir*. They were returned to their port of departure, Constanta in Romania (*Sandu*, *Assimi*) and Varna in Bulgaria, the first in March, the rest in April 1939. The ships were transporting more than 1200 refugees, Jews from Germany, Austria, Romania and Poland.[91] The procedure

---

[88] W. Żabotyński, *Państwo Żydowskie*, Warszawa–Kraków–Poznań–Łódź [1937], p. 144. This aspect was to also have significance after the war, as the British side noticed. Cf. TNA. CO 537/2398. *Illegal Immigration Review No. 2.* (16 VI–15 VII 1947), pp. 8–9 (*Selection is on political rather than humanitarian grounds. Almost invariably preference is given to young persons aged between 17 and 35, and to young mothers, either pregnant or with children. [...] Such human material is chosen in order to provide young and vigorous bodies capable of helping, with their labour and their services in the armed forces of Hagana, to establish, develop and defend a Jewish Palestine*). Aaron Zwergbaum writes that *the Zionist authorities treated this Aliyah Bet like regular migration*, selecting candidates appropriately in relation to their vocational work experience among other things. A. Zwergbaum, "From Internment in Bratislava and Detention in Mauritius to Freedom. The Story of the Czechoslovak Refugees of the Atlantic (1939–1945)" [in:] *The Jews in Czechoslovakia. Historical Studies and Surveys*. Vol. 2, Philadelphia 1971, p. 601.

[89] Quoted after: *Parliamentary Debates* (Commons), vol. 346, 26 IV 1939, col. 1127. Cf. also: "General R.H. Haining, formerly with the Palestine army command, to Sir John Shuckburgh, 13 August 1939, on measures that should be taken to curb illegal immigration" [in:] *The Rise of Israel*. Vol. 30: *The Holocaust and Illegal Immigration*, pp. 3–7.

[90] FRUS 1939. Vol. IV, p. 746: *The Consul General at Jerusalem (Wadsworth) to the Secretary of State. Jerusalem, 3 V 1939*; TNA. CO 733/394/1. *Memorandum on coastal patrolling. 5 XII 1938*; *Parliamentary Debates* (Commons), vol. 348, 14 VI 1939, col. 1295.

[91] There exist discrepancies with regard to the number of passengers – from 1217 to 1439. CZA. S 25/22701. *Telegram from High Commissioner for Palestine, Transjordan to Secretary of State.*

in each case was identical. The British upon detaining the vessel would take it to the port at Haifa. There it would be kitted out for the return journey. The Jewish Agency would supply the refugees with food while the port authorities would provide drinking water. The supplies were designed to last for 5 days. Then the steam ships would be escorted out to sea. The British escort would accompany them to the border with Palestinian territorial waters.[92]

It would happen that refugees, in order to force the Mandate to agree to a port of call in Palestine, would, at the very last moment, empty the containers of drinking water, destroy the food supplies and the documents they possessed, and even their own clothes.[93] In certain cases this resulted in violence. Weapons were used in the case of, for example, the Mossad transports of *Atrato*[94] and *Tiger Hill*. This last incident occurred exactly when the Second World War broke out in Europe.

*Tiger Hill*, an old freighter (launched in 1887) with a displacement of one thousand five hundred tons, set off from Constanta on the 3rd of August with around 750 people, on the whole young pioneers from Poland as well as refugees from Lithuania and Latvia. The ship was overcrowded. On route it took on board an additional 650 passengers in Beirut from the *Frossoula* charted by the Revisionists.[95] The *Frossoula* (*Frosula*) had also set off from Romania, but much earlier (at the end of May). In such a dilapidated state, it was unable to continue the voyage. The reloading drew the attention of British intelligence and when on the night of the 31st of August/1st of September 1939 *Tiger Hill* entered Palestinian territorial waters it was fired upon at a distance of half a mile from the shore (at the level of Jaffa) by a gun-

---

23 IV 1939 (1229 refugees); FRUS 1939. Vol. IV, p. 745: *The Consul General at Jerusalem (Wadsworth) to the Secretary of State. Jerusalem, 3 V 1939* (1217); W.R. Perl, *Operation Action*, p. 405 (1249); M. Naor, *Haapala*, p. 110 (1439). Cf. also: "Govt. to Prosecute Illegal Immigrants. Palestine in Parliament. 1220 Refugees Prevented Entry Between February and April." *The Palestine Post*, 26 IV 1939, p. 1.

[92] TNA. CO 733/394/2 (f. 127). *Telegram from FO to Sir M. Lampson (Cairo), Mr. Houstoun–Boswall (Bagdad), Sir R. Bullard (Jedda). 7 V 1939. Astir* after being turned back, sailed aimlessly on the Aegean for no port wanted to accept its passengers. Only in the middle of June, at Piraeus, was it possible to transfer the refugees to a small schooner, the *Marsis*. The boat was unable to stand up to the rigours of the journey and after two weeks with the threat of it sinking it was apprehended by the British. This time the refugees were not sent to Europe but interned in Palestine.

[93] M. Gilbert, *Exile and Return*, p. 227.

[94] This was already the sixth voyage for the ship in the service of *Aliyah Bet* (the first was in November 1938). According to the British report there were 405 refugees on board. The women and children were soon released, while the men were interned. TNA. CO 733/394/3 (f. 220). *Letter from the Deputy Inspector General (Criminal Investigation Department, Headquarters, Palestine Police) to High Commissioner for Palestine. Subject: Illegal Immigration – SS "Atrato." 5 VI 1939*; TNA. ADM 116/4312. *Capture of SS "Atrato," carrying Polish Jews by HMS "Sutton." 5 VI 1939*; FRUS 1939. Vol. IV, pp. 771–772: *The Consul General at Jerusalem (Wadsworth) to the Secretary of State. Jerusalem, 3 VI 1939*.

[95] In certain works one may come across other names for this ship: *Prosula* (D. Ofer, *Escaping the Holocaust*) and *Produla* (M. Naor, *Haapala*).

boat of the Marine Police. Two people were fatally wounded, and a third was to die later in hospital.[96]

By instantly increasing speed, *Tiger Hill* was able to escape the British. After 24 hours, on the evening of the 1st of September, it again tried to reach the shore, in the area of Tel Aviv. The departure commenced. Despite the late hour, hundreds of local Jews appeared on the shore ready to give help to the refugees. Before the police arrived, around 200 passengers had made it ashore, avoiding arrest. The remainder (1202 in total) were interned by the mandate authorities at the Sarafand camp between Tel Aviv and Jerusalem.[97]

The main place for the interning of *ma'apilim* was Atlit, 20 km to the south of Haifa. The camp at Atlit, which in time became one of the symbols of *ha'apala*, was situated near the Mediterranean coast and had originally been used for military purposes. The first illegal immigrants were sent here in 1939 when their number had significantly increased.[98] The camp's geographical location was not by chance, for the majority of the *ma'apilim* came by sea. Atlit also housed fighters from the underground Jewish organizations in armed struggle with the British. Tens of thousands of Jews passed through the camp.

The camp covered an area of 25 acres[99] and numbered 80 residential barracks, each of which could hold from 30 to 70 people. The entire space was surrounded by triple fencing with barbed wire and manned by British soldiers. Those interned had the opportunity to develop culturally and organize educational classes. Men and women were placed in separate sections of the camp. This solution, otherwise understandable, meant the separation of married couples.[100] The length of stay fluctuated from several days to a dozen or so months (though terms of internment could

---

[96]   TNA. CO 733/395/4 (pp. 29–30). *Telegram from the High Commissioner for Palestine to the Secretary of State for the Colonies. No. 1099. 3 IX 1939* (full text of the telegram published in: A. Patek, *Żydzi w drodze do Palestyny*, pp. 324–325); "1400 Refugees Land at Tel Aviv Beach. Three Killed by Marine Patrol Fire," *The Palestine Post*, 3 IX 1939, p. 1.

[97]   TNA. FO 371/24094/W 13553 (pp. 277–278). *Telegram from the High Commissioner for Palestine to the Secretary of State for the Colonies, 3 IX 1939*. For more detail see among others B. Habas, op.cit., pp. 91–103 as well the recollections of one of the organizers of the transport Ruth Klueger (Aliav): R. Aliav, P. Mann, *The Last Escape. The Launching of the Largest Secret Rescue Movement of All-Time*, London 1974, pp. 94–263. The United States consul in Jerusalem, Christian Steger incorrectly informs as if the vessel was to arrive in Tel Aviv 2 IX 1939: FRUS 1939. Vol. IV, p. 805: *The Consul at Jerusalem (Steger) to the Secretary of State. Jerusalem, 21 IX 1939*.

[98]   We can find the announcement for interning illegal immigrants at Atlit in a telegram of the High Commissioner for Palestine, Sir Harold MacMichael, to the Colonial Office dated the 3rd of May 1939: *I am arranging for special camp to receive any further illegal immigrants caught where they can be detained pending quarantine, interrogation and decision in their case*. CZA. S 25/22701. *Telegram from High Commissioner for Palestine, Transjordan to Secretary of State*.

[99]   An acre – a unit of land area equal to 4046.86 m².

[100]   On the basis of *Ma'apilim Detention Camp Atlit* (a two-sided leaflet issued by the Atlit Detention Camp for Illegal Immigrants museum; in the author's possession). See also: "Athlit, where refugees are cleared," *The Palestine Post*, 22 I 1940, p. 2.

be even longer). Those released made use of the immigrant certificate pools, thanks to which they could legally settle in Palestine.

Every now and then Yishuv opinion was shaken by reports of incidents at Atlit. Accusations came from both the British and Jewish sides. In the reports of the latter we read about the brutality of the guards, the beating of the interned, resounding anti-Jewish remarks (*Here is Dachau for you*), and otherwise making life unpleasant for the inmates (personal inspections, cutting off electricity and water).[101] In one of the accusations reference is made to so-called fitness trails.[102] The British claimed that these accusations were exaggerated. They justified searches and the applying of sanctions by the fact that the interned were liable to hide weapons and sabotage the guards' orders.[103]

Atlit served the British authorities until the very end of the mandate in 1948. After the creation of Israel the camp was changed into a transit point for new immigrants. It was to exist until the 1970s when it was abandoned and fell into ruin. In 1987 the Israeli government proclaimed the site to be a national monument. A museum was opened and a gradual programme of restoration work has been undertaken including the reconstruction of several barracks.[104]

In order to halt the flow of *ma'apilim*, the British put diplomatic pressure on those states where transports set sail and on those under whose flag the immigrant ships sailed. Interventions were made with the governments of Romania, Greece, Turkey as well as Panama.[105] British agents were active in the countries of the Balkans, trying to anticipate the *Aliyah Bet* organizers' intentions. They watched the ports of the Mediterranean and the local Jewish communities with particular vigilance. Those involved in illegal immigration were fined and imprisoned. For example, the owner of a ship ran the risk of a fine of up to £10,000 and 5 years in gaol; others had

---

[101]  CZA. Z 4/31066. *Translation of Report on Treatment of two Jewish Refugees at Athlit Camp* (30 III 1940), a copy of this report is also in: CZA. Z 4/31104; CZA. Z4/31066. *Bernard Joseph, Executive of the Jewish Agency to the Chief Secretary, Government Offices, Jerusalem* (2 IV 1940), full text published in: A. Patek, *Żydzi w drodze do Palestyny*, pp. 333–334; Rhodes House Library, Oxford (subsequently RHL). J.A. Dudley Nigg Papers. MSS. Medit. S 21. *Ill – usage of ex-detainees at Athlit Camp. Palestine 1948* (pp. 2–4).

[102]  *Suddenly they* [the detainees] *were ordered to pass from the prisoners' camp to the detainees' camp along the connecting road. On both sides of this road soldiers and policemen armed with batons and behind them a crowd of armed troops were standing. Every detainee and prisoner had to walk slowly between those lines and was beaten and searching* (quoted after: *Ill – usage of ex-detainees at Athlit Camp*, p. 3).

[103]  RHL. J.A. Dudley Nigg Papers. *Allegations made by ex-detainees of Athlit* (20 IV 1948), pp. 5–7.

[104]  *Atlit Detention Camp for Illegal Immigrants* (official leaflet of the museum at Atlit, without year of issue); *Atlit "Illegal Immigration Camp,"* Jewish Virtual Library (Internet – www.jewishvirtual-library.org/jsource/Immigration/athlit.html). More see: Z. Rotenberg, "The Atlit Detention Camp" [in:] M. Naor, *Atlit. "Illegal immigrant" detention camp. A story of a time and place*, Mikveh Israel 2010, pp. 5–6.

[105]  FRUS 1939. Vol. IV, p. 773: *The Minister in Rumania (Gunther) to the Secretary of State. Bucharest, 8 VI 1939*; B. Wasserstein, *Britain and the Jews of Europe 1939–1945*, London–Oxford 1979, p. 27.

to reckon with losses in the environs of £1000 and the prospect of two years behind bars (amendment to the Palestine Immigration Ordinance, 17th of April 1939).[106] Arrest and fines, and deportation from the Mandate, were also envisaged for the passengers. In practice they ended up at an interned persons camp, from where, after a certain time, they were released and allowed to make use of the immigration quotas.[107] As a result of the dramatic increase in the number of *ma'apilim*, in July 1939 Great Britain decided on an unprecedented step – the announcing of a temporary suspension of legal emigration to the Mandate for a six month period, starting from the 1st of October 1939.[108]

The tightening of immigration policy was accompanied by a series of events within Yishuv. In Haifa on the 23rd of April a strike was called. Protestors took to the streets. On the protest banners could be read: "Down with the British Empire" and "Open wide the gates of our homeland." Demonstrations took place in Jerusalem and other centres.[109] "Free Aliyah" was surely the most frequently used slogan during anti-British demonstrations in Yishuv at the end of the 1930s, and then throughout the following decade right up until the end of the mandate.

The tightening up of countermeasures resulted from Great Britain's political strategy in the Middle East and its sensitivity to the voice of the Arab side. The situation was incredibly difficult for anti-British feeling was spreading in the Muslim world, while in Palestine itself a state of heightened tension existed with a return to violence by no means ruled out. The Arabs did not believe that a country which presented itself as a great power was unable to cope with illegal Jewish immigration. Rumours speculated that the government in London was conducting a conscious policy[110] of playing the Zionist card *as a means of maintaining permanent British control over Palestine.*[111] The Arab press called for forceful opposition to illegal forms of Jewish influx. *Illegal immigration constitutes a crime against Palestine* – claimed *Falastin*, published in the Mandate, pointing to the fragile state of the economy and the high level of unemployment amongst the Arab population.[112]

High-ranking Arab civil servants in the Palestine service looked worriedly at the changing ethnic composition of the Mandate, submitting a memorandum to the

---

[106] FRUS 1939. Vol. IV, pp. 744–747: *The Consul General at Jerusalem (Wadsworth) to the Secretary of State. Jerusalem, 3 V 1939.* Cf. also: "Increased Penalties for Assisting 'Illegals,'" *The Palestine Post*, 24 VIII 1939, p. 1.

[107] TNA. CO 733/394/3 (f. 271). *Palestine: Illegal Immigration, 6 VI 1939.*

[108] AAN. MSZ 9933 (pp. 61–65). A note of the Foreign Office to the Polish ambassador in London, E. Raczyński of the 2 VIII 1939; "No Legal Immigration in the next Schedule Period," *The Palestine Post*, 13 VII 1939, p. 1.

[109] CZA. S 25/22701. *Telegram from High Commissioner for Palestine, Trans-Jordan to Secretary of State. 23 IV 1939.*

[110] CZA. S 25/22701. *Note by A.F. Giles, Inspector-General: "Illegal immigration." Secret. 7 IV 1939.*

[111] TNA. FO 371/45383/E 8593 (p. 4/237). *Great Britain and Palestine. Foreign Research and Press Service. Balliol College, Oxford, 18 II 1942.*

[112] CZA. S 25/22701. *Arabic Press. Extracts. 6.4.39. "Falastin" – Illegal immigration.*

High Commissioner for Palestine, Sir Arthur Wauchope, on the 30th of June 1936.[113] These fears were repeated by the Arab summit that took place in Syrian Bludan. In July of the following year the Prime Minister of Egypt, Mohammed Mahmud Pasha, in a conversation with the head of the Colonial Office, Malcolm MacDonald, made it clear that if Great Britain forced through a division of Palestine she would *lose important friends in the Arab world and India*.[114] Similar signals were being sent from other circles. The Arabs repeated their opposition to further Jewish immigration in February 1939 during the conference which ended in fiasco at St James's Palace in London. From their perspective, Jewish settlers were intruders, while the Jewish claims to Palestine were legally unfounded.

It was difficult not to notice that gradually the Palestinian matter had become a general Arab question. Besides ethnic and religious factors, geopolitical considerations also played a role in this. Palestine was a natural land bridge between Arab North Africa and the Arab Middle East. The Arabs feared that an independent Jewish State would not only end the geographic unity of their world but in mobilizing the support of the world Zionist movement and western countries it would become a base for foreign penetration into the region.[115] Followers of Islam found it difficult to accept that places that they considered holy (first and foremost the Temple Mount in Jerusalem, known by Muslims as Haram esh-Sharif, the Noble Sanctuary) would be under foreign control.

It was difficult to ignore Arab sentiment and this must have influenced the steps taken by London.[116] The activities of the Mandate government *have had a profound effect in Egypt as well as Arab States as proof of good faith and intentions* – Sir Sydney Waterlow, the British representative in Greece, telegraphed headquarters following talks with an envoy of Cairo's.[117] *Such concrete action had far more value in the eyes of an Oriental than any number of promises or agreements* – he added.

---

[113] The memorandum was signed by 137 Arab civil servants with only 7 allegedly not signing it. After: "Arab Gov't Officials Ask Immigration Stoppage. Full Text of Memorandum Submitted to High Commissioner," *The Palestine Post*, 10 VII 1936, pp. 1, 8 (a copy of the paper is also in the collections of AAN. The Embassy of the Polish Republic in London 140, p. 20 and onwards).

[114] Z.V. Hadari, op.cit., p. 57.

[115] TNA. FO 371/45383/E 8593 (p. 5/238). *Great Britain and Palestine. Foreign Research and Press Service. Balliol College, Oxford, 18 II 1942.*

[116] CZA. S 25/22701. *Telegram from Secretary of State to High Commissioner for Palestine, Transjordan. Immediate. 20 IV 1939.*

[117] TNA. CO 733/394/2 (f. 136). *Decypher from Greece (Sir S. Waterlow) to Foreign Office, 10 V 1939.* A copy of the document is also in the collections of CZA, in the file "Illegal immigration. Various doc. 1936–1939" [CZA. S 25/22701].

***

*Aliyah Bet* started off as a movement without formal organization. It was an immediate response to the situation of Jews in Europe and the immigration policy of the British Mandate. It was conditioned not only by political circumstances but also ideological and spiritual aspects. Therefore *ha'apala* incorporated into itself various circles and groups which did so for a number of different motives. Gradually *Aliyah Bet*, which still in the mid 1930s had been devoid of staff and resources, was to change itself into a political force. As Shaul Avigur has noted, *the modest start was an essential door to the large-scale operations and it was only its huge proportions which made clandestine immigration an important factor in the context of immigration in general, its success and its political pressure.*[118]

---

[118] Quoted after: M. Naor, *Haapala*, p. 32.

# Chapter IV: In the shadow of the "White Paper"

## 1. The reality of wartime

As it turned out, the first shots fired by British units at the moment the Second World War began were directed against Jewish refugees, passengers of the freighter *Tiger Hill*.[1] This incident opened up a bitter chapter in the British-Jewish struggle for the right to free immigration to Palestine. This was brought about not by anti-Semitism but the circumstances resulting from Great Britain's strategy in the Middle East. This strategy stipulated that MacDonald's "White Paper" was imperative if Great Britain intended to maintain its position in this dangerous region.[2]

The outbreak of the Second World War appeared to bring with it new political conditions. Many Jews were familiar with the dilemma of reconciling the resolutions of the "White Paper" with the figure of Great Britain as an ally in the battle against Hitler. *Fight the war as if there were no White Paper* – answered David Ben-Gurion – *and fight the White Paper as if there were no war*.[3] The chance for dialogue appeared not to be accepted. Great Britain opposed, among other things, the drafting of Jewish volunteers from Palestine into its army (in total 136,000 Jews expressed a willingness to fight) and only at the very end of the war in 1944 did it agree to the creation of a separate military unit under the name of the Jewish Brigade (within the framework of the British armed forces), which was then to fight in Italy.[4]

From the British perspective this restraint had its justifications: on the one hand the fear that a separate Jewish corps might become for the idea of Eretz Israel what (*toutes proportions gardées*) Piedmont became for Italian unity; on the other

---

[1]  B. Wasserstein, *Britain and the Jews of Europe 1939–1945*, London–Oxford 1979, p. 40. We recalled the incident in the chapter "On the eve of war."

[2]  B. Joseph, *British Rule in Palestine*, Washington 1948, p. 166.

[3]  G. Kirk, *The Middle East in the War*, 3rd ed., London–New York–Toronto 1954, p. 13; R. Balke, *Izrael*, Warszawa 2005, p. 53; Y. Bauer, *From Diplomacy to Resistance. A History of Jewish Palestine 1939–1945*, New York 1973, p. 72; M. Bar-Zohar, *Ben-Gurion*, London 1978, p. 100; D. Ben-Gurion, *Israel. A Personal History*, London 1972, p. 54.

[4]  London explained that it had to worry about the equal proportion between Jews and Arabs. While the recruitment of the latter was small, in a similar way to the small amount of motivation (different than for the Jews) to fight on the side of Great Britain against the Germans. Cf. M.N. Penkower, *The Jews were Expendable. Free World Diplomacy and the Holocaust*, Chicago 1983 (the chapter: "The Struggle for an Allied Jewish Fighting Force"); M. Beckman, *The Jewish Brigade. An Army with Two Masters, 1944–1945*, Staplehurst 1998.

the need to follow the Arab reaction and their potential rapprochement in sympathies with the Axis states.

The governments of the Arab states had confirmed their loyalty, yet there were various tendencies were clashing within these countries. That the fears were not groundless was confirmed by the anti-British coup in Iraq in 1941. The collaboration of the leader of the Palestinian Arabs, the Grand Mufti of Jerusalem, Haj Amin al-Husseini, with the Germans must have caused concern (in 1941 he was to take shelter in Italy and Germany from where he would call on Muslims to support the Axis powers).[5] The matter was serious as Palestine constituted an important supply area for the allied armies in the Middle East. The region's importance increased with the expansion of the theatre of war to include the Balkans and North Africa, and particularly after Germany's attack on the USSR. In the summer of 1940 and spring of 1941 there even existed the danger of a British withdrawal and German occupation, and the Italian air force bombed Haifa and Tel Aviv.[6] The threat of a German attack on Palestine in the form of the Afrika Korps was to remain real until the decisive British victory at El Alamein in Egypt in November 1942. Defense plans for the Mandate were even devised in the eventuality of the Afrika Korps closing the Suez Canal. If the Germans had managed to reach the Persian Gulf they would have cut Great Britain's lines of communication and deprived it of strategic supply sources (oil).

London decided to pursue if not the favour then at least the neutrality of the Arab world, whose natural resources had huge importance for the successful conduct of the war. Previous experience had shown that the British were able to maintain influence in countries which were strategically important for them despite the granting of formal independence. This was the intended policy with regard to Palestine. It was going to abandoned sooner or later and this was understood, though it was not desirable until the ground had been appropriately prepared. It was believed that this was possible only through the literal application of the "White Paper" of 1939, which[7] in effect limited Jews' ability to acquire land, leaving in their hands the managing of plots on a small patch of the Mandate (around 5% of the area, chiefly in a coastal strip and the environs of Jerusalem).[8]

---

[5] For more see: J. Schechtman, *The Mufti and the Führer. The Rise and Fall of Haj Amin el Huseini*, New York 1965; K. Gensicke, *Der Mufti von Jerusalem. Amin el-Husseini und die Nationalsozialisten*, Frankfurt am Main 1988.

[6] M. Gilbert, *Israel A History*, London 1999, p. 105; K. Gebert, *Miejsce pod słońcem. Wojny Izraela*, Warszawa 2008, s. 109–110.

[7] Cf. the collection of documents: *The Rise of Israel*. Vol. 28: *Implementing the White Paper 1939–1941*. Ed. by M.J. Cohen, New York–London 1987. For more see: R.W. Zweig, *Britain and Palestine During the Second World War*, Woodbridge 1986; D. Trevor, *Under the White Paper. Some Aspects of British Administration in Palestine from 1939 to 1947*, Jerusalem 1948; M.J. Cohen, *Palestine: Retreat from the Mandate. The Making of British Policy, 1936–1945*, New York 1978 (Chapter 6: "British Policy during the Critical Phase, 1939–1942").

[8] The "Land Transfers Regulations" published in February 1940 divided the Mandate into three zones: A (the management of land exclusively in the hands of the Arab population), B (an "Arab zone" with

This tightening up was reflected in the scale of Jewish immigration. The quantity of certificates issued during the war years did not even reach the upper limits envisaged by the "White Paper." Rather than the envisaged 75,000, the British allowed in a mere 50,000 together with those whose stay had been legalized. It is important to note that from October 1939 to March 1940 and then from October 1940 to March 1941 the issuing of certificates was totally suspended, this being explained by the dimensions of the illegal immigration that occurred in the course of 1939 as well as the fears that amongst the incomers from the Reich and other countries allied with it could be Nazi agents.[9]

In October 1939 the government Committee on Refugees devised guidelines by which Great Britain was to operate in its policy towards Jewish refugees during the period of the war. First – no cooperation with the Third Reich in the question of the emigration of Jewish German citizens. Secondly – no agreement on the accepting of refugees from countries under enemy occupation.[10]

It is a paradox that the policy of the "White Paper" was being realized by a government that from May 1940 had been headed by a man known for his sympathy for the Zionist movement and Jews. Let us recall that a year earlier Winston Churchill had condemned MacDonald's "Paper" (he had described it as an *act of repudiation*),[11] but within the Foreign Office and military circles its supporters had the advantage, such as the heads of diplomacy and the Colonial Office Anthony Eden and Malcolm MacDonald, Resident Minister in the Middle East Walter Edward Guinness, Lord Moyne, the commander-in-chief of the British forces in the Middle East General Archibald Wavell or the High Commissioner to Palestine Harold MacMichael.[12]

A chain of circumstances meant that British and Jewish arguments were completely at loggerheads. Many matters looked different viewed through British or Jewish eyes. What appeared an act in defense of the Empire from London's perspective was perceived by the other side as heartlessness. Furthermore, Great Britain really did find itself in an awkward situation. From the 3rd of September it had been in a state of war with Germany while at the same time opposing Jewish immigrants, refugees from Germany or countries under its occupation. The drama was deepened by the fact that these events occurred at the time of the Holocaust. As the Jewish

---

the possibility for limited Jewish purchase of land) and C (the "Jewish zone"). Zone A covered 63% of the area of Palestine. For text see: British White Paper, *Palestine Land Transfers Regulations. Letter to the Secretary-General of the League of Nations, February 28, 1940*, London 1940; *The Rise of Israel*. Vol. 28: *Implementing the White Paper*, doc. 22, pp. 98–106.

[9] *The Jewish Case Before the Anglo-American Committee of Inquiry on Palestine as presented by the Jewish Agency for Palestine. Statements and Memoranda*, Jerusalem 1947, p. 295; G. Kirk, *The Middle East in the War*, p. 239.

[10] M.J. Cohen, *Churchill and the Jews*, London 1985, p. 274.

[11] "Speech by Winston Churchill in the House of Commons, 23 May 1939, and comments by other members of Parliament" [in:] *The Rise of Israel*. Vol. 27, doc. 28, pp. 331–337. See also Chapter 1, footnote 50.

[12] B. Wasserstein, *Britain and the Jews of Europe 1939–1945*, London–Oxford 1979, pp. 23, 31–33; M. Gilbert, *Churchill and the Jews. A Lifelong Friendship*, New York 2007, pp. 157–160.

Agency bitterly remarked: *There can be little doubt that substantial numbers who are dead today, certainly tens of thousands, might have been alive if the gates of Palestine had been kept open.*[13]

Yet this was not only about Palestine. An unwillingness to open their borders to refugees (not only Jewish) also characterized such countries as the USA and Canada. Fugitives from the Third Reich, and later from Nazi-occupied Europe, met with a high wall of bureaucratic heartlessness.[14] Compassion for the victims did not go hand in hand with immigration facilitation.

Events in and around Palestine heightened British-Jewish tensions. Irgun announced a truce, but the terrorist activities directed against the British were continued by its extreme fraction, the so called Stern group. Abraham Stern, the cofounder of Irgun (of Polish origin) considered Great Britain to be the main opponent of the Jews. In Great Britain's view he and his group were "fifth columnists" (from other sources it is known that Stern in his hatred of the British even undertook attempts to forge links with representatives of the Third Reich).[15] Although the efforts of the British police and intelligence led to the physical elimination of Stern in 1942 this did not prevent further activity by the group. Known also as Lohamei Herut Israel (Fighters for the Freedom of Israel, Lehi in short) they were to conduct armed struggle with the British to the very end of the Mandate, organising attacks on representatives of the Mandate administration, armed attacks on British military and government sites as well as acts of expropriation. After Stern's death one of the group leaders became Yitzhak Yezernitsky (Yitzhak Shamir, the future Prime Minister of Israel).[16]

---

[13]  Quoted after: [The Jewish Agency for Palestine], *The Jewish Case before the Anglo-American Committee of Inquiry on Palestine as presented by the Jewish Agency for Palestine. Statements and Memoranda*, Jerusalem 1947, p. 296. Cf. also the reflections of Mitchell Bard: *The gates of Palestine remained closed for the duration of the war, stranding hundreds of thousands of Jews in Europe, many of whom became victims of Hitler's Final Solution.* M. Bard, *British Restrictions on Jewish Immigration*, p. 3 [in:] Jewish Virtual Library (http://www.jewishvirtuallibrary.org/jsource/History/mandate.html).

[14]  For more see: R. Breitman, A.M. Kraut, *American Refugee Policy and European Jewry, 1933–1945*, Bloomington 1987; S.S. Friedman, *No Haven for the Oppressed. United States Policy toward Jewish Refugees, 1938–1945*, Detroit 1973; D.S. Wyman, *The Abandonment of the Jews: America and the Holocaust, 1941–1945*, New York 1984 (Polish translation: *Pozostawieni swemu losowi. Ameryka wobec Holocaustu 1941–1945*, Warszawa 1994); H.L. Feingold, *The Politics of Rescue. The Roosevelt Administration and the Holocaust 1938–1945*, New Brunswick, NJ 1970; I. Abella, H. Troper, *None Is Too Many. Canada and the Jews of Europe, 1933–1948*, New York 1983.

[15]  Such an attempt was made in January 1941, offering the Germans cooperation against Britain. L. Brenner, *The Iron Wall. Zionist Revisionism from Jabotinsky to Shamir*, London 1984, pp. 195–197; H.M. Sachar, *A History of Israel. From the Rise of Zionism to Our Time*, New York 1988, p. 247.

[16]  For more see: J. Heller, *The Stern Gang. Ideology, Politics and Terror, 1940–1949*, London 1995. Cf. Y. Shamir, *Summing Up. An Autobiography*, Boston–New York–Toronto–London 1994 (the Chapter "Freedom Fighters," pp. 32–50).

Towards the end of the war Irgun was also to join in the struggle against the Mandate. And its fighters were to plague the enemy with methods similar to Lehi. Admittedly Irgun and Lehi constituted the periphery of Yishuv military activity, yet their actions caused the British major losses.

A different tactic was adopted by Hagana, which accepted short-term cooperation with Great Britain. It was the German offensive in North Africa that induced the British to agree in 1941 to the formation of Hagana assault battalions (Palmach) and the training of Jewish commandos, who were to conduct acts of sabotage behind enemy lines. Hagana became a semi-official ally of London for a short time, when the German-Italian threat had passed, the authorities demanded a return of the weapons. Hagana again went underground although the military experience gained was to prove extremely useful. The Palmach units were de facto regular military units, and their fighters were to become a cadre of the Israeli armed forces.[17] Tactical cooperation with the Mandate did not mean giving up on the struggle against the "White Paper."

During the war not many more than 16,000 refugees made it to Palestine within the framework of *ha'apala*, chiefly in the period 1939–1940 and in 1944.[18] Significantly fewer than in the years 1934–1939. A further few thousand immigrants, for whom the transit point was Istanbul, were issued with the relevant certificates by the Mandate after arriving in Turkey in 1944, which enabled them to legally travel on to Palestine. Over 2,500 refugees never reached their destination, dying either in transports at sea or at the hands of the Germans.

The limitation on the number of *ha'apala* was certainly influenced by the rigorous countermeasures and strengthening of defenses of the Palestinian coast employed by the Mandate. A fundamental role was played by objective difficulties arising during the period of war and associated problems of organising transports, obtaining finances, and guaranteeing security. Ship-owners took advantage of the opportunity to charge exorbitant prices for the chartering of a vessel, as the risk involved in the undertaking had risen considerably. Money was lacking. The possibility of organizing groups of refugees from Central Europe became increasingly difficult together with their transportation to Mediterranean or Black Sea ports; a significant part of Europe was under occupation. Italy's entry into the war in June 1940 also markedly limited possibilities. Balkan countries progressively began to view the passage of subsequent waves of Jewish refugees through their territories unfavour-

---

[17]  Y. Bauer, *From Diplomacy to Resistance*, pp. 139–152, 195–211. E.N. Luttwak, D. Horowitz, *The Israeli Army 1948–1973*, Cambridge, Mass. 1983, pp. 19–21; M.J. Cohen, *Palestine: Retreat from the Mandate*, p. 98 onwards.

[18]  M. Naor, *Haapala, Clandestine Immigration 1931–1948*, [Tel Aviv 1987], p. 104. According to the calculations of CINM (the part "Ha'apala – Clandestine Immigration 1934–1948") the number of *ma'apilim* was 16,456 persons. This figure is supported by Dalia Ofer, "Die illegale Einwanderung nach Palästina. Politische, nationale und persönliche Aspekte (1939–1941)" [in:] S. Heim et al. (Hg.), *Flüchtlingspolitik und Fluchthilfe*, Berlin 1999, p. 17.

Table 12. *Ha'apala* from Europe during the war

| Time of organized transport | Number of transports | Immigrants (1000s) |
|---|---|---|
| 1939 (September–December) | 4 (+ 3)* | 2.8 (+ 2.9) |
| 1940 | 7 | 6.8–7.6 |
| 1941 | 4 | 1.6 |
| 1942 | 7 | 0.2 |
| 1943 | 1 | ? |
| 1944 | 11 | 4.6–5.0 |

* Transports which set off in August 1939 yet reached Palestine already after the outbreak of the war.

Author's study. The list also covers transports that did not reach Palestine.

ably. Who would guarantee these people's passage? Even if they succeeded, there was Great Britain's reaction to deal with. And how would the Third Reich react?[19]

The matter was not helped by the fact that *ha'apala* was organized by various circles, which acted independently of each other – Mossad, the Revisionists, Konfino. To which were added the aforesaid dilemmas: should they focus on the image of Great Britain as the enemy in Palestine or as an ally in the war with Germany?

Arguments were advanced for and against the continuation of *Aliyah Bet*. Arguments of an economic, moral and political nature. It was feared that subsequent transports of illegal immigrants could damage the tactical agreement with the British e.g. in the matter of creating a Jewish military unit. Opponents claimed that *ha'apala* was taking place at the cost of regular *aliyah* and that it reduced possibilities for the most desired individuals to come, the most sought-after from an economic point of view in relation to Yishuv's requirements and needs. In 1940, *Aliyah Bet* had clearly become less important in the thinking of the Jewish Agency. Not without significance here was Winston Churchill's taking of power in May 1940; he was perceived as a Zionist sympathizer and an opponent of the "White Paper." The objective difficulties of wartime mentioned above, including the severe lack of finance, also played their part. *Today, aliyah is not in our hands* – said Ben-Gurion at the Jewish Agency forum on the 14th of April 1940, *the seas are ruled by the British navy* [...], *what we need now is a militant Zionism that will strengthen and build up the Zionist movement.*[20]

During the first phase of the war Mossad had independently organized only two transports with illegal immigrants, the first at the beginning of 1940 (*Hilda*), the sec-

---

[19] D. Ofer, "Illegal Immigration During the Second World War: Its Suspension and Subsequent Resumption," *Studies in Contemporary Jewry* (New York–Oxford). Ed. by J. Frankel. Vol. VII: 1991, pp. 225–226.
[20] Ibidem, p. 233.

ond (*Darien II*) a year later. Both had been taken by the British. The attempt to help the refugees held on the Danube by ice at the Yugoslavian port of Kladovo ended in failure. It was also impossible to prevent the deportation by the Mandate of one and a half thousand Jewish refugees to Mauritius.[21] These events most certainly did not create an encouraging atmosphere for *Aliyah Bet*.

When the hope placed in Great Britain did not materialize, and the dramatic news of the Holocaust started to come out of Europe, the tactics employed by the leaders of Yishuv had to change. War events also played favourably into the hands of *Aliyah Bet*. After the defeat of the Germans at Stalingrad and the opening of a second front (1943) the initiative passed into Allied hands. In 1944 there emerged the possibility of evacuating Jews through the territory of Romania and Bulgaria, whose governments had started to look for ways of coming to an agreement with the West.

# 2. Through the "green border"

Although the majority of *ma'apilim* came from Europe by sea, there did exist a parallel dropping of Jews by land routes, chiefly the "green border" from the Syrian and Lebanese side. The operations were coordinated by Mossad emissaries in the Middle East: David Nameri (Syria and Lebanon), Enzo Sereni (Iraq), Moshe Averbuch (Iran) and Ruth Klueger (Egypt). In order to slip past the British patrols the refugees were dressed in Arab clothes and provided with Arab documents. The operation generally comprised two stages. First the refugees had to be smuggled into the countries of the Levant; and then from there onwards to the Mandate. Some made it on foot, others on camels or in vehicles, while others still were transported by fishing boat from one of the Lebanese ports.

Amongst those smuggled were many Jews from Iraq. The possibility for legal emigration from this country was limited. The government in Baghdad, in solidarity with the Palestinian people, had introduced restrictions before the war. In June 1941, following the overthrow by the British army of the pro-German government of Rashid Ali al-Gaylani (he had taken power on the 1st of April as a result of a military coup), there occurred a wave of anti-Jewish riots, in the course of which 179 Jews were killed and hundreds injured. These events without doubt created an atmosphere conducive to emigration. Emissaries from Yishuv, Enzo Sereni, Ezra Kaduri, Munya Mardor worked towards this end.[22] The future immigrants, on the whole young people, were trained before departure, in utmost secrecy, how to

---

[21] See more in the next Chapter.

[22] E. Meir-Glitzenstein, *Zionism in Arab Country. Jews in Iraq in the 1940s*, London–New York 2004, pp. 64–66; J. and D. Kimche, *The Secret Roads. The "Illegal" Migration of a People, 1938–1948*, London 1954, pp. 60–63.

handle weapons, were taught Hebrew, were proselytized to Hagana, etc. Help was provided in their redeployment by, among others, employees of the Baghdad branch of the construction company Solel Boneh belonging to Histadrut as well as Jewish soldiers serving in the British units in Iraq. Some "lent" the immigrants documents or even uniforms, others "employed" them as, for example, drivers. The possibilities were immense but this particular route could only be taken by individuals and not larger organized groups.[23]

The smuggling route most often went through Syria. This was helped by the terrain (mountainous), as well as the fact that in the countries of the Levant there were concentrations of Jewish people. The desert borderland with Transjordan was devoid of these advantages. The operation was beset with numerous dangers: firstly – the significant distances, 1000 to 1500 km; secondly – the numerous military checkpoints. One land or rail transport could be stopped and checked several times. The smuggling required the investment of increasing amounts of money. The difficulties meant that the *Aliyah Bet* from Iraq did not take on a large scale dimension. *After all our efforts, we have not broken open the road to aliyah for the eastern lands* – admitted the head of Mossad.[24]

Some made it to Syria legally as tourists or students – and were not to return to Iraq. The Mandate's border was crossed in various ways. Sometimes a bribe was enough, and sometimes a well forged passport. More often the services of smugglers were employed, though this involved risk. It happened that the smugglers, having collected their substantial fee, would suddenly disappear or denounce the immigrants to the authorities. It was relatively easy to smuggle across young people not afraid of the risk, though children were also smuggled.[25] With time the work of the Mossad emissaries ran into increasing difficulties. Iraq was practically occupied by the British army, which was to protect it from foreign invasion. The strategic importance of the country meant that British intelligence was interested in what went on. Mossad's field of manoeuvre was limited to such a degree that it had to temporarily remove its people from Iraq.

*Aliyah bet* from the countries of the Levant, directly bordering the Palestinian Mandate, was somewhat easier. Following the crossing of the border the route onwards usually took in the nearby kibbutzim of Kfar Giladi (the Lebanese-Syrian-Palestinian borderland) and Ayelet ha'Shahar in the region of Rosh Pina.[26] It could

---

23  The British contracted the company Solel Boneh for road and construction works in Iraq. M. Naor, *Haapala*, pp. 83–85; E. Meir-Glitzenstein, op.cit., pp. 159–175. The Jewish Agency was able to bring in a part legally. CZA. Z 4/30523. *Refugees cross desert to reach haven in Palestine. 26/6/1942.*

24  In a letter to the Histadrut secretariat of April 1944. Quote after: E. Meir-Glitzenstein, op.cit., p. 163.

25  "Yani Avidov relates how Jewish children were smuggled into Eretz Yisrael from Syria" [in:] L. Soshuk, A. Eisenberg (eds.), *Momentous Century. Personal and Eyewitness Accounts of the Rise of the Jewish Homeland and State 1875–1978*, New York–London 1984, pp. 232–235; M. Naor, *Haapala*, pp. 83–85.

26  R. Pearse, *Three Years in the Levant*, London 1949, pp. 192–193.

happen that even several hundred Jews monthly would be dropped from Syria.[27] In total, according to Mossad data, 3,300–3,500 Jews were smuggled from countries of the Middle East: 75% from Syria, the rest (about 850 people) from Iraq, Iran and Turkey. Some came on their own.[28]

The secret smuggling of Jews from countries of the Orient was an integral part of *ha'apala*, but in the popular imagination it is less important than that from Europe. It has drawn the attention of the media and historians to a much lesser degree. There are several reasons for this: 1) the numbers brought by sea easily exceeded those transported by land; 2) the maritime *ha'apala* was far more spectacular and could be used politically to a greater degree 3) after the war the sympathy and compassion experienced by a significant part of society was directed towards the Jews after the Holocaust – and amongst the ranks of the post-war *ma'apilim* the greatest number are indeed victims of Shoah.


# 3. From Anders' Army

A separate chapter was constituted by those who came to Palestine together with the units of the Polish Army of General Władysław Anders, which was evacuated from the USSR in 1942.[29] The army was first sent to Iran, then transferred to Iraq. The Second Polish Army Corps, created from within the ranks of Anders' army as a separate force of about 53,000 soldiers, was regrouped in Palestine in summer 1943. These Polish detachments were operationally subordinate to British command. The purpose of the regrouping was to retrain the Corps as a fighting force

---

[27]  J. and D. Kimche, op.cit., p. 60.

[28]  E. Meir-Glitzenstein, op.cit., p. 165. The number of all illegal immigrants who came to Palestine from Muslim countries during the war is estimated by the authors of the *Encyclopedia of Jewish History* (New York–Oxford 1986, p. 176) to be 12,000. Shaul Avigur claims that up until 1948 a total of 8,700 Jews were smuggled from North Africa and countries of the Orient (S. Avigur, *S pokoleniyem khagany*, Tel Awiw 1976, p. 40), Mordechai Naor writes about 7,500 illegal immigrants, of which 2,000 from North Africa (*Haapala*, p. 105), while Yehuda Bauer and Nana Sagi cite 8,402 *ma'apilim* in total by 1948 ("Illegal Immigration" [in:] *New Encyclopedia of Zionism and Israel*. Vol. 1. Ed. by G. Wigoder, London–Toronto 1994, p. 649).

[29]  After the attack on Poland on the 17th of September 1939, the USSR occupied a half of the territory of the Polish Republic. Between 180,000 to 230,000 soldiers, while around 320,000 Polish citizens were taken prisoner and deported into the heart of the Soviet Union (1940–1941). Amongst those repressed were many Jews. Following the German invasion of the USSR on the 22nd of June 1941 and the agreement reached between Moscow and the Polish Government-in-Exile (30th July 1941) the situation of these people changed. On the basis of this agreement the Soviet government agreed to create a Polish Army on its territory as well as to release Polish citizens from prisons and camps. Command was taken by General Anders on his release from prison. This army was evacuated to Iran in 1942. In total (together with civilians) over 115,000 people left. For more see: P. Żaroń, *Armia Andersa*, Toruń 1996.

and to prepare for military operations on the Italian front, where it would be sent via Egypt at the end of 1943. Auxiliary units remained in Palestine.

According to the estimates of Tomasz Gąsowski, at least 4300 soldiers and 3070 civilians of Jewish nationality – citizens of pre-war Poland – left the USSR. A significant part of the soldiers deserted (up until March 1944 in total 2972 individuals, the so called *aliyah vav*, from the Hebrew word *va-yivrah* meaning "escape") not encountering much in the way of complications on the part of the Polish command.[30] Others legally discharged themselves from the army. *I did not allow a search for deserters, and not a single deserter was arrested by us* – General Anders was to say years later, not without a sense of pride.[31] *I considered that they had a dual loyalty, one towards Palestine and the other towards Poland.* The Polish military police only drew up lists which they in turn handed over to the British authorities.

This approach represented a certain understanding of the situation that the Jews found themselves in, partly fugitives from the Germans and partly deportees from the USSR. Many had experienced the nightmare of Soviet labour camps and life in exile. The arrival of the Polish Army in Palestine opened up possibilities for desertion as the Jews found themselves in their own country and felt obliged to fight for its independence. In the face of the reports coming in about the Holocaust, they tied their future to Palestine. They felt that there was nobody to return to, for their families had been killed. In such conditions loyalty to the Polish uniform was replaced by loyalty to Eretz Israel. This is why the command had no intention of using force in apprehending these soldiers. Another reason for desertion was the anti-Semitic behaviour and attitudes of certain sections of the Polish Army. The Jewish side pointed to unfair treatment and discrimination in advancement, the malice displayed by Polish soldiers in relation to their Jewish comrades-in-arms. These incidents led to a sense of bitterness and indignity amongst the Jews, all the more so that they recurred while the army was in Palestine. A part of the Poles also harboured grudges; not understanding the specifics of the situation they accused the deserters of being unwilling to fight the Germans, and disloyalty towards the army which had helped them leave the USSR.[32]

---

[30] T. Gąsowski, *Pod sztandarami Orła Białego. Kwestia żydowska w Polskich Siłach Zbrojnych w czasie II wojny światowej*, Kraków 2002, pp. 136, 171. There exist discrepancies in the literature on the subject with regard to the number of Jews evacuated from the USSR (T. Gąsowski, op.cit. pp. 135–136).

[31] W. Anders, *Bez ostatniego rozdziału. Wspomnienia z lat 1939–1946*, Bydgoszcz 1989, p. 176 (reprint of the London edition of 1959); Z.S. Siemaszko, "Rozmowa z gen. Andersem w dniu 31 lipca 1967 roku," *Kultura* (Paryż), Nos. 7–8 (274–275): 1970, p. 36.

[32] This matter can be only touched on here. For more see: I. Gutman, "Jews in General Anders' Army in the Soviet Union," *Yad Vashem Studies* (Jerusalem). Vol. XII: 1977, pp. 231–333; T. Gąsowski, op.cit., pp. 146–176; K. Zamorski, "Dezercje Żydów z Armii Polskiej," *Zeszyty Historyczne* (Paris). No. 104: 1993, pp. 5–22; H. Sarner, *Generał Anders i żołnierze II Korpusu Polskiego*, Poznań 2002, pp. 144–156 (translation from English: *General Anders and the soldiers of The Second Polish Corps*, Cathedral City, Calif. 1997). See also: D. Levin, *Alija „waw." Masowa dezercja żołnierzy żydowskich z Armii Andersa w Palestynie w latach 1942–1943* [in:] idem, *Żydzi wschodnioeuropejscy podczas*

The deserters in part went to Hagana, others strengthened the ranks of Irgun. A part (around 1000) joined the British Army, swelling the ranks of the Jewish Brigade formed in the autumn of 1944. It was known that this army offered better opportunities for advancement, while service within its ranks made legal settlement in Palestine easier. Around 400–500 found themselves in the Palestinian auxiliary police. The rest settled down to civilian life. An ideal place for shelter were the kibbutzim, where there was a need for people with vocational and military experience.[33] Many had friends or family in Palestine and could count on their support.

The deserters were helped by Hagana and Irgun, and also the Jewish Agency. Views on whether and to what degree the decision to desert was motivated by agitation on their part are divided. Certainly this was in their vested interests. Moshe Shertok, the head of the Political Department of the Jewish Agency, denied that the Agency organized desertion, but admitted that help was provided to those soldiers who did desert. In turn Polish intelligence considered such agitation to have been a certainty.[34] *The operation of enticing desertion and hiding deserters was conducted by the secret military organisation Hagana* – noted the deputy head of the Second Unit (intelligence) of Anders Army command, Lt Col Bronisław Mokrzycki.[35] *Having expressed a willingness to desert they received an address as well as an identification sign, the deserter was taken to the Hagana office situated at Merkaz-Aliyah* [The Central provider of aid to Jewish Immigrants closely connected with the Histadrut party]*, a Jewish social welfare and charity organisation. There the deserter changed into civvies and was taken by Jewish auxiliary police car to a designated kibbutz. After 2–3 weeks [...] he would be registered to the Jewish army. In the meantime Hagana would obtain for the deserter an identity card in an assumed name.*[36]

At the same time the Polish command, in secret from its British ally, would grant several Jewish soldiers "leave" from the army. This referred to individuals linked to the New Zionist Organisation, with which good relations had been maintained since before the war. Amongst those given leave was rifleman Menachem Begin, a leader of Betar in pre-war Poland, and a future Prime Minister of Israel. After the Soviet Union's attack on Poland, Begin was arrested in 1940 by Soviets and sent to Siberia. He

---

*II wojny światowej*, Warszawa 2005, pp. 117–140 (translation from English: "Aliyah 'vav'. The Mass Desertion of Jewish Soldiers from the Polish Army in Palestine, 1942–1943" [in:] *Shvut. Studies in Russian and East European Jewish History and Culture* (Tel Aviv–Beer Sheva). Vol. 5 (21): 1997, pp. 144–170). "*Vav*" is the sixth letter of the Hebrew alphabet.

[33]  H. Sarner, op.cit., pp. 145, 169; E. Kossoy, "Żydowskie podziemie zbrojne w Palestynie i jego polskie powiązania," *Zeszyty Historyczne* (Paris). No. 157: 2006, p. 89; A. Zvielli, "A Soldier's Dilemma," *The Jerusalem Post*, 6 I 1991, p. 5; "W sprawie dezercji Żydów z Armii Polskiej. Ściśle tajne" [in:] "Dezercje Żydów z Armii Polskiej na Wschodzie," *Zeszyty Historyczne* (Paris). No. 103: 1993, pp. 138–139 (report of the Office for Near and Middle East Studies of September 1943).

[34]  K. Zamorski, *Dezercje Żydów...*, p. 11; PISM. A49/1. *Facts concerning attempted disaffection among Jewish and Orthodox soldiers in the Polish Army in Great Britain*, pp. 4–5.

[35]  Note of 9 XII 1942. Quote after: T. Gąsowski, op.cit., p. 161.

[36]  Ibidem.

gained his freedom at the end of 1941 following the concluding of the Polish-Soviet political agreement. He joined Anders' Army and together with it reached Palestine. At the end of 1943 he took over the leadership of Irgun. Begin did not want to desert from the Polish Army as he considered desertion contrary to a soldier's honour and knew that as a deserter he would not be able to stand at the head of the Irgun Zvai Leumi.[37] As the American author Harvey Sarner claims (the grandson of Jewish immigrants from Volynia), in order to hide Begin's legal demobbing from the British, documents were drawn up in which it was affirmed that he had been granted leave of a year's duration from which he had not returned to service.[38]

*Aliyah Vav* was undoubtedly a major boost in strength for the Jewish underground in Palestine. It is worth adding that the fighters from Irgun were extremely well-disposed towards Poles and advised them to clearly mark their vehicles, thanks to which they avoided being targeted as British troops.


# 4. "The only alternative is to maintain the existing procedures"

The outbreak of the war limited the possibilities for *Aliyah Bet* from Europe, but did not stop it. Now there was only one route that came into the equation – through Romania and Bulgaria. From their ports set forth new transports with refugees. The route went through Istanbul, where the Palestine Office of the Jewish Agency was located (its responsibilities included the distribution of immigration certificates) and where it was hoped to receive permission from the Mandate authorities to enter Palestine. The crew was on the whole recruited from Greek, Romanian and Bulgarian sailors.

The British attempted to counteract *Aliyah Bet* indirectly (by placing diplomatic pressure on the governments of those countries which allowed for the organisation or transit of immigrant groups) or directly through the use of force. In December 1939 the Foreign Office warned the authorities in Sofia not to allow Jewish immigrants to use Bulgarian vessels or they would be returned and Bulgaria would be forced to take them back.[39] London's pressure on Romania was sufficiently successful that in January 1940 Bucharest refused transit to 900 "potentially illegal immigrants" from Austria and Slovakia as well as banning Romanian sailors from serving on

---

[37]  As the lawyer Marek Kahan, cooperating with Begin, claimed, *by the nature of things it was not possible to disclose the attempts to free Begin as he headed Irgun and this would have resulted in British repression. On the other hand a sense of basic loyalty and a genuine respect for the military oath and civil responsibilities demanded an honest approach to matters without misleading and revealing the whole truth.* Quoted after: K. Zamorski, *Dwa tajne biura 2. Korpusu*, London 1990, pp. 109–110.

[38]  Cf. H. Sarner, op.cit., pp. 16–17; K. Zamorski, *Dwa tajne biura*, pp. 108–118; E. Kossoy, op.cit., pp. 84, 89.

[39]  TNA. FO 371/24096/W 17689 (p. 347). *Telegram from FO to Mr Rendel (Sofia). No. 306. 6 XII 1939.*

*Aliyah Bet* ships.[40] A certain tightening of, e.g., passport control was also promised by Yugoslavia, which pledged itself to introduce a ban on the transit of those Jews who did not have appropriate travel documents.[41] In total Great Britain attempted to intervene at governmental level in twelve Mediterranean countries.[42] These efforts did not, however, bring about the desired effect. Of course it was more difficult to organize transports, and the matter now required larger amounts of money, but the problem still remained.

The Colonial Office, in agreement with the Admiralty, therefore decided on an unconventional measure. Officially the matter concerned the checking of whether vessels with illegal immigrants were involved in contraband and transporting agents from enemy countries.[43] There were theoretical premises for this – for the transports did set off from the ports of countries cooperating with the Third Reich, while the organisation of a part of the transportations involved the participation of the Viennese Zentralstelle. If it turned out that these premises had rational bases then the British would gain a trump card of real weight. How did they intend to prove the suspicions?

Units of the Naval Contraband Control Service were authorized to stop one of the *Aliyah Bet* transports at sea, while still outside Palestinian territorial waters. Having been towed to the port in Haifa it was to be subjected to a thorough control and search.[44] This operation (otherwise in violation of international law) was intended to be carried out on the Bulgarian ship *Rudnitchar*, which departed from Varna at the end of December 1939. The steamer was sent by Baruch Konfino, and on board were a little over 500 refugees. This was the fourth voyage of the ship in the service of *Aliyah Bet* (the first had taken place in August 1939) and so far it had always managed to reach its destination successfully.[45] Now it was supposed that

40     TNA. FO 371/25238/W 1082 (pp. 279–286). *Employment of Roumanian seamen on ships engaged in illegal immigration traffic. 20 I 1942.*

41     TNA. FO 371/25239/W 2743 (p. 237). *Telegram from FO to Sir P. Loraine (Rome). No. 28. 27 II 1940*; TNA. FO 371/25240/W 3207 (pp. 84–88). *Yugoslav measures to control intending illegal immigrants into Palestine. 23 II 1940.*

42     TNA. FO 371/25239/W 2500 (p. 153). *Memorandum by J.E.M. Carvell, Section for Refugees in the Foreign Office. Proposal to extend the powers of the High Commissioner for Palestine to enable effective action to prevent illegal immigration of Jews. 5 II 1940.*

43     Cf. "Correspondence between the Admiralty and the Foreign Office, 5 and 21 November 1939, on the use of the Naval Contraband Control Service to intercept illegal immigrants" [in:] *The Rise of Israel*. Vol. 30: *The Holocaust and Illegal Immigration*, pp. 26–31.

44     TNA. FO 371/24096/W 16515 (pp. 123–124). *Use of Contraband Control Service in prevention of illegal immigration into Palestine. Cypher telegram from the Secretary of State for the Colonies to the High Commissioner for Palestine. No. 911. 10 XI 1939*; TNA. FO 371/25238/W 38 (pp. 145–146). *Use of Contraband Control Service to discourage illegal immigration into Palestine. Cypher telegram from the Secretary of State for the Colonies to the High Commissioner for Palestine. No. 1030. 28 XII 1939.*

45     TNA. FO 371/24096/W 16036 (pp. 59–62). *Intending illegal immigrants into Palestine on board S.S. "Rudnitchar." 28 X 1939*; ibidem, W 16279 (p. 92). *Transport of illegal immigrants into Palestine on S.S. "Rudnitchar." 7 XI 1939.*

the vessel would be confiscated, the captain and officers arrested, and the passengers returned to Bulgaria or possibly interned in Palestine.[46] The assumption was that this procedure would dissuade the organizers of illegal immigration from continuing. The plan, however, failed. The *Rudnitchar* was able to outpace the British. The refugees were transferred at sea to smaller motor boats, which took them ashore. The Mandate authorities were admittedly able to arrest these people but it turned out that only one individual presented Bulgarian documents as a Bulgarian citizen while the rest were on the whole without citizenship (mainly fugitives from the Reich). Deportation to Bulgaria did not come into the equation and the refugees were interned in Palestine.[47] The majority were released shortly afterward.

It is also difficult to talk about success in relation the application of this policy against subsequent transports. Although it was admittedly possible to seize the *Hilda* sent by Mossad (January 1940)[48] as equally the *Sakarya* prepared by the Revisionists (February 1940)[49], the end result was nonetheless the release of all passengers, around 3,000, into Palestine after a shorter or longer period of internment, while the circumstances surrounding the incidents changed Great Britain's image.[50] Attention was drawn to the fact that both ships were de facto under British guard when in international waters, immediately after passing the Dardanelles, and were escorted all the way to Haifa. On this basis the Turkish owners of *Sakarya*, sailing under a Turkish flag, successfully argued in court that their ship was in fact taken to Palestine (its point of destination had officially been South America). In effect the Mandate had to free the crew and return the craft.[51]

---

[46]  TNA. FO 371/25238/W 184 (pp. 150–164). *Illegal immigration into Palestine: arrest of S.S. "Rudnitchar."* 3 I 1940; TNA. ADM 116/4312. *Landing of Jewish immigrants from S.S. "Rudnitchar." From CO.*

[47]  B. Wasserstein, *Britain and the Jews of Europe*, pp. 54–55; FRUS 1940. Vol. III, p. 834: *The Consul General at Jerusalem (Wadsworth) to the Secretary of State, Jerusalem 24 I 1940.*

[48]  TNA. FO 371/25238/W 1157 (pp. 300–305). *Arrest of S.S. „Hilda" by Contraband Control Service. 22 I 1940*; ibidem, W 1371 (pp. 372–391). *Detention of S.S. „Hilda" in connection with illegal immigration traffic to Palestine. 25 I 1940*; TNA. ADM 116/4312. *S.S. „Hilda." Report of voyage to Haifa under armed guard while carrying Jewish refugees (16–23 I 1940). 9 II 1940.*

[49]  TNA. FO 371/25238/W 843 (pp. 264–268). *Proposed detention of S.S. "Sakarya" of the contraband control service. 17 I 1940*; TNA. ADM 116/4659. *S.S. "Sakarya." Report on voyage to Haifa, 15 II 1940* (author – J.B. Shillitoe, Royal Navy Reserve Officer in Charge of Guard). One may also encounter the form "Sakariya." Sakarya – a river in the Asian part of Turkey, flowing into the Black Sea (824 km length); also a province and town on the shore of the Black Sea in Asia Minor.

[50]  Women and children were released from internment the earliest. In relation to the 15 suspected of operating for the enemy or for other reasons deemed "undesirable" separate proceedings were initiated. TNA. CO 733/429/1 (pp. 104–105). *From High Commissioner for Palestine, Jerusalem, to the Right Honourable The Lord Lloyd of Dolobran, His Majesty's Principal Secretary of State for the Colonies. 20 VIII 1940.*

[51]  D. Ofer, *Escaping the Holocaust. Illegal Immigration to the Land of Israel, 1939–1944*, New York 1990, p. 84; Y. Lapidot, *The Irgun's Role in Illegal Immigration*. Jewish Virtual Library (http://www.jewishvirtuallibrary.org/jsource/History/irgunill.html), p. 3.

It is worth pointing out that the First Lord of the Admiralty of the time, Winston Churchill, did not support this approach. As is clear from his letter to the Secretary of State for the Colonies, Malcolm MacDonald, he agreed to this course of action only with regard to *Rudnitchar*.[52] Significantly, approach was to be rejected a few days before Churchill took up the position of prime minister in May 1940, which could have been decided as much by the position of the head of the Admiralty (for the *Hilda* and *Sakarya* had been seized with his knowledge) as the final fiasco in the handling of matters by the Naval Contraband Control Service.

*Sakarya* was the biggest, to date, *Aliyah Bet* transport and its seizure by the Mandate authorities paralyzed Revisionist *ha'apala* to a significant degree, the more so since amongst those arrested was Eri Jabotinsky, son of the movement's leader.[53]

The internment at Atlit usually lasted several months, but certain groups of immigrants had to spend there over a year there.[54] There was an unwritten principle which supposed that these people, after a certain time, could count on a legalized stay in Palestine making use of the immigration quotas in force. These quotas were fixed by the Mandate every few months (until the end of 1942 every six months) but their magnitude was not constant and would change in accordance with the political and social situation.

Illegal immigration put Great Britain in conflict with the Jews and the Arabs, the governments of the countries of Southern Europe and world public opinion. A range of dilemmas came into being which were far from easy to resolve. Equally for Jews. Supporting *Aliyah Bet* meant being in opposition to Great Britain, an ally in the struggle against the Third Reich. In turn short term cooperation with (and what did it matter if unenthusiastically) Zentralstelle, resulted in serious problems for London in the Middle East and this was exactly what Hitler was after. Suspending *ha'apala* for the duration of the war would have meant de facto giving up entirely on attempts to rescue thousands of fellow Jews as well as agreeing to MacDonald's "White Paper". In London it was understood that an ideal situation simply did not exist. Immediate considerations would have to take priority.

---

[52] "Winston Churchill, First Lord of the Admiralty, to Colonial Secretary Malcolm MacDonald, 4 January 1940, refusing general use of Contraband Control to intercept Jewish illegal immigrants" [in:] *The Rise of Israel*. Vol. 30: *The Holocaust and Illegal Immigration*, pp. 32 onwards; M.J. Cohen, *Churchill and the Jews*, pp. 277–279.

[53] After the entire transport was taken by the Mandate, Eri Jabotinsky was arrested but freed after a few months. Cf. E. Jabotinsky, *The Sakariya Expedition. A Story of Extra-Legal Immigration into Palestine*, Johannesburg 1945; W. Perl, *Operation Action. Rescue from the Holocaust*. Revised and enlarged edition, New York 1983, pp. 271–340; L. Epstein, *Before the Curtain Fell*, Tel Aviv 1990, pp. 37–53.

[54] *Ma'apilim Detention Camp Atlit* (leaflet issued by the Atlit Detention Camp for Illegal Immigrants Museum).

Table 13. *Rudnitchar*, *Hilda* and *Sakarya* in the Mandate's official statistics[55]

|  | Rudnitchar | Hilda | Sakarya |
|---|---|---|---|
| Refugees total | 519 | 729 | 2229 |
| Citizens of: |  |  |  |
| Germany | 3 | 491 | 1229 |
| Czechoslovakia | 15 | 90 | 133 |
| Poland | – | – | 103 |
| Romania | 1 | 45 | – |
| Hungary | – | – | 23 |
| Other states | 7* | 14 | 11 |
| Stateless | 493 | 89 | 730 |

\* Including 6 with Turkish citizenship and one with Bulgarian.

The table created from data reported in: TNA. CO 733/429/1 (pp. 104–105). *From High Commissioner for Palestine, Jerusalem, to the Right Honourable The Lord Lloyd of Dolobran, His Majesty's Principal Secretary of State for the Colonies. 20 VIII 1940.*

In March 1940 the methods employed against *Aliyah Bet* were intensified. The seizure of vessels with immigrants outside of Palestinian territorial waters was sanctioned, envisaging subjection to restrictions on a par with those for transports which had knowingly crossed this maritime border. And hence – confiscation of the vessel, hefty fines and imprisonment terms more severe for crews (even up to 8 years) milder for refugees (six months).[56] Could this bolstering constitute an effective countermeasure? Certainly not from the perspective of potential immigrants. For many Jews in war-torn Europe the prospect of a six-month internment in Palestine

---

[55] Other data on the number of passengers of the *Sakarya* may be found in D. Ofer (*Escaping the Holocaust*, 2,200 persons on p. 83 and 2,228 on p. 326), B. Wasserstein (*Britain and the Jews of Europe*, 2,176 on p. 57), S. Horev (*Sefinot be-terem shahar. Sipuran shel sefinot ha-ma'apilim mi "Vilus" ad "Kerav Emek Ayalon." Leksikon ha-ha'apalah 1934–1948*, Hefa 2004, 2,385 on p. 92) and W. von Weisl (*Illegale Transporte* [in:] J. Fraenkel (ed.), *The Jews of Austria. Essays on their Life, History and Destruction*, London 1967, 2, 400 on p. 174).

[56] "Select British Documents on the Illegal Immigration to Palestine (1939–1940)." Introduced by L. Yahil, *Yad Vashem Studies* (Jerusalem). Vol. X: 1974 (subsequently: *Select British Documents*), doc. 1: *Jewish Illegal Immigration into Palestine (Memorandum prepared jointly by the Foreign Office and Colonial Office. December 1939–January 1940). 17 I 1940*, p. 256 (document from the TNA. FO 371/25238/W 766, pp. 241–242); "Severer Measures Against Illegal Immigration. Regulations supplemented," *The Palestine Post*, 20 III 1940 (text of the article in: CZA. Z 4/31104).

was nothing in comparison with what they could come across under German occupation.[57]

For this reason, the Colonial Office considered the application of other solutions – from the return of unwanted arrivals to their country of origin through deporting them somewhere outside of the Palestine Mandate, to some British colony or dependent territory.[58] For, as was aptly observed, the *imprisonment of illegal immigrants in Palestine is no deterrent. Their object is to get into Palestine. They realize that, once there, they cannot be kept indefinitely in prison, and a spell of internment is probably no great hardship in comparison with their previous conditions of life.*[59] In order to stop the stream of immigrants it was intended to announce that those interned at Atlit would not be able to count on legalized residence in the Mandate and would, after the war, be sent back to Europe. An adherent of this solution was, among others, the head of the Colonial Office, Malcolm MacDonald.[60]

What was the reasoning behind the line taken by London? The uncontrolled increase in Jewish immigration (and for the Arabs it was of no matter if the immigration was legal or illegal) meant increasing dissatisfaction on the part of the Arab population. In a time of war this was the last thing the British wanted. They could see that the development of events in the Mandate was being observed by neighbouring Arab states. And they knew that damage to the British position in this troublesome area would be exploited to the fullest possible extent by the Axis powers, who had only just started their campaign in North Africa. Ernest Bevin, the Minister of Labour and National Service in Churchill's wartime cabinet (and later head of the Foreign Office) admitted frankly in a conversation with Chaim Weizmann, that despite full sympathy for the Jews and their political programme *we could not afford to do anything which might make our relations with the Arab countries more difficult.*[61] In practice this was equivocal to slamming the door in the face of the Jewish refugees.

Deportation as a stopgap preventative measure would certainly solve a number of matters. The problem lay in the fact that it was just this – a stopgap. This was most clearly understood for – as John S. Bennett of the Colonial Office admitted – this step had been contemplated *on more than one occasion in the last twelve months.*[62]

---

[57] As Eliahu Ben-Horin aptly puts it: *The refugees gladly preferred to be under British arrest, rather than dwell "in freedom" under Hitler* (E. Ben-Horin, *The Middle East. Crossroads of History*, New York 1943, pp. 177–178).

[58] B. Wasserstein, *Britain and the Jews of Europe*, pp. 58–59; *Select British Documents*, doc. 6: *From the letter of J.S. Bennett (CO) to Major MacKenzie (War Office). 21 III 1940*, p. 267.

[59] Quote after: *Select British Documents*, doc. 1: *Jewish Illegal Immigration into Palestine (Memorandum prepared jointly by the Foreign Office and Colonial Office. December 1939–January 1940). 17 I 1940*, pp. 257–258.

[60] M. Gilbert, *Exile and Return. The Emergence of Jewish Statehood*, London 1978, p. 245.

[61] CZA. Z 4/31145. *Report of interview with the Right Hon. Ernest Bevin, P.C., M.P., at lunch at The Dorchester Hotel, January 23th, 1941, at 1.30 p.m. London, 30 I 1941* (pp. 1–3).

[62] *Select British Documents*, doc. 6: *From the letter of J.S. Bennett…*, p. 267.

Considerations of a *humanitarian nature* spoke out in opposition.[63] The returning of refugees to Europe where war was raging was tantamount to sentencing them to death. Deportation would arouse serious discontent amongst the Jewish population of Palestine. The British found themselves at a dead end.

If not deportation, then what was the alternative? If the aspirations of the Jews with regard to Palestine could not be fulfilled then maybe it was worth considering the idea of a *second Jewish National Home (or even a State)*[64] in some other territory subject to the British Crown? For some time the Foreign Office examined the possibility of settling Jewish refugees in British Guiana, in South America. It was calculated that "asylum for Jews" in Guiana or some other British colony would reduce the level of illegal immigration (for it would deprive the organizers of the important argument that they were directed exclusively by a humanitarian motive) as well as weakening the opposition of the Zionists to the policy of the "White Paper." Would this solution (*a second Jewish National Home*) not, however, be in opposition to the letter of the Balfour Declaration? London explained the matter by emphasising that the declaration had not been a commitment to all Jews but merely one made to the Zionist movement. Moreover the commitment had been limited in its scope for it had not envisaged the creation of a Jewish state but merely the establishment of a *national home* with the simultaneous guarantee of rights for the indigenous Arab population.[65] This argumentation proved that the enigmatic nature and ambiguity of the declaration made by the head of Britain's diplomacy had not been a matter of chance.

This project had no chance of success. And this was well understood by the Colonial Office. It was difficult to suppose that Jews could consider their homeland to be a country for which they had no historical or emotional attachment. The locating of refugees in Guiana, or anywhere else for that matter, would only have had a realistic effect on the influx of illegal immigrants if their motivation for illegal immigration had been derived simply from their refugee status without any other context whatsoever.[66]

Meanwhile news was abroad of the preparation for new transports…

---

[63] TNA. FO 371/25239/W 2500 (p. 151). *Memorandum by J.E.M. Carvell, Section for Refugees in the Foreign Office. Proposal to extend the powers of the High Commissioner for Palestine to enable effective action to prevent illegal immigration of Jews. 5 II 1940.*

[64] *Having found ourselves unable to meet the Jewish aspiration for a State in Palestine […] we have a moral obligation to provide a "second Jewish National Home" (or even a State) in British territory elsewhere.* Quote after: "Colonial Office memorandum, June 1940, on 'A Second Jewish National Home' in British Guiana in which to settle Jewish refugees" [in:] *The Rise of Israel.* Vol. 30, p. 64 (document from the collections of TNA. FO 371/24568, pp. 319–325).

[65] Ibidem, pp. 67.

[66] Cf. also L. London, *Whitehall and the Jews, 1933–1948. British immigration policy, Jewish refugees and the Holocaust*, Cambridge 2003, p. 140; M. Gilbert, *British Government Policy towards Jewish Refugees*, pp. 153–154.

# Chapter V: *The Atlantic* – Mauritius

## 1. The story of the passengers of the *Atlantic*

The question of deportation was the order of the day in October 1940, when three ships, the *Milos*, *Pacific* and *Atlantic* had chosen a course for Palestine. They had set off from the Romanian port of Tulcea, and were carrying around 3600 Jews, refugees from Germany, Austria, Danzig and occupied Poland and Czechoslovakia. As the organizer of the transportations was Berthold Storfer, who cooperated with Zentralstelle für jüdische Auswanderung, and these people had been transported along the Danube by German steamers serviced by Deutsche Donau Schiffahrt-gesellschaft (DDSG), the British did not rule out the possibility that enemy agents[1] might be amongst the fugitives. In official proclamations London often explained that these groups – fugitives from Nazi occupied Europe – were susceptible to infiltration by enemy agents.[2] This argument was put forth during the scarce allocation of immigration certificates and used to justify the firm policy line adopted in relation to *Aliyah Bet*.

The places taken into consideration as deportation destinations included Cyprus, British Honduras (Belize) and Trinidad in the Caribbean. The final decision fell on Mauritius, a British colony in the Indian Ocean, to the east of Madagascar.[3] London hoped this drastic move would halt illegal immigration and that subsequent refugees would not risk being sent to a remote island in the tropics.[4]

---

[1] *Select British Documents*, doc. 7: *Cypher Telegram to High Commissioner Palestine, 15 X 1940*, p. 268; ibidem, doc. 8: *Cypher Telegram to Governor Mauritius, 15 X 1940*, p. 269. It is worth noting that, among others, Chaim Weizmann does not consider this argumentation groundless. M.J. Cohen, *Churchill and the Jews*, London 1985, pp. 280–281; [B. Dugdale], *Baffy. The Diaries of Blanche Dugdale 1936-1947*. Ed. by N.A. Rose, London 1973, p. 178.

[2] TNA. FO 371/29160/W 188 (pp. 48–50). *Use made by the Enemy of Illegal Immigration. 6 I 1941*; *Parliamentary Debates (Commons)*, vol. 371, 29 V 1941, coll. 2001–2002.

[3] *Select British Documents*, doc. 9: *Cypher Telegram from Governor Mauritius, 17 X 1940*, p. 270; "Colonial Office to the High Commissioner of Palestine, 9 November 1940, on accommodations for intercepted illegal immigrants on the Island of Mauritius" [in:] *The Rise of Israel*. Vol. 30: *The Holocaust and Illegal Immigration*, pp. 76–78.

[4] Cf. FRUS 1940. Vol. III, p. 848: *The Chargé in the United Kingdom (Johnson) to the Secretary of State. London, 19 XI 1940 (They consider this action necessary to discourage further traffic of this character)*.

All three ships were flying under the Panamanian flag[5] and all were overcrowded. It was to be the *Atlantic*, which had set off the earliest (the 7th of October, with the *Pacific* and *Milos* 4 and 12 days later), that was to arrive at the designated spot the last. The dramatic course of the voyage emerges from passenger accounts.[6]

Three kitchens and a few disgusting latrines had to suffice for over 1700 persons. There was not enough room to sleep. A rancid stuffiness reigned below deck. When on the 16th of October it called in at port at Iraklion on Crete to stock up on coal what was intended as a short stopover lengthened in duration. There was not enough fuel, water and food, typhus appeared amongst the passengers, and on the 28th of October Greece and Italy found themselves in a state of war. It seemed that under the new circumstances continuing the journey would be impossible, the more so given that the captain and the majority of the Greek crew, fearing for their lives, wanted to remain in Crete. With the help of the local Jewish community the fuel situation was resolved and the *Atlantic* was able to weigh anchor. However, immediately after departing Iraklion the captain and his men threw overboard a significant part of the coal and pulled into another port on the island. It was then that the Hagana members on board the vessel decided to take over the helm. Thus on the 8th of November, 23 days later, the *Atlantic* finally set off. However, the diminished supplies of coal did not allow them to reach Palestine. Drinking water and food also started to run out. A course was reluctantly set for Cyprus, a British Crown Colony. But it was to turn out to be too far. When the coal ran out the furnace room was supplied with wooden masts, chairs, beds, boards taken from walls and floors. After a time the *Atlantic* recalled a metal shell rather than a real ship.[7]

In that state it was taken by the British and towed into the port of Limassol in Cyprus. According to the medical staff present at the scene, there was some danger of an immediate outbreak of typhoid on an epidemic scale, which would have taken a heavy death toll among the passengers. As the *Cyprus Post* reported, seven passengers had died of typhus since the departure from Crete.[8] After re-supplying with

---

[5]  TNA. FO 371/29160/W 98 (p. 22). *Use of Panamanian ships in Illegal traffic of emigrants to Palestine. Minute by Sir C. Barclay. 27 XII 1940.*

[6]  Cf. E. Enoch, R. Hirsch, E. Kovac, *History of the "Atlantic,"* London 19 VI 1942 (TNA. CO 733/466/15, pp. 17–22); K. Lenk, *The Mauritius Affair. The Boat People of 1940/1941.* Edited and translated from the original German by R.S. Lenk, Brighton 1993, pp. 19–60; R. Sander-Steckl, *Á bientôt en Eretz Israël. L'odyssée des réfugiés de l'Atlantic (décembre 1939–avril 1942). Journal traduit de l'allemand par Sonia Combe.* Commenté par M. Daëron, Paris 2002.

[7]  A. Zwergbaum, "Exile in Mauritius," *Yad Vashem Studies* (Jerusalem). Vol. IV: 1960, pp. 195–201 (the chapter "The Voyage of the S.S. 'Atlantic'"); B. Wasserstein, *Britain and the Jews of Europe 1939–1945,* London–Oxford 1979, pp. 61–62; W.R. Perl, *Operation Action. Rescue from the Holocaust.* Revised and enlarged edition, New York 1983, pp. 242–245; TNA. FO 371/25242/W 12017 (p. 117). *Telegram from Governor of Cyprus to Colonial Office. No. 556. 18 XI 1940.*

[8]  "1875 Refugees Fight Death in Mediterranean. Fleeing from Nazi Tyranny 7 Die on Voyage from Crete," *Cyprus Post* (Nicosia), 16 XI 1940, p. 3; a copy of the text of the article is in the collections of the Yad Vashem Archives in Jerusalem (subsequently YVA). O2/635.

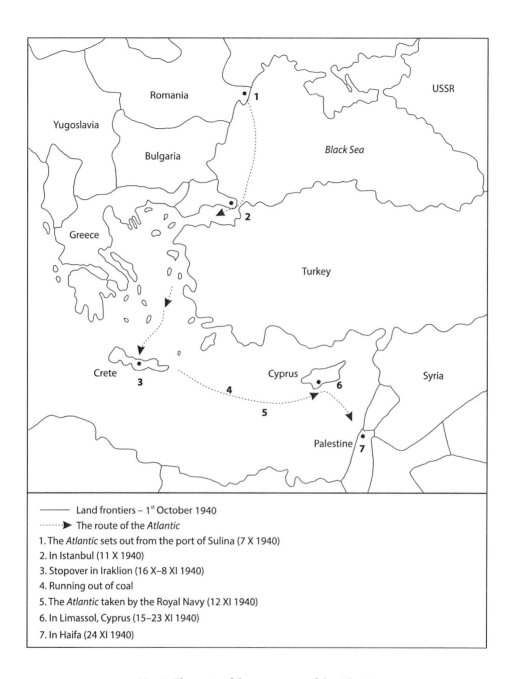

**Map 3. The route of the passengers of the *Atlantic***

Author's study. See also A. Zwergbaum, "Exile in Mauritius," *Yad Vashem Studies* (Jerusalem).
Vol. IV: 1960, p. 200

fuel and food – for which the refugees had to pay – the *Atlantic*, under British naval escort, set off for Haifa.[9]

Earlier, the passengers of the *Milos* and the *Pacific* had arrived. When both crafts entered Palestinian territorial waters, which happened in the first week of November 1940, they were seized by British coastal patrols and under guard were towed to Haifa. There in port the *Patria* was already waiting, which was to transport the refugees to Mauritius. This was a sizeable French ship taken over by the British Navy after the capitulation of France in June 1940.[10] The passengers of the *Milos* and the *Pacific* were refused permission to leave their crafts. When it was officially announced on the 19th of November that the refugees were to be deported to Mauritius, where they were to remain until the end of the war, Jewish circles in Palestine and also in the USA protested. A general strike was called in Yishuv. In order to prevent potential unrest and attempts at escape the British surrounded the port with military and police units.[11] They would shortly transfer the refugees to the *Patria*…

## 2. The *Patria*

In the meantime, on the 24th of November, the third of the transports, the *Atlantic*, arrived in Haifa and its passengers started to be transferred to the *Patria*. By the morning of the following day – about 130 had been transferred. Both sides – the Mandate authorities and the Yishuv – understood that the departure of this ship with such a sizeable number of passengers on board could have key importance for *Aliyah Bet* and the future of Palestine. Neither therefore intended to capitulate. Hagana fighters took the decision to stop the departure of the *Patria*. The plan involved seriously damaging the craft.[12] This would force the British to take the refugees ashore and make the necessary repairs. It was hoped that the outcome

---

9    The epopee of the passengers of the *Atlantic* is shown in the documentary film *La dérive de l'Atlantique* (2002, directed by Michael Daëron), a French-Israeli-Austrian joint production. A. Patek, "Alija bet w filmie," *Kwartalnik Filmowy* (Warszawa). No. 69 (129): 2010, p. 210.

10   TNA. CO 733/446/4. *Patria Commission of Enquiry. Report. Haifa, 31 I 1941*, p. 1.

11   *Select British Documents*, doc. 10: Chaim Weizmann, *Memorandum on the Refugee Ships in Haifa Bay, 26 XI 1940*, pp. 271–274; S. Teveth, *Ben-Gurion and the Holocaust*, New York–San Diego–London 1996, p. 246.

12   For more see: E. Feld, "The Story of the S/S Patria," *The Jewish Magazine*. No. 46 (http://www.jewishmag.com/46mag/patria/patria.htm); M. Chazan, "The Patria Affair. Moderates vs. Activists in Mapai in the 1940s," *Journal of Israeli History* (Neisbury Park). Vol. 22: 2003. No. 2, pp. 61–95; E.G. Steiner, *The Story of the Patria*, New York 1982 (a novel). Cf. also: D. Geffen, "The Sinking of the Patria," *The Jerusalem Post*, 23 XI 1990; W.R. Perl, *Operation Action*, pp. 243–253. It follows to separately mention the documentary materials (accounts, press articles, etc.) in the collection of *La Haapala. Compilación de notas y documentos de la Inmigración "Ilegal" a Eretz Israel 1933–1948*. La Selección del material por Moshé Kitrón, Jerusalem 1953 (part VI: "Patria," pp. 120–141).

of events would play out in the immigrants' favor. It would also be important to draw the attention of international opinion to the Palestinian problem.

An explosive device was smuggled on board even prior to the arrival of the *Atlantic*, on the 22nd of November. The man who brought the bomb on board was Munya Mardor, officially an assistant in the port repair team, but in actual fact an undercover member of Hagana.[13] He acted in cooperation with the leader of the refugees, Hans Vanfel. The first attempt at detonation was unsuccessful and the whole operation had to be started anew. This time the device was of better manufacture, and had a much stronger blast. Vanfel was to set the device off at the arranged time. The operation was planned for the morning of the 25th of November. The plan was endorsed by Eliyahu Golomb and Shaul Avigur, with support also being given by Moshe Shertok.[14] However, as a result of miscalculations and a lack of foresight on the part of the conspirators, the whole undertaking turned into a tragedy. When the lower deck rocked with the detonation, not all the passengers had managed to make it to the top by the indicated hour. The explosion tore off a part of the side. The ship quickly started to take in water and within 15 minutes had sunk.

The *Patria*, despite a reasonable outward appearance, was a well-worn vessel (it had been launched in 1913), a fact which may have exacerbated the magnitude of the catastrophe. Mardor himself was a witness. *The next morning, November 25th, I was again at the port and working in accordance with the normal harbour schedule. I was intensely nervous and agitated. It was almost impossible to take my eyes away from the spectacle of the "Patria," where she lay at anchor near the break water. Suddenly, a few minutes after nine o'clock, I heard the dull thud of an explosion. It sounded as if coming from far away. But then the "Patria" began to list. A din of screaming sirens broke loose over the harbour. Dozens of rowboats and launches began scurrying in the direction of the ship, which now lay on its side steadily sinking. [...] Everyone available, including British police, British soldiers, Arab and Jewish port workers, was engaged in rescue work. On the break water, and at the side of the ship clear of water, stood crowds of immigrants who had escaped being trapped below deck. Workers from the port engineering shops were actively boring large holes into the side of the ship in order to gain access to the people trapped inside.*[15] At the moment of the explosion, according to the official British report, there were 1,904 Jewish refugees on board.[16]

It is difficult to establish the exact number of victims. Generally it is accepted that around 250 died, of whom about 200 were immigrants, the rest mostly crew

---

[13] Mardor presents his part in the events in the memoirs: *Strictly Illegal*, London 1964 (Chapter VIII: "The Patria," pp. 56–76). A Hebrew edition of the book, with a foreword by David Ben-Gurion, appeared in 1957.

[14] M. Chazan, op.cit. (a shortened version of the article is also available on the Internet at: http://cat.inist.fr/?aModele=afficheN&cpsidt=13682290); M. Mardor, *Strictly Illegal*. Foreword by D. Ben-Gurion, London 1964, p. 72.

[15] Quote after: M. Mardor, op.cit., p. 74.

[16] TNA. CO 733/446/4. *Patria Commission of Enquiry. Report. Haifa, 31 I 1941*, p. 1.

members and British soldiers. A further 172 were injured. The British recovered 156 bodies, while 112 refugees were classified as missing. Some survivors may have taken advantage of the confusion and managed to make it to port and sneak into the town.[17] The scope of the tragedy is shown by the fact that bodies were being recovered a month after the vessel sank.[18]

The *Patria* incident highlighted differences in positions within the Yishuv leadership (and in the strongest party, Mapai) in relation to the way of fighting against the "White Paper." As Meir Chazan has written, two camps emerged, the "activists" and the "moderates." The former were the spokesmen for decisive methods including the use of force. The latter stood for political activity and exerting pressure on the Mandate. The "moderates" opposed the intended sabotage on the *Patria*, arguing that the operation could result in more harm than good.[19]

The catastrophe's consequences were to reverberate deeply.[20] Some attributed the deaths of these people to the British. The British in turn suspected either Irgun and Jewish extremists, or Hagana, and as a motive pointed to the attempts to exert pressure on the Mandate authorities to change their policy towards immigration. A special investigation commission set up by the British was to explain the circumstances of the catastrophe.[21] The investigation lasted six weeks, with 58 witnesses called, but the actual perpetrators were not identified. *Damage to the "Patria" –* we read in the final commission report issued on the 31st of January 1941 – *was committed by Jewish sympathizers ashore with the cooperation of at least one person aboard.*[22] British military intelligence MI5 (Military Intelligence Department, War Office Counter Espionage) was convinced that Hagana stood behind the explo-

---

[17]  After: TNA. CO 733/446/4 (p. 3). *Patria Commission of Enquiry. Report. Haifa, 31 I 1941.* In certain works there can be found a higher number of victims – 251 (W. Benz, "Illegale Einwanderung nach Palästina" [in:] *Exilforschung. Ein Internationales Jahrbuch* (München). Band 19: 2001, p. 138), 252 (G. Kirk, *The Middle East in the War*, 3rd ed., London–New York–Toronto 1954, p. 241; J. and D. Kimche, *The Secret Roads. The "Illegal" Migration of a People, 1938–1948*, London 1954, p. 54), 260 (A. Koestler, *Promise and Fulfilment. Palestine 1917–1949*, London 1983, p. 61), 267 (D. Ofer, *Escaping the Holocaust. Illegal Immigration to the Land of Israel, 1939–1944*, New York 1990, p. 35). According to Ehud Avriel (*Open the Gates! A Personal Story of "Illegal" Immigration to Israel.* Preface by G. Meir, New York 1975, p. 112) 240 refugees were to have died as well as 50 crew members and British policemen. In Mordechai Naor (*Haapala. Clandestine Immigration 1931–1948*, [Tel Aviv 1987], p. 36) we read of 216 victims on the Jewish side.

[18]  Cf. "Patria Roll Growing. Total Number of Dead Now 137," *The Palestine Post*, 30 XII 1940, p. 3.

[19]  M. Chazan, op.cit.

[20]  Cf. "Refugee Ship Off Palestine Is Sunk by Blast," *The New York Times*, 26 XI 1940 (the text of the article in: R. Sanders, *Shores of Refuge. A Hundred Years of Jewish Emigration*, New York 1989, p. 494); "Explosion Wrecks Liner at Haifa," *The Times*, 26 XI 1940; "Patria Sinks in Haifa Harbour," *The Palestine Post*, 26 XI 1940.

[21]  "Patria Enquiry Opened," *The Palestine Post*, 13 XII 1940, p. 1.

[22]  Quote after: *Patria Commission of Enquiry. Report. Haifa, 31 I 1941*, p. 19 (TNA. CO 733/446/4); also: ibidem, *Code Telegram from High Commissioner for Palestine. No. 173. 10 II 1941*, p. 1.

sion.[23] Some did not exclude that some determined passengers could themselves have caused the tragedy.[24]

A fuller picture of the course of events was only to become available in 1950. The facts of the case were then written about and revealed by, among others, David Flinker, the Israeli correspondent of the New York paper the *Jewish Morning Journal* (in the issue for the 27th of November 1950) and Menachem Begin on the pages of his book about his activities in Irgun.[25] The final uncertainties in the matter were cleared up by the publication of Munya Mardor's memoirs in 1957.

The *Patria* affair aroused various discussions beyond the facts of the incident itself. It was used to attack the Zionists, being presented as the practical application of an "ends justify the means" philosophy. It was claimed that the Zionists were prepared to sacrifice the lives of innocent people in order to *show the world that we do not accept solutions that forbid us access to Palestine.*[26] It was speculated that their main aim was the incitement of anti-British feelings and the propaganda victory derived from the incident.

The place that should be allotted to the memory of the *Patria* was another subject of discussion. For Berl Katznelson the incident was historical in its scope, comparable to the battle at Tel Hai in which Trumpeldor died. Others claimed that *Patria* had become a "symbol of resistance" and "national martyrdom," and that the victims had not died in vain. But there was also no shortage of those who opposed the *glorification of the bloody action* and claimed that Hagana had had no right to risk the lives of immigrants and entangle them in its political tactics against the Mandate authorities.[27]

## 3. Deportation to Mauritius

Both groups of refugees, those from the *Patria* and those from the *Atlantic*, were temporarily transferred to Atlit (a portion of the men spent a few days at Acre

---

[23] TNA. FO 371/25124/W 12493/ G (p. 190). *MI5. 9 XII 1940*.

[24] Cf. *The passengers blew up their ship. (…) These people had become allergic to barbed wire.* Quote after: A. Koestler, op.cit., p. 61.

[25] *The Patria never sailed. Jewish "terrorists" placed a bomb to prevent its departure.* Quote after: M. Begin, *The Revolt*, Jerusalem 1951, pp. 35–36. Begin's memoirs first appeared in Hebrew entitled *Mered* (Yerushalayim 1950).

[26] A.M. Lilienthal, *Druga strona medalu*, Warszawa 1970, pp. 141–142. Alfred M. Lilienthal, an American political scientist of Jewish descent, a consultant to the American delegation at the founding conference of the United Nations in San Francisco in 1945, was a firm opponent of Zionism. His work (first published in the USA entitled *The Other Side of the Coin. An American Perspective of the Arab-Israeli Conflict*, New York 1965) has a clearly anti-Zionist character. Cf. also A. Lilienthal, *The Zionist Connection II*, New Brunswick, NJ 1982, p. 359.

[27] B. Habas, *The Gate Breakers*, New York–London 1963, pp. 126–149 (Cf. the characteristic title of chapter VII: "S.S. Patria – Symbol of Resistance"); M. Mardor, op.cit., p. 57; N. Fridman, "Nuestro 'Patria' ha triunfado" [in:] *La Haapala. Compilación de notas y documentos*, pp. 128–130.

prison). The two groups were kept apart, however. Chaim Weizmann and Zionist leaders from the USA intervened on their behalf.[28] After a time the British authorities agreed for the survivors to remain in Palestine, using up a portion of the immigration quotas. The British called their decision an *exceptional act of mercy*.[29] One supporter of an amicable solution was Prime Minister Winston Churchill, while Sir Thomas Ingram Lloyd of the Colonial Office and General Archibald Wavell were opposed. The Commander-in-Chief of the British forces in the Middle East explained that a milder line in relation to illegal immigrants would result in a growth in Arab dissatisfaction, which in the face of an Italian offensive (in September 1940 the Italians attacked the territory of Egypt from Libya) could potentially be dangerous.[30] This consideration on the one hand was balanced by the fact that this *act of mercy* did not extend to the remaining passengers of the *Atlantic*, who were, in their number of 1600 or so, to be deported to Mauritius.[31] On the other hand–upon the hardening of London's position, which made it clear that this approach (deportation) would not only be maintained but intensified, as those deported could not be sure of legal settlement in Palestine, even after the end of the war and within the official immigration quotas.[32]

The deportations to Mauritius were carried out on the 9th of December, i.e., two weeks after the *Patria* catastrophe, and as the head of the Palestine Police admitted, it was a *distasteful task*.[33] The refugees practiced passive resistance. They refused to pack their things, dress, and leave the barracks. The police used batons, and several people were roughed up. Half-naked people were carried out by their hands and feet. All were loaded onto lorries which were to take them to the port in Haifa. Objects

---

[28]  CZA. A 406/55. *Statement on behalf of the Emergency Committee for Zionist Affairs* (no date); CZA. Z 4/31066. *Prof. B.L. Namier to G. Hall, CO*, 9 XII 1940.

[29]  Quoted after: FRUS 1940. Vol. III, p. 854: *The Consul General at Jerusalem (Wadsworth) to the Secretary of State. Jerusalem, 10 XII 1940*. Cf. also *Parliamentary Debates (Commons)*, vol. 367, 4 XII 1940, col. 520; "Cabinet discussion, 27 November 1940, on the 'Patria' tragedy and the decision to allow survivors to remain in Palestine as an exceptional act of mercy" [in:] *The Rise of Israel*, vol. 30, pp. 95–96; "Survivors of Patria to Remain. Official Communique. Position Regarding Other 'Illegals' Unchanged," *The Palestine Post*, 5 XII 1940, p. 1.

[30]  Cf. the Churchill – Wavell correspondence: "General Archibald Wavell, commander in chief, Middle East, to the War Office, 30 November 1940, objecting to the Cabinet decision to allow survivors of the 'Patria' to remain in Palestine" [in:] *The Rise of Israel*, vol. 30, p. 106; "Winston Churchill to General Wavell, 1 December 1940, chiding the general for suggesting that Arabs will rebel if "Patria" survivors are allowed to stay in Palestine" [in:] *The Rise of Israel*, vol. 30, pp. 107–108.

[31]  TNA. CO 733/466/15 (pp. 2–65). *Transport Arrangements. Treatment of "Atlantic" Passengers*; TNA. CO 733/466/16 (pp. 2–37). *Treatment of "Atlantic" Passengers*; *Parliamentary Debates (Commons)*, vol. 368, 22 I 1941, col. 207.

[32]  TNA. CO 733/431/1 (p. 2). *Draft. Secretary of State. 6 XII 1940*; Cf. also: "Foreign Office to Marquess of Lothian, British ambassador to Washington, 10 December 1940, on policy toward illegal immigrants following the 'Patria' disaster" [in:] *The Rise of Israel*, vol. 30, p. 114.

[33]  B. Wasserstein, *Britain and the Jews of Europe*, p. 75. Menachem Begin suggests the police brutality was intended *to teach the "illegal" immigrants a lesson*. M. Begin, *The Revolt*, p. 35.

that were considered dangerous, such as knives and razors, but also cameras, crockery, bottles, etc. were confiscated from the refugees. Financial compensation for the confiscated articles was to be granted a few years later when the matter was made public by Diaspora circles in the USA (in April 1945 the Mandate authorities allocated £3000 for this purpose).[34]

The preparations for deportation were accompanied by Yishuv protests. In Haifa there was a protest strike which, the next day (10th of December) spread to the whole country. The British actions were condemned by Vaad Leumi (National Council), the Palestinian Jews executive organ of self government,[35] the Jewish Agency and Histadrut.[36] The Czechoslovakian government in exile also protested against the deportations. Amongst those deported were many citizens of pre-war Czechoslovakia.[37]

The refugees reached Mauritius[38] on board two Dutch passenger liners, *Nieuw Zeeland* and *Johan de Witt*. The transports were accompanied by a British escort composed of several war ships. 41 immigrants died while the ships were still at sea. 22 of them were victims of typhoid. The journey, via the Suez Canal and the Red Sea, lasted 17 days, until the 26th of December 1940.[39]

# 4. Five years of exile

From the European point of view, Mauritius was a remote and exotic country, situated somewhere in the tropics between Africa and Asia, in the Indian Ocean. One lived here better than in many other countries in this part of the world. The relative prosperity was ensured by the island's main resource – Mauritius was a sizeable producer and exporter of sugar. The climate was not particularly deadly for the tropics, though the high rate of humidity was intense, especially for Europeans.

The refugees were interned at a camp at HM Central Prison on the outskirts of Beau Bassin, five miles from the capital of Port Louis. The camp covered an area of 12 acres and was surrounded by a high stone wall, almost five metres tall. The men were placed in two three-storey blocks. Each of them could hold 400 pris-

[34] CZA. Z 4/31103. *Evidence of an Eye-Witness. Translation from the Hebrew* (14 XII 1940); B. Wasserstein, *Britain and the Jews of Europe*, p. 75.

[35] FRUS 1940. Vol. III, p. 855: *The Consul General at Jerusalem (Wadsworth) to the Secretary of State. Jerusalem, 10 XII 1940*.

[36] CZA. Z 4/31104. Copies of the protest of the Jewish Agency and Histadrut, both dated 11 XII 1940; CZA. A 406/55. *Statement on behalf of the Emergency Committee for Zionist Affairs* (no date).

[37] B. Wasserstein, *Britain and the Jews of Europe*, p. 76.

[38] Mauritius covered an area of 1865 km$^2$ and according to the census of 1944 had a population of 419,200. Data after: *The Statesman's Year-Book. Statistical and Historical Annual of the States of the World for the Year 1947*. Ed. by S.H. Steinberg, London 1947, p. 310.

[39] Cf. R. Sander-Steckl, op.cit., pp. 115–136.

oners. The women lived in a separate part composed of 30 small tin huts. There was also a hospital within the area of the camp, workshops and an administrative area. Several acres were covered by gardens and orchards.[40]

In total 1,580 persons were interned on the island, of whom 849 were men, 635 women and 96 children.[41] These were citizens of various countries, including: Austria (640), Czechoslovakia (294), Poland (172), the Free City of Danzig (151), and Germany (84), as well as 192 without citizenship. The camp also contained Jews from Romania, the USSR, Hungary, Latvia and Turkey. Here were individuals from a variety of occupations and professions, different levels of education, the orthodox and the assimilated, Zionists and adherents of other political tendencies.

Up to the year 1945 the British authorities freed around 200 people, of whom 111 were volunteers to serve in Czechoslovak units, eight – in Polish, and the rest – in British units. Their relatives, however, had to stay on the island. A further several dozen were refused for health reasons. There were various motivations for joining the army: patriotic considerations, loyalty to one's country of birth, but also a desire to leave the camp.[42] In the autumn of 1944 there arose a different kind of motivation – the possibility of serving in the Jewish Brigade. From amongst the 78 volunteers the British accepted 56 men aged 18–35.[43] The British actions were characterized by particular caution. The fear was whether these future soldiers would be able to forget

---

[40] On the Mauritius odyssey have written, among others, G. Pitot, *The Mauritian Shekel. The Story of the Jewish Detainees in Mauritius, 1940–1945*, Port Louis (Mauritius) 1998; R. Friedmann, *Exil auf Mauritius. Report einer "demokratischen" Deportation jüdischer Flüchtlinge*, Berlin 1998; K. Lenk, *The Mauritius Affair. The Boat People of 1940/1941*; A. Zwergbaum, "Exile in Mauritius," pp. 191–257 (Lenk and Zwergbaum were amongst of those deported); A. Patek, "Żydowscy zesłańcy na Mauritius (1940–1945)" [in:] W. Bernacki, A. Walaszek (eds.), *Amerykomania*. Vol. 2, Kraków 2012, pp. 667–678. It is also worth looking at the annual British reports on the situation in the camp: *Colony of Mauritius. Interim Report on the Detainment Camp*, Port Louis, Mauritius (report for the period 1 X 1941–30 IX 1942 in the collections of TNA. CO 733/446/9; for the period 1 X 1942–30 IX 1943 in the collections of TNA. T 220/195). From amongst the archival accounts it follows to mention: YVA. O2/633. *Die Alijah von Bratislava nach Mauritius. Ein Tagebuch von Dr. A. Zwergbaum* (pp. 1–78); YVA. O2/636. *Meine Auswanderung in die zwangs-internierung von Mauritius. Erlebnisse des Herrn Hans Klein waehrend der Herrschaft der Nationalsozialisten* (pp. 1–9); TNA. CO 733/466/20. *The Case of the Mauritius deportees (A Report prepared on the basis of evidence from an ex-detainee)* [London, December 1944, pp. 1–9]; this same report in the collections of CZA. Z 4/30286 (pp. 1–8).

[41] Amongst the interned there was to be one person from *Patria* who was to have found themselves here "by mistake." In *Parliamentary Debates (Commons)* [Vol. 368. 22 I 1941, col. 207] talk is of the 1634 embarked on the Dutch liners. A different number (1645 persons) is given by the official CINM booklet.

[42] YVA. O2/633. *Die Alijah von Bratislava nach Mauritius. Ein Tagebuch von Dr. A. Zwergbaum* (part III, pp. 7–8; part IV, pp. 3–4); CZA. Z 4/30286. *Airgraph from South African Zionist Federation. Johannesburg, 16/5/1944*.

[43] In a letter to the Jewish Agency of the 15th of March 1945, Zwergbaum writes of 53 volunteers enlisted into the Jewish Brigade (CZA. Z4/30286).

about the humiliations experienced and be able to loyally help the British Army, the very same that had deported them to Mauritius.[44]

The camp was situated in buildings that previously had been a prison. The staff was fairly numerous and initially numbered 90. The officers were British and the guards were recruited from the local coloured population. Civilians also worked here – bookkeepers, warehousemen, and janitors, mainly island inhabitants. The camp was quite thoroughly guarded and there were no reported cases of escape. After all, where was there to escape to on a remote island?

Table 14. Interned at Beau Bassin, Mauritius 1940–1945

| Citizens | December 1940 | September 1943 | September 1944 |
|---|---|---|---|
| In total | 1,580 | 1,422 | 1,371 |
| of which: | | | |
| men | 849 | 729 | 659 |
| women | 635 | 611 | 603 |
| children | 96 | 82 | 109 |
| Citizens of: | | | |
| Austria | 640 | 604 | 571 |
| Czechoslovakia | 294 | 214 | 208 |
| Poland | 172 | 155 | 154 |
| Gdansk | 151 | 144 | 140 |
| Germany | 84 | 80 | 77 |
| USSR | 21 | 17 | total 39 |
| Romania | 15 | 15 | |
| Hungary | 6 | 5 | |
| Turkey | 3 | 2 | |
| Latvia | 2 | 2 | |
| Citizenless | 192 | 184 | 182 |

The table created from data reported in: G. Pitot, op.cit., p. 232; R. Friedmann, op.cit., pp. 101–103; A. Zwergbaum, *Exile in Mauritius*, pp. 208–209; TNA. T 220/195. *Colony of Mauritius. Interim Report on the Detainment Camp for the period 1st Oct., 1942, to 30th Sept. 1943*, Port Louis 1943, p. 9.

---

44 *Parliamentary Debates* (*Commons*), vol. 398, 15 III 1944, coll. 232–233.

It is notable that these individuals were not officially referred to as "internees" but "detainees" in a refugee camp without the right to leave voluntarily.[45] The fact that legally everyone was treated the same – citizens of allied Poland and Czecho-slovakia and those from Germany with whom Britain was in a state of war – is also striking. This may be why the status of the deportees was not clearly defined.

The British underscored that they would allow the detainees a certain amount of freedom so that they could develop culturally and spiritually.[46] On the other hand, correspondence was censored and no permission was given for the visits of relatives from abroad. These and other restrictions were at least dictated by war time matters of security and, to a greater or lesser extent, they also applied to the inhabitants of the colony. The matter obviously looked slightly different from the perspective of the internees. For them their stay at HM Central Prison did justice to the camp's original name. The relations between the refugees and the local population were harmonious and the Jews interned there generally retained warm memories of the Mauritians.[47]

There were many families in this camp society, and the division of the camp into separate sections for men and women of must have been difficult. The separation of married couples caused much dissatisfaction. The families met using the several hours of leave granted three or four times a week. With time the situation improved and married couples were granted longer daily periods together.[48]

The climatic conditions were conducive to the spread of malaria. In the summer of 1943 around 40% of those interned were to suffer from it. The high temperature and high air humidity weakened the health particularly of older people and those with poor hearts. Numerous cases of vitamin deficiency and dysentery were not-ed. Children were particularly susceptible to illness.[49] In the course of the first four weeks after deportation over 40 victims were claimed by an epidemic of typhoid. The disease had struck first on board the *Atlantic*, then again during the intern-ment at Atlit (the press noted one fatality),[50] only to reach its pinnacle on Mauri-tius, a development helped by insects and the initially disgusting sanitation (open

[45]  TNA. CO 733/466/20. *The Case of the Mauritius deportees (A Report prepared on the basis of evi-dence from an ex-detainee)* [London, December 1944], p. 2 (full text published in: A. Patek, *Żydzi w drodze do Palestyny 1934–1944. Szkice z dziejów aliji bet, nielegalnej imigracji żydowskiej*, Kraków 2009, pp. 352–367); CZA. Z 4/31104. Document without title – British guidelines on the status of the detained refugees, 10 XII 1940.

[46]  CZA. Z 4/30286. A letter of A. Zwergbaum to the "Zionist Review" in London, of the 5th of June 1943; TNA. CO 733/466/20. *The Case of the Mauritius deportees*, p. 3.

[47]  When in 1960 Mauritius was devastated by two cyclones, the former deportees organised a collec-tion of money in Israel for the victims of the cataclysm. G. Pitot, op.cit., p. 232.

[48]  TNA. CO 733/466/15. E. Enoch, R. Hirsch, E. Kovac, *History of the "Atlantic,"* p. 8 (the part "Family Life").

[49]  According to Harry Sacher, a trusted colleague of Chaim Weizmann's, malaria had affected 60% of those interned, dysentery 40–50%, and vitamin deficiency 90%. CZA. A289/75. H. Sacher, *The Mauritius detainees*, 1 II 1945 (p. 2).

[50]  "Refugee Dead of Typhoid," *The Palestine Post*, 13 XII 1940, p. 1.

latrines).[51] The increasingly weakened internees wrestled with psychiatric problems. Some suffered from the lack of privacy, while others were pushed into depression by the forced inactivity and the prison atmosphere. Medical treatment was provided by the camp hospital and was administered at an acceptable level. The refugees were treated by local specialists as well as the doctors who were companions in their misery. When the situation required it, treatment would take place at centres outside of the camp. Relatives and various Jewish organisations abroad helped the internees. in various ways – money transfers, packages with medicines, clothes, etc. A lot of support was shown by the Diaspora from Southern Africa.[52]

Many refugees took up vocational activities. Work was important not only because it brought in a concrete income but because it allowed one to forget, at least to a degree, about the monotony of life. For carpenters, mechanics, shoemakers and tailors, employment could be found in the camp workshops. Some worked outside of the camp, hired by private companies or as private teachers in the homes of the local elite.[53]

The refugees engaged in social and cultural activities.[54] Amongst those interned were teachers, musicians, rabbis, and people with degrees; it was they who first took charge of these activities. The camp authorities were sympathetic to the idea, regarding an active lifestyle as most conducive to a good psychic condition within the camp. The majority of those deported came from German language environments, which is why German dominated in the camp. From January 1941 to May 1942, a camp newspaper, *Camp News. Lager Zeitung,* was published.[55] Courses in Hebrew were organized, concerts given, and works of amateur dramatics performed. School lessons were organized by the internees themselves. The school played a special role, for its task was not simply providing remedial education but also protecting the younger generation from the demoralising influence of camp conditions. Religion, Jewish history, and Hebrew were taught among other subjects. Spiritual needs were satisfied by two synagogues, for Orthodox and Reform Jews.[56]

The refugees had the option of selecting a form of self-government called the "Detainment Area Committee." Its composition and names changed as members

---

[51] TNA. CO 733/466/15. E. Enoch, R. Hirsch, E. Kovac, *History of the "Atlantic,"* p. 4 (the part "The Typhoid Fever Epidemic"); K. Lenk, op.cit., p. 81.

[52] YVA. O2/633. *Die Alijah von Bratislava nach Mauritius* (part II, pp. 12–13; part V, p. 10); A. Zwergbaum, "Exile in Mauritius," p. 252.

[53] A pupil of one of the interned Jewesses was Geneviève Pitot (b. 1930), the author of the work *The Mauritian Shekel.*

[54] TNA. T 220/195. *Colony of Mauritius. Interim Report on the Detainment Camp for the period 1st Oct., 1942, to 30th Sept. 1943,* pp. 3–4; TNA. CO 733/466/15. *History of the "Atlantic,"* pp. 4–6 (the parts "Culture" and "School education").

[55] A copy of one of the issues (27 VI 1941) in the collections of YVA. O2/634 (pp. 7–11). The original at The Wiener Library in London, inventory number P.III.h (Mauritius). No. 778.

[56] TNA. T 220/195. *Colony of Mauritius. Interim Report on the Detainment Camp for the period 1st Oct., 1942, to 30th Sept. 1943,* p. 6.

ostentatiously resigned.[57] In October 1943 in a petition directed to the Colonial Office in London, the internees demanded their freedom and return to Palestine, arguing that further detainment of the refugees whose relatives were serving in the forces of Great Britain and her allies was unjust.[58] A resolution was subsequently adopted on the third anniversary of the deportation.[59] By means of the Jewish Agency and other Jewish institutions, attempts were made to attract the attention of international public opinion. The Agency officially approached the British authorities in 1942 asking them to enable the deportees to return to Palestine within the framework of the immigration quotas and limits imposed by the White Paper. It also inspired a question in the House of Commons.[60]

Around 70–75% of the adult inhabitants of the camp identified themselves with the principles of the Zionist movement.[61] Its sympathizers in May 1941 convoked the Zionist Association in Mauritius (ZAM), whose secretary became Dr Aaron Zwergbaum, born in 1913 in Brno, Moravia, later the author of works documenting the lot of this camp society.[62] The Association became the informal advocate of the internees. ZAM established correspondence with Jewish organisations in various countries. These included: the Jewish Agency, the World Jewish Congress, the Zionist Federation of Great Britain and Ireland. Closest relations were kept with the South African Diaspora. On the pages of *The South African Jewish Chronicle* reports and notes on the camp's inhabitants regularly appeared.[63] The Association also organized lively social activity. It is worth mentioning the collections for the Jewish National Fund (Keren Kayemet le'Israel). Vouchers called "Mauritius Substitute Shekels" were also distributed, endorsed by the Zionist World Organization, which raised money for furthering Zionist movement goals.[64]

---

[57]　TNA. CO 733/466/15. *History of the "Atlantic,"* pp. 4–5 (the part "Self-Government"); CZA. Z 4/30286. *Mauritius Detainees' Executive Committee. 19 IV 1944.*

[58]　Text: YVA. O2/635 (pp. 3–10). *Memorial submitted by the representatives of the Detainment Camp Beau Bassin to the Secretary of State for Colonies in London. 15.10.1943.*

[59]　For text see: CZA. Z 4/30286. *Zionist Association Mauritius to the Zionist Federation of Great Britain, 9 XII 1943.*

[60]　Cf. for example *Parliamentary Debates* (Commons), vol. 377, 21 I 1942, col. 370; ibidem, vol. 400, 14 VI 1944, coll. 1975–1976.

[61]　A. Zwergbaum, *Exile in Mauritius,* pp. 248–253; CZA. Z 4/31103. *Jewish Internees on Mauritius. Facts communicated by Mr. Sternheim, a Palestinian, who called at the Jewish Agency Office on 21.10.1941* (p. 2). Sternheim, a young Jew from Yishuv, was a shipwright on a British ship. He saw the camp in June 1941 when his ship was on route from Haifa to England and called in at port for a short time in Mauritius.

[62]　YVA. O1/213. *Protokoll über eine Besprechung mit Dr. Aaron Zwergbaum, Jerusalem, zum Thema "Mauritius" aufgezeichnet von Dr. Ball-Kaduri. Tel Aviv, 27 Februar 1958* (here is also a list of Zwergbaum's publications on the subject).

[63]　The author of a part was of these articles Dr Zwergbaum. Cf. the issues of 10 IV and 21 XI 1941, 26 IX 1942, 17 XI 1944. YVA. O1/213. *Protokoll...*

[64]　One of these vouchers is in the YVA. O2/634 (p. 6).

During the period of internment around 60 children were born, almost all in the period 1943–1945, when the separated couples were not hampered in their daily contacts. 126 people died (according to other data – 124);[65] 54 of whom passed away in the course of the first 10 months.[66] All were buried in the local cemetery of St. Martin's, where a Jewish section was set apart. After the deportees' return to Palestine, the cemetery was looked after by the Anglican bishop of Mauritius at their request; in 1946, care for the graves was entrusted to the South African Jewish Board of Deputies. The cemetery has since been renovated several times, including in 1960 after the cyclone. In May 2001 sixty six gravestones renovated with money provided by the South African Diaspora were unveiled. The ceremony took place with the participation of former deportees, a group whose numbers decrease with each passing year.[67]

The camp existed until the end of the war. The internees learnt about the possibility to travel to Palestine in February 1945.[68] They were to avail themselves of a portion of the immigration quotas. They were, however, forced to wait before traveling. The war was still underway. An appropriate vessel had to be obtained and the safe transportation of over 1000 people organized. In the meantime Mauritius was struck by a polio epidemic (Heine-Medina disease). Contact between the camp and the rest of the island became restricted. Despite the preventative measures, several of the internees fell ill. The departure had to be postponed. The final date was set for the 12th of August 1945. The Jews were to sail to Palestine on board the *Franconia*, a luxury British liner in the service of the Ministry of War Transport – the same ship which a few months earlier, during the Yalta conference, had been moored at Sevastopol and served the British delegation as headquarters.[69]

In August 1945 there were over 1300 Jews in the camp. When they were asked where they wanted to settle – 81% indicated Eretz Israel (of the rest, 40 people chose Austria and 20 Czechoslovakia). The journey from Mauritius to Palestine lasted 14 days. The *Franconia* reached Haifa on the 26th of August. Two days earlier, in Suez, officials of the Jewish Agency from the department of immigration had boarded to process the relevant formalities before disembarkation. Flats were prepared for the arrivals in Nahariya, Holon and Haifa. Those who required recuperation were housed in sanatoriums. Others were looked after by relatives, while those who had chosen not to connect their future with Palestine and wanted to join their families

---

[65] A list of the deceased see: R. Friedmann, op.cit., pp. 9–12. A. Zwergbaum writes about 124 deceased (*Exile in Mauritius*, p. 229); J. Sloame – about 128 (*Exile in Mauritius*), Jewish Virtual Library (http://www.jewishvirtuallibrary.org/jsource/vjw/Mauritius. html).

[66] *Parliamentary Debates* (*Commons*), vol. 377, 21 I 1942, col. 370.

[67] There are 127 graves at the cemetery, in 1989 there was buried here also one more person from the local Diaspora. G. Pitot, op.cit., p. 232; W. Pickett, "Mauritius Inmates Recall British Detention Camp," *The Jerusalem Post*, 6 X 1995.

[68] *Parliamentary Debates* (*Commons*), vol. 408, 21 II 1945, coll. 802–803.

[69] After "Mauritius Refugees Return," *The Palestine Post*, 27 VIII 1945, p. 2.

in Europe were taken care of by the UNRRA (United Nations Relief and Rehabilitation Administration).[70] This was the first numerous group of Jewish immigrants to settle in Palestine after the end of the war. The "Mauritian saga" is recognized as an important chapter in *ha'apala*.

---

[70] G. Pitot, op.cit., pp. 228–230; "Saga of Suffering Ended. Mauritius Refugees Do Not Smile," *The Palestine Post*, 27 VIII 1945, p. 3; A. Zwergbaum, "Exile in Mauritius," pp. 253–256; "Happy End of a Sad Odyssey. Saga of Mauritius Refugees," *The Palestine Post*, 27 VIII 1945.

# Chapter VI: If the gates to Palestine had been open...

## 1. The Kladovo group

One of the most tragic chapters of *ha'apala* was the fate of the so-called Kladovo group of Jewish refugees from Austria and Germany, who attempted to reach Palestine via the Danube and the Black Sea.[1] After the outbreak of war in September 1939, Mossad and Hehalutz activists in Austria began to fear that the Reich might change its policy on Jewish emigration, all the more as Jews from the Reich and Czech territory had already been deported to occupied Poland, to the General Gouvernement. Who could guarantee that this operation would not touch the rest? The decision was taken not to delay. The plan envisaged the transportation by rail from Vienna to Bratislava of around 1,000 Jews, mostly Hehalutz members from Austria, then taking them by means of Deutsche Donau – Schiffahrtgesellschaft to the Romanian port at Sulina, where a ship prepared by Mossad was to be waiting. The organizer of the undertaking was the Viennese associate of the Institute of B Immigration Georg Überall (Ehud Avriel). The Slovak visas were obtained with the help of Berthold Storfer.

The first group of refugees left Vienna on the 24th of November 1939. In Bratislava they were joined by others, from Slovakia, the Protectorate of Bohemia and Moravia, and Danzig. The success of the undertaking was to be decided by the preparation of a ship which would be able to take the Jews onwards, following their arrival in Romania, to Palestine. Mossad had problems, however, with obtaining a suitable vessel, while the DDSG conditioned the transportation of refugees to Romania on the guarantee that a ship would be ready and waiting for them in port. The situation became all the more critical as it appeared an early and severe winter was coming, and this meant that the Danube would be frozen over. A lot of money allowed for the hiring of three Yugoslav river vessels. They transported the refugees to Kladovo in Yugoslavia, the small port of the Danube close to the Romanian border, a few

---

[1] For more see: G. Anderl, W. Manoschek, *Gescheiterte Flucht. Der "Kladovo – Transport" auf dem Weg nach Palästina, 1939–1942*, Wien 2001; D. Ofer, H. Weiner, *Dead-End Journey. The Tragic Story of the Kladovo-Šabac Group*, Lanham, Md.–New York–London 1996; A. Douer (Hg.), *Kladovo. Eine Flucht nach Palästina. Escape to Palestine*, Jüdisches Museum Wien, Wien 2001. Also the documentary film made in Austria in 2001, *Kladovo–an Escape–Vienna–Palestine* directed by Alisa Douer.

days' journey from Sulina. The Danube started to freeze, and Bucharest would not allow the transport onto its territory, unsurprisingly, as nobody knew when – if at all – it would be possible to guarantee the departure of these people from Romania.[2]

The fugitives would wait out the winter in Kladovo and move on when spring had softened the ice. In reality, however, they found themselves interned, because the Yugoslav authorities recommended they stay on the steam ships. Meanwhile the vessels were not designed to hold so many people in winter conditions. The heating did not work, and basic conveniences like kitchens and toilets were lacking. Several people died. Problems emerged with supplying the vessels with food and medication. As a result of Kladovo's distance from the main communication routes, snow-blocked roads made contact difficult, and the supply of foodstuffs and medicines was affected.

The emigrants' misery attracted the interest of the British press, and mention of their plight was made in the House of Commons[3] and the House of Lords.[4] The Foreign Office expressed sympathy. The government of Great Britain explained, however, that it could not be held responsible for the policy of the Third Reich.[5]

The refugees did not leave with the onset of spring. Their forced stay in Kladovo continued. Fate appeared to have cast its sentence against them. When it had seemed that a Turkish ship was going to take them from Romanian Sulina, paid for by Mossad with serious money ($42,000), Ankara issued a new law which forbade the selling of Turkish vessels to foreigners. Then a heated discussion flared up over the next ship under consideration – this time the Greek vessel *Darien II* under a Panamanian flag – to be precise, over whether it should go into the service of *Aliyah Bet* or whether it should serve broader aims linked with the on-going war. This discussion reflected a dilemma that had, in the summer of 1940, manifested itself amongst the leadership of the Zionist movement – what was more profitable: short-term and immediate operations with a limited chance of success or a long-term policy of small steps with a view to future success?

Meanwhile the political and military situation in Europe was changing. In 1940 Italy had entered the war and France had capitulated. Great Britain was facing the prospect of a German invasion. Some Yishuv leaders supported tactical cooperation with Great Britain, including intelligence and sabotage operations in the Balkans.

---

[2]  G. Anderl, W. Manoschek, *Gescheiterte Flucht*, pp. 48–57. Cf. also E. Avriel, *Open the Gates! A Personal Story of "Illegal" Immigration to Israel*. Preface by G. Meir, New York 1975, pp. 99–107; B. Habas, *The Gate Breakers*, New York–London 1963, pp. 111–117; K.J. Ball-Kaduri, "Illegale Judenauswanderung aus Deutschland nach Palästina 1939/40 – Planung, Durchführung und internationale Zusammenhänge," *Jahrbuch des Instituts für deutsche Geschichte* (Tel Aviv). 4. Band: 1975, pp. 405–407.

[3]  TNA. FO 371/25238/W 454 (p. 205). *Plight of Jews on board ships marooned in the Danube*, 8 I 1940; *Parliamentary Debates (Commons)*, vol. 357, 7 II 1940, col. 236. Cf. also: "2000 Jewish Refugees Marooned on the Danube. MacDonald Refuses to Lift Palestine Ban," *The Palestine Post*, 8 II 1940, p. 1.

[4]  *Parliamentary Debates (Lords)*, vol. 115, 13 II 1940, coll. 528–529.

[5]  *Select British Documents*, doc. 4: *N.S. Ronald, FO, to V. Jabotinsky, 30 I 1940*, p. 264.

They calculated that this step would induce the Mandate authorities to revise its policy in relation to Yishuv's nationalist aspirations. With this aim, they intended to give the ship *Darien* to the British intelligence services,[6] which meant agreeing to the continued stay of the refugees in Yugoslavia. The country appeared to be a relatively safe haven, much safer than pro-Hitler Romania, or a ship in the Mediterranean which with Italy's entry into the war had become part of the theatre of war.

The Jewish Agency tried hard to ensure that the refugees would be allocated places based on immigration quotas and thereby legally travel to Palestine. Among those who appealed to the Mandate authorities was Moshe Shertok. These efforts had partial success. The British agreed to allow around 200 persons into the Mandate (half of whom were children), while the remainder as citizens of enemy countries had no chance.[7]

Significant funds were needed in order to support such a multitude of refugees. The Jewish Agency appealed for material help. The greatest amount came quickly from JOINT and the local Jewish community in Yugoslavia. The situation of those interned, now joined by other refugees, momentarily improved in September 1940 when they were moved to the town of Šabac on the Sava, 250 km to the west of Kladovo. Admittedly they were now separated by a greater distance from the Black Sea; but at least they were housed in a building on firm ground (most were located in a former mill converted into accommodation) and could move around the immediate environs.[8]

In the autumn of 1940 it seemed that the transport would soon be moving. At the beginning of November the *Darien II* dropped anchor at the port in Constanta to collect the refugees. The plan was that the ship would wait in Sulina, at the mouth of the central branch of the Danube, and from Šabac onwards they would be taken by Yugoslavian barges. The refugees packed and waited for the signal. The departure was, however, put off several times. Preparatory work on the *Darien* was taking longer than envisaged. When the *Darien* finally called in at the port in Sulina, the Yugoslav participants withdrew from the action. Winter was approaching and Belgrade feared that the barges would not manage to return before the Danube froze. *Darien II* waited a month in Sulina, after which it weighed anchor and returned to Constanta. The refugees remained in Šabac. It may have appeared the lesser of evils, as the war so far had spared Yugoslavia; but this conviction would turn out to be illusory.

---

6    Cf. D. Ofer, "The Kladovo-Darien Affair – Illegal Immigration to Palestine: Zionist Policy and European Exigencies" [in:] R.J. Cohen (ed.), *Vision and Conflict in the Holy Land*, Jerusalem–New York 1985, pp. 218–245.

7    G. Anderl, W. Manoschek, *Gescheiterte Flucht*, pp. 170–175.

8    D. Ofer, H. Weiner, op.cit., pp. 79–86; G. Anderl, W. Manoschek, *Herta Eisler und der jüdische "Kladovo – Transport" auf dem Weg nach Palästina* [in:] H. Halbrainer (Hg.), *Zwei Tage Zeit. Herta Reich und die Spuren jüdischen Lebens in Mürzzuschlag*, Graz 1998, pp. 51–55.

When the Third Reich attacked Yugoslavia in April 1941, there were around 1,100 Jews in Šabac. Several months later, in October, the Germans shot dead all of the men as revenge for the death of 21 of its soldiers killed by Yugoslavian partisans.[9] The women and children were taken in January 1942 to the concentration camp at Sajmište near Belgrade, where all were shortly to perish.[10] Paradoxically they were the same Jews who two years earlier had been mobilized by the Viennese Zentralstelle to leave the Third Reich.

Even in 1940, Jews were still able to leave the territory of the Third Reich and try to reach Palestine within the framework of *Aliyah Bet*. Berlin's policy was, however, moving towards the planned extermination of the Jewish population. At the conference in Wannsee (20th January 1942) near Berlin, the decision to exterminate all Jews inhabiting areas under the control of the Third Reich was taken. Their number was calculated to be eleven million. The operation euphemistically called the "final solution" (*Endlösung*), was to be headed and coordinated by the head of the Gestapo department for Jewish matters in the RSHA (*Reichssicherheitshauptamt*, the Reich Security Head Office), Adolf Eichmann.[11]

## 2. The case of the *Darien II*

The history of *Aliyah Bet* contains extraordinary incidents, one of which that of the *Darien II*, the last transport of *Aliyah Bet* during the war to reach Haifa, was one. Its journey was even more unusual in that they involved a ship which during the course of its mission was formally the property of the British secret service.[12]

*Darien II* was almost 50 years old. It had changed its name and owner several times. In the spring of 1940 it was bought by Mossad le'Aliyah Bet in Greece, with plans for *Darien* to transport the refugees of the so called Kladovo group. At

---

[9]   In 1959 the remains of those shot were transferred from Šabac to the Sephardic cemetery in Belgrade. Five years later the Jewish community in Vienna funded a monument which was placed on their grave. D. Ofer, H. Weiner, op.cit., pp. 157–163, 172–173.

[10]  Only two people were to have survived (G. Anderl, W. Manoschek, *Gescheiterte Flucht*, p. 287). Tad Szulc incorrectly states as if the SS execution of all, women and men, took place on the 7th of April 1941. T. Szulc, *The Secret Alliance. The Extraordinary Story of the Rescue of the Jews Since World War II*, New York 1991, p. 31. Cf. also M. Shelah, "Sajmište – An Extermination Camp in Serbia" [in:] *Holocaust and Genocide Studies. An International Journal* (Oxford–New York–Jerusalem). Vol. 2: 1987, pp. 243–260.

[11]  Y. Bauer, *Jews for Sale? Nazi-Jewish Negotiations, 1933–1945*, New Haven–London 1994, p. 53.

[12]  R. Aliav, P. Mann, *The Last Escape. The Launching of the Largest Secret Rescue Movement of All Time*, London 1974, pp. 444–459; W.R. Perl, *Operation Action. Rescue from the Holocaust*. Revised and enlarged edition, New York 1983, pp. 201–204, 212–216; B. Habas, op.cit., pp. 150–151 (here as *Dorian II*); I. Grinbaum, "Dorián II" [in:] *La Haapala. Compilación de notas y documentos de la Inmigración "Ilegal" a Eretz Israel 1933–1948*. La selección del material por M. Kitrón, Jerusalem 1953, p. 160.

the same time Hagana had decided to sell the vessel to the British SOE (Special Operations Executive).

The British had concrete plans for the *Darien*. They calculated that as an *Aliyah Bet* craft it would not arouse untoward suspicion on the part of the Germans. The ship, loaded up with scrap and explosives, was to be detonated on the Danube, blocking the transportation of Romanian oil to Germany.

The sale transaction was conducted in Cairo with the participation of representatives of Hagana and Mossad (David Hacohen, Yehuda Arazi, Moshe Agami, Ze'ev Shind).[13] When the board of Hagana recommended that *Darien* be turned over to the British (the boat was at the time moored at Sulina, awaiting the refugees from Šabac), some Mossad activists refused, pointing to the *Aliyah Bet* priority of rescuing the refugees. The main advocates of this position were Yehuda Braginski and Ruth Klueger.[14] *Darien* was not delivered to the British however, even though they had paid for the vessel. The activists of *Aliyah Bet* had other plans for the *Darien*.

They intended to use it for the transportation to Palestine of several hundred Jews, mainly Romanians and Bulgarians. The ship left Constanta on the 19th of February 1941. Other groups joined on route, at Varna and Istanbul. The *Darien* was carrying around 790 refugees.[15] Great Britain, as usual, asked the Turkish authorities to stop the transport. Turkey, however, refused. After an eight-day wait in Istanbul the ship continued its journey. On the 19th of March 1941, after reaching Haifa, the vessel was taken by the British. The passengers were to be sent to Mauritius, but the Mandate authorities did not have an appropriate means of transportation at their disposal.[16] The refugees were taken to Atlit, where they were to be interned for eighteen months. They luckily avoided deportation and in the summer of 1942 were

---

[13] Cf. "The Darien Story" [in:] *The Darien Dilemma*, pp. 4–8 (http://www.dariendilemma.com/eng/story/darienstory/); D. Ofer, *The Kladovo-Darien Affair*. Hacohen's wife was Bracha Habas (1900–1968), the author of one of the first attempts at a synthesis of *Aliyah Bet*: *The Gate Breakers* (New York–London 1963; a translation of the Hebrew edition of 1957).

[14] The dilemmas connected with the question of the ship are presented in the documentary film *The Darien Dilemma* by the Israeli director Erez Laufer (2006; Hebrew with English subtitles). A. Patek, "Ha'apala między historią a filmem," *Nowiny Kurier* (Tel Awiw), 19 III 2009, p. 15.

[15] According to data from the Colonial Office 793 persons, of which 464 were Romanian Jews and 252 Bulgarian, the remainder came from Germany, Hungary, Poland and Czechoslovakia. TNA. CO 733/446/8 (f. 56). *Release of "Darien" Passengers. London 1.12.1941*. This data is confirmed by Ronald W. Zweig (*Britain and Palestine During the Second World War*, Woodbridge 1986, p. 117). The Jewish Agency rounded up the passengers to 800 persons (CZA. F 38/1304. *Jewish Agency – Internment of Jewish Refugees in Athlit, Palestine 1942*). A higher number – 878 – we can find in P.H. Silverstone (*Our Only Refuge, Open the Gates! Clandestine Immigration to Palestine 1938–1948*, New York 1999, p. 7). In turn Dalia Ofer gives the number of refugees as once 786 (*Escaping the Holocaust. Illegal Immigration to the Land of Israel, 1939–1944*, New York 1990, p. 67), while another time as 789 (p. 326).

[16] TNA. CO 733/446/8 (f. 2). *CO draft. 18 I 1942*. Following its acquisition by the Royal Navy, the *Darien II* served as a refrigerator ship transporting, among other things, foodstuffs for the Allied units fighting at Tobruk.

given the chance to legally settle in Palestine.[17] An adherent of this very solution was Churchill himself, who in February 1942 appealed to Lord Walter Moyne of the Colonial Office to allow the refugees to settle in the Mandate.[18]

Whether Churchill's voice in the matter was decisive or not, the fact remains that the British Prime Minister took a stand that was beneficial to Jewish immigrants, and not for the first time (he had done so earlier in, among other examples, the matter of the *Patria* catastrophe). Many saw him as sympathetic to the Zionist movement. Churchill understood the need to change Great Britain's Palestinian policy to increasingly take Jewish aspirations into account. It was chiefly thanks to him that a Jewish military arm of the Jewish Brigade was formed in 1944. Hence it is a curious paradox that the government he headed was to take such an active role in counteracting *Aliyah Bet*. London's approach is usually explained by the course of political circumstances. In this context the figure of Churchill himself is ambiguous. Some, like Martin Gilbert, have lauded his services to the Jews, others (Michael J. Cohen) are more restrained in their assessment.[19]

Circumstances were increasingly disadvantageous to the Jews. After Romania's accession to the Axis Powers (Tripartite Pact) in the autumn of 1940, the Jewish inhabitants of Romania could no longer count on legally receiving an immigration certificate to Palestine. It should be remembered that the Diaspora here was second in magnitude only to that of Poland in Central-Eastern Europe. Circumstances in Europe and the Middle East were not favourable. On the one hand the infamous Wannsee Conference was approaching (January 1942). On the other – following the pro-German coup of Rashid Ali al-Gaylani in Iraq (April 1941), London had to tread carefully in the Middle East. This meant with regard to Palestine a further intensification of the policy against the illegal influx of Jewish immigrants.

---

[17]  TNA. CO 733/446/7 (p. 5). *Telegram to Palestine to High Commissioner (Sir H. MacMichael) from Secretary of State for the Colonies. No. 554. Secret. 20 V 1942*; Y. Bauer, *From Diplomacy to Resistance. A History of Jewish Palestine 1939–1945*, New York 1973, pp. 116–118. Following the release of the immigrants from the *Darien*, the camp at Atlit was momentarily empty. Jews were again interned here in 1945.

[18]  "Winston Churchill to Colonial Secretary Lord Moyne, 5 February 1942, urging him to allow 'Darien' passengers to stay in Palestine" [in:] *The Rise of Israel.* Vol. 30: *The Holocaust and Illegal Immigration*, p. 145. The Jewish Agency appealed for the internees' release. CZA. F 38/1304. *Memorandum on Jewish Refugees interned in Athlit, Palestine, submitted to His Excellency, Ambassador of Great Britain to the United States, 24 II 1942*.

[19]  M.J. Cohen, *Churchill and the Jews*, London 1985, particularly pp. 275–286. Cf. the telling title of Martin Gilbert's book, *Churchill and the Jews. A Lifelong Friendship* (New York 2007).

# 3. Catastrophes at sea (the *Pencho* and the *Salvador*)

Not all *Aliyah Bet* vessels were to reach their destination. Almost miraculously, the 500 or so passengers of the *Pencho,* mostly Jewish refugees from the Protectorate of Bohemia and Moravia or from Slovakia managed to emerge with their lives.[20] The ship, prepared by the Romanian Revisionists, set sail in May 1940 from Bratislava. For long weeks on end it meandered from one river port to another, between Yugoslavia, Romania and Bulgaria, attempting to secure food and water. On the Aegean, close to the Italian Dodecanese Islands, the engine failed. Navigation failures took place. A hole in the hull resulting from running aground on some shallows appeared, and the boat started gradually to leak.[21] The passengers were successfully evacuated onto one of the nearby uninhabited islands. After ten days, on the 18th of October 1940, they were found by an Italian warship. The refugees were taken to Rhodes, where they were interned.[22]

Italy tried to deport the Jews back to Germany and Slovakia. However, these countries refused to take them and in January 1942 the Italians settled them in the south of Italy at the Ferramonti di Tarsia camp, from where they were freed by the Allies in September 1943. This camp, founded in the summer of 1940, was intended exclusively for Jews, but unlike Nazi concentration camps was not a place of extermination. In the course of its three years of existence over 3,800 people were interned here.

The majority of the refugees from the *Pencho* found themselves in Palestine in 1944, still before the war's end. They arrived legally with the permission of the Mandate authorities. The most numerous group, 350 in number, was taken to Egypt by the Polish liner *Batory*, which after September 1939 had gone over to Allied service and operated as a military transporter. From Alexandria to Palestine the Jews travelled by rail.[23]

In December 1940 the sailing ship *Salvador* set off from the Bulgarian port of Varna. This Bulgarian tub, somewhat dilapidated and withdrawn from regular service, had earlier been named the *Tsar Krum*, in honour of the medieval Bulgarian ruler. The new name (*Salvador*, i.e. "saviour") was to symbolize the hopes and de-

---

[20] For more see: J. Bierman, *Odyssey*, New York 1984; K.J. Ball-Kaduri, op.cit., pp. 407–408; B. Habas, op.cit., pp. 120–123; D. Ofer, *Escaping the Holocaust*, pp. 85–88; W.R. Perl, *Operation Action*, pp. 261–267.

[21] More than likely another possible cause of damage to the ship was it hitting an Italian mine. M.R. Marrus, *The Unwanted. European Refugees from the First World Through the Cold War*, Philadelphia 2002, p. 276.

[22] Following the sinking of the *Pencho*, several young Jews took to sea in a dinghy. They were picked up by a British ship, having only made it to Cyprus and subsequently to Palestine. Cf. also TNA. FO 371/25242/W 11541 (pp. 76–78). *Movements of S.S. "Pentcho." Decode from Sir R. Hoare (Bucharest) to FO. No. 1479. 1 XI 1940*; CZA. L 22/922. *Leitung der Schiffbruechigen an die Jewish Agency, Genf. Rodi, Camp Stadione, 12 XI 1940*. In the file is a collection of telegrams about the refugees.

[23] J. Bierman, op.cit., pp. 230, 238.

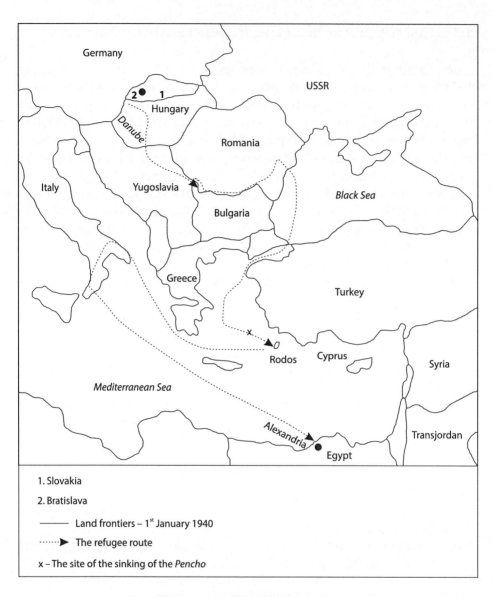

Germany

USSR

2● 1

Hungary

Danube

Romania

Italy

Yugoslavia

Black Sea

Bulgaria

Greece

Turkey

x

Rodos  Cyprus

Syria

Mediterranean Sea

Alexandria

Transjordan

Egypt

1. Slovakia

2. Bratislava

——— Land frontiers – 1ˢᵗ January 1940

·······▶ The refugee route

x – The site of the sinking of the *Pencho*

**Map 4. The *Pencho* passenger odyssey (1940–1944)**

Author's study

sires of the refugees. With time this became bitterly ironic. On board the schooner were about 350 immigrants (on the whole Bulgarian citizens),[24] about one hundred more than the boat should have taken, while there were plans to take on board a further 40–50 castaways from the *Pencho* waiting on Rhodes. The vessel was in need of a general overhaul, which was, unfortunately, not carried out. Even appropriate maps and compasses were lacking.[25]

In short, *Salvador's* departure was a real risk. This unfortunate undertaking was backed by Baruch Konfino. The leaders of Bulgaria's Jews appealed to him and his associates for caution. The British ambassador in Sofia, George William Rendel, also warned against setting sail.[26] Some passengers were also aware of the vessel's poor condition, but, determined to leave, they were prepared to run the risk.

The transport left Varna on the 3rd of December under a Uruguayan flag. As a result of the poor engine that had been installed, it was aided by a Bulgarian tug on the journey to Turkey. After eight days, the *Salvador* reached Istanbul. The Foreign Office, through the intermediacy of the British diplomatic posts in Ankara and Athens, undertook efforts to stop the vessel from sailing through the straits and the Aegean Sea. It was suggested to the Turkish authorities that the vessel could be detained on sanitary grounds. On the next day, the 12th of December, the *Salvador* sank during a storm on the Sea of Marmara.[27] Most of the passengers perished: over 200 people, including several dozen children. Some managed to swim ashore but many of these, exhausted and soaked through, froze to death. The majority of those saved, around 80 people, were returned to Bulgaria. The rest were allowed to stay in

---

[24]  The number of passengers is different depending on the source. Bernard Wasserstein (*Britain and the Jews of Europe 1939–1945*, London–Oxford 1979, p. 76) estimates it as 350–380 persons, Howard M. Sachar (*A History of Israel. From the Rise of Zionism to Our Time*, New York 1988, p. 237) writes of 350, Nicholas Bethell (*The Palestine Triangle. The Struggle between the British, the Jews, and the Arabs, 1935–1948*, London 1979, p. 97) of 380; Dalia Ofer once gives 350 (*Escaping the Holocaust*, p. 95), another time 320 passengers (p. 326). According to Paul H. Silverstone there were 327 people on board (*Our Only Refuge*, p. 7). The report of the Bulgarian Ministry of Foreign Affairs mentions 320 immigrants: YVA. M67/85 (pp. 6). Министерство на вънишнить работи и на изповъданията. Политическа дирекция – до Дирекцията на Полицията – Отдѣль Административна Полиция (София). 23 XII 1940.

[25]  B. Wasserstein, *Britain and the Jews of Europe*, pp. 76–77; "El desastre del 'Salvador'" [in:] *La Haapala. Compilación de notas y documentos*, pp. 159–160. The story of the passengers of the *Salvador* appeared in 2006 in an Israeli documentary film entitled *Salvador – The Ship of Shattered Hopes* directed by Nissim Mossek.

[26]  S. Shealtiel, "The Private Clandestine Immigration Operation of Dr. Baruch Confino, 1939–1940," *Shvut. Studies in Russian and East European Jewish History and Culture* (Tel Aviv–Beer Sheva). Ed. by B. Pinkus. Vol. 10 (26): 2001, pp. 101, 103 (here the surname – Randall – is incorrectly spelt).

[27]  M. Wischnitzer (*To Dwell in Safety. The Story of Jewish Migration Since 1800*, Philadelphia 1948, p. 241) incorrectly states that the *Salvador was under sail for five months* [sic!], *without being allowed to land its passengers, until early in 1940* [sic!] *it foundered on a rock in the Sea of Marmora*. It is indicative that a similar mistake is made by H.M. Sachar in his otherwise excellent synthesis of the history of Israel (op.cit., p. 237), maintaining as if the *Salvador* made it to Haifa and from there was returned to Bulgaria.

Istanbul where they were looked after by the Jewish Agency and the local Diaspora.[28] Some of them, two months later, were to undertake another attempt to reach to Palestine on board the *Darien II*.

The *Salvador* catastrophe was widely discussed, not only in Jewish circles. The leadership of the Bulgarian Jewish community considered Konfino to be partly responsible for the misfortune, and the Bulgarian authorities ordered him to temporarily leave Sofia. Yishuv was highly critical.[29] Konfino was accused of being driven by a desire for profit, and of allowing organisational disorder and engaging in activities "at odds with Zionist ethics." It is worth noting that in the course of the eighteen months of Konfino's activities the attitude of Yishuv and the Bulgarian Diaspora towards him had evolved and following the successful missions of the *Rudnitchar* transformed into something akin to goodwill. The catastrophe of the *Salvador* changed everything.[30]

The *Salvador* was the last *Aliyah Bet* transport organized by the ophthalmologist from Sofia and the last to leave a Bulgarian port during the Second World War. Several months later Sofia joined the Axis Powers and the German army entered the country; on the 6th of April the Germans attacked Yugoslavia and Greece from Bulgarian territory.

Konfino was certainly not an adventurist. He believed in the correctness of what he was doing, and he helped many people. But at a certain moment he lost his sense of perspective and put the lives of hundreds at risk.

Part of the blame lay with the Bulgarian authorities, who did nothing to prevent the departure of a vessel which seriously jeopardized the lives of its passengers. The sinking of the *Salvador* was publicized by the British, shouldering the Bulgarians with the blame for the catastrophe. The Foreign Office spoke of the *scandalous part played by Bulgarian authorities* and their *brutal methods* of dealing with the Jews.[31] The Yishuv press joined in the same tone.[32] Sofia was left to explain in an unconvincing manner that *the ship had been chartered by a group of travellers for a voyage to Constantinople*, while – according to the knowledge of the authorities –

---

[28]  The number of victims oscillates in various works from "over" 200 to 231. According to the report of Chaim Barlas, the long serving head of the immigration department of the Jewish Agency, the *Salvador* was transporting 352 refugees, from which only 119 people were saved. CZA. A 406/55. *Cable from Barlas, Turkey, to Zionists, New York. 24 XII 1940*. The Bulgarian side in a report of the 23rd of December 1940, states there were 103 victims, 95 missing. YVA. M67/85 (p. 6). Министерство на външнитъ работи и на изповъданията; ibidem (pp. 17–20), a list of 197 victims. Different data may be found in *The Palestine Post*, in the article "204 Jewish Emigrants Drowned in Storm. 66 Children Among Dead" (15 XII 1940, p. 1). According to this article there were 326 passengers on board.

[29]  Cf. the article in *The Palestine Post*, "Salvador Was Derelict Ship Without Maps or Instruments" (18 XII 1940, p. 3).

[30]  S. Shealtiel, "The private clandestine immigration," pp. 106–107.

[31]  TNA. FO 371/25242/W 12674 (p. 259). *Decypher from Mr Rendel (Sofia) to FO. No. 965. 18 XII 1940*.

[32]  "Bulgaria Responsible for Salvador Tragedy," *The Palestine Post*, 22 XII 1940, p. 1.

*there was no person travelling to Palestine* on board. Bulgaria emphasized that *Salvador* was not flying under a Bulgarian flag, indicating that it carried no responsibility for the wilful decision of the passengers and a foreign ship owner.[33]

In the months that followed, the stream of immigrants diminished significantly. Where in 1940 there had been seven large transports (with around 7,000 persons), in the following year there were two, with a fourfold reduction in passenger numbers.[34] The experiences of the *Atlantic*, and even more so the *Patria* and the *Salvador*, certainly played a role in this development. Equally if not more important, was the gradual evolution of the Third Reich's policy towards the "final solution to the Jewish question" and the limitation on the emigration of Jews from Europe.

# 4. The tragedy of the *Struma*

The ordeal of the *Struma*'s passengers is one of the more tragic threads that run through the story of *Aliyah Bet* and retains an important place in the memory of Jews.[35] The *Struma*, which had previously been called the *Macedonia*, was a well-

[33]  TNA. FO 371/29160/W 1039 (pp. 86–87). *From M. Momtchiloff (Bulgarian Legation) to Sir A. Cadogan. 29 I 1941.*

[34]  A. Patek, *Żydzi w drodze do Palestyny 1934–1944. Szkice z dziejów aliji bet, nielegalnej imigracji żydowskiej*, Kraków 2009, p. 236.

[35]  The first serious work concerning the tragedy of the *Struma* had appeared already in 1942 in the two-volume synthesis by Abraham Galante, *Histoire des Juifs d'Istanbul depuis la prise de cette ville, en 1453, par Fatih Mehmed II, jusqu'à nos jours*, 2 vol., Istanbul 1942 (Chapter XXII: "Le naufrage du bateau STRUMA," pp. 144–150). From amongst others mention can be given to: D. Frantz, C. Collins, *Death on the Black Sea. The Untold Story of the Struma and World War II's Holocaust at Sea*, New York 2003 (combining the features of an academic monograph with reportage); T. Carmely, *The Real Story of "Struma" or Breaking Down a 60 Years Old Conspiracy of Silence*, Haifa 2002 (copied computer printout – NLI, inventory no. S2 = 2002 B 3367); idem, *Dosarul "Struma"și dedesubturile sale*, Haifa 2005 (NLI, inventory no. S2 = 2006 B 4904); M. Stoian, *Ultima cursă de la Struma la Mefküre*, București 1995; Ç. Yetkin, *Struma. Bir dramin içyüzü*, Istanbul 2008; J. Feinstein, *Struma. Corabia vietii și a mortii*. Prefata de David Safran, Tel Aviv 1965; S. Gheorghiu, *Tragedia navelor "Struma" și "Mefkure,"* Constanța 1998; E. Ofir, *With No Way Out. The Story of the Struma. Documents and Testimonies*, Cluj-Napoca 2003; A. Ozer, "The Strumah Tragedy," *ROM-SIG News. The Journal of the Special Interest Group for Romanian Jewish Genealogy* (Greenwich, Conn.). Vol. 5: Spring 1997. No. 3 (also in the Internet at: http://www.turkishjews.com/struma); A. Patek, "Wokół zatonięcia statku 'Struma' (Morze Czarne, luty 1942 r.)," *Prace Komisji Środkowoeuropejskiej PAU* (Kraków), T. XIX: 2011, pp. 73–86; S. Rubinstein, "Asupra câtorva tragedii mici petrecute în cadrul unei tragedii mari, numită 'Struma,'" *Studia et Acta Historiae Iudaeorum Romaniae* (București). Vol. IV: 1999, pp. 193–207. This author also has prepared two additional works: *Personal Tragedies as a Reflection to a Great Tragedy Called Struma*, Jerusalem 2003 (of value as a result of the collection of eyewitness accounts; also in the Internet at: http://www.isro-press.net/Struma.Rubinstein/index.shtml) as well as it supplementation *Comments on Several Personal Tragedies that were part of the General Tragedy Called Struma*, Jerusalem 2002 (copied printout – NLI, inventory no. S2 = 2003 B 6596). Of a more literary nature are: M. Arsene [A. Leibovici], *Struma*, București 1972 as

worn two-master with a surface displacement of 146–180 tons, over 70 years old. Its owner was the Greek company Jean D. Pandelis et Co., run by businessman Jean Pandelis, who since 1939 had had a business relationship with the *Aliyah Bet* organizers. The ship, which was in fact a mere punt, sailed under the flag of Panama. It had earlier been used for river transport, including transport of cattle. Pandelis was able to interest operatives of the Romanian Revisionist branch in the aging vessel. As there was no shortage of people eager to leave Romania, the idea of organizing a transport to Palestine was seized upon. Between 769 and 791 Jewish refugees boarded the *Struma,* among them elite professionals – doctors, lawyers, and engineers – as well as students, merchants, and craftsmen. There were over 100 children. The great majority of the passengers were citizens of Romania.[36]

The aim was to reach Turkey where they expected to obtain permission from the Mandate authorities to enter Palestine. The state of the vessel and the conditions on board left a lot to be desired – cramped sleeping areas, the lack of a real kitchen, the wretched state of the engine, only one toilet and two lifeboats for several hundred people. The passengers did not hide their disappointment. They had paid handsomely for the journey. In the advertisements, which had appeared in the Romanian press, the organizer of the endeavour – a private travel agency – had promised them decent travel conditions. They had been assured that the vessel conformed to safety standards and that the obtainment of the immigration certificates was almost certain. Initially the plan had been to take a mere 100–200 people. The fact that the actual number was several times that of the initial planned figure was the result of pure profiteering on the part of the organizers. For there was no lack of those interested, with many willing to hand over their very last penny for a ticket.

The *Struma*, with the knowledge and agreement of the Romanian authorities, set out from Constanta on the 12th of December 1941.[37] The engine failed several times and the *Struma* was pulled into Istanbul by a Turkish ship. Turkey refused to allow the passengers ashore as it feared that the British would not issue immigration certificates, and the Turkish authorities had no intention of giving the refugees asylum. Turkey found itself in an especially delicate situation as, formally neutral, it tried to maintain a balance between the Allies and the Axis Powers. It was linked

---

well as M. Solomon, *Le Struma*, Toronto 1974 (English translation *The Struma Incident. A Novel of the Holocaust*, Toronto 1979). A collection of a dozen or so poems in Romanian and Hebrew come with the booklet published to commemorate the 30th anniversary of the catastrophe *Martirilor din fundul mării 1942–1972*. Culegere întocmită de I. Bar-Avi și I. Feinstein, Ierusalim 1972. Amongst the works available on the Internet cf. the block of accounts, articles, list of victims at: U. Friedberg-Valureanu (ed.), *Struma Tragedy* (http://www.alpas.net/uli/struma/struma_engl.htm).

[36] The ship was built in 1867. P.H. Silverstone, *"Our Only Refuge Open the Gates!" Clandestine Immigration to Palestine 1938–1948*, New York 1999, p. 7; A. Ozer, op.cit., p. 3. According to other sources it was even older, from 1830. D. Frantz, C. Collins, op.cit., p. 76; D. Ofer, *Escaping the Holocaust*, p. 149. Compare: *Struma General Specification* (http://www.alpas.net/uli/struma/Undeseafla.htm).

[37] We can find an incorrect date of sailing for the ship – February 1942 – in: J.J. Zasloff, *Great Britain and Palestine. A Study of the Problem before the United Nations*, München 1952, p. 22 as well as in W. Laqueur (*A History of Zionism*, London 1972, p. 535) – October 1941.

to Great Britain through the defense treaty it had signed in October 1939, and with the Third Reich by the friendship and non-aggression treaty concluded in June 1941 (it is worth noting that both were signed when the war was already underway). Besides the British and Turks, representatives of the Jewish Agency took part in the negotiations. The negotiations became drawn out. The Turkish side pointed out that the immigration limitations imposed by MacDonald's "White Paper" had not been exhausted and the passengers of the *Struma* could make use of the existing reserves. The British in reply noted that those individuals came from a country controlled by the Third Reich and as citizens of an enemy state were not entitled to Palestinian visas. Since the 7th of December 1941, Romania and Great Britain were at war.[38]

There were also other motivating factors. Allowing the passengers of the *Struma* to enter the Mandate for would have encouraged similar undertakings.[39] However, Polish, Yugoslavian and Greek refugees were arriving in Palestine,[40] also, at least in part, from territories controlled by Axis Power countries. The problem was that they were not Jews and did not intend to stay permanently while their presence – as we read in a confidential Foreign Office memorandum – did not bring with it the *risk of inciting dangerous repercussions amongst the non-Jewish peoples of the Middle East.*[41] The British feared that these "repercussions" would not be without influence on the future course of the war as they could lead to a loss of control over the Middle East.

Only a few individuals, who had expired Palestinian visas, were allowed to travel on to the Mandate (and one woman who, having had a miscarriage, was admitted to hospital).[42] There was a chance for children aged 11 to 16 to travel on, but the matter came to nothing as an impasse developed over how they would get to Palestine. The British did not want to send a vessel for them and the Turks refused to allow them transit through Turkish territory.[43]

---

[38]  TNA. FO 371/32661/W 2483 (p. 56). *Telegram from High Commissioner (Sir H. MacMichael) to Secretary of State for the Colonies. No. 190. 17 II 1942*; A. Ozer, op.cit., p. 4.

[39]  Cf. the comment of Alec Walter Randall of the Foreign Office: *what is perhaps worst of all, they will have succeeded in breaking through our policy, and this would certainly open the way for frequent repetitions of the same procedure.* TNA. FO 371/32661/W 2093. *FO minute (Alec Randall), 12 II 1942.* See also: R.W. Zweig, op.cit., pp. 117, 119.

[40]  In the war years, up to July 1943, according to Lord Robert Cranborne (Secretary of State for the Colonies, 1942), 2,400 non-Jewish refugees took shelter in Palestine. *Parliamentary Debates (Lords)*, vol. 128, 28 VII 1943, col. 866.

[41]  Quote after D.S. Wyman, *Pozostawieni swemu losowi. Ameryka wobec Holocaustu 1941–1945*, Warszawa 1994, p. 213. This aspect has been addressed by Lewis B. Namier (1888–1960), a British historian and Zionist, in an article highly critical of Great Britain "The Refugee Ships" published in the London *Time and Tide* (14 III 1942). Cf. *the same authorities had no qualms about Nazi agents when they admitted non-Jewish refugees from any of the Axis countries.*

[42]  This was Medea Salamovici (1919–1996). Her account is quoted by S. Rubinstein, *Personal Tragedies*, pp. 34–40.

[43]  TNA. FO 371/32661/W 2483 (pp. 52–53). *From High Commissioner (Sir M. MacMichael) to Secretary of State for the Colonies. No. 179. 15 II 1942* as well as *From Angora (Mr. Morgan) to Jerusalem. No. 14. 17 II 1942.*

Matters became more complicated when in January 1942 Panama declared war on Germany and her allies (including Romania and Bulgaria); it was under a Panamanian flag that the *Struma* had set sail. The captain and some of the crew had Bulgarian citizenship. The incident involved countries at war with each other. From the point of view of desiring to remain neutral, Turkey found itself in a most awkward position. The weakest player had to yield...

There is some question as to why Great Britain did not deport the refugees to Mauritius. Since 1940 no further groups of immigrants had been interned there, but this policy had not been formally revoked. Deportation, though morally questionable, would summarily have resolved many matters. It would at least have prevented the worst possible scenario – sending the people back to Europe where their future looked direst. The British were aware of the potential dangers. *The Black Sea is rough at this time of the year and the Struma may well founder* – noted Alec Randall from the Refugee Section of the Foreign Office.[44]

It is true that there were transportation problems (a war was on), but it is possible that the still-unsolved question of the passengers of the *Darien* was the key consideration here. If they were deported to Mauritius, then there would be no room left for the refugees from the *Struma*. A further consideration, possibly even more important, because dictated by pragmatics, was the fact that deportation to admittedly distant and remote, but peaceful Mauritius would have been less terrible than the Jews' situation in occupied Europe. It was thus unlikely to serve as a deterrent to further *Aliyah Bet*. But sending back refugees to the Old Continent could have just such an effect.[45]

The deadlock continued. Several hundred people were for two months *de facto* imprisoned on a small craft 7x20 metres in size, without amenities or professional medical care. After 71 days, on the 23rd of February 1942, the Turkish authorities took the decision to send the vessel back to the Black Sea.[46] The *Struma* had to immediately leave the port in Istanbul. The captain refused to follow the order while the passengers assembled on deck started to protest. The police intervened. Many Jews were roughed up and hurt. After the situation was brought under control a Turkish tug moved the craft into the Black Sea even though it did not possess adequate supplies of water, food and fuel and the engine was still damaged. The dejected refugees hung signs in English and Hebrew on the side of the *Struma* with the words: "SOS" and "Save us!" The following day, early in the morning of

---

44  TNA. FO 371/32661/W 2810. *Randall minute, 24 II 1942* (quoted after: R.W. Zweig, op.cit., p. 123).

45  An advocate of the thesis that Great Britain did what it could to persuade Turkey to force the *Struma* back to the Black Sea is R.W. Zweig (op.cit., pp. 125–126). Cf. also A. Koestler (*Promise and Fulfilment. Palestine 1917–1949*, London 1983, pp. 62–63). For the British point of view see: G. Kirk, *The Middle East in the War*, 3rd ed., London–New York–Toronto 1954, p. 244. Cf. Ch. Sykes, *Cross Roads to Israel. Palestine from Balfour to Bevin*, 2nd ed., London 1967, p. 238.

46  The Turkish point of view see: CZA. A 406/59. *Turkish Embassy, Washington, D.C., to Emmanuel Neumann, American Emergency Committee for Zionist Affairs, New York, 3 III 1942.*

the 24th of February, when the *Struma* was at a distance of 8–10 km off shore, it was struck by a forceful explosion. The Turkish rescue boats that came to the scene found only one survivor. The rest had perished.

How many victims were there? It is difficult to give an unequivocal answer. Usually in the literature on the subject we read that the *Struma* carried 769 Jewish refugees as well as 10 crew members (four [three?] Jews, five Bulgarians and a Hungarian; the nationality of one is disputed). Considering the fact that nine were allowed to leave the vessel while in Istanbul and only one person survived, a minimum of 769 must have died.[47] This figure has recently been questioned by Dr Samuel Aroni of California. Comparing the available information and contrasting it with archival materials he has claimed that the number of victims could even be 791.[48]

The Turkish authorities tried to play down the dimensions of the catastrophe. Significantly, the sole survivor – this being a 19-year old Romanian citizen, David Stoliar – was sent to prison for several weeks for having arrived on Turkish territory illegally, without the requisite visa. It should be remembered that he was in fact a castaway... In Stoliar's words: *I jumped into the sea and kept myself for some 24 hours. As I remember a Turkish Motor launch arrived and I was taken to hospital. I stayed in hospital two weeks and after my discharge from hospital I was taken to the Police, and I was imprisoned for a month and a half. After a certificate had been*

---

[47] The number of victims is different depending on the source. For example – 720 victims (Z.V. Hadari, *Second Exodus. The Full Story of Jewish Illegal Immigration to Palestine, 1945–1948*, London 1991, p. 5), 763 ([The Jewish Agency for Palestine], *The Jewish Case Before the Anglo-American Committee of Inquiry on Palestine as presented by the Jewish Agency for Palestine. Statements and Memoranda*, Jerusalem 1947, p. 296; A. Ozer, op.cit., p. 5), 767 (W.R. Perl, op.cit., p. 408; H.M. Sachar, op.cit., p. 237), 768 (M. Naor, *Haapala. Clandestine Immigration 1931–1948*, [Tel Aviv 1987], p. 38; G. Kirk, *The Middle East in the War*, p. 244; Ch. Lazar-Litai, *Af-'al-pi. Aliyah 2. shel tenu'at Z'abotinski*, Berit hayale ha-Etsel 1988, p. 128; D. Ofer, *Escaping the Holocaust*, p. 326; M. Wischnitzer, op.cit., p. 242; *Encyclopaedia Judaica*, vol. 8, col. 1249), 769 (Y. Bauer, N. Sagi, "'Illegal' Immigration" [in:] *New Encyclopedia of Zionism and Israel*. Vol. 1. Ed. by G. Wigoder, London–Toronto 1994, p. 648; H. Barlas, *Immigration to Palestine and Israel* [in:] *Encyclopedia of Zionism and Israel*. Vol. 1. Ed. by R. Patai, New York 1971, p. 537), 770 (K. Kubiak, *Pierwsza wojna bliskowschodnia 1947–1949 (studium polityczno-wojskowe)*, Wrocław 2006, p. 36; a mistake in the name of the ship – *Stuma*), and also 772 (T. Carmely, *The Real Story*, pp. 137 onwards) and 777 (E. Ofir, op.cit., pp. 100–102). And differently again (796 refugees) in: D. Cohn-Sherbok, D. El-Alami, *Konflikt palestyńsko-izraelski*, Warszawa 2002, p. 59. A list of 768 victims of the catastrophe was placed in the New York bulletin of the United Romanian Jews of America, *The Record* (25 IV 1942), in the YVA. O11/67 (p. 138).

[48] S. Aroni, "Who Perished on the Struma and How Many" [in:] D. Frantz, C. Collins, op.cit., pp. 295–335. For lists of victims see: T. Carmely, *The Real Story*, pp. 137–159; ibidem, *Dosarul Struma*, pp. 90–112; D. Frantz, C. Collins, op.cit., pp. 301–335; J. Feinstein, op.cit., pp. 143–151; E. Ofir, op.cit., pp. 323–346. Also in the Internet: *Struma's people* (http://www.alpas.net/uli/struma/Victimele.htm); *Struma: A Romanian Tragedy* (http://www.sephardicstudies.org/struma.html).

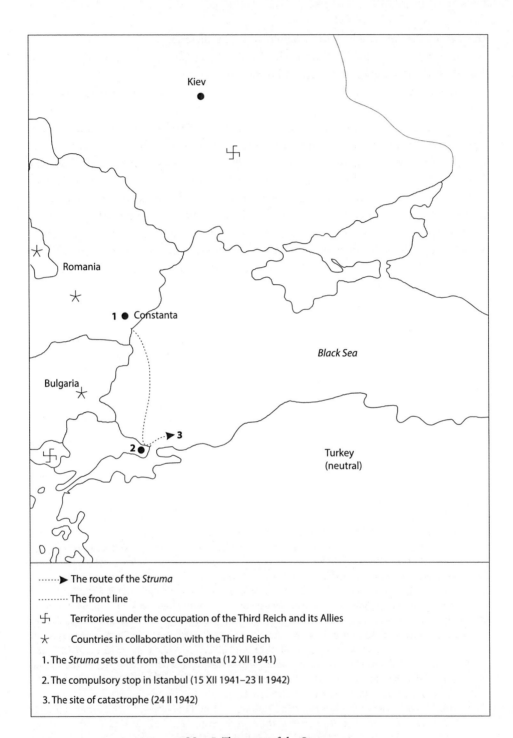

Kiev

Romania

1 ● Constanta

Black Sea

Bulgaria

2 ● ▶ 3

Turkey
(neutral)

······▶ The route of the *Struma*

·········· The front line

卐     Territories under the occupation of the Third Reich and its Allies

✲     Countries in collaboration with the Third Reich

1. The *Struma* sets out from the Constanta (12 XII 1941)

2. The compulsory stop in Istanbul (15 XII 1941–23 II 1942)

3. The site of catastrophe (24 II 1942)

**Map 5. The route of the *Struma***

Author's study. See also D. Frantz, C. Collins, op.cit., p. IV

*obtained for me I left Turkey, came to Palestine.*[49] The British allowed him into Palestine at the end of April 1942 "on humanitarian grounds."[50]

Possibly more could have been saved if help had arrived earlier. Stoliar claimed that for some time after the catastrophe he kept seeing people alive, holding onto pieces of the deck, coming up to the surface of the sea. One of them was a member of the crew, first mate Lazar Dikof (a Bulgarian). He and Stoliar, hanging onto a piece of wood, lasted many hours in the cold water. Dikof, however, lost his battle for survival.[51]

The causes of the catastrophe – which made the front pages of the newspapers[52] – aroused speculation and conjecture. It was suggested that the boat had been hit by a German torpedo, or that it could have run into a mine. It was deemed conceivable that the vessel was sunk by the passengers themselves, destitute and devoid of hope. This suggestion was taken up by the widely read "Manchester Guardian," otherwise sympathetic towards Jews, in an article signed by the "diplomatic correspondent" in London. *Whether the Struma struck a mine or whether the exiles themselves took desperate measures to forestall the consequences of their arrival at a Rumanian port will probably never be known.*[53]

During the period of the Cold War, Soviet propaganda attempted to hold one of the employees of the German embassy in Ankara of the time, Manfred Kleiber, responsible for the catastrophe. Kleiber was accused of having given the German navy the order to sink the *Struma.* These speculations were deliberately promulgated when Kleiber became a high-ranking government official in the Federal Republic of Germany, and their aim was to discredit the West German government.[54]

---

[49] TNA. CO 733/446/10 (pp. 26–27). *Statement of David Ben Yakov Stolar, Taken Down at 10.00 am this 3rd day of May 1942 at the offices of C.I.D., Jaffa* (photocopy at: YVA. O11/66. *Struma*). For a fragment of Stoliar's account see: S. Rubinstein, *Personal Tragedies*, pp. 32–34; M. Stoian, op.cit., pp. 166–171; M. Arsene, op.cit., pp. 367–372; A. Patek, "Wokół zatonięcia statku 'Struma,'" pp. 85–86 and also in the work of Simion Săveanu, *Save the Honour of Civilization!*, Tel Aviv 1996, pp. 24–27.

[50] Following arrival in Palestine Stoliar joined the British Army and served in North Africa (Egypt, Libya). In 1948 as a soldier of the Israel Defense Forces (Cahal) he took part in the war for Israeli independence. Later he settled in the USA. His profile is sketched by Nicholas Bethell in "The man who survived the Struma," *Sunday Times Magazine* (London), 9 III 1980, pp. 52–57 (the article is also in the collections of YVA. O11/66).

[51] D. Frantz, C. Collins, op.cit., pp. 195–197.

[52] "709 Refugees Lost in Struma. Ship Sinks in Black Sea," *The Palestine Post*, 27 II 1942, p. 1 (here is a mistaken report that speaks of 60 saved); "Jewish Refugee Tragedy. Disastrous Tragedy. Palestine Entry Barred," *Manchester Guardian*, 26 II 1942; "Loss of Refugee Ship in Black Sea. 760 Jews Drowned," *The Times*, 27 II 1942; "A Ship in the Black Sea Transporting 700 Victims Sailed into a Mine Field for Lack of Navigation Facilities," *The New York Times*, 28 II 1942; "The Struma Tragedy," *The New York Times*, 13 III 1942.

[53] "Jewish Refugee Tragedy. Disastrous Tragedy. Palestine Entry Barred," *Manchester Guardian*, 26 II 1942 (this cutting is also available in the TNA. FO 371/32661/W 2810).

[54] E. Ofir, op.cit., p. 173.

Another hypothesis, which Stoliar himself supported, posited that the *Struma* had been sunk by the Turks themselves. What would their aim have been? If the government in Ankara desired to maintain neutrality, helping Jewish refugees heading for Palestine was out of the question. It therefore followed to dissuade Jews from a transit route through Turkey. The sinking of a transport with hundreds of stranded immigrants would perfectly fulfill this goal. According to Stoliar, two factors point to a Turkish plot: (1) the directing of the *Struma* onto the Black Sea without a reliable engine and (2) the twenty-four hour delay in coming to the castaways' rescue.[55] In the absence of hard evidence it is difficult to consider this anything more than a hypothesis.

In the 1960s in the Federal Republic of Germany an attempt was made to solve the mystery. As a result of compensation suits against Germany being filed by relatives of the victims, a German court commissioned a historian, Jürgen Rohwer, to conduct an academic investigation into the matter and to determine the actual culprit in the sinking of the *Struma* (as well as another *Aliyah Bet* ship, the *Mefkura*, in August 1944). The fruit of this research was a detailed work, published in 1965, in which the author convincingly proves that the *Struma* could not have been torpedoed by a German submarine as there were no submarines operational in the area of the Bosphorus. As the likely perpetrator, he pointed to a Soviet submarine SC 213, which was actually active in that part of the Black Sea at the time.[56]

Considering the circumstances in which Rohwer undertook his research, the conclusions of the German historian may raise doubts. Confirmation came from the least expected quarter. In 1978 a book by Gennady I. Vaneev on the participation of the Black Sea Soviet fleet in the "Great Patriotic War" appeared in Moscow, published by the Ministry of Defense of the Soviet Union. The work was based on previously unpublished documents from Soviet military archives wherein we read that *on the morning of the 24th of February 1942 the submarine SC 213 under the command of lieutenant D.M. Deniezhko[57] and Political Commissar A.G. Rodimatsav localized the enemy transporter Struma, displacement 7 tons unarmed. A torpedo was fired which after covering 1111.18 metres hit the target and sank the ship.*[58] What seizes the reader's attention is the lack of reference to the passengers, the Jewish refugees.

---

[55]  N. Bethell, "The man who survived the Struma," p. 57.

[56]  J. Rohwer, *Die Versenkung der jüdischen Flüchtlingstransporter Struma und Mefkure im Schwarzen Meer (February 1942, August 1944)*, Frankfurt/Main 1965, pp. 71–72, 81–87. An unpublished version of this work (148 page typescript), with the subtitle *Gutachten bearbeitet im Auftrag des Oberstaatsanwaltes bei dem Landgericht Frankfurt/Main von Dr. Jürgen Rohver (1964)* is available at YVA. O11/71. *Gutachten von Dr. J. Rohwer*.

[57]  Dmitri M. Deniezhko was the commander of the Black Sea Soviet fleet from July 1939 to 23th of March 1942 (to his death during the German air-raid). E.A. Kovalev, *Koroli podplava v more chervonnykh valetov. Khronika nachal'nogo perioda sovetskogo podvodnogo plavaniia, 1918–1941 gg*, Moskva–St. Peterburg 2006, p. 265.

[58]  G.I. Vaneev, *Chernomortsy v velikoy otechestvennoy voyne*, Moskva 1978, p. 299. E. Ofir includes a reproduction of this page, op.cit., p. 174.

What were the USSR's motives for acting thus? Does the concept of a mistake come into play? Could the captain of the SC 213 have taken the transporter for an enemy vessel? Such a scenario is championed by, among others, Dalia Ofer and Jürgen Rohwer. In turn, Douglas Frantz and Catherine Collins suggest that the USSR acted under a secret directive of Stalin's to destroy ships heading towards the Black Sea shores of German satellites as they could be transporting materials of strategic significance. This would explain why at more or less the same time and in a nearby place a Turkish fishing boat, the *Çankaya*, also sank.[59] Did Moscow know about the *Struma*? Considering the active Soviet diplomacy on the Bosphorus it seems difficult to accept that it would have escaped their attention.[60]

Regardless of the direct causes of the sinking of the *Struma*, the ordeal of its passengers exposed the heartlessness and hypocrisy of many governments, for the matter of the extermination of the Jews in Nazi-occupied Europe was already known.[61] It also showed, on the one hand, the lack of imagination amongst those who decided to send off the *Struma*, and on the other hand, their and the passengers' determination to play for the highest stakes.

The tragedy of the *Struma* aroused immense unrest in Jewish circles.[62] Many asked why the refugees had not been allowed into the Mandate when the immigration quotas imposed were a long way from being exhausted. A one-day general strike was called in Yishuv, while the Jewish Agency and Vaad Leumi proclaimed a state of mourning.[63] The dismissal of the High Commissioner for Palestine, Sir Harold MacMichael, seen as the main person responsible for the tragedy, was called for. Warrants for MacMichael's arrest put out by the Jewish underground appeared on the streets of Palestinian towns. A likeness of the High Commissioner was accompanied by the inscription in Hebrew and English: *Wanted for Murder*.[64] The ex-

---

[59]  Cf. also D. Frantz, C. Collins, op.cit., pp. 253–254; A. Zvielli, "Soviet fire, cold hearts claimed 'Struma' passengers," *The Jerusalem Post*, 18 VIII 2000, p. 13; I.C. Butnaru, *The Silent Holocaust. Romania and its Jews.* Foreword by E. Wiesel, New York–London 1992, p. 143; T. Carmely, *The Real Story*, p. 119.

[60]  Cf. "Otchet sotrudnika politicheskogo departamenta pravleniya Yevreyskogo Agenstva dla Palestiny E. Epshteyna o besedakh s poslom SSSR v Turtsii S.A. Vinogradovym. 25 I 1942" [in:] *Sovetsko-izrailskiye otnosheniya. Sbornik dokumentov.* T. I: 1941–1953. Kniga 1: 1941–may 1949, Moskva 2000, pp. 28–38.

[61]  Cf. the telling title of Olivia Manning's article: "The Tragedy of the Struma. How the World Stood By and Watched 760 Jews Sail to their Deaths", *The Observer* (London), 1 III 1970. Also the article in a similar vein by M. Raizel, "'Struma' şi responsabilitatea internaţională," *Viata Noastra* (Tel Aviv), 2 III 1956, p. 5 (the newspaper available at YVA. O11/64).

[62]  Cf. CZA. Z 6/292. *Memorandum on the sinking of the refugee ship "Struma" and similar earlier disasters* (March 1942), p. 2; T. Carmely, *The Real Story*, pp. 85–90.

[63]  "Jewry Mourns and Protests," *The Palestine Post*, 27 II 1942, p. 1; "The White Paper and the Struma. Dr. Weizmann on Refugee Tragedy," ibidem, 9 III 1942, p. 3. CZA. Z4/30523. *The "Struma" disaster. Statement of the Executive of the Jewish Agency for Palestine, 25 II 1942.*

[64]  Poster available at TNA. CO 733/446/10. Reproduction in M. Naor, *Aliyah 2, 1934–1948: mekorot, sikumim, parashiyot nivharot vehomer 'ezer/ ha – 'orekh*, Yerushalayim 1988, p. 74; D. Frantz, C. Collins, op.cit., pp. 156/157; N. Bethell, *The Palestine Triangle*, pp. 80/81; E. Ofir, op.cit., p. 187.

treme right swore to kill both him and the Secretary of State for the Colonies, Lord Moyne, the "architects" of the struggle with *Aliyah Bet*. Moyne was indeed to die at the hands of Lehi in Cairo in 1944. Several assassination attempts were made on MacMichael, from all of which he managed to escape unharmed.[65]

Solidarity with the victims of the *Struma* was also shown by Jews from the Diaspora: in the USA, Mexico, New Zealand, Canada and Great Britain.[66] In the United States critical remarks were directed at London in many periodicals including *The New York Times*. Rallies were organized. David Ben-Gurion took part in one of these on his visit to the USA, in New York on the 13th of March 1942. The resolution submitted demanded that Great Britain implement changes in its Palestinian policy, free those interned on Mauritius and open the gates of Palestine to all Jewish refugees, and appealed to the American government to support these demands.[67] Intellectuals and politicians paid hommage to the victims. Albert Einstein, the author of the theory of relativity, claimed that the catastrophe *strikes at the heart of our civilisation*. Similarly strong words were used by the American First Lady, Eleanor Roosevelt, in speaking about the *atrocity which there are no words to describe*.[68] The wave of criticism addressed at Great Britain was so strong that it raised alarm in the British Embassy in Washington.[69]

The *Struma* affair also reached the British House of Commons, where it became the subject of a stormy debate. The Labour opposition openly criticized the Colonial Office. Emotions raged. Baron Josiah Clement Wedgwood (1872–1943), a Labour member of the House, sympathetic to Zionism and an advocate of creating a Jewish state on both banks of the Jordan, demanded the immediate dismissal of the "fascist" MacMichael.[70] Fuel to the flames was added by the firm, though somewhat undiplomatic, statement of the High Commissioner Sir Harold MacMichael. *Palestine* – he claimed – *was under no obligations toward them*, while he himself had acted in accordance with the *basic principle that enemy nationals from enemy or enemy-*

---

[65]  M.J. Cohen, "The Moyne Assassination, November 1944. A Political Analysis," *Middle Eastern Studies* (London). Vol. 15: 1979. No. 3, pp. 358–373; idem, *Palestine to Israel*, pp. 158–174; "Murder of Lord Moyne. Minister Resident Shot in Cairo," *The Palestine Post*, 7 XI 1944, p. 1.

[66]  E. Ofir, op.cit., pp. 231–238; D. Frantz, C. Collins, op.cit., pp. 220, 222.

[67]  "New York memorial meeting to "Struma" victims: demand for reorientation of British policy in Palestine," *Jewish Telegrafic Agency Bulletin*, 15 III 1942. In the TNA. FO 371/32661/W 3308 (p. 143).

[68]  Quoted after: D.S. Wyman, *Pozostawieni swemu losowi*, p. 213. Menachem Begin in his first address to the Knesset as Prime Minister (1977) emphasized the drama of the *Struma* as a *crime against humanity*. S. Săveanu, *Save the Honour of Civilization!*, Tel Aviv 1996, p. 15; N. Bethell, *The Palestine Triangle*, p. 113.

[69]  "Lord Halifax, ambassador to Washington, to the Foreign Office, 5 March 1942, reporting increased public agitation against the government's Palestine immigration policy following the sinking of the Struma in the Black Sea" [in:] *The Rise of Israel*, vol. 30, pp. 153–154.

[70]  *Parliamentary Debates* (Commons), vol. 377, 4 III 1942, col. 638; vol. 378, 11 III 1942, coll. 1048–1049; TNA. CO 733/446/11. *Palestine. Illegal Immigration. "Struma." Parliamentary Questions*; M. Solomon, op.cit., p. 172; "Struma Again Raised in Commons," *The Palestine Post*, 13 III 1942, p. 3.

*controlled territory should not be admitted to this country during war.* This principle was to be applied in equal measure to refugees.[71]

The bitter paradox was that all of these countries, politically so divided (Great Britain fighting against Hitler, Romania a German satellite, and neutral Turkey), spoke of the *Struma* in a similar voice – though conditioned by different considerations. Characteristically, the Romanian censor did not allow for more detailed press accounts, the British emphasized the cavalier thoughtlessness of the *Aliyah Bet* organizers, and Turkey attempted to lay the chief blame on Romania.[72] It is difficult to deny the impression that responsibility lay not on the waters of the Bosphorus but in the dusty corridors of Ankara, London and other capitals.

After the war, it looked as if Romania would conduct an investigation into the sinking of the *Struma*. Several people involved in preparing the transport were temporarily arrested. The lawyer for the families of the victims was Ion Gheorghe Maurer, subsequently president (1958–1961) and prime minister for many years (1961–1974) of communist Romania. However, the matter never went to court.[73]

In 2000, reports appeared that the wreck of the *Struma* had been located. Several months later a service for the victims was held on the site of the catastrophe, with the participation of their relatives, the Israeli ambassador to Turkey, and delegations from the USA and Great Britain.[74] A Canadian-British documentary film entitled *The Struma* (2001) directed by Simcha Jacobovici tells of the catastrophe and the search for the wreckage. The director was able to persuade David Stoliar to take part in the production.[75]

The drama of the *Struma* occupies an important place in the collective consciousness of the Jews. The memory of the victims is marked by, among others, monuments in Bucharest (at the Jewish cemetery) and at Holon in Israel. One of

---

[71] Quoted after: D. Frantz, C. Collins, op.cit., p. 216. Sir Harold MacMichael (1882–1969) was the High Commissioner for Palestine probably most disliked by Yishuv. He held the office from 1938 to 1944. Palestinian Jews saw in him someone morally responsible for the catastrophes of the *Patria* and *Struma*. In 1944 a Stern group organized an unsuccessful attempt on his life. Soon afterwards London transfers him to Malaya. B. Reich (ed.), *An Historical Encyclopedia of the Arab-Israeli Conflict*, London 1996, pp. 334–335. Ben-Gurion described him as *a petty, self-assured arrogant man.* [M. Pearlman], *Ben-Gurion Looks Back in talks with Moshe Pearlman*, New York 1965, p. 75.

[72] Cf. "Turkey Censures Rumania for Struma Sinking," *The Palestine Post*, 5 III 1942, p. 1; YVA. P6/20 (pp. 112–115). J. Hefter, *La fin tragique des emigrants du navire „Struma."*

[73] YVA. O11/64 (pp. 33–56). A collection of cuttings from the Romanian press (1946).

[74] D. Frantz, C. Collins, op.cit., pp. 5–10, 112–120, 258–290; D. Kemp, "Search for Jewish refugees' shipwreck," *The Independent* (London), 2 VIII 2000.

[75] The film ends with the bitter observation that *sometimes even your allies kill you.* Quoted after: I. Greenberg, "The 'Struma': Unsinking history," *The Jerusalem Post*, 14 XII 2001. Other films about the catastrophe of the vessel: *Struma* (2001, directed by Radu Gabrea, Romania), *Le Grand Akshan* (2002, directed by Ron Goldman, Israel) – both documentary. A. Patek, "Alija bet w filmie," *Kwartalnik Filmowy* (Warszawa). No. 69 (129): 2010, pp. 204–206.

the streets in Jerusalem bears the name of the ship.[76] For many Jews the sinking of the *Struma* constituted yet another proof, following MacDonald's "White Paper," of London's reluctance regarding plans for the creation of a Jewish state in Palestine. In this sense it strengthened Yishuv in its opposition to the Mandate authorities.

Conflict between the two sides was unavoidable when their positions were so difficult to reconcile. During the war the Jews required a national homeland as a place of shelter more than ever. Hence the Zionist movement in its search for an ally directed itself toward the United States, where a five-million strong Jewish community lived. This new strategy (one which had already been under development for a long time) was fixed by the *Biltmore Program*. Adopted in May 1942 at a conference initiated by Ben-Gurion, organized under the patronage of the American Zionist Emergency Council and attended by several hundred delegates from the USA, Yishuv and Europe, it went much further than the Balfour Declaration, envisaging as its goal the creation in Palestine of an independent Jewish state as well as unlimited immigration of Jews to Eretz Israel.[77] It was calculated that with the help of the USA, the leading Western power (and already for a few months an active member of the Ally coalition), it would be possible to force through a change in British Palestine policy.

This programme, rejecting the provisions of the "White Paper," and in effect setting itself the aim of forcing an end to the British Mandate, was from now on to constitute the guiding light for the activities of the Zionist movement, whose centre was now the USA. It did not yet signify confrontation with the Mandate authorities. The majority of Yishuv still saw support for Great Britain in the war against Germany and its allies as the most important issue. Local industry worked for the needs of the British Army. Many volunteers served in the UK armed forces. The key to relations between London and Yishuv were to lie, however, in the hands of the Mandate.

---

[76]   YVA. O11/64 (pp. 102, 182–190). The material concerns the unveiling of the monument in Bucharest (press cuttings, photographs, leaflets); A. Patek, "Tragedia Strumy," *Nowiny Kurier* (Tel Aviv), 6 XII 2007, p. 15.

[77]   For a full text of the programme see: [The Jewish Agency for Palestine], *Book of Documents submitted to the General Assembly of the United Nations relating to the Establishment of the National Home for the Jewish People*, New York 1947, pp. 226–227; J.C. Hurewitz, *The Middle East and North Africa in World Politics. A Documentary Record.* Vol. II, New Haven–London 1979, pp. 595–597; W. Laqueur, B. Rubin (eds.), *The Israel-Arab Reader. A Documentary History of the Middle East Conflict*, 4th ed., New York–Oxford 1985, pp. 77–79; B. Reich (ed.), *Arab-Israeli Conflict and Conciliation. A Documentary History*, London 1995, pp. 53–54. For more see: Y. Bauer, *From Diplomacy to Resistance* (Chapter 6: "Biltmore"); J.C. Hurewitz, *Struggle for Palestine*, New York 1976 (Chapter 12: "The Biltmore program"); A.R. Taylor, *Prelude to Israel. An Analysis of Zionist Diplomacy, 1897–1947*, New York 1959 (Chapter 8: "The Zionist search for American Support").

# Chapter VII: "The sole route to survival"

## 1. London's concessions

Following the sinking of the *Struma* Great Britain's immigration policy underwent a certain relaxation. In the Colonial Office the place of the principled Lord Moyne was taken by the more liberal Robert Arthur Gascoyne-Cecil, Viscount Cranborne. London still categorically opposed *Aliyah Bet* and based its policy on MacDonald's "White Paper," yet it desisted from deporting illegal immigrants, and in May of 1942 the government agreed *to admit and gradually release all refugees from Europe who got to Palestine on their own*.[1] Immigrants upon arrival were to be interned and if they did not constitute a "threat to the security of the Mandate,"[2] they could gradually be settled in Palestine, according to the immigration quotas. This procedure was applied to, among others, those passengers of the *Darien* who had been held at Atlit for eighteen months.[3] Given Great Britain's *extremely delicate position* in the Middle East, the government tried not to overly publicize these resolutions.[4]

At the beginning of July 1943 the Colonial Office lifted the ban on emigration to the Mandate by Jews from enemy-occupied countries, while those refugees who had managed to reach Turkey *under their own power* (the British never defined the meaning of the expression) could count on obtaining a Palestinian visa.[5] According to data from the Jewish Agency office in Istanbul, this visa was issued in the course of 1944 to a total of 6,869 Jews from European countries, the largest numbers

---

[1] Quote after: *The Jewish Case Before the Anglo-American Committee of Inquiry on Palestine as presented by the Jewish Agency for Palestine. Statements and Memoranda*, Jerusalem 1947, p. 296.

[2] CZA. Z 6/292. *Short note of meeting at Colonial Office, London, on Friday, May 22nd, 1942 at 12: Noon.*

[3] TNA. CO 733/446/7 (p. 5). *Telegram to Palestine to High Commissioner (Sir H. MacMichael) from Secretary of State for the Colonies. No. 554. Secret. 20 V 1942*; "Cabinet memorandum by the Colonial Secretary, 15 May 1942" [in:] *The Rise of Israel*. Vol. 30: *The Holocaust and Illegal Immigration*, pp. 155–156.

[4] As we read in the letter of Cranborne to Berl Locker from the Jewish Agency office in London (22 V 1942 r.): *in view of the extremely delicate position in the Middle East, His Majesty's are anxious that the new arrangements should have the minimum of publicity* (CZA. Z 6/292).

[5] FRUS 1943. Vol. I, p. 350: *The British Chargé (Campbell) to the Secretary of State. Washington, 9 IX 1943*; *Parliamentary Debates (Commons)*, vol. 393, 10 XI 1943, coll 1151–1154; R.W. Zweig, *Britain and Palestine During the Second World War*, Woodbridge 1986, pp. 145–146.

of whom came from Romania (4,433 persons) and Bulgaria (1,392), with smaller groups from Greece (599) and Hungary (163).[6]

It is typical that the decision to publish this information was not taken immediately, due to a fear of increasing the influx of immigrants. The House of Commons was officially informed several months later (10th of November 1943) while the Turkish authorities (the route for the majority of refugees from the Balkans ran through Turkey itself) only in January 1944.[7]

What caused the modification in London's position? The sufferings of the passengers of the *Patria*, *Salvador* and *Struma* certainly played their part, but other factors were decisive. Great Britain found itself in a far more awkward position as a result of the fact that the fourth (and penultimate) year under which the new immigration limits envisaged in the "White Paper" had passed, and a sizeable fraction of the places reserved for Jews had still not been used.[8] Worse still, the majority of European Jews had been excluded because they found themselves on territories controlled by Germany and its allies. This had led to a paradoxical situation whereby almost the entire Jewish emigration from Europe to Palestine would have to be illegal emigration. If, therefore, the low limits determined by the "White Paper" were to be realized then there was no other option than to distribute legal certificates among illegal immigrants. Pragmatism also played its role – in 1943 there was no threat of mass *Aliyah Bet* through Nazi-occupied Europe. It was also difficult to disregard the Zionist movement's new strategy (*The Biltmore Program*) and the rise in anti-British feeling within Yishuv.

## 2. With Romania and Turkey in the background

After the *Struma* catastrophe another seven *Aliyah Bet* transports were to leave Romanian ports by the end of 1942, though they only vaguely resembled the earlier efforts. These were small hookers. The largest, the *Vitorul*, which sailed out of Constanta in September 1942, had 120 refugees on board. On five others the number did not exceed 21. In total around 200–230 people were transported.[9]

The transports were prepared by the refugees themselves. A large part of the money was spent on bribes. The majority of these small boats shared the fate

---

[6]  PISM. A 11 E/87. *Report of the Intelligence Information Section of the Staff of the Commander in Chief to the Ministry of Foreign Affairs on Jewish affairs of the 25th of April 1945*, p. 1.

[7]  M.J. Cohen, *Churchill and the Jews*, London 1985, p. 275; *Parliamentary Debates (Commons)*, vol. 393, 10 XI 1943, coll. 1151–1154.

[8]  In February 1944 there still remained 27,500 certificates to be distributed. FRUS 1944. Vol. III, p. 28: *Report to the Secretary of State by Under Secretary Stettinius on His Mission to London, April 7–29, 1944 [Washington] 22 V 1944*.

[9]  D. Ofer, *Escaping the Holocaust. Illegal Immigration to the Land of Israel, 1939–1944*, New York 1990, p. 167.

of the *Struma* and the *Salvador*, and sank off the coast of Turkey. Such was the case for the *Euxenia* (March 1942) and the *Dordeval* (April 1942). Luckily the refugees were saved. The *Vitorul* was in such a disastrous state of repair that it had to stop its voyage in Istanbul. Only two transports made it to Palestine, the *Mihai* and the *Mircea*, which departed in March and April 1942. On board the two were not many more than 50 refugees. The passengers were initially interned by the British at Atlit. In time they made use of a portion of the immigration certificates and could legally settle in Palestine.[10]

The fate of those, castaways or passengers of the *Vitorul* who were unable to reach the Mandate in their boats, and for various reasons had to end their journeys in Turkey, varied. According to the line adopted by London in May 1942 they could not be sure of entry into Palestine. Turkey threatened to deport refugees to Romania and Bulgaria. The Jewish Agency attempted to intervene in their name. Finally Great Britain took the decision to temporarily intern them on Cyprus, then a British colony. The cost of transportation to the island was covered by the Jewish Agency.[11] London tried not to publicize this approach, emphasising that the "Cypriot variant" was merely an isolated incident and would not repeat itself with all immigrants who landed in Turkey in the future.[12]

In the middle of May 1943 there were 224 interned Jews on Cyprus. The British deliberated over their deportation to Mauritius, which did not come to pass, chiefly as a result of wartime transportation difficulties.[13] The Jewish Agency appealed for the refugees' release, as did American Jews.[14] These attempts at intervention were so successful that by March 1944 the last internees had left the island, gaining permission to legally settle in Palestine within the immigration quotas.[15] One way or the other, these people successfully avoided deportation, a feat of more than symbolic significance.[16]

---

[10]  Ibidem, p. 168; *Walka o prawo powrotu do Ojczyzny (maapilim)*. Ed. by Ichud Hanoar Hacijoni-Akiba, Łódź 1948, p. 36.

[11]  TNA. CO 537/1813 (f. 38). *Draft Supplementary Brief for Secretary of State. Top Secret. Illegal Immigration. XII 1946*; R.W. Zweig, op.cit., p. 134; D. Trevor, *Under the White Paper. Some Aspects of British Administration in Palestine from 1939 to 1947*, Jerusalem 1948, pp. 36–37.

[12]  CZA. Z 6/292. *Telegram from Linton, London, to Jewish Agency for Palestine, 26 V 1942*; ibidem, *Short note of meeting at Colonial Office, London, on Friday, May 22nd, 1942 at 12: Noon*.

[13]  TNA. CO 733/466/12 (f. 10). *Telegram from FO to Angora. No. 247. 16 II 1943*; ibidem, f. 24. *Telegram to Mauritius (Sir D. Mackenzie Kennedy) from S. of S. Secret. No. 368. 15 V 1943*.

[14]  CZA. Z 5/10819. *Memorandum from Dr. S. Bernstein to Judge Louis Levinthal, 6 I 1943*; ibidem, Dr. S. Bernstein, Director Palestine Bureau, to Mr S.A. Sternklar, Bronx, New York, 13 I 1943.

[15]  TNA. CO 733/466/12 (f. 50). *Draft R.L.M. James, Esq, Treasury Chambers. 10 III 1944*; TNA. CO 537/1813 (f. 38). *Draft Supplementary Brief for Secretary of State. XII 1946*.

[16]  Cyprus was also to figure in the post-war history of *ha'apala*. For the years 1946–1949 the British interned here in total over 51,500 *ma'apilim*. TNA.CO 67/364/4. Report upon the administration of the Cyprus Camps for illegal Jewish immigrants by Roland E. Turnbull, Acting Governor, 24 III 1949, pp. 2–3 (51,594 *ma'apilim* + 1,916 children who were born there). For more see: D. Schaary, *Gerush Kafrisin, 1946–1949 (The Cyprus Detention Camps*

From the point of view of *Aliyah Bet*, Romania was to play a special role during the final period of the Second World War. The only real route for Jews escaping Europe was through Romanian territory. The situation of the Jewish population in the country had dramatically deteriorated after the outbreak of war, and the Romanian dictator Ion Antonescu was a loyal ally of Hitler, yet Romania still had to some degree a free hand in its treatment of its Jewish citizens. Despite Nazi pressure, there was no mass annihilation of Romanian Jews. *Ironically Romania, which had refused the emancipation of its Jewish subjects prior to the First World War and which during the interwar period had enacted anti-Semitic policies, witness to the growth of the strongest form of indigenous fascist movement in the whole of Eastern Europe, turned out to be safer for Jews than* [occupied] *Hungary, Poland, Czechoslovakia and the Baltic states.*[17]

That said, on the eve of 1941 the campaign against Jewish citizens noticeably intensified. Gradually racist laws were introduced and the fascist Iron Guard carried out a series of attacks on Jews. In these circumstances Mossad's emissaries, threatened with arrest, had to suspend their activities in Romania (Ruth Klueger managed to leave the country literally at the very last moment). Romania's policy toward the Jews started to improve after the defeat of the Third Reich at Stalingrad. The view that it was better not to burn bridges on the road to an understanding with the Western Allies started to gain the upper hand. For *Aliyah Bet* this constituted a green light. Between March and December 1944 eleven boats departed from the Romanian port of Constanta, on board which there were, according to various estimates, around 4700–4900 refugees.[18]

All sailed for Istanbul where the passengers would transfer to trains and reach Palestine through Turkey. The operation was coordinated by Mossad emissaries from their post on the Bosphorus. As mentioned earlier, in the summer of 1943 the British had eased their policy in relation to *ha'apala* and those immigrants who

---

for Jewish "Illegal" Immigrants to Palestine 1946–1949), Yerushalayim 1981 (in Hebrew, in the appendix are several documents in English); idem, "The Social Structure of the Cyprus Detention Camps: 1946–1949," *Studies in Zionism* (Tel Aviv). No. 6: Autumn 1982, pp. 273–290; N. Bogner, *Iy ha-gerush: mahanot ha-ma'apilim be-Kafrisin 1946–1948*, Tel Aviv 1991 (*Deportation Island: The Camps of the Illegal Immigrants in Cyprus 1946–1948*, in Hebrew); M. Laub, *Last Barrier to Freedom. Internment of Jewish Holocaust Survivors on Cyprus, 1946–1949*, Berkeley, Cal. 1985 (Morris Laub was the head of the permanent Joint mission on Cyprus); D. Ofer, "Holocaust Survivors as Immigrants. The Case of the Cyprus Detainees," *Modern Judaism* (Baltimore). Vol. 16: 1996. No. 1, pp. 1–23. In Polish see: A. Patek, „Brytyjskie obozy na Cyprze dla deportowanych imigrantów żydowskich (1946–1949)," *Portolana. Studia Mediterranea* (Kraków). Edited by D. Quirini-Popławska. Vol. 1: 2004, pp. 233–245; I.E. Thomas, „Brytyjskie obozy pracy na Cyprze dla nielegalnych żydowskich imigrantów," *Midrasz* (Warszawa). No. 12: 2009, pp. 21–29.

[17] Quoted after: E. Mendelsohn, *Żydzi Europy Środkowo-Wschodniej w okresie międzywojennym*, Warszawa 1992, p. 288.

[18] According to D. Ofer (*Escaping the Holocaust*, pp. 326–327) – 4728 persons, according to P.H. Silverstone – 4924 (*Aliyah Bet Project, List 1: 1934–1945*, pp. 9–10).

managed to reach Turkey could count on being allowed into the Mandate.[19] This situation opened up new possibilities for Mossad.

Discussions about the role and nature of illegal immigration had already been going on for a long time, as is borne out by the "Draft of a plan for *Aliyah Bet*" developed in August 1943. Its author was probably Eliyahu Golomb. The project contained a plan of action for after the war. It presupposed the arrival of 150,000–200,000 Jews from the Diaspora, appropriately prepared *nationally, morally, ideologically and militarily*.[20] These people were to be smuggled in by sea in close consultation with Hagana, responsible for the preparing of crafts, the training of crews and the sending of emissaries to Europe. The emissaries' tasks included the training of immigrants, as well as the technical side of operations. They foresaw the establishment of contacts in European countries at various levels, with representatives of central and local administration, the police etc. The plan was a crucial point of reference for Hagana after 1945.

Turkey, geographically close to both the Balkans and Palestine, naturally had a significant role to play in the plans of *Aliyah Bet*, constituting as it did a bridge between occupied Europe and the Middle East. The country's neutral status gave it manifold possibilities. The diplomatic posts of opposite camps were active here, and the diplomats, spies and businessmen of many nationalities and political affiliations would mingle and meet. The Jewish Agency, as well as JOINT, the Revisionists, Histadrut and others had their emissaries here. Despite objective difficulties, they were active on many fronts. They maintained contacts with Jewish circles in Europe (the West, the Balkans, the Reich, the Polish lands, Hungary, Slovakia). They acted as intermediaries in the transfer of cash, medicines, and foodstuffs. They smuggled false passports and visas and helped to organize legal and illegal immigration to Palestine: Ze'ev Shind and Moshe Averbuch (Agami) were responsible for the latter.[21] The young emissaries Venia Pomerantz and Theodor (Teddy) Kollek, later the long-serving mayor of Jerusalem,[22] cooperated with them.

---

[19] FRUS 1944. Vol. III, p. 28: *Report to the Secretary of State by Under Secretary Stettinius on His Mission to London…*

[20] D. Ofer, "Illegal Immigration During the Second World War: Its Suspension and Subsequent Resumption," *Studies in Contemporary Jewry* (New York–Oxford). Ed. by J. Frankel. Vol. VII: 1991, pp. 242–243.

[21] D. Ofer, "The Activities of the Jewish Agency Delegation in Istanbul" [in:] Y. Gutman, E. Zuroff (eds.), *Rescue Attempts during the Holocaust. Proceedings of the Second Yad Vashem International Historical Conference, Jerusalem. April 8–11, 1974*, Jerusalem 1977, pp. 435–450; D. Porat, "Istanbul Emissaries" [in:] W. Laqueur (ed.), *The Holocaust Encyclopedia*, New Haven–London 2001, pp. 326–329; S.J. Shaw, *Turkey and the Holocaust. Turkey's Role in Rescuing Turkish and European Jewry from Nazi Persecution, 1933–1945*, New York 1993, pp. 268–269.

[22] Kollek presents this part of his biography in the memoirs *For Jerusalem. A Life by Teddy Kollek with his son, Amos Kollek*, London 1978, pp. 37–53 (the chapter "Interlude in Istanbul"). After the war Kollek was, among other things, the head of Prime Minister D. Ben-Gurion's chancellery, and then for 28 years (1965–1993) the mayor of Jerusalem. Pomerantz dedicated himself to nuclear physics and would be one of the founders of the Ben-Gurion University of the Negev at Beer Sheva. He

The Istanbul post of Mossad managed to smuggle several hundred (up to a thousand) Greek Jews. The operation was organized in cooperation with Greek partisans and the Greek resistance. The refugees were taken on fishing boats, each carrying no more than a few or a dozen or so people. In return the partisans were given food, clothing and medications. The route was across the Aegean archipelago to the western coast of Turkey in the region of Izmir. There the refugees were looked after by the local Jewish community. Meanwhile emissaries from Yishuv attempted to arrange Palestinian visas for the refugees in Istanbul, thanks to which the majority of them found themselves legally in Palestine before the end of 1944.[23]

Here in Istanbul the War Refugee Board, an American government agency called into being on the 22nd of January 1944 by President Franklin Delano Roosevelt, also had its mission. Its aim was to help victims of the Second World War, chiefly Jews from the occupied part of Europe and countries cooperating with Germany. The Istanbul office was headed by Ira Arthur Hirschmann, a New York businessman.[24] He remained in close contact with the United States ambassador to Turkey, Laurence A. Steinhardt. Both were in contact with Mossad emissaries and provided them with support. The War Refugee Board provided financial help and organized supplies of foodstuffs and medicines, as well as the transportation of refugees. Hirschmann acted as an intermediary in obtaining Turkish transit visas, negotiated with the British embassy, and kept in contact with both diplomats accredited on the Bosphorus and the agents of secret services.[25]

The activity of the Board and Hirschmann enabled around seven thousand Jews, chiefly Bulgarian and Romanian, to reach Palestine. This figure could have been larger if it had not been for the unwillingness of the Turks to plan and create a "salvation route" across their country.[26] Turkey did not trust the British and wanted as-

---

published under the name of Ze'ev Venia Hadari the book *Second Exodus. The Full Story of Jewish Illegal Immigration to Palestine, 1945–1948*, London 1991 (with a foreword by T. Kollek).

[23] H. Ziffer, *Rescuing Greek Jews under German occupation* (http://www.sefarad.org/publication/lm/050/html/page20.html). The author, born in Vienna, lived from 1933 in Izmir. During the war he cooperated with representatives of the Jewish Agency. According to him, between December 1943 and August 1944 a total of over 1000 Jews were successfully smuggled out of Greece, of which 859 found sanctuary in Palestine.

[24] The War Refugee Board had its missions also in Lisbon, Geneva and Stockholm. D.S. Wyman, *Pozostawieni swemu losowi. Ameryka wobec Holocaustu 1941-1945*, Warszawa 1994, Part IV: "War Refugee Board" (pp. 275–399); D. Ofer, *Escaping the Holocaust*, pp. 270–285; M.N. Penkower, *The Jews were Expendable. Free World Diplomacy and the Holocaust*, Chicago 1983, Chapter V: "The creation of the US War Refugee Board" (pp. 122–147); T. Szulc, *The Secret Alliance. The Extraordinary Story of the Rescue of the Jews Since World War II*, New York 1991, pp. 47–55 as well as Hirschmann's memoires: *Life Line to a Promised Land*, New York 1946.

[25] In the The American Jewish Joint Distribution Committee Archives in Jerusalem there is a collection of documents (the so called Istanbul Collection), on the involvement of the American embassy and its head Laurence Steinhardt in help for Jewish refugees (Box 1. File 11. Ambassador Laurence A. Steinhardt, American Embassy, Ankara 1944–1945).

[26] S.J. Shaw, op.cit., pp. 292–298.

surance that the refugees really were moving on to Palestine and would not remain on the Bosphorus.

It is worth asking the question: what did the Palestinian Jews of the time know of the cataclysm that had befallen their European brethren? News of the Holocaust obviously did reach them, but it was patchy and did not give any concept of the immensity of the tragedy. The British had no vested interest in propagating such information as this would provide Yishuv with an additional political weapon. Jewish leaders, with Ben-Gurion at the head, also maintained discretion. They approached matters with the premise that Palestinian Jews were unable to do much to help their kin in Europe anyway. The matter boiled down to *preserving all the energy needed for the future fight for a sovereign state and to avoid any feeling of helplessness which could damage this struggle.*[27] It was considered that the society there was not yet sufficiently developed *to allow itself the luxury of despair.*[28]

Meanwhile, in Romania, Mossad emissaries formed a special body called the Official Rumania Expeditini Transportoi Bucureşti Colea (ORAT), independent of Jewish circles in Romania and subordinated to the cell in Istanbul, at the end of 1943. Through its intermediacy Mossad was to cooperate with the Romanian authorities.[29]

The reality was not so simple, however. The idea of *Aliyah Bet* aroused widely divergent attitudes amongst Jewish leaders in Romania. Its protagonists concentrated themselves around Shmuel Enzer, the head of the Palestine Office in Bucharest (a branch of the Jewish Agency responsible for, among other things, the distribution of immigration certificates and the technical side of Jewish immigration to Palestine), while the opponents gravitated toward the leader of the local Zionists, Misho Benvenisti. Among the latter the memory of the *Struma* was still very much alive, together with fears that its fate could be repeated.

Another problem was the lack of unity. The Jewish population in Romania was internally divided. Controversy revolved around the figure of Jean Pandelis, who was responsible for the technical side of the undertaking and served in ORAT. For some a competent organizer with wide-ranging contacts and possibilities; for others a conman and low-lifer, morally co-responsible for the tragedy of the *Struma* (he had been a co-organizer of the transport). Pandelis was opposed by Benvenisti (in the end he and his people withdrew from the operation) and Abraham Leib Zissu, a Revisionist activist, writer and journalist.[30] The latter was to play an important

---

[27] Quoted after: E. Barbur, K. Urbański, *Właśnie Izrael*, Warszawa 2006, pp. 43.
[28] Ibidem, pp. 44–45. For more see: D. Porat, *The Blue and the Yellow Stars of David. The Zionist Leadership in Palestine and the Holocaust, 1939–1945*, Cambridge, Mass. 1990.
[29] A. Ettinger, *Blind Jump. The Story of Shaike Dan*, New York–London–Toronto 1992, pp. 96–121.
[30] For more see: D. Ofer, *Escaping the Holocaust*, pp. 253–259; E. Ofir, *With No Way Out. The Story of the Struma. Documents and Testimonies*, Cluj-Napoca 2003, pp. 285–291.

role in obtaining the Romanian authorities' approval for *Aliyah Bet* but as a radical nationalist was unable to gain the trust of the Mossad emissaries.[31]

Difficulties mounted. In January 1944, as a result of German intrigue, Romanian Zionist activists, including Enzer and Benvenisti, were arrested. They were accused, among other things, of helping refugees to illegally cross the border and of cooperating with enemy centers abroad. The Germans in turn commandeered the Bulgarian ship *Marica*, on which Mossad had planned to transport immigrants to Istanbul. The ship's arrest was only lifted a few weeks later on Bucharest's insistence.

These and other problems meant that the first transport of *Aliyah Bet* – via the Bulgarian vessel *Milka* (chartered for a huge fee) – set off on the 23rd of March 1944. Over subsequent weeks, until the middle of May, another four plied a course for Istanbul. They were followed by the *Marica* (4th of April 1944), the *Bela-Christa* (21st of April, as the only one to sail under the protection of the International Committee of the Red Cross), again *Milka* (27th of April) and once again *Marica* (15th of May). In total they transported, according to various sources, around 1400–1600 Jews.[32] It was a miracle that these small craft, overloaded and sailing without appropriate safety standards, managed to reach their destination without any problems. The next step was taken by the Mossad office in Istanbul. With the help of the United States Embassy and the War Refugee Board the refugees were, after a time, placed on trains to Palestine. This did not pass, however, without complications. The Turkish authorities did not allow the first group of refugees to come ashore, maintaining that giving such permission would result in a whole wave of refugees, amongst whom would also be spies. The resolute intervention of ambassador Steinhardt helped in the matter, but it was clear that one could forget about mass transports of refugees.[33] Subsequent transports were planned, but in May 1944 the Germans confiscated almost the entire Mossad flotilla moored at Varna. Only the *Marica* was saved, as at this time it was in Istanbul.

Mossad agents were able to secure a few Turkish vessels. The first of these, the *Kazbek,* with over 700 refugees, set off at the beginning of July 1944. A month later, on the 3rd of August, sailed the *Bulbul, Morina* and *Mefkura.* Amongst the 1,000 or more passengers were around 300 Jewish orphans from Transnistria (a region between the Dniestr and the Boh occupied by Romania during the war).[34]

---

[31] YVA. P6/24 (pp. 46–47). A letter of I.A. Hirschmann to Wilhelm Filderman, the head of Uniunea Evreilor Romăni (The Union of Romanian Jews), 5 IX 1944.

[32] I.A. Hirschmann, *Life Line to a Promised Land*, New York 1946, pp. 82–87; E. Avriel, *Open the Gates! A Personal Story of "Illegal" Immigration to Israel*. Preface by G. Meir, New York 1975, pp. 140–145; I.C. Butnaru, *Waiting for Jerusalem. Surviving the Holocaust in Romania*, Westport, Conn.–London 1993, pp. 174–175; M.N. Penkower, op.cit., pp. 166–167.

[33] D.S. Wyman, op.cit., p. 287. For more on the activities of Steinhardt see: B. Rubin, "Ambassador Laurence A. Steinhardt. The Perils of a Jewish Diplomat," *American Jewish History* (New York). Vol. 70: 1981, pp. 332–344.

[34] Cf. E. Avriel, op.cit., pp. 169–170; B. Habas, *The Gate Breakers*, New York–London 1963, pp. 303–306; J. Rohwer, *Die Versenkung der jüdischen Flüchtlingstransporter Struma und Mefkure im*

Table 15. The largest *Aliyah Bet* sea transports during the war

| Name of ship | Number of immigrants | Date | Organizer |
|---|---|---|---|
| *Sakarya* | 2175–2400 | II 1940 | Revisionists |
| *Atlantic* | 1771–1880 | X–XI 1940 | Storfer |
| *Pacific* | 1000–1100 | X–XI 1940 | Storfer |
| *Taurus* | 958 | XII 1944 | Mossad |
| *Darien II* | 789–800 | II–III 1941 | Mossad |
| *Struma* | 769–801 | XII 1941–II 1942 | Revisionists |
| *Kazbek* | 725–735 | VII 1944 | Mossad |
| *Hilda* | 728–729 | XII 1939–I 1940 | Mossad |
| *Milos* | 702–709 | X–XI 1940 | Storfer |

Developed on the basis of the works of M. Naor, D. Ofer and P.H. Silverstone.

# 3. The sinking of the *Mefkura*

Turkey, previously formally neutral, yet in fact engaged in an alliance with both fighting blocs and precariously balancing itself between them, undertook, on the 2nd of August, the decision to break off diplomatic relations with the Third Reich. It had not yet declared war on Germany (it was to do so only on the 23rd of February 1945), but it had in fact gone over to the Allied side. The Turkish flag on *Aliyah Bet* transports could now constitute an additional danger. And who could guarantee that the Germans would not attack a flotilla heading for a country that had just broken off diplomatic relations? Hence the dilemma – to sail or to wait for the further development of the situation? All the more so as Berlin was putting pressure on the Romanian authorities to stop the boats.

It was decided not to delay. All three vessels – the *Bulbul*, *Morina* and *Mefkura* – left the port at Constanța the same evening (3rd of August), one shortly after the other. The *Mefkura* sailed out last, slower and more decrepit than the others. An hour after she weighed anchor, her engine failed and needed repair.[35] More problems

---

*Schwarzen Meer (Februar 1942, August 1944)*, Frankfurt/Main 1965, pp. 46–56; M. Stoian, *Ultima cursă de la Struma la Mefküre*, Bucureşti 1995, pp. 278, 281–283; *Referat Priveste: Plecarea vaselor „Bulbul," „Morino" şi „Mefkurie,"* Bucureşti, 5 VIII 1944 (YVA. O11/69, p.1c).

[35] YVA. O11/69 (pp. 33–34). *Report on the sinking of the M/V "Merkure"* [sic!]. Istanbul, 9.9.1944, pp. 1–2. Text of the report published in A. Patek, *Żydzi w drodze do Palestyny 1934–1944. Szkice z dziejów aliji bet, nielegalnej imigracji żydowskiej*, Kraków 2009, pp. 345–350. Photocopy in:

appeared in the night. First the *Bulbul* was stopped by a German navy patrol, but moved on after documents were checked. The worst was to come after midnight. When the *Mefkura* left Bulgarian territorial waters and found itself on the same longitude as Ahtopol – Igneada, 7 to 15 miles from shore, it was hit by a torpedo and started to sink. The majority of passengers, sound asleep, died instantly. The others jumped overboard in panic without lifejackets. The captain and four members of the crew managed to evacuate to safety in the only lifeboat. At the same time the sinking wreck was fired upon. Only five of the 320–350 refugees survived the catastrophe.[36] The castaways were saved by the passengers of the *Bulbul*.[37] A third of the victims were children. The sinking of the *Mefkura* was reported by the press in many countries, although the fact of war meant that the reports were not precise and appeared with some delay.[38]

Who attacked the *Mefkura* and why? To this day there is no clear-cut answer.[39] The final report of the special commission called to discover the causes of the capsize admitted its failure to do so. The commission was convoked by the Jews, who delegated the head of the Institute of B Immigration Shaul Meirov to take part in it as a member of the Palestine Rescue Committee in Istanbul, along with Chaim Barlas of the Istanbul mission of the Jewish Agency and Reuben B. Resnik on be-

---

A. Finkelstein, *The Mefkure Tragedy (An inquiry into the slayers' identity)*, Paris [1989] (unpublished, NLI, S2=89 B 2684 as well as at YVA O11/69).

[36] In the relevant literature one may find various data on the number of passengers: 295 (D.S. Wyman, op.cit., p. 286), 300 (W. Benz, "Illegale Einwanderung nach Palästina" [in:] *Exilforschung. Ein Internationales Jahrbuch* (München). Band 19: 2001, p. 132), 306 (I.A. Hirschmann, op.cit., pp. 93–96; M. Wischnitzer, *To Dwell in Safety. The Story of Jewish Migration Since 1800*, Philadelphia 1948, p. 256; according to the latter 6 passengers were to have emerged with their lives), 350 (P.H. Silverstone, *Aliyah Bet Project*, p. 10; A. Ozer, "The Strumah Tragedy," *ROM-SIG News. The Journal of the Special Interest Group for Romanian Jewish Genealogy* (Greenwich, Conn.). Vol. 5: Spring 1997. No. 3, p. 7), 379 (*The Holocaust Encyclopedia*, p. 325), 390 (J. and D. Kimche, *The Secret Roads. The "Illegal" Migration of a People, 1938–1948*, London 1954, p. 69); 394 (M. Naor, *Haapala. Clandestine Immigration 1931–1948*, [Tel Aviv 1987], p. 39, as "Mafkura"); 430 (H. Barlas, *Immigration to Palestine and Israel* [in:] *Encyclopedia of Zionism and Israel*. Vol. 1. Ed. by R. Patai, New York 1971, p. 537). It is characteristic that Dalia Ofer in her otherwise meticulous monograph writes three times about the number of passengers and each time gives a different figure: 320, 350 and 379 (cf. pp. 196, 264 and 327).

[37] YVA. O11/69 (pp. 34–35). *Report on the sinking of the M/V "Merkure,"* pp. 2–3.

[38] Cf. for example: J.M. Levy, "Refugee Boats Attacked," *The New York Times*, 17 VIII 1944, p. 9; "U-Boat Sank Refugee Ship," *The Palestine Post*, 20 VIII 1944, p. 1 (the name of the ship in the form *Mafrouka*); "246 żydowskich uchodźców utonęło w Morzu Czarnym," *Dziennik Polski i Dziennik Żołnierza* (London), 8 VIII 1944, p. 4 (here information that 4 refugees were saved).

[39] On the catastrophe of the *Mefkura* see: A. Finkelstein, op.cit.; M. Resel, *Tik Mefkura*, Tel Aviv 1981; M. Stoian, op.cit., pp. 281–345; T.P. Maga, "Operation Rescue: The Mefkure Incident and War Refugee Board," *American Neptune. A Quarterly Journal of Maritime History and Arts* (Salem, Mass.). Vol. 43: 1983. No. 1, pp. 31–39; M. Schrager-Costin, "Am fost pe 'Mefkure' – zguduitoarea spovedanie a unei supraviețuitoare," *Facla* (Tel Aviv), 8 VIII 1979, pp. 3, 13; A. Patek, "Dramat 'Mefkury' (1944 r.)," *Nowiny Kurier* (Tel Aviv), 7 V 2008, pp. 12–13.

half of JOINT. It was supposed that two, or possibly three, submarines operating on the surface had taken part in the attack on the *Mefkura*. It was also claimed that immediately before the attack the enemy had fired a warning flare.[40] On many points, however, the statements of the captain and the passengers were contradictory. Had the captain correctly reacted to the warning or ignored it? Were the attackers submarines as the captain claimed or gunboats similar to those used by the Germans at the port of Constanta?[41] And why was only the *Mefkura* sunk when there were two other boats with Jews in the vicinity? These questions have remained unanswered.

It was generally assumed that the Germans were to blame. It appeared so from the accounts of the castaways. Some claimed that the sound of German voices came from the direction of the attacking vessels. Others added that before the *Mefkura* sailed it had been photographed by Germans in the port at Constanta.[42] It was speculated that the fact that the *Mefkura* alone was torpedoed was no mere coincidence for it had been secretly smuggling Polish officers of the Home Army (the most important structure of the Polish Underground Government, existing from 1942–1945) as well as Yugoslav partisans. This thesis is based on copies of an unsigned report of the intelligence section of German naval command dated the 8th of August 1944, and in the possession of the Yad Vashem Archives in Jerusalem. Here we can read that *the Jews are continuing to send Polish and Serbo-Croatian partisans for the Allied forces in the Near East through their emigration offices, placing them on boats used for transporting emigrants.*[43] As the report shows, this information was given to the Germans by Romanian counter-intelligence. There were five Poles, including two majors and a captain, on board the *Mefkura*.[44] *We allowed the ships to depart* – we read further – *in order not to draw the suspects' attention.* The report ends with the claim that none of the passengers made it to their destination.

This line of thought remains, for the moment, an interesting hypothesis (Dalia Ofer presents such a position). We know from other sources that following September 1939 a significant wave of Polish war refugees fled to Romania including many soldiers. This was the route fugitives took to the Polish army in the West, a fact which Romanian intelligence must have known. The historian Ion C. Butnaru, working in the USA, is an adherent of this putative course of events; he claims that *the presence of the Poles on the deck of the "Mefkure" signed the death sentence for all*

---

[40] YVA. O11/69 (pp. 35–36). *Report on the sinking of the M/V "Merkure,"* pp. 3–4.

[41] The captain of the vessel was Kazim Turan. His account is at YVA. O11/69 (pp. 23–25).

[42] YVA. O11/69 (p. 35). *Report on the sinking of the M/V „Merkure,"* p. 3.

[43] YVA. O11/69 (p. 6). A copy of this document was to have been given to the Jewish side by one of the employees of the Turkish embassy in Bucharest (cf. YVA. O11/69, pp. 1–2). Fragments of the report have been included in English translation by D. Ofer (*Escaping the Holocaust*, p. 197), I.C. Butnaru (*Waiting for Jerusalem*, pp. 187–188) and A. Finkelstein (doc. 1, full text). The versions in translation differ from each other.

[44] The report gives the surnames in a version which is less or more distorted: Vladimir Bielicki, Sladec Szimanowski, Petre Croning, Tadek Baer and Vladek Ostrowski.

*the emigrants.*[45] This is a most unfortunate generalization. (As an aside – would it not have been easier to simply detain these people in port, under any pretext whatsoever, given that their identities were known?).

Attempts to answer the question as to who sank the *Mefkura* have been undertaken many times since the war. According to the findings of the German researcher Jürgen Rohwer, the boat was sunk by a Soviet submarine, presumably unintentionally mistaking *Mefkura* for a German transporter ship.[46] Rohwer has proven that at the time no German submarines were operating in this region, for Berlin had withdrawn them some time earlier, not wishing to envenom relations with Ankara after the *Kriegsmarine* had mistakenly torpedoed Turkish boats. He considered the accounts of the castaways to be more than likely subjective projections: as Germans were natural enemies for such people. Rohwer considers the Soviet vessel SC 215 to be a possible perpetrator, a version of events that also seems to find confirmation in the work of the Soviet historian Vladimir I. Dmitrev, published almost at the same time in Moscow by the publishing house of the Soviet Ministry of Defense.[47] This author wrote that on the night of the 5th of August the Soviet submarine SC 215 on the same longitude as Burgas *destroyed with artillery fire a large schooner, on board which were 200 armed people, and a barge.*[48]

Burgas is a port on the southern part of the Bulgarian coast, a few dozen kilometres from the border with Turkey. This roughly corresponds to the area of the catastrophe determined by the commission of three. But the passengers of the *Mefkura* were not armed. This in itself does not disqualify this account but raises the need for further questions. Butnaru suggests that the Soviets may have torpedoed a German transport ship evacuating the remains of the Wehrmacht troops from the Crimea, which had been taken by the Red Army.[49] Albert Finkelstein, the author of the cited source monograph about the *Mefkura* catastrophe, was convinced that the Germans deliberately attacked the ship. He devoted many years to collecting documents on the matter and meeting with eyewitnesses to the events in question. Finkelstein was particularly interested in solving the mystery of the sinking of the *Mefkura* as one of the victims had been his sister, Sophie.[50]

The *Bulbul* and the *Morina* both reached Turkey, but only the latter managed to reach the port of Istanbul directly. The *Bulbul* had to return because of a storm. Though the ship was only a short distance from the Bosphorus, it was decided not to take the risk. The ship dropped anchor at the small Turkish port of Igneada, five

---

[45] We should remember that the report also talks of Yugoslavian partisans. I.C. Butnaru, *Waiting for Jerusalem*, pp. 188–189.

[46] J. Rohwer, op.cit., pp. 72–74, 92–95.

[47] V.I. Dmitrev, *Atakuyut podvodniki*, Moskva 1964.

[48] Ibidem, p. 327. This page is reproduced by A. Finkelstein in his work, op.cit., doc. 13.

[49] I.C. Butnaru, *Waiting for Jerusalem*, p. 190.

[50] A. Finkelstein, op.cit., p. 5. We can also read about the Germans being at fault in the booklet *Walka o prawo powrotu do Ojczyzny*, p. 38 (here the ship has the name *Mafkura*).

kilometres from the Bulgarian border. There the passengers went ashore and took the rest of the journey by land. They reached Istanbul after eight days, on the 14th of August.[51] They found themselves in Palestine several weeks later.

Meanwhile, on the 23rd of August, there was a coup in Romania. Marshal Antonescu was arrested and on the 25th of August King Michael II declared war on Germany. By the end of the month the Russians and the Red Army were already in Bucharest.[52] In such circumstances *Aliyah Bet* had to be suspended.

# 4. The arrival of the USSR

In September 1944 neighbouring Bulgaria also found itself within the sphere of Soviet influence. Both countries, Bulgaria and Romania, had played a special role in the history of *Aliyah Bet*. The local Jews, though persecuted and humiliated, had managed here to save themselves to a much greater degree than in other countries allied with the Third Reich or under its occupation. *The survival of Bulgarian Jewry – we read in The Holocaust Encyclopedia – despite Bulgaria's pro-Nazi regime and the physical presence of German troops on Bulgarian soil – represents a unique chapter in European Jewish history during the World War II era.*[53]

The Jewish population in Bulgaria was numerically small (less than one percent of the entire population) and did not play a significant role. The Bulgarian anti-Semitic legislation that was adopted in 1940, though admittedly turning Jews into second class citizens, was based on a religious rather than an ethnic basis, and consequently freed Christian Jews from persecution. Many took advantage of this lifeline. Later, when the outcome of the war appeared to already be decided, the easing of the policy toward Jews was dictated by hopes of milder treatment from the Allies. In September 1944, following the collapse of the German-backed government, Jews gained full civil rights; but many of them already had placed their hopes on emigration to Palestine.[54]

The socio-political conditions in Romania and Bulgaria meant that many Jews from occupied Poland, Hungary and Slovakia made their way here. Emissaries from Yishuv and people organising emigration to Palestine were able to operate here in relative freedom given war conditions. What would happen now that both these countries found themselves within the Soviet sphere? Would the Kremlin's ideologi-

---

[51]  YVA. 011/69 (p. 35). *Report on the sinking of the M/V „Merkure,"* p. 3.

[52]  M. Willaume, *Rumunia (Historia Państw Świata w XX wieku)*, Warszawa 2004, pp. 162–165.

[53]  Quoted after: W. Laqueur (ed.), *The Holocaust Encyclopedia*, p. 97 (headword: "Bulgaria"). See the collection of documents: T. Todorov, *The Fragility of Goodness. Why Bulgaria's Jews Survived the Holocaust*, London 2000. Cf. also A. Koen, A. Assa, *Saving of the Jews in Bulgaria, 1941–1944*, Sofia 1977; F.B. Chary, *The Bulgarian Jews and the Final Solution 1940–1944*, Pittsburgh 1972.

[54]  CZA. L 15/1139. *Zionisten Verein "Dr Theodor Herzl."* Sofia, 31 X 1944 (an official letter in German about the departure of Bulgarian Jews to Palestine via Turkey).

cal anti-Zionism[55] influence *Aliyah Bet* from the part of Europe it controlled? Or was Moscow intending to use the aims of the Zionist movement to realize its own political plans for the Middle East?

It was difficult to answer these questions unequivocally in the autumn of 1944. On the other hand the increased interest of the USSR in the Middle East was unquestionable. The Comintern had fought Zionism as a Jewish nationalist movement, but towards the end of the war it was possible to observe a gradual change in Soviet tactics with regard to the Zionist movement.[56] This turnaround was spectacularly in evidence in 1947 when the Kremlin supported the creation of a Jewish state. Support for the Zionist movement constituted part of a broader anti-British and anti-Western strategy adopted by the USSR. Moscow's main aim was to drive Great Britain out of the Middle East and to take over its position. It was calculated that the anti-British feelings of Palestinian Zionists would make them a logical ally for Moscow, while the future Israeli state could adopt a pro-Soviet orientation.[57]

For the moment, in the autumn of 1944, from the point of view of *Aliyah Bet* it was hoped that the new Romanian authorities and the USSR would agree to allow a new refugee transport to leave the port at Constanta. This was the *Salah-a-din*, and on board there were over 540 immigrants.[58] It departed at the end of October 1944. *Salah-a-din* reached Istanbul and the rest of the scenario was the same as before (transit via Turkey to Palestine). When this plan was successfully brought to fruition the *Taurus* set off in the steps of the *Salah-a-Din* (*Taurus* – 958 passengers, almost half of whom were children).[59] This Greek ship, the property of Pandelis, was the last of the *Aliyah Bet* sea transportations to set sail during the war.

Among those who cooperated with Mossad was Yesheyahu Trachtenberg, better known by the pseudonym of Shaike Dan.[60] He came from Romania and his knowledge of the local realia, as well as the language, turned out to be very helpful. He gained Avigur's trust. In 1944 he found himself among a 32-person group of volunteers that the British had trained in Egypt as a special parachute formation for

---

[55]  See, for example, B. Pinkus, *The Jews of the Soviet Union. The History of a National Minority*, Cambridge 1988, pp. 49–51, 127–137, 161–170; J.B. Schechtman, "The USSR, Zionism and Israel" [in:] L. Kochan (ed.), *The Jews in Soviet Russia since 1917*, London 1972.

[56]  PISM. A 11.3/Bł. Wsch./3c. *Aktywność sowiecka na Bliskim i Środkowym Wschodzie*. Reports of the Office for Near and Middle East Studies (sent to London 22 VI 1943); M. Buchwajc, "Obserwacje i wrażenia z Palestyny" [in:] K. Zamorski, *Dwa tajne biura 2. Korpusu*, London 1990, pp. 72–73.

[57]  For more see: A. Krammer, *The Forgotten Friendship. Israel and the Soviet Bloc, 1947–1953*, Urbana–Chicago–London 1974, pp. 32–53; G. Lenczowski, *The Middle East in World Affairs*, New York 1952 (the chapter "Russian activities during and after World War II," pp. 419–422).

[58]  "541 Refugees Arrive in Istanbul from Rumania," *The Palestine Post*, 30 X 1944, p. 1. A different number of passengers (547) is to be found in B. Habas (op.cit., p. 309) and M. Naor (*Haapala*, p. 112). Different again – 370 persons – in D. Ofer (*Escaping the Holocaust*, pp. 286, 301; but on p. 327 the same author writes of already 547 passengers).

[59]  An incorrect name for the ship (*Storus*) in L. Epstein, *Before the Curtain Fell*, Tel Aviv 1990, p. 83.

[60]  See: A. Ettinger, op.cit.

missions in occupied Europe. The group was to be involved in sabotage as well as organising help for Jews beyond enemy lines.[61] After being dropped in the Balkans, Trachtenberg made contact with Mossad emissaries and was to play a significant role in organizing the emigration of Jews from Romania and Bulgaria, including after World War II when both countries found themselves behind the "Iron Curtain."[62]

Some of the refugees tried to go by land, through Bulgaria and Turkey. Usually the groups were small, a few families or so. However, in the autumn of 1944 there were plans to transport over 1,500 Jews in this way. It was becoming increasingly difficult to obtain new ships (the *Smyrni*, which Mossad had adapted to its purposes, was taken by the Russians, who refused to return it), and signals were coming from London and Ankara that the existing Jewish policy of the two countries might undergo a change. Significantly, Great Britain in December 1944 informed the Turkish authorities that immigrants who reached Turkey could no longer count on the automatic issue of a Palestinian visa. These people, the British explained, were no longer in any danger since the expulsion of the German army from Bulgaria and Romania.[63]

Transit through Bulgaria appeared to be a solution of sorts, at least temporarily. In November 1944, after travelling by rail to Stara Zagora (central Bulgaria), the Jews were interned there. Soon their fate was shared by other groups, including 360 refugees detained in the vicinity of Ruse on the Danube. In Stara Zagora a total of over 600 Jews were interned. Half came from Polish territory, while the remainder were Romanian, Hungarian and former Czechoslovak citizens. David Ben-Gurion, on a visit to Bulgaria at the time, tried to intervene on behalf of the detained refugees. As could have been foreseen, everything was decided by the USSR (to be precise, the Soviet representative in charge of the Allied Control Commission supervising Sofia's fulfilment of the conditions of the armistice concluded on the 28th of October 1944). Moscow explained that the refugees could include Red Army deserters and Soviet citizens and therefore the matter needed to be cleared up.[64]

---

[61] Amongst the volunteers was Enzo Sereni, who had cooperated with Mossad, and Hannah Szenes, a 23 year old poetess. Both died during the mission. T. Szulc, op.cit., pp. 64–66; M. Gilbert, *Israel. A History*, London 1999, p. 119.

[62] Cf. A. Ettinger, op.cit., pp. 207–231; Z.V. Hadari, Z. Tsahor, *Voyage to Freedom. An Episode in the Illegal Immigration to Palestine*, London 1985, pp. 114–119.

[63] Z.V. Hadari, op.cit., p. 7.

[64] T. Friling, "The 'King of the Jews' in Bulgaria. David Ben-Gurion's Diary, December 1944," *Shvut. Studies in Russian and East European Jewish History and Culture* (Tel Aviv–Beer Sheva). Vol. 10 (26): 2001, pp. 201, 257; F.B. Chary, op.cit., p. 178; PISM. A. 11 E/87. The reports of the Intelligence Information Section of the Staff of the Polish Commander-in-Chief to the Ministry of Foreign Affairs, Polish Government-in-Exile, entitled *Podróż Ben-Guriona* (*The journey of Ben-Gurion*, 17 I 1945) and: *Emigracja żydowska* (*Jewish emigration*, 22 I 1945). On the visit of Ben-Gurion to Sofia see also: E. Avriel, op.cit., pp. 193–197; "Mr. Ben-Gurion in Bulgaria," *The Palestine Post*, 3 XII 1944, p. 1.

The Kremlin wanted to make it understood that the emigration of Jews from Balkan countries depended entirely upon its goodwill. The requirements of tactical considerations meant that the decision would not be taken too quickly. Moscow freed those interned only after a month, in the second half of December. This was not the end of the refugees' problems, for they were then held by Turkish border guards. Turkey agreed to let them onto their territory under the condition that the British grant them the right to enter Palestine.[65] Such permission was issued by London a few days later, justifying its move by *humanitarian considerations,* and asserting that these individuals would be able to take advantage of the pool of immigration certificates designated for January 1945.[66]

Great Britain had consented to this reluctantly and under the pressure of events. The British understood that the mass emigration of Jews from Balkan countries to Palestine would undermine the bases of British order in the Middle East. On the one hand it would increase Arab dissatisfaction, on the other it would work in the USSR's favor. For Moscow would support *aliyah* from the Balkans not so much to help the Jews as to damage Great Britain. The more Jews there were in the Mandate, the greater Arab aversion to the Mandate authorities would be. This would push them to look elsewhere for support, e.g. in Moscow. Any concession to the Arabs, which could only be achieved at the expense of the Jewish population, resulted in an intensification of anti-British feeling amongst the latter. An immensely complex situation had taken shape.[67]

# 5. In lieu of summing up

Great Britain's conduct in relation to matters Palestinian was subordinated to the broader political strategy of the Foreign Office. The Middle East was of particular importance to London. Here the British had military bases (Alexandria, Suez, Cyprus, Aden, Basra in Iraq); they considered this region to be the main front in the defense of their empire. They believed, with some justification, that destabilization of this area would have an influence on British interests globally. Experience to date

---

[65]  TNA. FO 371/42825/WR 2126 (p. 69). *Telegram to Palestine (Field Marshal Viscount Gort) from S. of S. Colonies. No. 1731. 28 XII 1944*; ibidem (p. 63). *Cypher from Angora (Sir M. Peterson) to FO. No. 2136. 26 XII 1944*.

[66]  Ibidem; TNA. FO 371/42825/WR 2125 (p. 57). *Cypher from Mr Houston Boswall (Sofia) to FO. No. 290. 26 XII 1944*.

[67]  "Minute by R.M.A. Hankey, 29 November 1944, warning that massive illegal immigration from the Balkans into Palestine will create a crisis for the British in the Middle East" [in:] *The Rise of Israel*. Vol. 30: *The Holocaust and Illegal Immigration*, pp. 333–334 (document from the collections of TNA. FO 371/42825); PISM. A. 11 E/87. *Żydowskie źródła polityczne o międzynarodowej sytuacji żydostwa (Jewish political sources on the international situation of Jewry)*. Report of the Ministry of Foreign Affairs, Polish Government-in-Exile, London, 12 II 1945, p. 4.

had forced them to base their Middle East strategy on cooperation with the Arabs which therefore implied a specific attitude to the principles of the Zionist movement. At the same time, aspirations for full independence had increased amongst the Arabs. This was particularly visible in Egypt, an important pillar of the British security system. Faced with this situation, Great Britain started to consider a tactic of official support for the pan-Arab movement, counting on thereby maintaining *pax Britannica* in the Arab East. This tactic can be seen in the support for the Arab League founded in March 1945, among other things.[68]

The end of 1944 in some way recalled the situation from the last few months before the war. At both junctures multitudes of Jews desired to leave Europe. In 1939 they wanted to escape Hitler and the threat of armed conflict. Five years later – because they were unable to live where the Shoah had taken place. The majority of those who came to the countries of the Balkans arrived believing that it would be easier for them to emigrate from there.

The resolution of Asefat ha'Nivharim (the Assembly of Representatives) raised the matter of unlimited Jewish immigration to Palestine; this was ratified on the 6th of December 1944.[69] It demanded that the Jews themselves decide, without any legal restrictions whatsoever, on whether a given group of Jews could or could not come.[70]

At the same time the situation within the Mandate had dramatically worsened. The chances of an agreement between the Jewish and Arab inhabitants of Palestine diminished with every passing year. The Jews based their rights to Eretz Israel on the "Biblical mandate" and considered that centuries of persecution and the Holocaust justified the necessity to create a Jewish state. The Arabs claimed that the building of a "Jewish National Home" was occurring at the expense of their society. We are becoming "foreigners in our own country," said Musa Alami, a delegate of the Palestinian Arabs at the Arab summit in Alexandria (5th of October 1944).[71] Many of his compatriots shared this view.

---

[68]  W.R. Louis, *The British Empire in the Middle East 1945–1951. Arab Nationalism, The United States, and Postwar Imperialism*, Oxford 1988, pp. 128–146 (also the map on pp. XVIII–XIX); A. Patek, *Wielka Brytania wobec Izraela w okresie pierwszej wojny arabsko-izraelskiej maj 1948–styczeń 1949*, Kraków 2002, pp. 30, 66–68.

[69]  PISM. A. 11 E/87, *Report of the Intelligence Information Section of the Staff of the Polish Commander in Chief to the Ministry of Foreign Affairs of the Polish Government-in-Exile, 18 I 1945*.

[70]  Ibidem, p. 1.

[71]  Quoted after: Z.V. Hadari, *Second Exodus*, p. 59.

# Final remarks

"Type B" immigration combined elements of Zionism with political struggle. Its most serious opponent was not a totalitarian regime, but a country with democratic traditions, Great Britain. In the beginning, no-one could have predicted the role *Aliyah Bet* was to play. There was no Jewish state, nor were there any formal structures such as an army, diplomacy, or a treasury to provide a measure of support, or any allies. The Zionists had just begun learning tactical warfare and how to overcome their difficulties. What turned out to be more important was something else – determination, and a sense of responsibility. After the conference at Evian in 1938 it became obvious that Jewish refugees from Nazi Germany could only rely on themselves. Conditions were extremely difficult, and the outbreak of war in 1939 made them even more complicated. Although many *Aliyah Bet* operations ended in failure, and several immigrant transports capsized, *ha'apala* gave diaspora Jews much-needed hope for a reversal of fortune. It was both an idea and a bridge between Jews in Europe and Yishuv, which simultaneously directed the attention of international opinion to the problem of Jewish refugees, decisively influencing the future of the Palestinian problem, though not until after the war.

In the period before September 1939 *Aliyah Bet* organized the relocation of about 21,600 people to Palestine via land, sea and air, and during the Second World War another 16,500, saving many human beings from the Holocaust. Most of the illegal immigrants came from the Old Continent, above all from the central and eastern parts – from Germany, Poland, Czechoslovakia, Austria, Lithuania, Romania and Bulgaria. Sea routes prevailed. Over 90% of the refugees were transported this way, on compact ships capable of taking at most a few dozen people and on freighters calculated to hold a few hundred passengers.

*Aliyah Bet* was conditioned both by factors within Yishuv and the diaspora and by others beyond the Jews' control. No less important than religious or ideological concerns was the role played by political circumstances. *Aliyah Bet* concentrated a great many elements which were part of the symbolism of Jewish history, and it was no accident that the components which gave it a dimension of reality included some products of tradition and religion – the idea of the Promised Land and the return of the exiles to Zion. *Ha'apala* therefore joined together diverse individuals and milieux, people of varying ideological stances and life experience.

The tone was set, understandably, by the Zionist movement, but this form of immigration did not obtain immediate support from the Jewish Agency, which was anxious that such activity could do tactical damage to its cooperation with British Mandate authorities. For this reason the Zionists-Revisionists were first to take the initiative. Both groups saw *Aliyah Bet* as a useful political tool. Mossad le'Aliyah Bet (Institute of B Immigration), linked with Yishuv leadership, emerged at the end of 1938 when the situation of the Jews in Europe was dramatically worsening, and Great Britain introduced severe limits on the influx of immigrants. Though their priority was saving their endangered European compatriots, it should be noted that short-term concerns relating to the refugees' usefulness in Palestine were also taken into account. Since candidates for emigration were expected to join in building the Jewish state, some were chosen with a view to their professional experience, physical fitness, and declared ideological sympathies.

Many supported *Aliyah Bet* because they attributed noble motives to the organization or were driven by ideological goals. But there were others (of diverse nationalities) who were planning to make a fast buck and took unscrupulous advantage of the refugees' predicament.

*Aliyah Bet* drew attention from many sides – the British mandatory, Palestinian Arabs and the governments of numerous European countries. The latter, such as Poland or Romania, saw in Jewish emigration a solution to their own internal societal problems. The Third Reich motivated a desire for governments to rid their territory of Jews. Arabs resisted the idea of a "Jewish national home," since it conflicted with their own political and national aspirations. Great Britain's position was dictated by political strategy and a view to playing the Arab card.

A nexus of circumstances set British and Jewish interests against each other. The British, to their credit, were not driven by prejudice or anti-Semitism, but they were strongly opposed to illegal immigration. From their perspective *Aliyah Bet* was unlawful and threatened to destabilize relations in the Palestinian Mandate; they worried that further influx of Jews would aggravate Arab frustration, which could cost Great Britain her position in the strategically vital Middle East. The Jews looked on the matter differently – for them, *Aliyah Bet* was salvation, hope, a way to fight for their own country. The Arabs had another view of the matter, viewing the Jewish settlers as unwanted intruders who were taking away their land and jobs. The drama was heightened by the fact that these events were occurring simultaneously with the persecution of the Jews, and then the Holocaust, in Europe. *Ha'apala* stripped bare the soulless hypocrisy of the many governments who treated Jewish refugees instrumentally. The sympathy for Jews proclaimed by governments was not accompanied by open borders, in countries which took pride in their democratic traditions.

# Appendices

### 1. Jewish immigration to Palestine 1934–1948

| Year | In total | Of which illegal immigration |
|------|----------|------------------------------|
| 1934 | 42,359 | 4,115 |
| 1935 | 61,854 | 3,804 |
| 1936 | 29,717 | 1,807 |
| 1937 | 10,536 | 681 |
| 1938 | 12,868 | 1,427 |
| 1939* | 27,561 | 11,156 |
| 1940 | 8,398 | 3,851 |
| 1941 | 5,886 | 2,239 |
| 1942 | 3,733 | 1,539 |
| 1943 | 8,507 | x |
| 1944 | 14,464 | x |
| 1945 | 13,121 | 370 |
| 1946 | 17,760 | 9,910 |
| 1947 | 21,542 | 14,252 |
| 1948** | 17,174 | 15,065 |
| Total | 295,480 | 70,216 |

The table created from data reported in: H. Barlas, "History of immigration since 1882" [in:] *Encyclopedia of Zionism and Israel*, pp. 536–538; *Great Britain and Palestine 1915–1945*, pp. 63–64; *The Political History of Palestine under British Administration. Memorandum by His Britannic Majesty's Government*, pp. 15, 33.

The list does not include those illegal immigrants who did not reach Palestine (among others those deported to Cyprus) as well as those that the Mandate authorities did not manage to register.

* – for the period September to December 1939 the total number of immigrants was 8422 persons of whom 4330 arrived without the required permission

** – up until 14th of May 1948

x – refugees from those years for which Istanbul was a stage point, who received the relevant certificates enabling their legal settlement in Palestine

# 2. Aliyah Bet sea transports organized for the years 1934–1944

A – vessel name, B – date, C – place of embarkation, D – organizer, E – number of passengers on board according to (1) Dalia Ofer, (2) Mordechai Naor and (3) Paul H. Silverstone, F – transport seized or turned back by the mandatory, G – sunk or met with disaster

| A | B | C | D | E | | | F | G |
|---|---|---|---|---|---|---|---|---|
| | | | | 1 | 2 | 3 | | |
| Velos 1 | VII 1934 | Greece | Hehalutz | 350 | 350 | 350 | | |
| Cappollo[1] | summer 1934 | Greece | Revisionists | | 107 | | | |
| Union | VIII 1934 | Greece | Revisionists | 117 | 117 | 117 | | |
| Velos 2 | IX–XI 1934 | Bulgaria | Hehalutz | 350 | 350 | 350 | X | |
| Af al pi (Kosta) | III–IV 1937 | Greece | Galili | 15 | 15 | 16 | | |
| Af al pi (Artemisia) | X 1937[2] | Albania[3] | Galili | 54 | 54 | 68 | | |
| Af al pi (Artemisia)[4] | XII 1937 | Greece | Galili | | | 120 | | |
| Poseidon 1 | I 1938 | Greece | Hehalutz | 68 | 65 | 65 | | |
| Af al pi (Panormitis?) | III 1938 | Greece[5] | Galili | 96 | 96 | 96 | | |
| Artemisia 1 | IV 1938 | Greece | Hehalutz | 128 | 128 | 126 | | |
| Poseidon 2 | V 1938 | Greece | Hehalutz | 65 | 65 | 65 | | |
| Af al pi (Artemisia?) | VI 1938 | Greece | Galili | | 380 | 386 | | |

[1] The crew in unsuccessfully trying to reach the Palestinian coast returned the ship to Greece.

[2] According to M. Naor, the transport happened in September 1937.

[3] According to P.H. Silverstone the ship set sail from Greece.

[4] This transport was not included by D. Ofer and M. Naor in their breakdowns.

[5] According to D. Ofer, the transport set sail from Italy.

| | | | | | | | |
|---|---|---|---|---|---|---|---|
| Artemisia 2 | VII 1938 | Greece | Hehalutz (Galili?)[6] | 157 | 157 | 158 | |
| Af al pi[7] | VIII 1938 | Greece | Galili | 156 | | | |
| Af al pi[8] | IX 1938 | Greece | Galili | 38 | | | |
| Draga 1/Artemisia[9] | IX–X 1938 | Yugoslavia | Perl | 140 | 180 | 220 | |
| Atrato 1 | XI 1938 | Italy | Hehalutz | 300 | 300 | 300 | |
| Draga 2[10] | XI–XII 1938 | Romania | Perl | 550 | 550 | 544 | |
| Eli[11] | XI–XII 1938 | Romania | Haller | 550 | 340 | 620 | |
| Geppo 1[12] | XII 1938 | Romania | Perl | 734 | 734 | 734 | |
| Delpa (Dalfa) | XII 1938–I 1939 | Romania | Revisionists | 250 | 250 | 224 | |
| Katina | I–II 1939 | Romania | Revisionists | 778 | 800 | 773 | |
| Artemisia[13] | II 1939 | | Revisionists | | | 237 | X |
| Atrato 2 | I 1939 | Italy | Hehalutz | 300 | 300 | 300 | |
| Atrato 3 | II 1939 | Italy | Hehalutz | 300 | 300 | 300 | |

6    According to D. Ofer, the transport was prepared by Hehalutz.

7    Transport included in D. Ofer's work, *Escaping the Holocaust*.

8    As above.

9    Composite operation. The passengers transferred at sea to the Greek vessel *Artemisia*. According to D. Ofer the vessel's name is in the form of *Daraga*.

10    Composite operation. A part of the passengers reached Palestine on board the *Artemisia*, a part on the *Eli*.

11    In P.H. Silverstone's work the vessel's name is in the form of *Elli*.

12    In the literature on the subject there exists also the name *Gippo* (Naor) and *Chepo* (Silverstone).

13    The boat was to bring the passengers of the *Katina* to Palestine in several phases. The transfer took place in the region of Cyprus.

| | | | | | | | |
|---|---|---|---|---|---|---|---|
| Geppo 2[14] | II–IV (?) 1939 | Romania | Perl | 750 | 750 | 750 | X |
| Colorado/Atrato 4 | III 1939 | Yugoslavia | Mossad | 400 | 378 | 400 | |
| Sandu | III 1939 | Romania | private | 270 | 270 | 269 | X |
| Aghios Nikolaos[15] | III 1939 | Romania | Flesch | | | 750 | |
| Astir | III–IV 1939 | Bulgaria | Revisionists | 724 | 724 | 720 | X |
| Assimi | III–IV 1939 | Romania | Mizrachi/Zionist youth | 470 | 470 | 369 | X |
| Aghia Zioni[16] | III–IV 1939 | France/Italy | Perl | 465 | 400 | 600 | |
| Astia | IV 1939 | Bulgaria | Flesch, Haller, Perl | 699 | 699 | | |
| Panagia Conasterio | IV 1939 | Greece | Revisionists | | | 176 | |
| Colorado/Atrato 5 | IV 1939 | Yugoslavia | Mossad | 388 | 408 | 388 | |
| Colorado/Atrato 6 | IV 1939 | Italy | Mossad | 372 | 337 | 337 | |
| Aghios Nikolaos[17] | IV–V 1939 | Bulgaria | Konfino | 800 | 800 | 600 | |
| Atrato 7[18] | V 1939 | Romania | Mossad | 390 | 400 | 430 | X |
| Kralitza Maria[19] | V–VI 1939 | Bulgaria | Konfino/Revisionists | 350 | 350 | 350 | |

14 D. Ofer and M. Naor state that *Geppo 2* sank on the 16 IV 1939.

15 Fired upon by a British patrol (one person died), it returned to Romania.

16 Also as *Aghia Dezioni* (Ofer), *Aghia – Juni* (Naor).

17 A part of the refugees, already after disembarkation, were held by the British and interned at the camp at Sarafand. Naor states (incorrectly) that the vessel set sail from Romania.

18 According to M. Naor the transport had departed from Greece.

19 In the studies also as *Karaiza Maria* (Ofer), *Calitza – Maria* – (Naor).

| Ship | Date | Country | Organizer | | | | | |
|---|---|---|---|---|---|---|---|---|
| *Colorado* | V–VI 1939 | Romania | Mossad | 379 | 379 | 379 | | |
| *Dimitrios* | V–VI 1939 | | J. Aron | 244 | 244 | 244 | X | |
| *Liesel* | V–VI 1939 | Romania | Revisionists | 921 | 921 | 906 | X | |
| *Frossoula*[20] | V–VIII 1939 | Bulg. (Rom.?) | Aron, Stavsky | 654 | 654 | 658 | | |
| *Marsis* | VI 1939 | Greece | Revisionists | | | 724 | X | |
| *Las Perlas* | VI–VII 1939 | Romania | Flesch, Haller | 370 | 370 | 370 | X | |
| *Aghios Nikolaos*[21] | VI–VII 1939 | Bulgaria | Revisionists | | | 693 | | |
| *Niko* | VI–VII 1939 | Romania | Perl, Haller | 560 | 560 | 560 | X | |
| *Rim* | VI–VII 1939 | Romania | Revisionists | 600 | 600 | 801 | | X |
| *Colorado* | VII 1939 | Romania | Mossad | 388 | 377 | 378 | X | |
| *Dora* | VII–VIII 1939 | Holland | Mossad | 480 | 480 | 500 | | |
| *Parita* | VII–VIII 1939 | Romania | Revisionists | 850 | 850 | 800 | | |
| *Rudnitchar* | VII–VIII 1939 | Bulgaria | Konfino | 305 | 305 | 305 | | |
| *Aghios Nikolaos* | VIII 1939 | Romania | Konfino/Revision. | 795 | 795 | 809 | | |
| *Osiris (Syros)* | VIII 1939 | Italy (Bulgaria?)[22] | Aron, Stavsky | 650 | 650 | 593 | | |
| *Krotova*[23] | VIII 1939 | Bulgaria | Aron, Stavsky | 650 | 650 | 650 | | |
| *Tripoli* | VIII 1939 | Bulgaria | Aron, Stavsky | 700 | 700 | 700 | | |

20  In the studies also as *Prosula* (Ofer), *Produla* (Naor), *Frosula*.

21  According to Silverstone, 560 passengers of this transport transferred at sea to the *Niko*.

22  According to P.H. Silverstone and W. Perl, *Osiris* was the last *Aliyah Bet* transport to leave Italy before the outbreak of war. While D. Ofer claims that the vessel left from Bulgaria.

23  In studies also as *Cartova* (Ofer), *Karatova* (Naor).

| | | | | | | | | |
|---|---|---|---|---|---|---|---|---|
| *Tiger Hill* | VIII–IX 1939 | Romania | Mossad | 1417 | 1417 | 1417 | X | |
| *Naomi Julia* | VIII–IX 1939 | Romania | Revisionists | 1130 | 1130 | 1136 | X | |
| *Rudnitchar 2* | IX 1939 | Bulgaria | Konfino | 371 | 371 | 368 | | |
| *Rudnitchar 3* | X–XI 1939 | Bulgaria | Konfino | 457 | 457 | 457 | | |
| *Rudnitchar 4*[24] | XII 1939–I 1940 | Bulgaria | Konfino | 505 | | | | |
| *Hilda* | I 1940 | Romania | Mossad | 728 | 677 | 729 | X | |
| *Sakarya* | II 1940 | Romania | Revisionists | 2228 | 2400 | 2175 | X | |
| *Pencho (Pentcho)* | V–X 1940 | Slovakia | Revisionists | 510 | 500 | 514 | | X |
| *Libertad* | VI–VII 1940 | Bulgaria | Konfino | 355 | 700 | 700 | X | |
| *Salvador* | XII 1940 | Bulgaria | Konfino | 320 | 180 | 327 | | X |
| *Atlantic* | X–XI 1940 | Romania | Storfer | 1780 | 1880 | 1771 | X | |
| *Pacific* | X–XI 1940 | Romania | Storfer | 1062 | 1100 | 1000 | X | |
| *Milos* | X–XI 1940 | Romania | Storfer | 709 | 671 | 880 | X | |
| *Darien II* | II–III 1941 | Romania | Mossad | 789 | 800 | 878 | X | |
| *Hainarul (Hoinar?)*[25] | IV 1941 | Romania | | | | 19 | | |
| *Struma* | XII 1941–II 1942 | Romania | Revisionists | 769 | 769 | 767 | X | X |
| *Mihai* | III–V 1942 | Romania | private | 15 | | 13 | X | |
| *Euxenia* | III 1942 | Romania | private | 11 | 12 | 12 | | X |

[24] The ship managed to escape the British but the passengers were captured and interned.

[25] Silverstone also recalls a small motor boat (*Crai Nou*, 12 persons), which in May 1941 was to depart Romania and reach Cyprus. This information could not be confirmed (also about the *Hainarul*) in other materials.

| | | | | | | | |
|---|---|---|---|---|---|---|---|
| Mircea | IV–V 1942 | Romania | private | 40 | | 40 | X |
| Dordeval (Dor de Val) | IV 1942[26] | Romania | private | 20 | | 14 | X |
| Dora | VIII–IX 1942 | Romania | private | | | 15 | |
| Europa | IX 1942 | Romania | private | | | 21 | X |
| Vitorul | IX 1942 | Romania | private | 120 | 120 | 120 | |
| Lily | VIII 1943 | Romania | private | ? | | | X |
| Milka 1 | III 1944 | Romania | Mossad | 239 | 239 | 410 | |
| Marica 1 | IV 1944 | Romania | Mossad | 244 | 224 | 244 | |
| Bela-Christa[27] | IV 1944 | Romania | Mossad | 273 | | 273 | |
| Milka 2 | IV–V 1944 | Romania | Mossad | 317 | 517 | 433 | |
| Marica 2 | V 1944 | Romania | Mossad | 318 | 318 | 266 | |
| Kazbek | VII 1944 | Romania | Mossad | 735 | 735 | 725 | |
| Morina | VIII 1944 | Romania | Mossad | 308 | | 308 | |
| Bulbul | VIII 1944 | Romania | Mossad | 410 | 410 | 410 | |
| Mefkura | VIII 1944 | Romania | Mossad | 379 | 394 | 350 | X |
| Salah-a-din | X 1944 | Romania | Mossad | 547 | 547 | 547 | |
| Taurus | XII 1944 | Romania | Mossad | 958 | 958 | 958 | |

26 Silverstone incorrectly dates the journey as July 1942.

27 In the studies there is a marked absence of agreement as to the name of this vessel: Bella-Chita, Bela-Christa, etc.

The list of sea transports created from data reported in: D. Ofer, Escaping the Holocaust, pp. 323–327; M. Naor, Haapala, pp. 109–112; P.H. Silverstone, Aliyah Bet Project. List 1: 1934–1945; A. Tartakower, K.R. Grossmann, The Jewish Refugee, pp. 70–71; W.R. Perl, Operation Action, pp. 405–408.

# Selected bibliography

## I. Archives collections

### 1. The National Archives (former Public Record Office), London

#### a. Admiralty Records (ADM)

ADM 116/4312 – Palestine: efforts to curtail illegal immigration of Jews, 1939–1940
ADM 116/4659 – Palestine. Illegal immigration of Jews, 1940–1942

#### b. Colonial Office Records (CO)

CO 67/364/4 – Jewish Camps in Cyprus. Detention of Illegal Immigrants in Cyprus, 1949
CO 537/2398 – Palestine. MI5, Illegal Immigration Reviews, 1947
CO 733/255/11 – Palestine. Immigration Report by Mr. E. Samuel, 1934
CO 733/331/3 – Palestine. Illegal immigration, 1937
CO 733/394/1 and 2 – Illegal immigration of Jews into Palestine, 1939
CO 733/395/1 – Illegal immigration. Measures in Palestine: setting up of refugee camps, 1939
CO 733/395/4 – Illegal Immigration: "Tiger Hill," 1939
CO 733/429/1 – Palestine. Situation and counter measures, 1940
CO 733/429/4 – Palestine. Illegal immigration. The Low Countries, 1940
CO 733/431/1 – Palestine. Illegal immigration. Publicity, 1940
CO 733/446/4 – Palestine. Illegal immigration. Commission of Enquiry into explosion and sinking of SS "Patria," 1941
CO 733/446/7 and 8 – Palestine. Illegal immigration. "Darien" ship, 1942
CO 733/446/9 – Palestine. Illegal immigration. Interim Reports on the Detainment Camp in Mauritius, 1942–1943
CO 733/446/10 – Palestine. Illegal immigration. M.V. "Struma," 1942
CO 733/446/11 – Palestine. Illegal immigration. M.V. "Struma." Parliamentary Questions, 1942
CO 733/454/2 – Jewish illegal immigration into Palestine, 1944–1945
CO 733/466/12 – Illegal immigration of Jews into Palestine through Turkey, 1943–1944
CO 733/466/15 and 16 – Palestine. Illegal immigration. Transport arrangements. Treatment of "Atlantic" passengers, 1944
CO 733/466/18 – Illegal immigration. Detainees in Mauritius. Conditions in camp. Applications for release, etc., 1944
CO 733/466/20 – Palestine. Illegal immigration. Detainees in Mauritius. Conditions in camp and applications for release, 1944

### c. Foreign Office Records (FO)

FO 371/24094 and 24096 – Political. Western. Refugees 1939. General question of settlement for refugees

FO 371/25124 – Political. Western. Co-ordination, 1940

FO 371/25238 and 25239, 25240, 25241, 25242 – Political. General. Refugees 1940. Illegal immigration into Palestine

FO 371/29160 – General. Refugees 1941. Illegal immigration into Palestine

FO 371/32661 – General. Refugees 1942. Illegal immigration into Palestine

FO 371/42825 – Jewish immigration into Palestine (via Istanbul), 1944

FO 371/45383 – Palestine and Transjordan, 1945

FO 371/61812 – Illegal immigration into Palestine: control of suspect shipping, 1947

### d. Treasury Records (T)

T 161/1107 – Palestine. Measures to prevent illegal immigration. Maintenance of refugees who are refused admission, 1933–1943

T 220/195 – Palestine. Measures to prevent illegal immigration, 1944–1951

### e. War Office Records (WO)

WO 275/60 – On board the Exodus 1947

## 2. Central Zionist Archives, Jerusalem

### a. Central Offices of the World Zionist Organization and of the Jewish Agency for Palestine / Israel abroad

Z4/30286 – Mauritius detainees, 1943–1945

Z4/30523 – Immigration into Palestine, 1942

Z4/31046 – Memorandum: a Positive Program. Suggestions for Agenda of World Zionist Congress, Geneva, August 1939

Z4/31066 – Illegal Immigration (including materials on the "Atlantic" as well as the refugees interned at Atlit and on Mauritius, 1940, 1941)

Z4/31096 – "Struma," 1942

Z4/31103 and 31104 – Refugees, 1940–1942

Z4/31107 and 31108 – including correspondence of Moshe Shertok (1939–1940)

Z4/31145 – correspondence of Chaim Weizmann, Berl Locker and Ivor Linton with Ernest Bevin and Arthur Creech-Jones (1941–1944)

Z5/10819 – Cyprus cases, 1942/1943

Z6/292 – Nahum Goldmann's offices in New York and Geneva. Confidential documents (1941–1944)

Z6/1567 – European Jewish refugees before World War II (1954)

### b. Departments of the Executive of the World Zionist Organization and the Jewish Agency for Palestine/ Israel in Jerusalem, Tel Aviv and Haifa

S25/22701 – Political Department. Illegal immigration. Various documents (1936–1939)

### c. Archives of Zionist federations, organizations and associations and collections of documents on the history of Zionism in the United States

F38/1304 – Internment of Jewish Refugees in Athlit, Palestine, 1942

d. **Affiliated offices of the World Zionist Organization and the Jewish Agency and institutions established by them**

L15/1139 – Immigration Department, Office in Istanbul (Aliyah from Balkan countries via Turkey, 1943–1944)

L22/922 – "Pencho" (1940, 1943)

e. **Personal Papers**

A289/75 – Harry Sacher: *The Mauritius detainees*, 1 II 1945

A406/55 and 59 – Robert Szold. Various documents (1940–1942)

f. **Minutes of the Jewish Agency**

S100/25 b – Vol. 25 (for the period 2 X 1938–1 I 1939)

# 3. Yad Vashem Archives, Jerusalem

a. **Archives in Bulgaria files**

M67/85 – including documents on the sinking of the "Salvador" in 1940

b. **Kurt Jakob Ball-Kaduri collection of testimonies and reports on German Jewry**

O1/213 – Protokoll über eine Besprechung mit Dr. Aron Zwergbaum, Jerusalem, zum Thema "Mauritius" aufgezeichnet von Dr. Ball-Kaduri. Tel Aviv, 27 Februar 1958

c. **Records of The Wiener Library, London**

O2/633 – "Die Alijah von Bratislava nach Mauritius." Ein Tagebuch von Dr. A. Zwergbaum

O2/634 – Mauritius: Documents and newspaper cuttings

O2/635 – Mauritius: petitions and cutting from *Cyprus Post*

O2/636 – Hans Klein, London (late of Vienna): "My emigration into forced Internment of Mauritius"

d. **Collection about Romania**

O11/64 and 66, 67 – "Struma"

O11/69 – "Mefkure," 1944

O11/70 – S.S. "Mefküre." S.S. "Patria"

O11/71 – "Struma" und "Mefkure." Gutachten von Dr. J. Rohver

e. **Records of the Wilhelm Filderman Archive (Chairman, Union of Jewish Communities in Romania)**

P6/20, P6/24, P6/117 – including documents on *Aliyah Bet* from Romania (1942, 1944)

# 4. Atlit Detention Camp for Illegal Immigrants Museum, Atlit

a. **booklet** *Atlit Detention Camp for Illegal Immigrants*. Ed. Atlit Detention Camp for Illegal Immigrants [without year of issue]

b. **leaflet** *Maʾapilim Detention Camp Atlit*

# 5. The National Library of Israel, Givat Ram, Jerusalem

**Unpublished works:**

Carmely T., *The Real Story of Struma or Breaking Down a 60 Years Old Conspiracy of Silence*, Haifa 2002 (inventory no. S2 = 2002 B 3367)

Carmely T., *Dosarul "Struma" și dedesubturile sale*, Haifa 2005 (inventory no. S2 = 2006 B 4904)

Finkelstein A., *The Mefkure Tragedy (An inquiry into the slayers' identity)*, Paris 1989 (inventory no. S2 = 89 B 2684)

Rubinstein S., *Comments on Several Personal Tragedies that were part of the General Tragedy Called Struma*, Jerusalem 2002 (inventory no. S2 = 2003 B 6596)

Shealtiel S., *Emigration and Illegal Immigration to Palestine from Bulgaria and via Bulgaria in the years 1939–1945*. Vol. 1–2, Tel Aviv University 2001 (inventory no. S2 = 2003 A 1581; PhD thesis in Hebrew, summary and additional title in English)

# 6. Rhodes House Library, Oxford

Dudley Nigg Papers, MSS. Medit/21 (*Ill – usage of ex-detainees at Athlit Camp, Palestine*)

# 7. The Polish Institute and General Sikorski Museum in London

Records: Ref. A.11 E/87 – Ministry of Foreign Affairs. Jews in Palestine 1945

Ref. A. 11/3/Bl. Wsch. – including analysis and reports of the Bureau for Near and Middle East Studies of the Polish Government-in-Exile

Ref. A. 49/1 – Polish Consulate in Tel Aviv. General political relations with Poland

# 8. Archiwum Akt Nowych (The Central Archives of Modern Records), Warsaw

**a. Records of the Ministry of Foreign Affairs (Ministerstwo Spraw Zagranicznych, MSZ)**

MSZ 9909 – The problem of Jewish emigration – legal and illegal including to Palestine 1938–1939 [microfilm B 26319]

MSZ 9916, 9918 – V. Jabotinsky's New Zionist Organization – activities, contacts with the Polish government, 1938–1939 [B 26326, B 26328]

MSZ 9933 – Emigration of Jews to Palestine. Activities of Jewish organizations. Question of youth military training etc., 1939 [B 26343]

MSZ 9935 – The "Hehalutz – Pioneer" organization in Poland. Tourist emigration to Palestine. Minutes of conferences at Ministry of Foreign Affairs, 1939 [B 26345]

MSZ 10004 – Problem of Jewish emigration. Resolutions of the New Zionist Organization, 1937–1939 [B 26414]

MSZ 10008 – Report of an official trip to Palestine, 1939 [B 26418]

b. Records of the Polish Central Police Command (Komenda Główna Policji Państwowej, KGPP)

KGPP 258 – Illegal emigration of Jews to Palestine. Memos of the Polish Ministry of Internal Affairs, correspondence, photocopies of declarations, records of statements, 1938–1939

c. Records of the Polish Embassy in London

140 – Palestine. Political system, government, parliament. Arab-Jewish conflict and government policy etc., 1936–1939

271 – Palestine. Movement of population. Immigration (including from Poland). Reports, statistical tables, 1932–1935

902 – Emigration of national minorities. Polish Jews in Canada, Palestine, South Africa etc., 1920–1938

d. Records of the Polish Diplomatic Mission in Bern

153 – Palestine. Internal situation and the problem of dividing the country. World Zionist Congress in Geneva. Reports of the Polish Diplomatic Mission in Bern and the Polish Consulate in Tel Aviv, correspondence, aide-memoires, 1939

e. Records of the Ministry of Internal Affairs (Ministerstwo Spraw Wewnętrznych, MSW)

MSW 1069 – Documents on the evacuation of Jews from Gdansk, 1938
MSW 1508 – Deporting of Polish citizens to Poland from Palestine, 1925–1939

# II. Published primary sources

Begin M., *Jedyna droga*, Warszawa 1936

British White Paper, Cmd. 1700 of 1922: *Palestine. Correspondence with the Palestine Arab Delegation and the Zionist Organization*, London 1922

British White Paper, Cmd. 3692 of 1930: *Palestine: Statement of Policy by His Majesty's Government in the United Kingdom*, London 1930

British White Paper, Cmd. 5957 of 1939: *Correspondence between Sir Henry McMahon, His Majesty's High Commissioner at Cairo, and the Sherif Hussein of Mecca, July 1915–March 1916*, London 1939

British White Paper, Cmd. 6019 of 1939: *Palestine: Statement of Policy*, London 1939

British White Paper, Cmd. 6180 of 1940: *Palestine Land Transfers Regulations. Letter to the Secretary – General of the League of Nations, February 28, 1940*, London 1940

Butler R. and Bury J.P.T. (eds.), *Documents on British Foreign Policy 1919–1939*. Series I. Vol. VIII: *1920*, London 1958

[Colony of Mauritius], *Interim Report on the Detainment Camp for the period 1st Oct., 1941, to 30th Sept., 1942*, Port Louis, Mauritius 1942

[Colony of Mauritius], *Interim Report on the Detainment Camp for the period 1st Oct., 1942, to 30th Sept., 1943*, Port Louis, Mauritius 1943

"Dezercje Żydów z Armii Polskiej na Wschodzie," *Zeszyty Historyczne* (Paris). No. 103: 1993, pp. 131–144

*Documents on German Foreign Policy 1918–1945*. Series D. Vol. V: *Poland; The Balkans; Latin America; The Smaller Powers. June 1937–March 1939*, London 1953

*Foreign Relations of the United States. Diplomatic Papers*

    *1937*. Vol. II: *The British Commonwealth, Europe, Near East and Africa*, Washington 1954

    *1939*. Vol. IV: *The Far East, The Near East and Africa*, Washington 1955

    *1940*. Vol. III: *The British Commonwealth, The Soviet Union, The Near East and Africa*, Washington 1958

    *1943*. Vol. I: *General*, Washington 1963

    *1944*. Vol. III: *The British Commonwealth and Europe*, Washington 1965

*Haapala, La. Compilación de notas y documentos de la Inmigrácion "Ilegal" a Eretz Israel 1933–1948.* La selección del material por M. Kitrón, Jerusalem 1953

Herzl T., *The Jewish State*, New York–London 1988 (translation from German, Leipzig–Wien 1896)

Hurewitz J.C., *Diplomacy in the Near and Middle East. A Documentary Record: 1914–1956.* Vol. II, Princeton 1956

Hurewitz J.C., *The Middle East and North Africa in World Politics. A Documentary Record.* Vol. II: *British-French Supremacy 1914–1945*, New Haven–London 1979

[The Jewish Agency for Palestine], *Book of Documents submitted to the General Assembly of the United Nations relating to the Establishment of the National Home for the Jewish People*, New York 1947

[The Jewish Agency for Palestine], *The Jewish Case before the Anglo-American Committee of Inquiry on Palestine as presented by the Jewish Agency for Palestine. Statements and Memoranda*, Jerusalem 1947

[The Jewish Agency for Palestine], *Memorandum submitted to the Palestine Royal Commission on behalf of the Jewish Agency for Palestine*, London 1936

Laqueur W., Rubin B. (eds.), *The Israel-Arab Reader. A Documentary History of the Middle East Conflict*, 4th ed., New York–Oxford 1985

*Palestine Mandate*, Cmd. 1785, London 1922

*Palestine Royal Commission. Report. Presented by the Secretary of State for the Colonies to Parliament by Command of His Majesty. July, 1937*. Cmd. 5479, London 1937

"Palestine Statement of Policy by H.M.G. Official Communique No. 2/39," *The Palestine Post*, 18 V 1939, p. 3

*Palestine. Termination of the Mandate 15th May, 1948. Statement prepared for public information by the Colonial Office and Foreign Office*, London 1948

*Parliamentary Debates. House of Commons. Official Report. 5th Series.* Vol. 298, London 1935; Vol. 346, London 1939, Vol. 347, London 1939; Vol. 348, London 1939; Vol. 350, London 1939; Vol. 351, London 1939; Vol. 356, London 1939; Vol. 357, London 1940; Vol. 367, London 1940; Vol. 368, London 1940; Vol. 377, London 1942; Vol. 378, London 1942; Vol. 393, London 1943; Vol. 398, London 1944; Vol. 400, London 1944; Vol. 408, London 1945

*Parliamentary Debates. House of Lords. Official Report. 5th Series.* Vol. 115, London 1940; Vol. 128, London 1943

Patek A. (ed.), "Żydowska 'emigracja turystyczna' z Polski do Palestyny w 1939 roku –dokumenty," *Studia Historyczne* (Kraków). No. 1 (213): 2011, pp. 81–98

*The Political History of Palestine under British Administration. (Memorandum by His Britannic Majesty's Government presented in July, 1947, to the United Nations Special Committee on Palestine)*, Jerusalem 1947

Reich B. (ed.), *Arab-Israeli Conflict and Conciliation. A Documentary History*, London 1995

*Report of the Commission on the Palestine Disturbances of August 1929 presented by the Secretary of State for the Colonies to Parliament by Command of His Majesty*, London 1930

*The Rise of Israel. A Documentary Record from the Nineteenth Century to 1948. A Facsimile Series Reproducing Over 1.900 Documents in 39 Volumes.* General Editor H.M. Sachar, New York 1987

Vol. 7, 8: *Britain Enters into a Compact with Zionism 1917.* Ed. by I. Friedman

Vol. 16: *The Jewish Yishuv's Development in the Interwar Period.* Ed. by A.S. Klieman

Vol. 19: *Zionist Political Activity in the 1920s and 1930s.* Ed. by A.S. Klieman

Vol. 24: *The Royal Commission Report, 1937.* Ed. by A.S. Klieman

Vol. 27: *The Darkest Year 1939.* Ed. by A.S. Klieman

Vol. 28: *Implementing the White Paper, 1939–1941.* Ed. by M.J. Cohen

Vol. 30: *The Holocaust and Illegal Immigration, 1939–1947.* Ed. by M.J. Cohen

"Select British Documents on the Illegal Immigration to Palestine (1939–1940)." Introduced by L. Yahil, *Yad Vashem Studies on the European Jewish Catastrophe and Resistance* (Jerusalem). Vol. X: 1974, pp. 241–276

*Sovietsko-izrailskiye otnosheniya. Sbornik dokumientov.* T. I: *1941–1953.* Kniga 1: *1941–May 1949*, Moskva 2000

*A Survey of Palestine. Prepared in December 1945 and January 1946 for the Information of the Anglo-American Committee of Inquiry.* Vol. 1, Jerusalem 1946

Todorov T., *The Fragility of Goodness. Why Bulgaria's Jews Survived the Holocaust*, London 2000

Tomaszewski J. (ed.), "Ministerstwo Spraw Zagranicznych Rzeczypospolitej Polskiej wobec Żydów, 1938–1939 (dokumenty)," *Polski Przegląd Dyplomatyczny* (Warszawa). Vol. 3: 2003. No. 1 (11), pp. 197–235

Wight M., *British Colonial Constitutions 1947*, Oxford 1952

Woodhead J., "The Report of the Palestine Partition Commission," *International Affairs* (Oxford). No. 2: 1939, pp. 171–193

Żabotyński W., *Państwo Żydowskie*, Warszawa–Kraków–Poznań–Łódź [1937]

Żebrowski R., *Dzieje Żydów w Polsce 1918–1939. Wybór tekstów źródłowych*, Warszawa 1993

# III. Diaries and memoirs

Aliav R., Mann P., *The Last Escape. The Launching of the Largest Secret Rescue Movement of All Time*, London 1974

Anders W., *Bez ostatniego rozdziału. Wspomnienia z lat 1939–1946*, Londyn 1959 (reprint: Bydgoszcz 1989)

Avigur S., *S pokoleniyem khagany*, Tel Awiw 1976 (Hebrew edition: *Im dor ha-Haganah*, Tel Aviv 1962)

Avriel E., *Open the Gates! A Personal Story of "Illegal" Immigration to Israel.* Preface by G. Meir, New York 1975 (also the Italian edition: *Aprite le porte. La drammatica storia dell' immigrazione clandestina in Israele*, Milano 1976)

Barbur E., Urbański K., *Właśnie Izrael. „Gadany" przewodnik po teraźniejszości i historii Izraela*, Warszawa 2006

Begin M., *The Revolt*, Jerusalem 1951 (7th ed.: Jerusalem–Tel Aviv–Haifa 1977; Hebrew edition: *Mered*, Yerushalayim 1950)

Ben-Gurion D., *Israel. A Personal History*, London 1972 (translation from the Hebrew, Tel-Aviv 1969)

Ben-Gurion D., *Rebirth and Destiny of Israel*. Edited and translated from the Hebrew under the supervision of M. Nurock, New York 1954

Bentwich N. and H., *Mandate Memories 1918–1948*, New York 1965

Braginsky Y., *Am hoter el hof*, Tel-Aviv 1965

Drymmer W.T., "Zagadnienie żydowskie w Polsce w latach 1935–1939 (Wspomnienie z pracy w Ministerstwie Spraw Zagranicznych)," *Zeszyty Historyczne* (Paris). No. 13: 1968, pp. 55–75

[Dugdale B.], *Baffy. The Diaries of Blanche Dugdale 1936–1947*. Edited by N.A. Rose. Foreword by M. Weisgal, London 1973

Epstein L., *Before the Curtain Fell*, Tel-Aviv 1990

Feinber Ch., "Nach fünfzehn Jahren… 'Patria' – Gedanken. Aus den Erinnerungen eines Geretteten," *Jedioth Chadashoth* (Tel-Aviv), 25 XI 1955, p. 6

Friling T., "The 'King of the Jews' in Bulgaria. David Ben-Gurion's Diary, December 1944," *Shvut. Studies in Russian and East European Jewish History and Culture* (Tel-Aviv–Beer Sheva). Ed. B. Pinkus. Vol. 10 (26): 2001, pp. 182–279

Hirschmann I.A., *Life Line to a Promised Land*, New York 1946

Kollek T., *For Jerusalem. A Life by Teddy Kollek with his son, Amos Kollek*, London 1978

Konfino B., *Aliyah Bet. Nielegalna imigraciya. Kratk ocherk za izvshenite nielegalni transporti za Palestina prez 1939/40 god*, Sofiya 1946 (Hebrew edition: *Aliyah Bet me-hofe Bulgaryah*, Yerushalayim-Tel Aviv 1965)

Laub M., *The Last Barrier to Freedom. Internment of Jewish Holocaust Survivors on Cyprus, 1946–1949*, Berkeley, Cal. 1985

Lenk K., *The Mauritius Affair. The Boat People of 1940/1941*. Edited and translated from the original German by R.S. Lenk, Brighton 1993

Marcus E., "The German Foreign Office and the Palestine Question in the Period 1933–1939," *Yad Vashem Studies* (Jerusalem). Vol. II: 1958, pp. 179–204

Mardor M.M., *Strictly Illegal*. Foreword by D. Ben-Gurion, London 1964 (Hebrew edition: *Shelihut alumah*, Tel-Aviv 1957)

Meir G., *My Life*, 6th ed., London 1978

Nameri D., *Sipuro shel Davidka*, Tel Aviv 1974

Pearse R., *Three Years in the Levant*, London 1949

[Pearlman M.], *Ben Gurion Looks Back in talks with Moshe Pearlman*, New York 1965

Perl W.R., *Operation Action. Rescue from the Holocaust*. Revised and enlarged edition, New York 1983 (1st ed.: *The Four-Front War. From the Holocaust to the Promised Land*, New York 1979)

Sander-Steckl R., *À bientôt en Eretz Israël. L'odyssée des réfugiés de l'Atlantic (décembre 1939–avril 1942). Journal traduit de l'allemand par Sonia Combe*. Commenté par Michel Daëron, Paris 2002

Shamir Y., *Summing Up. An Autobiography*, Boston–New York–Toronto–London 1994

Siemaszko Z.S., "Rozmowa z gen. Andersem w dniu 31 lipca 1967 roku," *Kultura* (Paris). No. 7–8 (274–275): 1970, pp. 26–39

Soshuk L., Eisenberg A. (eds.), *Momentous Century. Personal and Eyewitness Accounts of the Rise of the Jewish Homeland and State 1875–1978*, New York–London 1984

Weizmann Ch., *Trial and Error. The Autobiography of Chaim Weizmann*, London 1950

# IV. Contemporary press articles (selection)

"204 Jewish Emigrants Drowned in Storm. 66 Children among Dead," *The Palestine Post*, 15 XII 1940

"246 żydowskich uchodźców utonęło w Morzu Czarnym," *Dziennik Polski i Dziennik Żołnierza* (London), 8 VIII 1944

"400 Refugees Rescued from Blazing Vessel off Rhodes," *The Palestine Post*, 6 VII 1939

"541 Refugees Arrive in Istanbul from Romania," *The Palestine Post*, 30 X 1944

"709 Refugees Lost in Struma. Ship Sinks in Black Sea," *The Palestine Post*, 27 II 1942

"840 Refugees from Rhodes Land Here. Rim Disaster Victims and Others in 3 Small Boats," *The Palestine Post*, 20 VIII 1939

"1400 Refugees Land at Tel Aviv Beach. Three Killed by Marine Patrol Fire," *The Palestine Post*, 3 IX 1939

"1875 Refugees Fight Death in Mediterranean. Fleeing from Nazi Tyranny 7 Die on Voyage from Creta," *Cyprus Post* (Nicosia), 16 XI 1940

"2000 Jewish Refugees Marooned on the Danube. MacDonald Refuses to Lift Palestine Ban," *The Palestine Post*, 8 II 1940

"Abril Refugees Deported," *The Palestine Post*, 10 III 1947

"Af-al-pi-magbit," *Trybuna Narodowa* (Kraków–Lwów–Warszawa), 9 XII 1938

"Arab Gov't Officials Ask Immigration Stoppage. Full Text of Memorandum Submitted to High Commissioner," *The Palestine Post*, 10 VII 1936

"Are There Nazi Jews?," *The Palestine Post*, 25 III 1940

"Athlit, where refugees are cleared," *The Palestine Post*, 22 I 1940

"Britain's Blow Will Not Subdue Jews. Statement of the Jewish Agency for Palestine," *The Palestine Post*, 18 V 1939

"Bulgaria Responsible For Salvador Tragedy," *The Palestine Post*, 22 XII 1940

"Explosion Wrecks Liner at Haifa," *The Times* (London), 26 XI 1940

"Govt. to Prosecute Illegal Immigrants. 1220 Refugees Prevented Entry Between February and April," *The Palestine Post*, 26 IV 1939

"Happy End of A Sad Odyssey. Saga of Mauritius Refugees," *The Palestine Post*, 27 VIII 1945

"Hundreds of Homeless in Cellars and Ship's Holds," *The Palestine Post*, 14 VI 1939

"Increased Penalties For Assisting 'Illegals,'" *The Palestine Post*, 24 VIII 1939

"Jewish Agency and Aid to 'Illegals,'" *The Palestine Post*, 2 VIII 1939

"Jewish Refugee Tragedy. Disastrous Voyage. Palestine Entry Barred," *Manchester Guardian*, 26 II 1942

"Jewry Mourns and Protests," *The Palestine Post*, 27 II 1942

Levy J.M., "Refugee Boats Attacked," *The New York Times*, 17 VIII 1944

"Loss of Refugee Ship in Black Sea. 760 Jews Drowned," *The Times*, 27 II 1942

"Mauritius Refugees Return," *The Palestine Post*, 27 VIII 1945

"Mr. Ben Gurion in Bulgaria," *The Palestine Post*, 3 XII 1944

"Murder of Lord Moyne. Minister Resident Shot in Cairo," *The Palestine Post*, 7 XI 1944

Namier L.B., "The Refugee Ships," *Time and Tide* (London), 14 III 1942

"No Legal Immigration in the Next Schedule Period," *The Palestine Post*, 13 VII 1939

"Parita Refugees Released," *The Palestine Post*, 1 IX 1939

"Patria Enquiry Opened," *The Palestine Post*, 13 XII 1940

"Patria Roll Growing. Total Number of Dead Now 137," *The Palestine Post*, 30 XII 1940.

"Patria Sinks in Haifa Harbour," *The Palestine Post*, 26 XI 1940

"Refugee Dead of Typhoid," *The Palestine Post*, 6 XII 1940

"Refugee Ship off Palestine Is Sunk by Blast," *The New York Times*, 26 XI 1940

"Salvador Was Derelict Ship Without Maps Or Instruments," *The Palestine Post*, 18 XII 1940

"Severer Measures Against Illegal Immigration," *The Palestine Post*, 20 III 1940

"A Ship in the Black Sea, Transporting 700 Victims, Sailed into a Mine Field for Lack of Navigation Facilities," *The New York Times*, 28 II 1942

"The S.S. Parita Beached at Tel Aviv on Tuesday," *The Palestine Post*, 24 VIII 1939

"Struma Again Raised in Commons," *The Palestine Post*, 13 III 1942

"The Struma Tragedy," *The New York Times*, 13 III 1942

"Survivors of Patria to Remain. Official Communique. Position Regarding Other 'Illegals' Unchanged," *The Palestine Post*, 5 XII 1940

"Turkey Censures Romania for Struma Sinking," *The Palestine Post*, 5 III 1942

"U-Boat Sank Refugee Ship," *The Palestine Post*, 20 VIII 1944

"The White Paper and the Struma. Dr. Weizmann on Refugee Tragedy," *The Palestine Post*, 9 III 1942

"White Paper not in Accordance with League's View of Mandate," *The Palestine Post*, 25 VIII 1939


# V. Monographs and articles

Abella I., Troper H., *None Is Too Many. Canada and the Jews of Europe, 1933–1948*, New York 1983

Aharonson R., *Rothschild and Early Jewish Colonization in Palestine*, Lanham 2000

Anderl G., "Die Zentralstelle für jüdische Auswanderung in Wien, 1938–1943," *David – Jüdische Kulturzeitschrift* (Wien). Jg. 5: 1993, H. 16, pp. 12–19

Anderl G., "Die 'Zentralstellen für jüdische Auswanderung' in Wien, Berlin und Prag – ein Vergleich," *Tel Aviver Jahrbuch für deutsche Geschichte* (Tel Aviv). 23. Band: 1994, pp. 275–299

Anderl G., "Berthold Storfer: Retter oder Kollaborateur? Skizzen einer umstrittenen Persönlichkeit. Ein Beitrag zur Geschichte der 'sogenannten illegalen Einwanderung' in das britische Mandatsgebiet Palästina," *David – Jüdische Kulturzeitschrift* (Wien). Jg. 9: 1997, H. 35, pp. 15–30

Anderl G., Manoschek W., *Gescheiterte Flucht. Der "Kladovo-Transport" auf dem Weg nach Palästina, 1939–1942*, Wien 2001

Anderl G., Manoschek W., "Herta Eisler und der jüdische 'Kladovo-Transport' auf dem Weg nach Palästina" [in:] *Zwei Tage Zeit. Herta Reich und die Spuren jüdischen Lebens in Mürz-zuschlag*. H. Halbrainer (Hg.), Graz 1998, pp. 38–62

Anderl G., Rupnow D., *Die Zentralstelle für jüdische Auswanderung als Beraubungsinstitution*. Unter redaktioneller Mitarbeit von A.-E. Wenck, Wien–München 2004

Anderson E.W., *The Middle East. Geography & Geopolitics*, London 2000

Antonius G., *The Arab Awakening. The Story of the Arab National Movement*, London 1945

Arendt H., *Eichmann in Jerusalem. A Report on the Banality of Evil*, New York 1964 (Polish edition: *Eichmann w Jerozolimie. Rzecz o banalności zła*, Kraków 1987)

Aroni S., "Who Perished on the Struma and How Many" [in:] D. Frantz, C. Collins, *Death on the Black Sea. The Untold Story of the "Struma" and World War II's Holocaust at Sea*, New York 2003, pp. 295–335

Arsene M. [A. Leibovici], *Struma*, Bucureşti 1972

Avneri A.L., *Mi – "Velos" 'ad "Taurus." Asor rishon le-ha'apalah be-darkhe ha-yam, 1934–1944*, Tel Aviv 1985.

Avineri S., *The Making of Modern Zionism. Intellectual Origins of the Jewish State*, New York 1981

Avneri A.L., *The Claim of Dispossession. Jewish Land-Settlement and the Arabs 1878–1948*, New Brunswick–London 1984

Aumann M., *Land Ownership in Palestine 1880–1948*, 3rd rev. ed. Jerusalem 1976.

Balke R., *Izrael*, Warszawa 2005 (translation from the German, München 2002)

Ball-Kaduri K.J., "Illegale Judenauswanderung aus Deutschland nach Palästina 1939/40 – Planung, Durchführung und internationale Zusammenhänge," *Jahrbuch des Instituts für deutsche Geschichte* (Tel Aviv). 4. Band: 1975, pp. 387–421 (also an abridged version in Hebrew in: *Yalkut Moreshet* (Tel Aviv) 1968. Vol. 8, pp. 127–144)

Barnawi E., "60 lat samotności (the interview was conducted by J. Alia, H. Guirchoun, R. Backmann," *Forum* (Warszawa). No. 5: 2008, pp. 12–21

Bar-Zohar M., *Ben-Gurion*, London 1978 (translation from the Hebrew, Tel Aviv 1977)

Batmaz Ş., "Illegal Jewish – Immigration Policy in Palestine (Periods of 1st and 2nd Constitutional Monarchy)," *Turkish Studies* (Ilford). Vol. 3/1: Winter 2008, pp. 219–229

Bauer Y., *American Jewry and the Holocaust. The American Jewish Joint Distribution Committee, 1939–1945*, Detroit 1981

Bauer Y., *Flight and rescue: Brichah*, New York 1970

Bauer Y., *From Diplomacy to Resistance. A History of Jewish Palestine 1939–1945*, New York 1973

Bauer Y., *My Brother's Keeper. A History of the American Jewish Joint Distribution Committee, 1929–1939*, Philadelphia 1974

Bauer Y., *Jews for Sale? Nazi-Jewish Negotiations, 1933–1945*, New Haven–London 1994

Bauer Y., Sagi N., "'Illegal' Immigration" [in:] *New Encyclopedia of Zionism and Israel*. Vol. 1. Ed. by G. Wigoder, London–Toronto 1994, pp. 647–649

Baumkoller A., *Le mandate sur la Palestine*, Paris 1931

Beckman M., *The Jewish Brigade. An Army with Two Masters, 1944–1945*, Staplehurst 1998

Ben-Gurion D., *The Peel Report and the Jewish State*, London 1938

Ben-Horin E., *The Middle East. Crossroads of History*, New York 1943

Bentwich N., *The Refugees from Germany, April 1933 to December 1935*, London 1936

Benz W., "Illegale Einwanderung nach Palästina" [in:] *Exilforschung. Ein Internationales Jahrbuch* (München). Band 19: 2001 ("Jüdische Emigration zwischen Assimilation und Verfolgung, Akkulturation und jüdischer Identität"), pp. 128–144

Bernstein I., *Włodzimierz Żabotyński jako pisarz i myśliciel. Studjum psychologiczno-literac-kie*, Warszawa 1935

Bethell N., "The man who survived the Struma," *The Sunday Times Magazine* (London), 9 III 1980, pp. 52–57

Bethell N., *The Palestine Triangle. The Struggle between the British, the Jews, and the Arabs, 1935–1948*, London 1979

Bierman J., *Odyssey*, New York 1984

Binder J., *Von Wien zum Schwarzen Meer. Eigenverlag der DDSG*, Wien 1972

Black E., *The Transfer Agreement. The Untold Story of the Secret Pact between the Third Reich and Jewish Palestine*, New York 1984

Bogner N., *Iy ha-gerush: mahanot ha-ma'apilim be-Kafrisin 1946-1948*, Tel Aviv 1991

Bogoslovskiy V.V. et al. (ed.), *Syjonizm – teoria i praktyka*, Warszawa 1975 (translation from the Russian, Moskva 1973)

Bojko K., "Emigracja polskich Żydów do Palestyny i Państwa Izrael od końca wieku XIX do czasów współczesnych," *Portolana. Studia Mediterranea* (Kraków). Ed. by D. Quirini-Popławska, Vol. 3: 2007. pp. 387–404

Bowden T., "Arab Rebellion in Palestine 1936–1939," *Middle Eastern Studies* (London). Vol. 11/2: 1975, pp. 147–174

Breitman R., Kraut A.M., *American Refugee Policy and European Jewry, 1933–1945*, Bloomington 1987

Brenner L., *The Iron Wall. Zionist Revisionism from Jabotinsky to Shamir*, London 1984

Brenner L., *Zionism in the Age of the Dictators*, Westport, Conn. 1983

Bronsztejn Sz., *Ludność żydowska w Polsce międzywojennej. Studium statystyczne*, Wrocław 1963

Brzoza Cz., *Kraków między wojnami. Kalendarium 28 X 1918–6 IX 1939*, Kraków 1998

Buchwajc M., *Mandat Ligi Narodów nad Palestyną*, Kraków 1939

Burstein M., *Self-government of the Jews in Palestine since 1900*, Tel Aviv 1934 (reprint: Westport, Conn 1976)

Butnaru I.C., *The Silent Holocaust. Romania and Its Jews.* Foreword by Elie Wiesel, New York–London 1992

Butnaru I.C., *Waiting for Jerusalem. Surviving the Holocaust in Romania*, Westport, Conn.–London 1993

Carmichael J., Weisgal M.W. (eds.), *Chaim Weizmann. A Biography by Several Hands*, London 1962

Cesarani D., *Eichmann. His Life and Crimes*, London 2004 (Polish edition, Zakrzewo 2008)

Chary F.B., *The Bulgarian Jews and the Final Solution 1940–1944*, Pittsburgh 1972

Chazan M., "The Patria Affair. Moderates vs. Activists in Mapai in the 1940s," *Journal of Israeli History* (Neisbury Park, UK). Vol. 22: 2003, No. 2, pp. 61–95 (version in Hebrew: *Siyywn* (Jerusalem). Vol. 66: 2001. No. 4, pp. 495–530)

Chmielewski W., "Bojownicy Ziemi Świętej. W II RP przygotowywali się do walki o powstanie Izraela," *Nowiny Kurier* (Tel Aviv), 26 V 2006, pp. 10–11

Chojnowski A., Tomaszewski J., *Izrael* (*Historia Państw Świata w XX wieku*), Warszawa 2001

Cohen E.J., *Rescue. 2.500.000 Jews Were Liberated by Mossad From Europe, North Africa and Asia – 1932–1990. 300 Stories and Photographs*, New York 1991

Cohen M.J., *Churchill and the Balfour Declaration: The Interpretation, 1920–1922* [in:] U. Dann (ed.), *The Great Powers in the Middle East 1919–1939*, New York–London 1988, pp. 91–108

Cohen M.J., *Churchill and the Jews*, London 1985

Cohen M.J., "The Moyne Assassination, November 1944. A Political Analysis," *Middle Eastern Studies* (London). Vol. 15: 1979. No. 3, pp. 358–373

Cohen M.J., *Palestine to Israel. From Mandate to Independence*, London 1988

Cohen M.J., *Palestine: Retreat from the Mandate. The Making of British Policy, 1936–1945*, New York 1978

Cohn-Sherbok D., El-Alami D., *Konflikt palestyńsko-izraelski*, Warszawa 2002 (translation from the English, Oxford 2001)

Daniels R., *Coming to America. A History of Immigration and Ethnicity in American Life*, New York 1990

Dann U. (ed.), *The Great Powers in the Middle East 1919–1939*, New York–London 1988

Douer A. (Hg.), *Kladovo. Eine Flucht nach Palästina. Escape to Palestine*, Wien 2001

Eckert B. (Hg.), *Die jüdische Emigration aus Deutschland 1933–1941. Die Geschichte einer Austreibung*, Frankfurt/Main 1985

El-Eini R., *Mandated Lanscape. British Imperial Rule in Palestine, 1929–1948*, London 2006

Elpeleg Z., *The Grand Mufti Haj Amin al-Hussaini, founder of the Palestinian National Movement*, London 1993

[Esco Foundation for Palestine], *Palestine: A Study of Jewish, Arab and British Policies*. Vol. I–II, New Haven 1947

Ettinger A., *Blind Jump. The Story of Shaike Dan*, New York–London–Toronto 1992 (translation from the Hebrew: *Tsenihah' iveret*, Tel Aviv 1986)

Feilchenfeld W., Michaelis D., Pinner L., *Haha'avarah – Transfer nach Palästina*, Tübingen 1972

Feingold H.L., *The Politics of Rescue. The Roosevelt Administration and the Holocaust 1938–1945*, New Brunswick, NJ 1970

Feinstein J., *Struma. Corabia vietii şi a mortii*. Prefata de David Safran, Tel Aviv 1965

Feiwel T.R., *L'Anglais, le Juif et l'Arabe en Palestine*, Paris 1939

Frantz D., Collins C., *Death on the Black Sea. The Untold Story of the "Struma" and World War II's Holocaust at Sea*, New York 2003

Friedman I., *The Question of Palestine. British-Jewish-Arab Relations, 1914–1918*, 2nd ed., New Brunswick 1992

Friedman S.S., *No Haven for the Opressed. United States Policy toward Jewish Refugees, 1938–1945*, Detroit 1973

Friedmann R., *Exil auf Mauritius 1940 bis 1945. Report einer "demokratischen" Deportation jüdischer Flüchtlinge*, Berlin 1998

Fromkin D., *A Peace to End all Peace. The Fall of the Ottoman Empire and the Creation of the Modern Middle East*, London 2000

Galante A., *Histoire des Juifs d'Istanbul depuis la prise de cette ville, en 1453, par Fatih Mehmed II, jusqu'à nos jours*. 2 Vol., Istanbul 1942

Gąsowski T., *Pod sztandarami Orła Białego. Kwestia żydowska w Polskich Siłach Zbrojnych w czasie II wojny światowej*, Kraków 2002

Gebert K., *Miejsce pod słońcem. Wojny Izraela*, Warszawa 2008

Geffen D., "The Sinking of the Patria," *The Jerusalem Post*, 23 XI 1990

Gensicke K., *Der Mufti von Jerusalem. Amin el-Husseini, und die Nationalsozialisten*, Frankfurt am Main 1988

Gervasi F., *The Life and Times of Menahem Begin. Rebel to Statesman*, New York 1979

Gheorghiu S., *Tragedia navelor "Struma" şi "Mefkure,"* Constanţa 1998

Gilbert M., "British Government Policy towards Jewish Refugees (November 1938–September 1939)," *Yad Vashem Studies* (Jerusalem). Vol. XIII: 1979, pp. 127–167

Gilbert M., *Churchill and the Jews. A Lifelong Friendship*, New York 2007

Gilbert M., *Exile and Return. The Emergence of Jewish Statehood*, London 1978

Gilbert M., *Israel. A History*, London 1999

Glubb Bagot J., *Britain and the Arabs. A Study of Fifty Years 1908 to 1958*, London 1959

Goldscheider C., *Israel's Changing Society. Population, Ethnicity and Development*, Boulder, Col. 1996

Golomb E., *The History of Jewish Self-defence in Palestine (1878–1921)*, Tel Aviv [1947?]

*Great Britain and Palestine 1915–1945*. Ed. by The Royal Institute of International Affairs. Information Papers No. 20, London–New York 1946

Greenberg I., "The 'Struma': Unsinking history," *The Jerusalem Post*, 14 XII 2001

Greenfield M.S., Hochstein J.M., *The Jews' Secret Fleet. The Untold Story of North American Volunteers Who Smashed the British Blockade*, Jerusalem 1987 (rev. ed. Jerusalem–New York 1999)

Gutman I., "Jews in General Anders' Army in the Soviet Union," *Yad Vashem Studies* (Jerusalem). Vol. XII: 1977, pp. 231–333

Gvati Ch., *A Hundred Years of Settlement. The Story of Jewish Settlement in the Land of Israel*, Jerusalem 1985

*Ha'apala – clandestine immigration 1934–1948*. Published by State of Israel – Ministry of Defence, I.D.F. Museum [without year of issue]

Habas B., *The Gate Breakers*, New York–London 1963 (Hebrew version: *Portzei ha-shearim. Sipur korotehah shel Aliyah Bet*, Tel Aviv 1957)

Hadari Z.V., *Second Exodus. The Full Story of Jewish Illegal Immigration to Palestine, 1945–1948*, London 1991 (Hebrew version: *Pelitim menatshim imperyah: parashiyot 'Aliyah 2, 1945–1948*, Tel Aviv–Beer Sheva 1985)

Hadari Z.V., Tsahor Z., *Voyage to Freedom. An Episode in the Illegal Immigration to Palestine*, London 1985 (Hebrew version: *Oniyot o medinah: korot oniyot ha-ma'apilim "Pan York" u-"Pan Kresent,"* Tel Aviv–Beer Sheva 1981)

Halamish A., *The Exodus Affair. Holocaust Survivors and the Struggle for Palestine*, London 1998 (Hebrew edition: *Eksodus. Ha-Sippur ha-amiti*, Tel Aviv 1990)

Halamish A., "Illegal Immigration: Values, Myth and Reality," *Studies in Zionsim. An International Journal of Social, Political and Intellectual History* (Tel Aviv). Vol. 9: 1988. No. 1, pp. 47–62

Halpern B., Reinharz J., *Zionism and the Creation of a New Society*, New York–Oxford 1988

Hanna P.L., *British Policy in Palestine*, Washington 1942

Hattis S.L., *The Bi-National Idea in Palestine During Mandatory Times*, Haifa 1970

Heller J., *The Stern Gang. Ideology, Politics and Terror, 1940–1949*, London 1995

Hillgruber A., "The Third Reich and the Near and Middle East, 1933–1939" [in:] U. Dann (ed.), *The Great Powers in the Middle East 1919–1939*, New York–London 1988, pp. 274–282.

Hirszowicz Ł., *III Rzesza i arabski Wschód*, Warszawa 1963 (English edition: *The Third Reich and the Arab East*, London–Toronto 1966)

Horowitz D., Lissak M., *Origins of the Israeli Polity. Palestine under the Mandate*, Chicago 1978

Hoskins H.L., *The Middle East. Problem Area in World Politics*, New York 1954

Hoter E., "Avigur (Meirov) Shaul" [in:] *New Encyclopedia of Zionism and Israel*. Vol. 1. Ed. by G. Wigoder, London–Toronto 1994, p. 148

Huneidi S., *A Broken Trust. Herbert Samuel, Zionism and the Palestinians 1920–1925*, London 2001

Hurewitz J.C., *The Struggle for Palestine*, New York 1976

Hyamson A.M., *Palestine under the Mandate, 1920–1948*, London 1950

Joseph B., *British Rule in Palestine*, Washington 1948

Kamenec I., *Po stopách tragédie*, Bratislava 1991

Kamm J., *The Story of Sir Moses Montefiore*, London 1960

Kaniuk Y, *Und das Meer teilte sich. Der Kommandant der Exodus*, München 1999 (among others also the English edition: *The Commander of the Exodus*, New York 1999, French: *Il commanda l'Exodus*, Paris 2000 and Hebrew: *Ha-Saga shel mefaked ha-Eksodus*, Tel Aviv 2001)

Katz S., *Lone Wolf. A Biography of Vladimir (Ze'ev) Jabotinsky*, New York 1996

Kedourie E., *England and the Middle East. The Destruction of the Ottoman Empire 1914–1921*, London 1956

Kedourie E., *In the Anglo-Arab Labyrinth. The McMahon – Husayn Correspondence and Its Interpretations, 1914–1939*, Cambridge–New York 1976 (2nd ed.: London–Portland, Or. 2000)

Kemp D., "Search for Jewish refugees' shipwreck," *The Independent* (London), 2 VIII 2000

Kimche J., *The Unromantics. The Great Powers and the Balfour Declaration*, London 1968

Kimche J. and D., *The Secret Roads. The "Illegal" Migration of a People, 1938–1948*, London 1954 (also the German edition: *Des Zornes und des Herzens wegen. Die illegale Wanderung eines Volkes*, Berlin [West] 1956)

Kirk G., *The Middle East in the War*, 3rd ed., London–New York–Toronto 1954

Kirk G., *A Short History of the Middle East. From the Rise of Islam to Modern Times*, 7th ed., London 1964

Klieman A.S., *Foundation of British Policy in the Arab World. The Cairo Conference of 1921*, Baltimore 1970

Klugman A., *Izrael ziemia świecka*, Warszawa 2001

Koen A., Assa A., *Saving of the Jews in Bulgaria, 1941–1944*, Sofia 1977

Koestler A., *Promise and Fulfilment. Palestine 1917–1949*, London 1983 (1st ed., 1949)

Kossoy E., "Żydowskie podziemie zbrojne w Palestynie i jego polskie powiązania," *Zeszyty Historyczne* (Paris). No. 157: 2006, pp. 62–100

Kovalev E.A., *Koroli podplava v more chervonnykh valetov. Khronika nachal'nogo perioda sovetskogo podvodnogo plavaniia, 1918–1941 gg*, Moskva–St. Peterburg 2006

Krammer A., *The Forgotten Friendship. Israel and the Soviet Bloc, 1947–1953*, Urbana–Chicago–London 1974

Krasuski J., *Historia Rzeszy Niemieckiej 1871–1945*, 4th ed., Poznań 1986

Kubiak K., *Pierwsza wojna bliskowschodnia 1947–1949 (studium polityczno-wojskowe)*, Wrocław 2006

Kula M., "Porozmawiajmy jeszcze raz, na spokojnie, o syjonizmie," *Dzieje Najnowsze* (Warszawa). No. 2: 1987, pp. 89–124

Laqueur W., *A History of Zionism*, London 1972

Lazar H., *The Revisionist Immigration* [in:] M. Naor, *Haapala. Clandestine Immigration 1931–1948*, [Tel Aviv 1987], pp. 8–26

Lazar-Litai Ch., *Af-'al-pi. Sefer Aliyah Bet*, Tel Aviv 1957 (2nd ed.: *Af-'al-pi. Aliyah 2. shel tenu'at Z'abotinski*, Berit hayale ha-Etsel 1988; also the English edition: *Despite it all*, New York 1984)

Lenczowski G., *The Middle East in World Affairs*, New York 1952

Levin D., *Alija „waw." Masowa dezercja żołnierzy żydowskich z Armii Andersa w Palestynie w latach 1942–1943* [in:] D. Levin, *Żydzi wschodnioeuropejscy podczas II wojny światowej*, Warszawa 2005, pp. 117–140 (also in English: "Aliyah 'vav'. The Mass Desertion of Jewish Soldiers from the Polish Army in Palestine, 1942–1943," *Shvut. Studies in Russian and East European Jewish History and Culture* (Tel Aviv–Beer Sheva). Vol. 5 (21): 1997, pp. 144–170)

Liebreich F., *Britain's Naval and Political Reaction to the Illegal Immigration of Jews to Palestine, 1945–1948*, London 2005

Lilienthal A.M., *The Other Side of the Coin. An American Perspective of the Arab-Israeli Conflict*, New York 1965 (Polish edition: *Druga strona medalu*, Warszawa 1970)

Lilienthal A.M., *The Zionist Connection II*, New Brunswick, NJ 1982

Lipscher I., *Die Juden im Slowakischen Staat 1939–1945*, München–Wien 1980 (Slovak edition: *Židia v slovenskom štáte 1939–1945*, Bratislava 1992)

London L., *Whitehall and the Jews, 1933–1948. British immigration policy, Jewish refugees and the Holocaust*, Cambridge 2003

Louis W.R., *The British Empire in the Middle East 1945–1951. Arab Nationalism, The United States, and Postwar Imperialism*, Oxford 1988

Luttwak E.N., Horowitz D., *The Israeli Army 1948–1973*, Cambridge, Mass. 1983

Maga T.P., "Operation Rescue: The Mefkure Incident and War Refugee Board," *American Neptune. A Quarterly Journal of Maritime History and Arts* (Salem, Mass.). Vol. 43: 1983. No. 1, pp. 31–39

Mandel N.J., *The Arabs and Zionism before World War I*, Berkeley, Cal. 1976

Manning O., "The Tragedy of the Struma. How the World Stood By and Watched 760 Jews Sail to their Deaths," *The Observer* (London), 1 III 1970

Marlowe J., *The Seat of Pilate. An Account of the Palestine Mandate*, London 1959

Marrus M.R., *The Unwanted. European Refugees from the First World War Through the Cold War*, Philadelphia 2002

*Martirilor din fundul mării 1942–1972*. Culegere întocmită de I. Bar-Avi și I. Feinstein, Ierusalim 1972

"The Mauritius exile: Victims of a paradise," *The Jerusalem Post*, 16 IX 1988

Medding P.Y., *Mapai in Israel. Political Organization and Government in a New Society*, Cambridge 1972

Meir-Glitzenstein E., *Zionism in Arab Country. Jews in Iraq in the 1940s*, London–New York 2004

Mejcher H. (Hg.), *Die Palästina Frage 1917–1948. Historische Ursprünge und internationale Dimensionen eines Nationenkonflikts.* 2. Auflage, Poderborn–München–Wien–Zurich 1993

Melzer E., *No Way Out. The Politics of Polish Jewry, 1935–1939*, Cincinnati 1997 (translation from the Hebrew, Tel Aviv 1982)

Mendelsohn E., *Żydzi Europy Środkowo-Wschodniej w okresie międzywojennym*, Warszawa 1992 (translation from English, Bloomington 1983)

Miller S., Ogilvie S.A., *Refuge Denied. The St. Louis Passengers and the Holocaust*, Madison 2006

Miller Y.N., *Government and Society in Rural Palestine 1920–1948*, Austin 1985

Milotová J., "Die Zentralstelle für jüdische Auswanderung in Prag. Genesis und Tätigkeit bis zum Anfang des Jahres 1940" [in:] M. Kárný, M. Kárná, R. Kemper (Hg.), *Theresienstädter Studien und Dokumente*, Prag 1997, pp. 7–30

Monroe E., *Britain's Moment in the Middle East 1914–1956*, London 1963 (2nd ed.: *Britain's Moment in the Middle East 1914–1971*, Baltimore, Mar. 1981)

Morris B., *The Road to Jerusalem. Glubb Pasha, Palestine, and the Jews*, London 2003

Moser J., *Die Zentralstelle für jüdische Auswanderung in Wien* [in:] K. Schmid, R. Streibel (Hg.), *Der Pogrom 1938. Judenverfolgung in Österreich und Deutschland. Dokumentation eines Symposiums der Volkshochschule Brigittenau*, Wien 1990, pp. 96–100

Mossek M., *Palestine Immigration Policy under Sir Herbert Samuel. British, Zionist and Arab Attitudes*, London 1978

Naor M., *Aliyah 2, 1934–1948: mekorot, sikumim, parashiyot nivharot vehomer 'ezer/ ha – 'orekh*, Yerushalayim 1988

Naor M., *Atlit. "Illegal immigrant" detention camp. A story of a time and place*, Mikveh Israel 2010

Naor M., *Haapala. Clandestine Immigration 1931–1948*, [Tel Aviv 1987]

Nedava J., *Vladimir Jabotinsky. The Man and his Struggles*, Tel Aviv 1986

Nevakivi J., *Britain, France and the Arab Middle East 1914–1920*, London 1969

Nevo J., *King Abdallah and Palestine. A Territorial Ambition*, Oxford 1996

Nicosia F.R., *The Third Reich and the Palestine Question*, New Brunswick–London 1985

Ofer D., "The Activities of the Jewish Agency Delegation in Istanbul" [in:] Y. Gutman, E. Zuroff (eds.), *Rescue Attempts during the Holocaust. Proceedings of the Second Yad Vashem International Historical Conference, Jerusalem. April 8–11, 1974*, Jerusalem 1977, pp. 435–450 (also in: M.R. Marrus (ed.), *The Nazi Holocaust. Historical Articles on the Destruction of European Jews*, Westport, Conn. 1989, Vol. 8, pp. 629–657)

Ofer D., *Escaping the Holocaust. Illegal Immigration to the Land of Israel, 1939–1944*, New York 1990 (Hebrew version: *Derekh ba-yam: Aliyah 2 bi-tekufat ha-Sho'ah, 1939–1944*, Yerushalayim 1988)

Ofer D., "The Historiography of Aliyah Bet" [in:] Y. Gutman, G. Grief (eds.), *The Historiography of the Holocaust Period. Proceedings of the Fifth Yad Vashem International Historical Conference, Jerusalem, March 1983*, Jerusalem 1988, pp. 585–607

Ofer D., "Holocaust Survivors as Immigrants. The Case of the Cyprus Detainees," *Modern Judaism* (Baltimore). Vol. 16: 1996. No. 1, pp. 1–23

Ofer D., "Die illegale Einwanderung nach Palästina: Politische, nationale und persönliche Aspekte (1939–1941)" [in:] S. Heim et al. (Hg.), *Flüchtlingspolitik und Fluchthilfe*, Berlin 1999, pp. 9–38

Ofer D., "Illegal Immigration During the Second World War: Its Suspension and Subsequent Resumption," *Studies in Contemporary Jewry* (New York–Oxford). Ed. by J. Frankel. Vol. VII: 1991 ("Jews and Messianism in the Modern Era: Metaphor and Meaning"), pp. 220–246

Ofer D., "The Kladovo – Darien Affair – Illegal Immigration to Palestine. Zionist Policy and European Exigencies" [in:] R.J. Cohen (ed.), *Vision and Conflict in the Holy Land*, Jerusalem–New York 1985, pp. 218–245

Ofer D., "The Rescue of European Jewry and Illegal Immigration to Palestine in 1940 – Prospects and Reality. Berthold Storfer and the Mossad le'Aliyah Bet," *Modern Judaism*

(Baltimore). Vol. 4: 1984. No. 2, pp. 159–181 (also in: M.R. Marrus (ed.), *The Nazi Holocaust. Historical Articles on the Destruction of European Jews*. Vol. 9, Westport, Conn. 1989, pp. 199–222)

Ofer D., Weiner H., *Dead-End Journey. The Tragic Story of the Kladovo-Šabac Group*, Lanham, Md.–New York–London 1996 (Hebrew version: *Parashat Kladovo-Sabac. Hamas'a shelo higi'a 1939–1942*, Tel Aviv 1992)

Ofir E., *With No Way Out. The Story of the Struma. Documents and Testimonies*, Cluj-Napoca 2003

Ovendale R., *Britain, The United States, and the End of the Palestine Mandate 1942–1948*, London 1989

Ovendale R., *The Origins of the Arab-Israeli Wars*, 3rd ed., London–New York 1994

Ozer A., "The Strumah Tragedy," *ROM-SIG News. The Journal of the Special Interest Group for Romanian Jewish Genealogy* (Greenwich, Conn.). Vol. 5: Spring 1997. No. 3.

Paetz A., Weiss K. (Hg.), "*Hachschara.*" *Die Vorbereitung junger Juden auf die Auswanderung nach Palästina*, Potsdam 1999

Patek A., "Alija bet w filmie," *Kwartalnik Filmowy* (Warszawa). No. 69 (129): 2010, pp. 201–213

Patek A., "Brytyjskie obozy na Cyprze dla deportowanych imigrantów żydowskich (1946–1949)," *Portolana. Studia Mediterranea* (Kraków). Vol. 1: 2004. Ed. by D. Quirini-Popławska, pp. 233–245

Patek A., "Dramat 'Mefkury' (1944 r.)," *Nowiny Kurier* (Tel Aviv), 7 V 2008, pp. 12–13

Patek A., "Emigracja typu B (alija bet) do Palestyny przed II wojną światową" [in:] *Żydzi i judaizm we współczesnych badaniach polskich*. T. IV. Ed. by. K. Pilarczyk, Kraków 2008, pp. 293–308

Patek A., "Ha'apala między historią a filmem," *Nowiny Kurier* (Tel Aviv), 19 III 2009, pp. 14–15

Patek A., "Nielegalna emigracja żydowska z II Rzeczypospolitej do Palestyny," *Zeszyty Naukowe Uniwersytetu Jagiellońskiego. Prace Historyczne* (Kraków). No. 136: 2009, pp. 113–125

Patek A., "O swobodną imigrację do Erec Israel. Z dziejów aliji bet," *Nowiny Kurier* (Tel Aviv), 14 VI 2007, pp. 8–9, 14

Patek A., "Tragedia 'Strumy,'" *Nowiny Kurier* (Tel Aviv), 6 XII 2007, pp. 14–15

Patek A., *Wielka Brytania wobec Izraela w okresie pierwszej wojny arabsko-izraelskiej, maj 1948–styczeń 1949*, Kraków 2002

Patek A., "W kręgu wiary i zbiorowej świadomości. Z kart Aliji Bet (1938–1948)," *Portolana. Studia Mediterranea* (Kraków). Ed. by D. Quirini-Popławska, Vol. 2: 2006, pp. 297–310

Patek A., "Wokół zatonięcia statku 'Struma' (Morze Czarne, luty 1942 r.)," *Prace Komisji Środkowoeuropejskiej PAU* (Kraków). T. XIX: 2011, pp. 73–86

Patek A., "Żydowscy zesłańcy na Mauritus (1940–1945)" [in:] W. Bernacki, A. Walaszek (eds.), *Amerykomania*. Vol. 2, Kraków 2012, pp. 667–678

Patek A., *Żydzi w drodze do Palestyny 1934–1944. Szkice z dziejów aliji bet, nielegalnej imigracji żydowskiej*, Kraków 2009

Penkower M.N., *The Jews were Expendable. Free World Diplomacy and the Holocaust*, Chicago 1983

Perlmutter A., *The Life and Times of Menachem Begin*, Garden City, N.Y. 1987

Peters J., *From Time Immemorial. The Origins of the Arab-Jewish Conflict Over Palestine*, London 1985

Pickett W., "Mauritius Inmates Recall British Detention camp," *The Jerusalem Post*, 6 X 1995

Pinkus B., *The Jews of the Soviet Union. The History of a National Minority*, Cambridge 1988

Pitot G., *The Mauritian Shekel. The Story of the Jewish Detainees in Mauritius, 1940–1945*, Port Louis (Mauritius) 1998

Porat D., *The Blue and the Yellow Stars of David. The Zionist Leadership in Palestine and the Holocaust, 1939–1945*, Cambridge, Mass. 1990

Porat D., "Palestinian Jewry and the Jewish Agency. Public Response to the Holocaust" [in:] R.J. Cohen (ed.),*Vision and Conflict in the Holy Land*, Jerusalem–New York 1985, pp. 246–273

Prinz A., "The Role of the Gestapo in Obstructing and Promoting Jewish Emigration," *Yad Vashem Studies* (Jerusalem), Vol. II: 1958, pp. 205–218

Pułaski M., "Próba podziału Palestyny w roku 1937 a problem emigracji Żydów" [in:] A. Pankowicz (ed.),*Wojna i polityka. Studia nad historią XX wieku*, Kraków 1994, pp. 109–120

Rabinovich A., "In the Name of Isaiah and Balfour," *The Jerusalem Post*, 22 V 1991

Raizel M., "'Struma' și responsabilitatea internațională," *Viata Noastra* (Tel Aviv), 2 III 1956, p. 5 (also in *Lumea Noastra* [Tel Aviv], 4 III 1956, p. 4)

Reinharz J., *Chaim Weizmann. The Making of a Zionist Leader*, New York–Oxford 1985

Resel M., *Tik Mefkura*, Tel Aviv 1981

Reynolds Q., Katz E., Aldouby Z., *Minister of Death. The Adolf Eichmann Story*, London 1961

Rohwer J., *Die Versenkung der jüdischen Flüchtlingstransporter Struma und Mefkure im Schwarzen Meer (Februar 1942, August 1944)*, Frankfurt/Main 1965

Rose N., *Chaim Weizmann. A Biography*, London 1987

Rosenkranz H., *Verfolgung und Selbstbehauptung. Die Juden in Österreich 1938–1945*, Wien 1978

Rotenberg Z., "The Atlit Detention Camp" [in:] Naor M., *Atlit. "Illegal immigrant" detention camp. A story of a time and place*, Mikveh Israel 2010, pp. 5–6

Rubin B., "Ambassador Laurence A. Steinhardt. The Perils of a Jewish Diplomat," *American Jewish History* (New York). Vol. 70: 1981, pp. 332–344

Rubinstein S., "Asupra câtorva tragedii mici petrecute în cadrul unei tragedii mari, numită 'Struma,'" *Studia et Acta Historiae Iudaeorum Romaniae* (București). Vol. IV: 1999, pp. 193–207

Rubinstein S., *Personal Tragedies as a Reflection to a Great Tragedy Called Struma*, Jerusalem 2003

Sachar H.M., *The Emergence of the Middle East 1914–1924*, London 1970

Sachar H.M., *Europe Leaves the Middle East 1936–1954*, New York 1972

Sachar H.M., *A History of Israel. From the Rise of Zionism to Our Time*, New York 1988

Sanders R., *The High Walls of Jerusalem. A History of the Balfour Declaration and the Birth of the British Mandate for Palestine*, New York 1984

Sanders R., *Shores of Refuge. A Hundred Years of Jewish Emigration*, New York 1989

Sarner H., *Generał Anders i żołnierze II Korpusu Polskiego*, Poznań 2002 (also in English: *General Anders and the soldiers of the Second Polish Corps*, Cathedral City, Cal. 1997)

Săveanu S., *Save the Honour of Civilization!*, Tel Aviv 1996

Schaary D., *Gerush Kafrisin, 1946–1949 (The Cyprus Detention Camps for Jewish "Illegal" Immigrants to Palestine 1946–1949)*, Yerushalayim 1981

Schaary D., "The Social Structure of the Cyprus Detention Camps: 1946–1949," *Studies in Zionism* (Tel Aviv), No. 6: Autumn 1982, pp. 273–290

Schechtman J.B., *The Life and Times of Vladimir Jabotinsky*. Vol. 1–2, Silver Spring, Mar. 1986

Schechtman J.B., *The Mufti and the Führer. The Rise and Fall of Haj Amin el-Husseini*, New York 1965

Schechtman J.B., "The USSR, Zionism and Israel" [in:] L. Kochan (ed.), *The Jews in Soviet Russia since 1917*, London 1972

Schrager-Costin M., "Am fost pe 'Mefkure' – zguduitoarea spovedanie a unei supravieţuitoare," *Facla* (Tel Aviv), 8 VIII 1979, pp. 3, 13

Schwadran B., *The Middle East Oil and the Great Powers*, 3rd ed., New York 1974

Segev T., *One Palestine, Complete: Jews and Arabs under the British Mandate*, London 2000

Shafir G., *Land, Labor and the Origins of the Israeli-Palestinian Conflict 1882–1914*, Cambridge 1989 (updated ed.: Berkeley, Cal. 1996)

Shapira A. (ed.), *Haapalah: measef letoladot ha-hazalah, ha-berihah, ha-haapalah usheerit ha-peleitah*, Tel Aviv 1990

Shapiro S., "Smugglers with a cause," *The Jerusalem Post*, 4 IX 1998

Shapiro Y., *The Formative Years of the Israeli Labour Party. The Organization of Power, 1919–1939*, London 1976

Shavit Y., *Jabotinsky and the Revisionist Movement 1925–1948*, London 1988

Shaw S.J., *Turkey and the Holocaust. Turkey's Role in Rescuing Turkish and European Jewry from Nazi Persecution, 1933–1945*, New York 1993

Shealtiel S., "The Private Clandestine Immigration Operation of Dr. Baruch Confino, 1939–1940," *Shvut. Studies in Russian and East European Jewish History and Culture* (Tel Aviv–Beer Sheva). Ed. by B. Pinkus. Vol. 10 (26): 2001, pp. 57–123

Sheffer G., *Principles of Pragmatism: A Revaluation of British Policies toward Palestine in the 1930s* [in:] U. Dann (ed.), *The Great Powers in the Middle East 1919–1939*, New York–London 1988, pp. 109–127

Shelah M., *Ha-kesher ha-Yugoslavi. Yugoslavyah ve-Aliyah Beth, 1938–1948* (*The Yugoslav Connection. Yugoslavia and the Illegal Jewish Immigration 1938–1948*), Tel Aviv 1994

Shelah M., "Sajmište – An Extermination Camp in Serbia," *Holocaust and Genocide Studies. An International Journal* (Oxford–New York–Jerusalem). Vol. 2: 1987, pp. 243–260

Shepherd N., *Ploughing Sand. British Rule in Palestine 1917–1948*, London 1999

Sherman A.J., *Island Refuge. Britain and Refugees from the Third Reich, 1933–1939*, London 1973

Silver E., *Begin. A Biography*, London 1984

Silverstone P.H., *"Our Only Refuge Open the Gates!" Clandestine Immigration to Palestine 1938–1948*, New York 1999

Sjöberg T., *The Powers and the Persecuted. The Refugee Problem and the Intergovernmental Committee on Refugees*, Lund 1991

Slutsky Y., *Khagana – Evreyskaya boevaya organizatsiya v Eretz-Israel'*, kn. 1–2, Tel-Awiw 1978 (Hebrew version: *Sefer Toldot ha-Haganah*, Tel Aviv 1972)

Slutsky Y., Bauer Y., *"Illegal" immigration and the Berihach* [in:] *Immigration and Settlement*, Jerusalem 1973, pp. 35–49

Sobczyński M., *Państwa i terytoria zależne. Ujęcie geograficzno-polityczne*, Toruń 2006

Solomon M., *The Struma Incident. A Novel of the Holocaust*, Toronto 1979 (also published in French: *Le Struma*, Toronto 1974)

St. John R., *Ben-Gurion. A Biography*, Garden City, NJ 1971

Stein L., *The Balfour Declaration*, New York 1961

Stein L., *The Land Question in Palestine 1917–1939*, Chapel Hill 1984

Stein L., *Zionism*, London 1932

Steiner E.G., *The Story of the Patria*, New York 1982 (also published in German: *Die Geschichte der "Patria,"* Tel Aviv 1973)

Stewart N., *The Royal Navy and the Palestine Patrol*, London–Portland, Or 2002

Stoian M., *Ultima cursă de la Struma la Mefküre*, Bucureşti 1995

Strauss H.A., "Jewish Emigration from Germany. Nazi Policies and Jewish Responses," *Leo Baeck Institute Year Book* (London). Vol. 25: 1980, pp. 313–361, Part II – Vol. 26: 1981, pp. 343–409

Sykes Ch., *Cross Roads to Israel. Palestine from Balfour to Bevin*, 2nd ed., London 1967

Sykes Ch., *Orde Wingate*, London 1959

Syrkin M., *Blessed is the Match. The Story of Jewish Resistance*, Philadelphia 1947

Szczepański W., *Palestyna po wojnie światowej. Światła i cienie*, Kraków 1923

Szulc T., *The Secret Alliance. The Extraordinary Story of the Rescue of the Jews Since World War II*, New York 1991

Szyndler A., "Leon Schönker i jego plan emigracji Żydów z rejencji katowickiej z końca 1939 roku," *Studia Judaica* (Kraków). Nos. 1–2: 2009, pp. 237–274

Tartakower A., *Jewish Migratory Movements in Austria in Recent Generations* [in:] J. Fraenkel (ed.), *The Jews of Austria. Essays on their Life, History and Destruction*, London 1967, pp. 285–310

Tartakower A., Grossmann K.R., *The Jewish Refugee*, New York 1944

Tauber E., *The Arab Movements in World War I*, London 1993

Taylor A.R., *Prelude to Israel. An Analysis of Zionist Diplomacy, 1897–1947*, New York 1959 (rev. ed. Beirut 1970)

Teveth S., *Ben-Gurion and the Holocaust*, New York–San Diego–London 1996

Teveth S., *Ben-Gurion. The Burning Ground 1886–1948*, Boston 1987

Thomas G., *Operation Exodus. A Perilous Journey from the Nazi Camps to the Promised Land… and Back*, London 2010

Thomas G., Morgan Witts M., *Voyage of the Damned*, New York 1974 (Polish edition: *Rejs wyklętych*, Zakrzewo 2010)

Thomas I.E., "Brytyjskie obozy pracy na Cyprze dla nielegalnych żydowskich imigrantów," *Midrasz* (Warszawa). No. 12: 2009, pp. 21–29

Tomaszewski J. (ed.), *Najnowsze dzieje Żydów w Polsce w zarysie (do 1950 roku)*, Warszawa 1993

Tomaszewski J., "Początki prześladowania Żydów słowackich," *Zeszyty Majdanka* (Lublin), T. 11: 1993, pp. 5–17

Trevor D., *Under the White Paper. Some Aspects of British Administration in Palestine from 1939 to 1947*, Jerusalem 1948

Tzahor Z. (review), Shapira A. (ed.), "Ha'apalah: measef letoladot hahazalah, haberihah, haha'apalah usheerit hapeleitah" ("Ha'apalah: Studies in the History of Illegal Immigration into Palestine 1934–1948"), Tel-Aviv: Am Oved 1990,' *Studies in Contemporary Jewry*. Vol. IX: "Modern Jews and Their Musical Agendas." Ed. by E. Mendelsohn, New York 1993, pp. 362–364

Udelson J.H., *Dreamer of the Ghetto. The Life and Works of Israel Zangwill*, London 1990

Vaneev G.I., *Chernomortsy v vielikoy otechestvennoy voyne*, Moskva 1978

*Walka o prawo powrotu do Ojczyzny (maapilim)*. Ed. by Ichud Hanoar Hacijoni-Akiba, Łódź 1948

Wasserstein B., *Britain and the Jews of Europe 1939–1945*, London–Oxford 1979

Wasserstein B., *The British in Palestine. The Mandatory Government and the Arab-Jewish Conflict 1917–1929*, London 1978

Wasserstein B., *Herbert Samuel. A Political Life*, Oxford 1992

Weinbaum L., *A Marriage of Convenience. The New Zionist Organization and the Polish Government 1936–1939*, New York 1993

Weisl von W., *Illegale Transporte* [in:] J. Fraenkel (ed.), *The Jews of Austria. Essays on their Life, History and Destruction*, London 1967, pp. 165–176

Willaume M., *Rumunia* (*Historia Państw Świata w XX wieku*), Warszawa 2004

Wilson M.C., *King Abdullah, Britain and the Making of Jordan*, Cambridge 1987

Wischnitzer M., *To Dwell in Safety. The Story of Jewish Migration Since 1800*, Philadelphia 1948

Wyman D.S., *The Abandonment of the Jews. America and the Holocaust, 1941–1945*, New York 1984 (Polish edition: *Pozostawieni swemu losowi. Ameryka wobec Holocaustu 1941–1945*, Warszawa 1994)

Yetkin Ç., *Struma. Bir dramin içyüzü*, Istanbul 2008

Zalewska G., "Sprawa emigracji żydowskiej z Polski w drugiej połowie lat trzydziestych w świetle materiałów polskiego MSZ," *Dzieje Najnowsze* (Warszawa). No. 1: 1988, pp. 85–120

Zamorski K., "Dezercje Żydów z Armii Polskiej," *Zeszyty Historyczne* (Paris). No. 104: 1993, pp. 5–22

Zamorski K., *Dwa tajne biura 2. Korpusu*, Londyn 1990

Zasloff J.J., *Great Britain and Palestine. A Study of the Problem before the United Nations*, München 1952

Zertal I., *From Catastrophe to Power. Holocaust Survivors and the Emergence of Israel*, Berkeley–Los Angeles–London 1998 (Hebrew edition: *Zehavam shel ha-Yehudim. Ha-Hagirah ha-Yehudit ha-mahtartit le-Erets Yisra'el, 1945-1948*, Tel Aviv 1996)

Ziemiński J. [J. Wagner], *Problem emigracji żydowskiej*, Warszawa 1937

Zucker N.L., Flink Zucker N., *The Guarded Gate. The Reality of American Refugee Policy*, New York 1987

Zvielli A., "A Soldier's dilemma," *The Jerusalem Post*, 6 I 1991

Zvielli A., "Soviet fire, cold hearts claimed 'Struma' passengers," *The Jerusalem Post*, 18 VIII 2000

Zweig R., *Britain and Palestine During the Second World War*, Woodbridge 1986

Zwergbaum A., "Exile in Mauritius," *Yad Vashem Studies* (Jerusalem). Vol. IV: 1960, pp. 191–257

Zwergbaum A., "From Internment in Bratislava and Detention in Mauritius to Freedom. The Story of the Czechoslovak Refugees of the Atlantic (1939–1945)" [in:] *The Jews of Czechoslovakia. Historical Studies and Surveys*. Vol. 2, Philadelphia 1971, pp. 599–654

Żaroń P., *Armia Andersa*, Toruń 1996

# VI. Reference books and general works

Bachi R., *The Population of Israel*, Jerusalem 1974

Comay J., *Who's Who in Jewish History after the Period of the Old Testament*, 3rd ed. Revised by L. Cohn-Sherbok, London 2002

Edelheit H., Edelheit A.J., *History of Zionism. A Handbook and Dictionary*, Boulder, Col.–Oxford 2000

*Encyclopaedia Judaica*. Vol. 1–16, 4th ed., Jerusalem 1978 (new ed., Detroit–New York–San Francisco–New Haven–Waterwille–London 2007)

*Encyclopedia of Zionism and Israel*. Vol. 1–2. Ed. by R. Patai, New York 1971

Gilbert M., *The Dent Atlas of the Holocaust*, London 1992 (Polish edition: *Atlas historii holokaustu*, Kryspinów [2001])

Gilbert M., *The Routledge Atlas of the Arab-Israeli Conflict*, 9th ed., London–New York 2008

Gilbert M., *The Routledge Atlas of Jewish History*, 5th ed., London 1993 (Polish edition: *Atlas historii Żydów*, Kryspinów 1998)

Gilbert M., *The Routledge Historical Atlas of Jerusalem*, 4th ed., London–New York 2008

Horev S., *Sefinot be-terem shahar. Sipuran shel sefinot ha-maʼapilim me "Vilus" ad "Kerav Emek Ayalon." Leksikon ha-haʼapalah 1934–1948* (*Dawning Ships. The Story of the Clandestine Immigration Ships From "Vilus" to "Ayalon Valley Battle." Dictionary of the Clandestine Immigration 1934–1948*), Hefah 2004

Jones P. (ed.), *Britain and Palestine 1914–1948. Archival Sources for the History of the British Mandate*, Oxford–London 1979

Lange de N., *Atlas of the Jewish World*, Oxford 1992 (Polish edition: *Wielkie kultury świata. Świat żydowski*, Warszawa 1996)

Laqueur W. (ed.), *The Holocaust Encyclopedia*, New Haven–London 2001

Meniker V., *Osnovnye pokazateli ekonomicheskogo i sotsialnogo razvitiya Izrailya 1948–1991. Statisticheskiy obzor*, Yerusalim 1992

*New Encyclopedia of Zionism and Israel*. Vol. 1–2. Ed. G. Wigoder, London–Toronto 1994

Reich B. (ed.), *An Historical Encyclopedia of the Arab-Israeli Conflict*, London 1996

Shamir I., Shavit S. (eds.), *Encyclopedia of Jewish History. Events and Eras of the Jewish People*, New York–Oxford 1986

*The Statesman's Year-Book. Statistical and Historical Annual of the States of the World for the Year 1947*. Ed. S.H. Steinberg, London 1947

# VII. INTERNET sources (most important websites)[1]

*Atlit "Illegal Immigration Camp."* Jewish Virtual Library (http://jewishvirtuallibrary.org/jsource/Immigration/atlit.html)

Bard M., *British Restriction on Jewish Immigration*. Jewish Virtual Library (http://www.jewishvirtuallibrary.org/jsource/History/mandate.html)

---

[1]  The list is actual as of 15th May 2012.

Brenner L., *Zionism in the Age of the Dictators*, Westport, Conn. 1983 (including chapter 23: *Illegal Immigration*). International Secretariat of the Association des Anciens Amateurs de Recits de Guerre et d'Holocauste (AAARGH)
(http://www.vho.org/aaargh/engl/zad/zad.html)

Chazan M., "The Patria Affair" (abridged version of the article which appeared in: *Journal of Israeli History* [Neisbury Park, UK], Vol. 22: 2003. No. 2, pp. 61–95)
(http://cat.inist.fr/?aModele=afficheN&cpsidt=13682290)

Feld E., "The Story of the S/S Patria." *The Jewish Magazine*
(http://www.jewishmag.com/46mag/patria/patria.htm)

Friedberg-Valureanu U. (ed.), *Struma Tragedy* [block of first hand accounts, articles, list of victims, etc.]
(http://www.alpas.net/uli/struma/struma_engl.htm)

Haapalah Aliyah Bet database
(http://wertheimer.info/family/GRAMPS/WEBINDEX/haapalahindex.html)

Lapidot Y., *The Irgun's Role in Illegal Immigration*. Jewish Virtual Library
(http://www.jewishvirtuallibrary.org/jsource/History/irgunill.html)

Ozer A., "The Struma Tragedy." Turkish Jews (electronic version of the article which appeared in the *Turkish Times* [Washington] in February 1992 on the 50th anniversary of the sinking of the *Struma*)
(http://www.turkishjews.com/struma)

Rubinstein S., *Personal Tragedies as a Reflection to a Great Tragedy Called Struma*, Jerusalem 2003
(http://www.isro-press.net/Struma.Rubinstein/index.shtml)

Silverstone P.H., *Aliyah Bet Project*
(http://www.paulsilverstone.com/immigration/Primary)

Sloame J., *Exile in Mauritius*. Jewish Virtual Library
(http://www.jewishvirtuallibrary.org/jsource/vjw/Mauritius.html)

*Struma: A Romanian Tragedy*. Foundation for the Advancement of Sephardic Studies and Culture
(http://www.sephardicstudies.org/struma.html)

"Struma's people / Cei ce au fast pe Struma" [in:] U. Friedberg-Valureanu (ed.), *Struma Tragedy* [list of victims]
(http://www.alpas.net/uli/struma/Victimele.htm)

*The Darien Dilemma*
(http://www.dariendilemma.com/eng)

"The Mossad's People" [in:] *The Darien Dilemma*
(http://www.dariendilemma.com/eng/people/mossad/)

*The Sinking of the Struma (February 1942)*. Jewish Virtual Library
(http://www.jewishvirtuallibrary.org/jsource/History/struma.html)

Ziffer H., "Rescuing Greek Jews under German occupation," *Los muestros. La voix des sépharades – the sepharadic voice*, mars 2003
(http://www.sefarad.org/publication/lm/050/html/page20.html)

# VIII. Filmography

*Atlantic Drift / La dérive de l'Atlantique* (2002, directed by Michel Daëron, France–Israel––Austria)

*The Danube Exodus* (1998, directed by Péter Forgács, Holland)

*The Darien Dilemma* (2006, directed by Erez Laufer, Israel)

*Le Grand Akshan* (2002, directed by Ron Goldman, Israel)

*Kladovo – an Escape – Vienna – Palestine* (2001, directed by Alisa Douer, Austria)

*Salvador – The Ship of Shattered Hopes* (2006, directed by Nissim Mossek, Israel)

*The Struma* (2001, directed by Simcha Jacobovici, Canada-Great Britain)

*Struma* (2001, directed by Radu Gabrea, Romania)

*Unlikely Heroes* (2003, directed by Richard Trank, USA)

*Voyage of the Damned* (1976, directed by Stuart Rosenberg, Great Britain)

# List of tables

# List of maps

# Index*

---

* Ship names are given in *italics*.

**B**

Bachi, Roberto  27, 80
Backmann, René  50
Baer, Tadek  163
Baghdad  103, 104
Balfour, Arthur James  22
Balfour Declaration  22–24, 26, 35–37, 114, 152
Balkans  71, 76, 92, 98, 101, 132, 154, 157, 167–169
Balke, Ralf  22, 97
Ball-Kaduri, Kurt-Jakob  74, 85, 128, 132, 137
Bar-Avi, Israel  142
Bar-Kochba, Shimeon  18
Bar-Zohar, Michael  32, 97
Barbur, Eli  159
Barclay, C.  116
Bard, Mitchell  100
Bari  83
Barlas, Chaim (Hayim)  13, 140, 145, 162, 173
Barnawi, Eli  50
Barpal, Yosef  45, 66
Basle  18
Basra  168
Bateman, Charles H.  70
Batmaz, Şakir  40
*Batory*  137
Bauer, Yehuda  9, 35, 53, 65, 69, 72, 73, 77, 85, 97, 101, 105, 134, 136, 145, 152
Baumkoller, Abraham  24
Beau Bassin  123, 125
Beck, Józef  56, 57
Beckman, Morris  97
Beer Sheva  157
Begin, Menachem  60, 107, 108, 121, 122, 150
Beirut  40, 71, 90
*Bela-Christa*  160, 179
Belgium  51, 52, 54, 60
Belgrade  71, 134
Belgrade = Yugoslavia  133
Belize (British Honduras)  115
Ben-Gurion, David  14, 31, 34, 45, 65, 66, 69, 78, 97, 102, 119, 150–152, 157, 159, 167

*Ben Hecht*  68
Ben-Horin, Eliahu  87, 112
Bennett, John S.  113
Bentwich, Helen  25
Bentwich, Norman  25, 49
Benvenisti, Misho  159, 160
Benz, Wolfgang  120, 162
Berlin  76
Berlin = Germany  50, 72, 73, 77, 134, 161, 164
Bern  13
Bernacki, Włodzimierz  124
Bernstein, I.  47
Bernstein, S.  155
Betar (Brit Trumpeldor, Trumpeldor Alliance)  44, 46–48, 52, 53, 60, 81, 88, 107
Bethell, Nicholas  24, 33, 35, 139, 147–150
Bethlehem  34
Bevin, Ernest  113
Bielicki, Vladimir  163
Bierman, John  137
Biltmore Program (1942)  152, 154
Binder, Johannes  74
Black, Edwin  73
Black Sea  10, 12, 74, 101, 110, 131, 133, 144, 148, 149
Bludan  94
Bogner, Nahum  156
Bogoslovskiy, Viktor V.  77
Boh  160
Bojko, Krzysztof  56
Bosphorus  71, 148, 149, 151, 156, 158, 159, 164
Bowden, Tom  33
Braginski, Yehuda  45, 66, 68, 135
Braila  54
Bratislava  75, 76, 83, 131, 137, 138
Brazil  49, 77, 86
Breitman, Richard  51, 100
Brenner, Lenni  31, 48, 88, 100
Brest on the Bug  56, 59, 60
Brindisi  83
Brno  128
Bronsztejn, Szyja  55
Brzoza, Czesław  61
Bucharest  64, 71, 76, 151, 152, 159, 163, 165

Kovalev, Erik A. 148
Krakow 15
*Kralitza Maria* 176
Krammer, Arnold 166
Krasuski, Jerzy 72
Kraut, Alan M. 51, 100
*Krotova* 177
Krum, khan of Bulgaria 137
Kubiak, Krzysztof 145
Kula, Marcin 49
Kurnikowski, Zdzisław Kazimierz 42

**L**
Lampson, Miles 90
Land Transfers Regulations (1940) 98
Lapidot, Yehuda 47, 53, 54, 110
Laqueur, Walter 18, 22, 24, 28, 36, 78, 85, 142, 152, 157, 165
*Las Perlas* 177
Latvia 71, 90, 124, 125
Laub, Morris 156
Laufer, Erez 135
Lazar, Haim 47, 48, 53, 54
Lazar-Litai, Chaim 11, 52, 53, 85, 145
League of Nations 23, 24, 26, 31, 36, 40, 56, 79
Lebanon 10, 21, 23, 24, 34, 40, 47, 54, 71, 79, 80, 103, 104
Leibovici, Arthur, *see* Arsene, Maria
Lenczowski, George 17, 166
Lenk, Karl 116, 124, 127
Lenk, Rudolf S. 116
Levin, Dow 106
Levinthal, Louis 155
Levy, Joseph M. 162
Liberia 86
*Libertad* 178
Libya 122, 147
Liebman, M. 68
Liebreich, Fritz 9, 65, 79, 80
*Liesel* 86, 177
Lilienthal, Alfred M. 121
*Lily* 179
Limassol 116, 117
Linton, Joseph Ivor 155
Lipscher, Ladislav 75

Lisbon 158
Lissak, Moshe 25
Lithuania 90, 171
Lloyd, Thomas Ingram 122
Lloyd of Dolobran, George Ambrose 110, 112
Locker, Berl 153
Lodz 70
Lohamei Herut Israel (Lehi, Fighters for the Freedom of Israel) 100, 101, 150
London 11–13, 19, 20, 35, 38, 50, 64, 93, 94, 111, 126–128, 143, 147, 151, 153, 167
London = Great Britain 10, 21–24, 26, 32–35, 37, 79, 94, 97–99, 101, 108, 111, 113–115, 122, 136, 150–155, 168
London, Louise 77, 114
Loraine, Percy Lyham 109
Lothian, Philip Henry Kerr, Marquess of 122
Louis, William Roger 169
Luttwak, Edward Nicolae 42, 101

**M**
MacDonald, James Ramsay 24, 33, 35
MacDonald, Malcolm 35, 81, 89, 94, 99, 111, 113
MacMichael, Harold 36, 91, 99, 136, 143, 149–151, 153
Madagascar 57, 115
Mafdal (National Religious Party) 68
Maga, Timothy P. 162
Mahmud, Pasha Mohammed 94
Malaya 77, 151
Mandel, Neville J. 20
Mann, Peggy 14, 91, 134
Manning, Olivia 149
Manoschek, Walter 131–134
Mapai (Mifleget Poalei Eretz Israel, Party of the Workers of the Land of Israel) 31, 44, 46, 68, 78, 120
Mapam (Mifleget Ha'Poalim Ha'Meuhedet, United Workers' Party) 68
Marcus, Ernst 73
Mardor, Munya M. 14, 38, 103, 119, 121
*Marica* 160, 179
Marlowe, John 25

TECHNICAL EDITOR
Jadwiga Makowiec

PROOFREADER
Monika Zapała

TYPESETTER
Katarzyna Mróz-Jaskuła


Jagiellonian University Press
Editorial Offices: Michałowskiego St. 9/2, 31-126 Krakow
Phone: +48 12 631 18 81, +48 12 631 18 82, Fax: +48 12 631 18 83